Nonprofit and Civil Society Studies

An International Multidisciplinary Series

Series Editors
Paul Dekker
Institute for Social Research, The Hague, The Netherlands

Annette Zimmer
Universität Münster Institut für Politikwissenschaft, Münster, Germany

For further volumes:
http://www.springer.com/series/6339

Lesley Hustinx • Johan von Essen • Jacques Haers
Sara Mels
Editors

Religion and Volunteering

Complex, Contested and Ambiguous
Relationships

Editors
Lesley Hustinx
Department of Sociology
Ghent University
Ghent
Belgium

Johan von Essen
Institute for Civil Society Studies
Ersta Sköndal University College
Stockholm
Sweden

Jacques Haers
Universitair Centrum Sint-Ignatius
Antwerpen
Antwerp
Belgium

Sara Mels
Universitair Centrum Sint-Ignatius
Antwerpen
Antwerp
Belgium

ISSN 1568-2579
ISBN 978-3-319-04584-9   ISBN 978-3-319-04585-6 (eBook)
DOI 10.1007/978-3-319-04585-6
Springer Cham Heidelberg New York Dordrecht London

Library of Congress Control Number: 2014938102

© Springer International Publishing Switzerland 2015
This work is subject to copyright. All rights are reserved by the Publisher, whether the whole or part of the material is concerned, specifically the rights of translation, reprinting, reuse of illustrations, recitation, broadcasting, reproduction on microfilms or in any other physical way, and transmission or information storage and retrieval, electronic adaptation, computer software, or by similar or dissimilar methodology now known or hereafter developed. Exempted from this legal reservation are brief excerpts in connection with reviews or scholarly analysis or material supplied specifically for the purpose of being entered and executed on a computer system, for exclusive use by the purchaser of the work. Duplication of this publication or parts thereof is permitted only under the provisions of the Copyright Law of the Publisher's location, in its current version, and permission for use must always be obtained from Springer. Permissions for use may be obtained through RightsLink at the Copyright Clearance Center. Violations are liable to prosecution under the respective Copyright Law.
The use of general descriptive names, registered names, trademarks, service marks, etc. in this publication does not imply, even in the absence of a specific statement, that such names are exempt from the relevant protective laws and regulations and therefore free for general use.
While the advice and information in this book are believed to be true and accurate at the date of publication, neither the authors nor the editors nor the publisher can accept any legal responsibility for any errors or omissions that may be made. The publisher makes no warranty, express or implied, with respect to the material contained herein.

Printed on acid-free paper

Springer is part of Springer Science+Business Media (www.springer.com)

Preface

In December 2011, the University Centre Saint Ignatius Antwerp (UCSIA) organized an international interdisciplinary academic workshop on the topic of volunteering, religion and social capital. UCSIA convened a select group of researchers and practitioners to investigate how the idea of volunteering in religious, faith-based and secular organizations changed over time and what were and are people's motives in putting themselves forward as volunteers. Now, two years later, and thanks to the academic commitment of Lesley Hustinx and Johan von Essen, we are happy to present this collection: *Religion and volunteering: Complex, contested and ambiguous relationships.* We wish to thank all the authors who contributed; without their dedication and expertise, this volume would not exist.

The contributors examine the relationship between religion and volunteering in its complexity and depth. They add to the current discussions between academics and practitioners about the 'religious' dynamics of volunteering as well as the role of religion in contemporary society. They critically analyse the so-called 'default position' that expects a harmonious causal relationship between religion and volunteering. In this way, readers are led to a more varied and more contextual understanding of the role of religion in contemporary society, taking into account processes of secularization and pluralization.

This anthology explores the maze of religion and volunteering in great detail. The interactions between religion and volunteering require a variety of research perspectives. Therefore, we attempt to cover a wide range of theoretical and methodological approaches and include a variety of disciplinary accounts, including theology, philosophy, sociology, political science, anthropology and architecture.

What readers will not find here is an all-embracing theory or a conclusive synthesis. On the contrary, we hope to provoke discussion. The book is intended for scholars and students in the field of civil society and third sector research, focusing on the topics of volunteering and religion and its importance for social capital, politics and identity formation. It also contributes to the ongoing interdisciplinary discussion about the post-secular society and will appeal to sociologists, political scientists, anthropologists and theologians. The approaches offered here may also tempt practitioners since they allow for a reinterpretation of existing realities and for the introduction of fresh perspectives in concrete situations where volunteers play an important role. They may provide ideas and tools to decision-makers in the field of volunteering. Additional non-academic interest in this book may come from the governmental policymakers and those in leadership positions in religious communities, since it studies and discusses religion in its relationship to social capital, societal order and political realities.

2 December 2013

Lesley Hustinx
Johan von Essen
Jacques Haers
Sara Mels

Contents

1 **Religion and Volunteering** 1
Johan von Essen, Lesley Hustinx, Jacques Haers and Sara Mels

Part I Theologies of Religion and Volunteering

2 **Christian Calling and Volunteering** 23
Jacques Haers and Johan von Essen

3 **If I Am Only for Myself, Who Am I?** 41
Lena Roos

4 **Philanthropic Virtue** 59
Mohammad Fazlhashemi

Part II Religion as a Determinant of Volunteering

5 **Religiosity and Formal Volunteering in Global Perspective** 77
Matthew R. Bennett

6 **A Cross-National Examination of the Motivation to Volunteer** 97
Lesley Hustinx, Ronan Van Rossem, Femida Handy
and Ram A. Cnaan

7 **Volunteering Among Church Attendees in Australia** 121
John Bellamy and Rosemary Leonard

Part III Religion and Volunteering in a (Post-)Secular Context

8 **Lost and Found in Secularization** 147
Johan von Essen

vii

viii

9 Making Church Happen 169
Roel De Ridder and Sylvain De Bleeckere

10 Restorative Justice and Volunteering in a Secular Age 191
Erik Claes and Emilie Van Daele

11 Short-Term Mission Voluntarism and the Postsecular Imaginary 217
Mary Hancock

Part IV Politics of Religion and Volunteering

12 Religion and Social Solidarity 241
Paul Lichterman

13 'Your Prayer Moves God' 263
Oleg Dik

14 Faith-Based Organizations and Civic Engagement in Egypt 283
Moustafa Khalil

15 'Going Back to Our Values' 305
Itamar Y. Shachar

16 Volunteering in Religious Communities 329
Welmoet Boender

Index 345

Contributors

John Bellamy Social Policy & Research Unit, Anglicare Sydney, Sydney, Australia

Australian Catholic University, Strathfield, Australia

Matthew R. Bennett Department of Sociology, University of Oxford, Oxford, England

Welmoet Boender Department of Philosophy and Religious Studies, Utrecht University, Utrecht, Netherlands

Erik Claes HUB, Pragodi, Campus Erasmus, Brussel, Belgium

Ram A. Cnaan School of Social Policy and Practice, University of Pennsylvania, Philadelphia, Pennsylvania, USA

Graduate Institute for Peace, Kyunghee University, Seoul, Korea

Sylvain De Bleeckere ArcK, Hasselt University, Diepenbeek, Belgium

Roel De Ridder Arck, Hasselt University, Diepenbeek, Belgium

Faculty of Architecture, KU Leuven, Brussels & Ghent, Belgium

Oleg Dik Department of Religious Studies and Intercultural Theology, Humboldt University, Berlin, Germany

Mohammad Fazlhashemi Department of Theology, Studies in Faith and Ideologies, Systematic Theology and Studies in World Views, Uppsala University, Uppsala, Sweden

Jacques Haers University Centre Saint-Ignatius Antwerp, Antwerp, Belgium

Mary Hancock Departments of Anthropology and History, University of California, Santa Barbara, California

Femida Handy School of Social Policy and Practice, University of Pennsylvania, Philadelphia, Pennsylvania, USA

Lesley Hustinx Department of Sociology, Ghent University, Ghent, Belgium

Moustafa Khalil Institute of Development Policy and Management, University of Manchester, Manchester, U. K.

Rosemary Leonard School of Social Sciences, University of Western Sydney, Penrith, Australia

Ecosystem Sciences, Commonwealth Scientific and Industrial Research Organisation (CSIRO), Acton ACT, Australia

Paul Lichterman University of Southern California, Los Angeles, CA, USA

Sara Mels University Centre Saint-Ignatius Antwerp, Antwerp, Belgium

Lena Roos Department of Theology, Uppsala University, Uppsala, Sweden

Itamar Y. Shachar Department of Sociology, Ghent University, Ghent, Belgium

Emilie Van Daele Socius, Steunpunt Sociaal-Cultureel Volwassenenwerk, Brussel, Belgium

Ronan Van Rossem Department of Sociology, Ghent University, Ghent, Belgium

Johan von Essen Institute for Civil Society Studies, Ersta Sköndal University College, Stockholm, Sweden

About the Editors

Sara Mels is project-coordinator at the University Centre Sint-Ignatius Antwerp.

Lesley Hustinx is assistant professor at the Department of Sociology of Ghent University.

Johan von Essen is Doctor of Divinity and Researcher at the Institute for Civil Society Studies, Ersta Sköndal University College.

Jacques Haers is director of academic affairs at the University Centre Sint-Ignatius Antwerp.

About the Authors

Lena Roos is Associate professor at the History of Religions Department of Theology at Uppsala University.

Mohammad Fazlhashemi is professor of Islamic Theology and Philosophy at the Department of Theology, Research group "Studies in Faith and Ideologies; Systematic Theology and Studies in World Views" at Uppsala University.

Matthew Bennett is a PhD student at the Department of Sociology, University of Oxford, England. He is interested in the causes and consequences of prosocial behavior.

Lesley Hustinx is assistant professor at the Department of Sociology at Ghent University, and a member of the Center for Social Theory and the research group Participation, Opportunities, Structures (POS+). Her major research interests include societies in transition, and the consequences of recent social change for the nature of citizenship and citizen-based solidarity, with a special interest in the study of volunteering. Lesley Hustinx is a board member of the International Society for Third Sector Research (ISTR) and the Flemish Sociological Association (VVS). She is a member of the Senior Editorial Committee of Voluntas and the Journal of Civil Society.

Ronan Van Rossem is associate professor of Sociology at Ghent University, and chair of the research group Participation, Opportunities, Structures (POS+). His research focuses on social networks and social capital and their effects, the dynamics of the global system and how this affects economic, political and human development, and on reproductive health issues, including AIDS prevention and female genital mutilation.

Femida Handy is Professor of Social Policy at the University of Pennsylvania. Her research interests are focused on various aspects of the economics nonprofit sector and also include nonprofit entrepreneurship, human resource management, microfinance, and volunteerism, comparative and international aspects of volunteering sector. She has published many articles and books and her research has won several awards. She is currently working in the area of global philanthropy.

Dr. Handy is the Editor-in-Chief of the *Nonprofit and Voluntary Sector Quarterly*, the top ranked journal in its field.

Ram A. Cnaan is a Professor and Director of the Program for Religion and Social Policy Research at the School of Social Policy & Practice, University of Pennsylvania. He is also the director of the Goldring Reentry Initiative that helps ex-prisoners settle in society. He serves as a Global Eminent Scholar at the Graduate Institute for Peace at Kyung Hee University in South Korea. Professor Cnaan's research focuses on serving disadvanged populations with special emphasis on religious social services and the use of nonprofit organizations and volunteers. Professor Cnaan serves on the editorial board of ten academic journals and he published extensively in all aspects of social welfare and social work.

John Bellamy PhD is a senior researcher with Anglicare, a social service agency of the Anglican Diocese of Sydney, and is an Honorary Fellow of Australian Catholic University. He was involved in the development of the five-yearly National Church Life Survey in Australia, one of the largest surveys of church life in the world. Since 1992 John has co-authored several books on religion and church life in Australia. More recently he has been involved in an Australian Research Council funded study researching social capital in churches. His areas of research include social welfare, service evaluation and church life and mission.

Rosemary Leonard PhD is an Associate Professor at the University of Western Sydney and currently works as a Senior Research Scientist with the CSIRO, Australia's national science agency. Her research and publications cover the fields of third-sector research, particularly volunteering and social capital; life-course and ageing; social dimensions of climate change. Rosemary is the Managing Editor of the peer reviewed, academic journal *Third Sector Review* and is a former Chair of Australian and New Zealand Third Sector Research. Since 2002 she has been involved in a number of Australian Research Council funded projects addressing third-sector issues, including social capital in churches.

Johan von Essen is Doctor of Divinity and Researcher at the Institute for Civil Society Studies, Ersta Sköndal University College.

Roel De Ridder (1982, Hasselt, Belgium), architect and PhD, obtained his architecture degree from PHL University College in 2007. In 2008 he started doing research on the future of the parish churches of Flanders with Sylvain De Bleeckere as his supervisor. He defended his doctoral thesis in February 2013. His research interests are (contemporary) architectural theory and the public and social aspects of architecture. De Ridder is currently a researcher at Hasselt University, a tutor at the new Faculty of Architecture (KU Leuven) and one of the two artistic directors of *Architectuurwijzer*, an architectural association without lucrative purpose.

Sylvain De Bleeckere (1950, Hasselt, Belgium), philosopher and PhD., teaches cultural sciences at the (former) Architecture department of PHL University College, which is currently being transformed into the Faculty of Architecture and Art of Hasselt University. He directs the master seminar on architecture and democracy and is a staff member of the research group ArcK. Since 1977, De Bleeckere has been publishing continuously in Flanders and abroad on themes such as the postmodern philosophy of culture in relation to democracy, architecture and meaning, phenomenology and dwelling.

Erik Claes studied Law and Philosophy at the KU Leuven. He obtained his doctoral degree in Law on 'Legality and Adjudication in the Criminal Law' (2001). His main research areas are restorative justice, and the philosophy of the criminal law. He lectures Philosophy, Law and Ethics at the HUB, School of Social Work. He is a member of the research group of social work (HUB). He currently coordinates two research projects on restorative justice, volunteers and active citizenship.

Emilie Van Daele studied Philosophy at the VUB. She obtained her doctoral degree in Philosophy on 'The community of those who have nothing in common: Levinas, community and the self' (2012). She was a researcher at the research group of social work (HUB). She currently works as a staff-member at Socius. Steunpunt Sociaal-Cultureel Volwassenenwerk.

Mary Hancock is Professor in the Departments of Anthropology and History at University of California, Santa Barbara. Her areas of research are in transnational cultural circulation, urban religiosity, gender and cultural memory. She has conducted ethnographic fieldwork in Tamil Nadu, India and in southern California in the U.S. Her published works include *Womanhood in the Making: Domestic Ritual and Public Culture in Urban South India* (Westview 1999) and *The Politics of Heritage from Madras to Chennai* (Indiana 2008), as well as numerous chapters and articles, published in journals that include *American Ethnologist, Modern South Asia, Environment and Planning D: Society and Space, Material Religion and the International Journal of Urban and Regional Studies*. She currently convenes a multicampus research group on Urban Place-Making and Religiosity (co-convenor, Smriti Srinivas), sponsored by the Humanities Network of the University of California (http://www.urbanreligions.net).

Paul Lichterman currently is Professor of Sociology and Religion at the University of Southern California, Los Angeles. A cultural sociologist and ethnographer, he has studied a variety of political and religious associations. He is the author of **Elusive Togetherness: Church Groups Trying to Bridge America's Divisions** (2005) and **The Search for Political Community** (1996), coeditor of **The Civic Life of American Religion** (2009), and has written a variety of scholarly articles. His book **Elusive Togetherness** won the Distinguished Book Award from the Society for the Scientific Study of Religion and the Distinguished Scholarship Award from the Pacific Sociological Association.

Oleg Dik has studied Theology, Religious Studies, Cultural Anthropology and Philosophy. He holds a MA in Biblical and Theological Studies from the University of Gloucestershire, UK and a MA in Religion and Culture from the Humboldt University, Berlin, Germany. From January 2010 until January 2011 Oleg was a research fellow at the Orient Institute in Beirut, Lebanon. Currently, Oleg is finishing his PhD at the Humboldt University in the department of Religious Studies and Intercultural Theology. His dissertation describes the emergence of the post war Charismatic/Pentecostal movement in Beirut and aims at providing a hermeneutical model for analyzing life worlds.

Moustafa Khalil earned his PhD degree in 2014 in Development Policy and Management at the Institute of Development Policy and Management in the University of Manchester in the UK. He graduated from the American University in Cairo with a degree in political science and economics in 2002. After that, he spent five years in Egypt working for several development agencies and media outlets including USAID and Egyptian National TV. In 2007, he moved to the UK where he resumed post graduate studies. His research interests are in the role of Faith-based Organizations in poverty reduction and his fieldwork has been concentrated in his native Egypt.

Itamar Y. Shachar is a doctoral fellow at the Department of Sociology, Ghent University. He is affiliated with the Centre for Social Theory and the research group "Participation, Opportunities, Structures". He currently works on a multi-sited ethnographic study of the emerging phenomenon of 'corporate volunteering'. His contribution to this volume is based on parts from his Master thesis, written at the University of Amsterdam.

Welmoet Boender is Assistant Professor in Islamic Studies at Utrecht University, Department of Philosophy and Religious Studies. From 2006 until 2011 she was senior researcher at Oikos Foundation (Utrecht, the Netherlands) where she manned the Knowledge Centre Religion and Development. She holds a PhD in Religious Studies from Leiden University. Between 2000 and 2005 she was a PhD fellow at the International Institute for the Study of Islam in the Modern World (ISIM). Her dissertation (in Dutch) is called *Imam in the Netherlands. Views about his religious role in society* (Amsterdam: Bert Bakker 2007). She obtained MA's in Cultural Anthropology and in Islamic Studies at Leiden University.

Chapter 1
Religion and Volunteering

Complex, Contested and Ambiguous Relationships

Johan von Essen, Lesley Hustinx, Jacques Haers and Sara Mels

Religion and Volunteering

At a time when financial cuts affect welfare systems and increasing migration leads to more heterogeneous societies, expectations are growing for civic engagement, and especially volunteering, to contribute more to welfare services and social cohesion. It therefore comes as no surprise that in recent decades research on volunteering has grown exponentially, reflecting a burgeoning interest among politicians and policymakers. The relationship between religion and volunteering has been a key focus in this research agenda since it has generally been assumed to be a strong and positive one (see for instance Cnaan et al. 1999; Lam 2002; Schwadel 2005; van Tienen et al. 2011; Verba et al. 1995; Yeung 2004). Religion is considered to be one of the key predictors of volunteer participation, both in religious and secular organizations: The more religious people are the more likely they are to volunteer. However, both volunteering and religion are multi-dimensional social phenomena and on closer inspection the relation between them appears to be more complex and ambiguous than was first assumed. This book represents a 'closer look' at this complex relationship.

Existing research indicates two major mechanisms for explaining the positive relationship between religion and volunteering: religious beliefs and religious practice. Religious belief teaches the values of altruism and caring for others, which

---

J. von Essen (✉)
Institute for Civil Society Studies, Ersta Sköndal University College, Stockholm, Sweden
e-mail: johan.vonessen@esh.se

L. Hustinx
Department of Sociology, Ghent University, Ghent, Belgium
e-mail: lesley.hustinx@ugent.be

J. Haers · S. Mels
University Centre Saint-Ignatius Antwerp, Antwerp, Belgium
e-mail: jacques.haers@ucsia.be

S. Mels
e-mail: sara.mels@ucsia.be

L. Hustinx et al. (eds.), *Religion and Volunteering,* Nonprofit and Civil Society Studies,
DOI 10.1007/978-3-319-04585-6_1, © Springer International Publishing Switzerland 2015

may easily find expression in acts of volunteering. The second strand of research suggests that religious practice, e.g. attendance of religious services, has been found to be of crucial importance. In the latter case, rather than religious conviction, religious networks play a determining role. Through these networks, people receive information about volunteering opportunities, have a higher likelihood to be invited and experience normative expectations and social pressure to volunteer. Scholars of religion and volunteering have found the most conclusive evidence in support of the network hypothesis (e.g. Vermeer and Scheepers 2011; Wuthnow 1996, 2004). Recently, the availability of cross-national data has made it possible to study the relationship between religion and volunteering at country level, examining the influence of a devout or secular national context on levels of volunteering, as well as the variable relationship between religion and volunteering within these different contexts (see chapters of Bennett and Hustinx and colleagues in this volume, also Ruiter and De Graaf 2006). Conclusive evidence at the contextual level is, however, still lacking, mainly due to methodological difficulties in measuring volunteering across different nations and cultures and in using national data as a proxy for local and regional network composition and diversity.

The hypothesis of a harmonious causal relationship between religion and volunteering enjoys considerable support in existing research and will also be found in this book. In fact, this perspective is so dominant that it seems to be the 'default' relationship' between both phenomena. But it should also be recognized that though we take the positive 'default relationship' as our point of departure there are tensions between religion and volunteering and that these are intensifying partly because of the changing role of religion in society.

One of these tensions seems to be fundamental since it is conceptual rather than empirical; it arises from volunteering being defined as consisting of actions carried out in freedom of choice. Such understanding of volunteering is at odds with the claims religions make on their followers to care for other individuals. From the viewpoint of Christian theology, this is the calling to neighborly love in the New Testament; in Judaism this claim is integrated in the law and for Islam it is written in the Koran. From a religious perspective, being of service to others constitutes an obligation, something the pious person has to do in obedience to God. Hence, it is not just a freely chosen act made by an autonomous individual and to understand volunteering from a religious perspective, there is a need for a theological examination of the religious foundations of neighborly love. To explore the rarely discussed contrast between religious calling and volunteering as a free choice, the first part of this book approaches the service to others from theological perspectives (chapters of Haers and von Essen; Roos and Fazlhashemi). Of course, there are more aspects of the relation between religion and volunteering that emerge if one investigates beyond the 'default' positive relationship. In order to uncover and discuss these aspects we will 'bring theology back in' and, hopefully, contribute to a more complete understanding of the relation between religion and volunteering.

Apart from religious obligation, religious change and the processes of secularization also determine tensions between religion and volunteering. The importance of religion in contemporary society seems to be weakening and the default relationship between religion and volunteering is becoming problematic. The question arises whether the shrinking importance of religions poses a threat to volunteering or whether there are other sources that can replace the privileged relationship of religion with volunteering. In this context, scholars have increasingly paid attention to the question of a possible 'spill-over' effect from religious to non-religious people and networks (e.g. Lim and MacGregor 2012; Ruiter and De Graaf 2006).

However, from a post-secular perspective, the secularization thesis has received ample criticism as the sole and traditional understanding of the fading away of religion in modernity. We will come back and develop the notion of the 'post-secular' further but here we simply state that it opens up new perspectives on the interaction between religion and volunteering, as demonstrated in particular chapters of this book (chapters of Hancock, Dik, De Ridder and De Bleeckere, Claes and Van Daele, von Essen).

These brief observations suggest that the relationship between religion and volunteering is not univocal—or 'default'—but differentiated and ambiguous. To further research a more complete in-depth and critical *re*-examination of the relationship between religion and volunteering is needed. What we have called the 'default relationship' is an important and productive perspective but just *one* of the many possible relationships between religion and volunteering. A key focus is to examine how the changing conditions and understandings of religion influence its interaction with volunteering. Consequently, this volume emphasizes the religious side of the relationship, even though there are some chapters that critically explore the volunteering side (see chapters of Lichterman and Shachar).

Religious Perspectives on Volunteering

Religion and volunteering are similar in the sense that in contemporary western societies both are expected to be apolitical and private, concerned with moral values rather than political aspirations. Volunteering is differentiated from social or political activism (Eliasoph 1997, 2013; Lyons et al. 1998; Musick and Wilson 2008) and religion has become a private matter (Casanova 1994). Of course, in reality neither volunteering nor religion are politically neutral phenomena and both impact on society. Among academics the alleged apolitical character of volunteering is often discussed. Janoski (2010), for instance, argues that the divide between volunteering and political activism acts to conceal the processes in civil society where volunteering can lead to political activism. Furthermore, the political structures that steer civic participation into apolitical forms of volunteering in welfare-providing organizations are disguised when they are backed up by an idea of spontaneous volunteering as a distinct form of participation in contrast to political or social activism (Goss 2010).

We will explore how actions that are held to be altruistic, politically neutral and motivated by religious beliefs can be used for political reasons. As some of the chapters in this volume will demonstrate, volunteering makes it sometimes possible for religion to transgress the limits of the private sphere and become politically significant (chapters of Hancock, Khalil, Roos and Fazlhashemi) and, conversely, religion can sometimes structure volunteering towards influencing the social order of a society (chapters of Dik and Shachar).

This similarity indicates that the relation between religion and volunteering goes deeper than the empirically demonstrated positive correlation between religion and volunteering and that the perspective of religion can contribute to shed some light on volunteering as a social phenomenon (see, for instance, Jacobsson 2014). If we define religion by its practices, rendering service to others becomes an expression of religiosity. That is why it is tempting to understand volunteering as a secular variation of piety (cf. Yinger 1970). Although there is a role for free choice in religious belief, which is thoroughly discussed in theology (see for instance the chapter of Haers and von Essen), there is, as mentioned above, a distinct difference between the obligatory character of the demands made by religions and secular volunteering as an act of free choice. The fact that religion and volunteering are both similar and different makes their relation interesting, both from the perspective of theology and the social sciences.

Volunteering also resembles religion because of its unstable character. Engagement in civil society is sometimes held to be an indicator of the strength of community spirit since it allows citizens to act in solidarity with others (Hustinx 2003). However, volunteering in Western societies (allegedly) has shifted from a collectively oriented and stable mode of involvement towards a more individualized and episodic type of engagement—which Putnam considers 'less serious' (Putnam 1995). One trend is the growing instrumentalization of volunteering by individual volunteers themselves (e.g. for career-building reasons) as well as by voluntary organizations and 'third parties' (e.g. professionalization of volunteer services at the expense of paid work, 'mandatory' volunteering for the long-term unemployed) (e.g. Haski-Leventhal et al. 2010; Hustinx and Meijs 2011; Hustinx 2010; Pick et al. 2011). Such a shift from collective and altruistic to individualistic and instrumental modes of involvement can, in a transferred sense, be seen as a form of secularization. Since both religion and volunteering are affected by individualism, both phenomena are changing in similar ways that are increasingly difficult to capture in academic definitions.

Volunteering is a complex and ambiguous phenomenon that is not clearly delineated and spans a wide variety of types of activities, organizations and sectors. If volunteering is defined as the unpaid activities that are performed out of free will for the benefit of others beyond kinship ties, it highlights the common elements in most definitions and in the public perception (e.g. Cnaan et al. 1996; Handy et al. 2000). Usually, these activities are carried out in the context of a formal organization, although informal volunteering exists as well. Both in research and public discourse, there is a tendency to de-politicize volunteer work and to emphasize its virtuous and compassionate nature. However, it has been argued that the boundaries between what definitely constitutes volunteering and what does not are socially constructed and thus permeable (Hustinx et al. 2010). Consequently, both the terminology and the connotations of volunteering differ between countries and civil

1 Religion and Volunteering

society regimes (Dekker and Halman 2003). It follows that a simple prediction of whether one volunteers or not leaves open the enormous heterogeneity of types of activities, styles of involvement and meanings attributed to volunteering. For academic research volunteering is an intriguing phenomenon because it is so complex and atypical in many ways. Since it is multidimensional (it is held to be an expression of altruism, a form of organizational behaviour and unpaid work, a voluntary act, etc.), volunteering speaks to the imagination of scholars in many disciplines. This need for a multidisciplinary approach is reflected in the contributions to this anthology.

The causes for volunteering constitute a recurrent interest, both in academic research and among policymakers. As noted above, studies have demonstrated that religion is one of the key determinants of volunteering. The significance of religion as regards the propensity to volunteer in religious communities as well as in secular organizations and on the motives for volunteering is further explored and discussed in the anthology (chapters of Bennett; Hustinx, Van Rossem, Handy and Cnaan; Bellamy and Leonard). In the search for the causes of volunteering, it seems as if religion has returned to the social sciences through the back door so to speak. Although it does not always have an interest in religion as such, this research has highlighted the significance of religion in contemporary society.

There is a presupposed link between the idea of religion as a cause of volunteering on the one hand, and the expectations of the benefits of volunteering on the other, that is seldom problematized. Since volunteering is expected to increase social solidarity and since it has been demonstrated that religious individuals have a propensity to volunteer and that they are unusually active 'social capitalists', to borrow a term from Joep de Hart, Paul Dekker and Loek Halman, there arises the anxiety that increased secularization may bring decreased social solidarity in society (de Hart et al. 2013; van Tienen et al. 2011). However, this presupposes that individuals are 'bearers' of religion and carry or represent their religion in uniform and well-defined ways. This reflects what Paul Lichterman calls the 'unitary actor model' and is implicitly assumed in the dominant approach to the study of religion and volunteering as described above. In his contribution, Lichterman critically scrutinizes the 'unitary actor model' and introduces the 'pragmatic model'. This model allows for a high degree of contingency and variability in the conventional 'chain of causality' by examining the ways in which religion is 'expressed' and 'performed' in different settings. This approach opens up a new field of research on the context-dependent strategic use and performative role of religion, with variable consequences for volunteering. Here, religion is situational and not some kind of overarching quality that unchangeably characterizes actors in various contexts.

Volunteering is most often studied from the perspective of its antecedents (preferably causes) and consequences. How volunteers experience the meaning of their efforts is not studied to the same extent (Wilson 2012). However, there are studies that indicate that volunteering is a means whereby individuals may form an identity (Grönlund 2011), enact a normative vision of society (Wuthnow 1991) and handle questions of meaning (von Essen 2008; O'Reagan 2009). Whether the content of a religious faith is involved in the process of making volunteering meaningful is less frequently studied. In the search for the role of religion in the perceived meaning of volunteering the content of faith or religious traditions is brought to the fore.

Religious Change

The contemporary and vital discussion about the return of religion is paradoxical since, as de Hart, Dekker and Halman (2013) remind us, religion never really disappeared. Furthermore, and also paradoxically, today's increased interest in religion seems to be compatible with secularization. These rather complex processes give rise to new forms of religion and new conditions for religiosity. Therefore, instead of deciding how to judge the present condition we shall talk of religious change in order to include both the return and the decline of religion. This is certainly not a novelty as religion has always been unstable and in constant flux throughout history.

The broad expression 'return of religion' can be seen as made up of three differentiated but related processes. Firstly, it can refer to a revival of religious beliefs, practices and religious communities, for example the recovery of churches and growth of religiosity in former socialist countries in Eastern Europe, the expanding Evangelical and Pentecostal movements in the Middle East, Africa and Latin America and the revitalization of Islam. Secondly, there is a reentrance of religion in the public sphere: its separation from politics is questioned (Habermas 2006; de Vries and Sullivan 2006), religion is invited by government to meet social needs and strengthen social cohesion (e.g. Chapman and Hamalainen 2011; Dinham and Lowndes 2009) and there is a revival of theology in the academic debate (Breckman 2005; Svennungsson 2004). Finally, there is a new visibility of, or attention to, religion, where the impact of religion on secular society because of a long history of religious dominance can be explored and discussed (e.g. Casanova 2009; Gillespie 2008). The religious heritage and influence on society becomes visible in the patterns of institutions and behaviours now naturalized and taken for granted and in which religion, through secularization, becomes just one social phenomenon among others (e.g. Joas 2009).

The return of religion and secularization constitute two simultaneous processes; this indicates that secularization, as the disappearance of religion, can no longer be simply perceived as the default outcome of modernity. Of course, this does not mean that the religious and social landscape would not have changed during and because of the modern era. Religion, particularly in the institutionalized form of a certain confession, does not occupy the same central and hegemonic position in society as it did in pre-modern society. This is most obvious in European countries where modernity separated religion from politics (Lilla 2007), where transnational immigration has transformed former religiously homogenous countries into landscapes of religious plurality (Kong 2010) and where there has been a definitive decline in regular church attendance, especially since the 1950s (Casanova 2009). So, what is secularization then, if not an overall fading away of religion? Generally, the concept refers to the decline of the social significance of religion (Wilson 1985). This rather

1 Religion and Volunteering

sweeping formulation can be nuanced by a more detailed analysis of secularization following Casanova (1994). According to Casanova, secularization consists of three independent components; firstly, differentiation of various spheres of the social system, where religion has lost its function as an overarching system of meaning and has become one sphere among others; secondly, a decline in religious beliefs and practices; and finally, secularization refers to the marginalization of religion into the private sphere. An adequate analysis of secularization in contemporary society must evaluate these three components separately and independently.

Furthermore, the secularization of European states and societies cannot be found to the same extent in Africa, Asia or America. The secularization of society that in Europe was seen as an inevitable outcome of modernization is rather an exception considering the vitality of religion outside Europe. Even among European countries, there are considerable differences in patterns of secularization (Casanova 2009). There is no monolithic European religious situation, even on a legal level (Brugger 2009). How religion relates to civil society in general and to volunteering in particular depends on how religion is embedded in society (see de Hart and Dekker 2013; chapters of Bennett and Hustinx, Van Rossem, Handy and Cnaan in this volume). '[J]ust as there are multiple forms of modernisation, so there are multiple forms of secularization' (Turner 2011). This becomes evident when one takes into consideration that the Latin concept *saeculum* (age) is a category that originated in medieval theology to differentiate the transcendent reality from the immanent temporal world. Secularization is therefore a particular Christian dynamic that has a history that preceded the origin of modernity. In fact, modernity itself has one of its early roots in Christian theology (Gillespie 2008). This means that the particular European Christian dynamic of secularization cannot be universalized to other world religions outside Europe, since they categorize religion and world, transcendence and immanence, in different patterns which give rise to other dynamics.

Through this nuanced analysis of secularization, its contingent and context-bound character becomes apparent but also its limits. Secularization did not originate in modernity as an inevitable result of the maturity of humankind. It has, just like religion, been there all the time, as a particular (European) dynamic between the realms of religion and the secular world. Because of the insight of the limits of secularization and the overall vitality of religion the very character of secular society has been questioned and there is a vital debate in academia whether we are living in a post-secular society (Habermas 2006).

Post-secular is a frequently used but also contested concept that should be used with caution (see for instance Beckford 2012 for a critical overview of the use of the concept). Sometimes, post-secular refers to the re-emergence model, i.e. an increased religiosity or even some kind of re-sacralization of the secular world. However, the concept can also refer to a situation where attention is paid to the importance and presence of religious communities in a continuously secularizing society. In the latter use of the concept, post-secular refers to religion becoming more visible in society, to a changed attitude of the secular state towards it and of the academic and political debates in the public sphere with respect to the continued existence of different manifestations of religion and their influence on society (Joas 2009). The three components of secularization, proposed by Casanova, fit in well with the three processes of the return of religion described above. Thus, in a post-secular perspective, secularity and religion are not regarded as two dichotomous concepts involved in a zero-sum-game, but as two dialectical concepts locked in ongoing dynamic of interaction and thus shaping society (see also Beaumont and Baker 2011).

However, religious change is not only about secularization or the return of religion, it also concerns the change from a traditional, organized and collective religiosity contained in organizations or communities and grounded in a common and inherited confession, towards individualistic, post-institutional and subjective forms of spirituality. This change is important for the relation between religion and volunteering. For instance, spirituality is said to imply a lower level of commitment, more directed to individual inner life than to political and social reality (de Hart and Dekker 2013; Heelas and Woodhead 2001; Turner 2011). Hence, one central issue concerns how new forms of religion are influencing religiously motivated volunteering.

To be able to capture the different forms of religion resulting from these changes, a broad definition of religion will be used. In the concept of religion, traditional religious meaning systems, organizations and practices, but also individualized (private) religious expressions outside of the traditional contexts and derived forms of religion in secular society are to be included. Therefore, religion is defined as a system of symbols that acts to establish powerful and enduring experiences and motives in individuals by conceptualizing perceptions of the ontological order of reality and turning those concepts into an objective reality so that experiences and motives are perceived as realistic (Geertz 1966). As the authors in this volume are interested in how individuals are influenced by religion and how they are influencing society, religiosity will be studied as well. That term is taken to refer to an individual's preferences, emotions, beliefs and practices that refer to either a traditional or self-made religion. The conception of religion consequently includes the traditional and collective forms of religiosity in congregations, belief in a transcendent God and practices like saying prayers and attending services. It also, however, involves both private and collective forms of religiosity expressed in secular venues, as, for instance, 12-steps programs, with invented or eclectic belief-systems referring to a God or other phenomena (satisfying the definition above) and rituals. Furthermore, it allows for civil religion as a collection of beliefs (in the nation and its ethos), symbols (flags) and rituals (traditions, sacrifices), all of which sanctify a society or the nation.

The Politics of Religion and Volunteering

Fiscal cuts in the welfare state and an increasing religious and cultural heterogeneity are obvious motives for using religion to foster volunteering. However, to study the impact of religion on volunteering from a post-secular perspective also opens up a variety of, sometimes unexpected, perspectives on the relation between religion and volunteering. It can involve a search for the return of overt religiosity as a reaction to secular society (chapter of Hancock), or it can show how a theological framework can contribute to the understanding of the meaning of secular volunteering (chapter of von Essen). It is notable that Casanova (2009) argues that one of two factors explaining the drastic decline of religious practices in Europe after the Second World War was the institutionalization of welfare states across Western Europe since these entailed a transference of collective identification from the imagined community of the church to the nation-state. Many years later, with the welfare state inviting partners in civil society to help meet social needs, religion is ironically slipping in again by the back door, as a possible supplier of welfare services. In this process religious communities and organizations try to legitimize themselves by proving themselves as efficient service providers (chapter of Boender).

A post-secular perspective also admits that religion can withdraw from places and discourses, and this withdrawal can create new conditions and possibilities for volunteering. When parish churches in the North-west of Europe become empty, abandoned as a result of secularization, the buildings become open spaces that provoke local participation in the future of the church buildings (chapter of De Ridder and De Bleeckere). Here secularization as the withdrawal of religion creates new opportunities for volunteering. Secularization also threatens ideas and ideologies that have historically been associated with, or influenced by, religion and thus excluded secular volunteers, with obsolescence. In such a situation a certain ideology has to be re-interpreted so that it becomes independent of its religious heritage and consequently can include secular volunteers as well. In this anthology the case of restorative justice is discussed (chapter of Claes and Van Daele), but there are a lot of formerly religious organizations and ideologies that survive in spite of secularization and have to find a secular rationale to be able to include secular volunteers.

Traditionally, in modern liberal western societies, state institutions and religious communities and organizations have been separated to a varying degree in constitutional and legal terms. Even in civil societies, religiously motivated opinions and actions have been regarded with suspicion or even hostility. However, there are exceptions to this opposition towards expressions of religion outside of religious communities; one notable example is religiously motivated volunteering. Hence, volunteering is one practice that allows religious conviction and faith to act outside the realms of faith. Volunteering consequently contributes to the re-entrance of religion in the public sphere. One reason for this is the allegedly private and altruistic character of religiously motivated volunteering that makes it politically neutral. This neutral character can be used to give religion legitimacy in political processes. This transference from the realm of private religious altruism to political aspiration is discussed in some of the chapters (chapters of Khalil, Fazlhashemi and Roos). The private and neutral character of religiously motivated volunteering can also be used for political reasons (chapters of Hancock and Shachar). Even unwittingly and unexpectedly, religion can motivate and structure volunteering so that it has a broad impact on society since it influences individualization, the significance of free choice and the creation of bridging social capital (see the chapter of Dik).

The aim of this anthology is to contribute to a richer, more complex and variable understanding of how religion and volunteering interrelate. Hence, it will open up for complexity, contestation and ambiguity. Here, the reader will not find a new synthesizing framework or overarching theoretical perspective. Rather, we offer different and sometimes conflicting perspectives and thus contribute to the discussion among academics and policymakers about the many faces of religion and volunteering. More specifically, the book addresses the following questions: How do the relationships between types of religions/religiosity and types of volunteering vary within and across nations? What recent changes in our understanding of society, religion, and volunteering challenge the default view on their interactions? What other aspects of religion and volunteering can be studied apart from the traditional, default and in some instances instrumental perspective on religion and volunteering? What other enactments, reasons and consequences can be explored?

An Interdisciplinary Discussion

The aim of this anthology is to examine the relationship between religion and volunteering in its fuller complexity and depth. By this aim we want to contribute to the discussion among academics and practitioners on the dynamics of volunteering from the perspective of religion, but also on the role of religion in contemporary society. Therefore, interdisciplinary perspectives are necessary, and in the various chapters contributions from philosophy, theology, sociology, political science, anthropology, and even architecture are included.

We have consciously introduced the viewpoints of theologians, not because we think that volunteering should be understood as a mere religious phenomenon or practice but because we have become more aware that theological perspectives add to the scientific study of volunteering. Among other topics, they point to the need to elaborate on the meaning of the expression 'free choice', a crucial part of the definition of volunteering, and on how the understanding of free will cannot be taken for granted. In fact, how people understand the notion of free will determines how they conceive of the societies in which they live and how they practice volunteering. This means that, depending on their understanding of free will—as revealed in the questions they ask during their interviews—researchers may well reach different conclusions on volunteering or understand religious experiences differently. In this way theological perspectives may contribute to a more nuanced understanding of the interplay between religions, societies and volunteering.

We have included both quantitative and qualitative approaches so as to illustrate the multiple methodological features of research on religion and volunteering. Some quantitative contributions use datasets that allow for cross-national comparisons and examine the influence of various aspects of national contexts. But the anthology also includes qualitative research that uses phenomenological approaches or participant observation to unravel how individuals understand their commitments. Hence, our collection boasts a diversity of methodological approaches so as to grasp the relation between religion and volunteering in its full complexity and depth.

We are aware of the importance of geographical, religious and cultural contextuality when studying the relationships between religion and volunteering, but we do not offer a systematic representation from different regions or religious traditions in this book. For instance, readers will not find here texts discussing volunteering in the Eastern European Orthodox context. Nevertheless, we think it is important to offer contributions from the perspective of the three Abrahamic religions (Judaism, Christianity and Islam) and also to include contributions from outside western liberal societies. The context of the Middle East seemed important to us in this respect. Taking into consideration the role of religion in politics and conflicts in this region allows us to offer material to study the relation between religion and volunteering and its influence in societies in conflict and from other than western liberal perspectives.

We hope that the various approaches and methodologies will illustrate the need for diversified perspectives in the complex and diverse field of religion, society and volunteering and invite readers to follow up on the research that we offer.

Introducing the Chapters

In the first part of this anthology 'Theologies of religion and volunteering' we try to contextualize the relationships between religion and volunteering from the theological perspectives of the so-called Abrahamic religions. The contributions included in this section illustrate the importance of a diversified reflection on the idea of 'free will' that is constitutive for the understanding of both religion and volunteering. Religions impose 'claims' on their followers, such as neighbourly love or the obedience to the law, and these claims shape the meaning of the free will that is crucial to volunteering. From a religious perspective free will cannot be understood merely as the capacity for making an individual choice in isolation. Theological study, then, illustrates the complex forms of volunteering that may exist, precisely from the little-researched perspective of free will. The religious perspective on volunteering reminds us that in the study of free will altruism and social relationships also play an important role, a fact that is equally important in secularized societies.

In 'Christian Calling and Volunteering', Johan von Essen and Jacques Haers show how, in various Christian perspectives such as the Lutheran and Roman Catholic traditions, the invitation to neighbourly love calls the faithful to volunteer and thus, as it were, imposes an understanding of volunteering on the basis of religious adherence. Free will, a crucial concept in the history of ideas in the western world and a key element in all definitions of volunteering, is understood in the Christian tradition as taking responsibility in the common life and requires processes of discernment that clarify the deep bonds and interactions that characterize both creation and the understanding of the future world. The presentation of the Lutheran and Ignatian traditions shows the variety of perspectives that are possible in the Christian faith and its churches, while also illustrating how religious faith offers possibilities to clarify motivations for volunteering even in a highly secularized world in which, more often than not, the idea of free will has come to be equated with individual choice.

In her contribution 'If I Am Only for Myself, Who Am I? Volunteering and Righteousness in Judaism', Lena Roos discusses volunteering from a Jewish theological perspective by describing volunteering in Israel as carried out by the ultraorthodox Haredi community. She studies volunteer efforts as related to three important commandments—caring for the poor, the dead and the sick. The Haredis are involved in volunteering due to their piety and willingness to follow the commandments of the Torah. Therefore, seen from the religious perspective, volunteering is not entirely a free choice; it is a religious duty to fulfil God's commandments. Because of their volunteering, however, the Haredis are becoming secularized since they are confronted with secular Israeli society and have to educate themselves to be able to carry out their tasks. They are also increasing their influence and power in Israeli society because of the sheer extent of their volunteering activities. It demonstrates how an ultra-orthodox group is gaining power through apolitically and religiously motivated volunteering.

In the third contribution of this first part, 'Philanthropic Virtue', Mohammed Fazlhashemi studies the importance of the virtue of compassion in the Islamic tradition. Compassion can be pursued from the perspective of the reward it will offer to those who practice it, or from the perspective of the intrinsic value of the ethical norm. As a theological quality it is at the service of needy and suffering people and represents a challenge both at the individual and at the collective levels, while the need arises for a social safety net. In the course of history, the need to organize both this safety net and the volunteers who serve it became entangled with political organization and the power at play in societies. Decline in the capacity of political rulers to organize compassion opened the way for Islamic scholars to assume responsibility at this level. The commandment to be compassionate, therefore, determines volunteering in its individual and collective features.

In contemporary research the 'default position' on the issue of the relationship between religion and volunteering sees the former, taken as a social phenomenon and in its capacity to further welfare services and social cohesion, as a cause of the latter. In research, religious belief is frequently treated as a set of mental states that cause or facilitate actions such as volunteering and analyses bear on such self-reported motives. In an alternative approach, 'motive talk' and values are considered instead as the expression of cultural resources. This alternative approach is used when motives for volunteering are discussed in the second section, 'Religion as a Determinant of Volunteering'. Furthermore, we include findings at the country-level concerning the influence of religion on the overall probability to volunteer, i.e. how religious and organizational factors influence volunteering in any particular given context. Finally, findings on how individual and collective dimensions of volunteering are influenced in the context of a religious community are also presented in this section.

While building on previous studies, Matthew R. Bennett's contribution, 'Religiosity and Formal Volunteering in Global Perspective', explores the role played by religion at the individual and contextual levels on the likelihood of formal volunteering across 113 countries contained in the Gallup World Poll. He finds that religiously affiliated people are more likely to volunteer than the unaffiliated, and

1 Religion and Volunteering

that religious service attendance accounts to a significant degree for this association. Controlling for service attendance, respondents with a Hindu and Jewish affiliation are no more likely to volunteer than the unaffiliated. Bennett confirms the curvilinear relationship between country-level devoutness and volunteering: People in secular *and* devout countries are more likely to volunteer. This research also points out that a diverse religious context is positively associated with volunteering and that belonging to a religious minority group in a country is associated with an increased likelihood of volunteering.

In their contribution 'A Cross-National Examination of the Motivation to Volunteer: Religious Context, National Value Patterns, and Nonprofit Regimes' Lesley Hustinx, Ronan Van Rossem, Femida Handy and Ram A. Cnaan use the 1990 World Values Survey to investigate cross-nationally the influence of inner human drivers and contextual characteristics on the motivation to volunteer. They study the context at the levels of individual background characteristics, religious reality and institutional context variables, so as to answer the question: Is it possible on the basis of these factors to distinguish clearly between altruistic and self-interested motivations for volunteering? The conclusions point to the importance of contextual realities such as religious and cultural understandings, besides the traditionally researched individual psychological factors. The conclusions highlight that the secularization process observed in western societies is not at odds with altruistic motivations for volunteering and that religion cannot therefore be seen as the sole source of such altruistic motivations.

In the last chapter of this part 'Volunteering Among Church Attendees in Australia: Individual and Collective Dimensions', John Bellamy and Rosemary Leonard examine the relationship between involvement in the churches and individual volunteering activity in the wider community in Australia, using a survey of more than 3,000 (core) church attendees across all the major Christian denominations in Australia. The bridging capacity of Christian denominations is studied both at the individual and congregational level and the study also includes measures of (perceived) congregational bonding, congregational bridging and collective efficacy. The findings confirm the importance of the degree of a person's church involvement and the role of Christian theological orientation and denomination in predicting individual volunteering by church attendees in the wider community. Church attendees' stated reasons for volunteering form a pattern which did not vary for different types of volunteering. However, a distinction emerges in the findings between individual volunteering activity and collective involvement by the congregation. The sense of collective efficacy among church attendees was strongly associated with the extent of congregational bridging to the wider community but did not predict individual volunteering activity. The role of collective efficacy raises questions about the focus of congregations and the need for vision and goal setting as key ingredients in congregational life.

Processes of religious change and secularization have an impact on the understanding of religion itself and on the relationships between religion and volunteering. Sometimes this is perceived as a threat at the same time as religious change opens up new opportunities for religion to re-articulate itself and to inspire people in new ways towards volunteering. In this third section 'Religion and Volunteering in a (Post-) Secular Context', the reader will find contributions that offer empirical evidence concerning the complex and sometimes unexpected impact of religious change on volunteering. In a post-secular perspective the modern divide and incompatibility between religion and secularization is overcome and theology can be used as a framework to interpret even secular volunteering.

In his chapter 'Lost and Found In Secularization: A Religious Perspective on the Meaning of Volunteering', Johan von Essen's starting point is the observation that in post-secular societies, secularization and the increasing role of religion in society can go hand in hand. Of course, this entails a renewed understanding of religion as part of culture, relating to and not incorporating other cultural phenomena. He then explores, through interviews with volunteers in traditional Swedish volunteer organizations, whether it makes sense to frame the meaning they lend to their volunteering in religious terms, particularly with respect to how they perceive the altruistic motives for volunteering while at the same time reaping the rewards of gratitude and fulfilment for their actions as volunteers. From a theological point of view and in the Swedish context, he asks the question whether traditions of Lutheranism, particularly those concerning the notion of a calling, continue to shape contemporary secularized society and the understanding of volunteering. The contribution ends with suggestions about how these ideas can be further tested and researched.

In their contribution 'Making Church Happen: Architectural Methods for Transforming the Parish Churches of Flanders into Civic Collectives', Roel De Ridder and Sylvain De Bleeckere address issues of social capital and volunteering from an architectural point of view, studying the case of Flemish parish churches. Due to diminishing numbers of priests, increasing costs and decreasing church attendance, (political) questions are raised regarding the future of these church buildings. To answer these challenges, the authors study the interface between architecture (more precisely 'spatial agency') and the social sciences (more precisely 'actor-network theory' and the 'hybrid forum') both theoretically and practically, focusing on one particular case study. The research shows that even in a highly secularized context it is possible to stimulate a renewed interest in and re-appropriation of nearly empty church buildings. By involving local communities in a public deliberation process on the future of church buildings, old and new forms of civic participation are elicited. The involvement of both religious and secular citizens in the process further demonstrates that the meaning of a church building is not necessarily related to people's religiosity: In secularized societies, the remembrance of former religiosity can still form a solid basis for the voluntary commitment of citizens.

In 'Restorative Justice and Volunteering in a Secular Age' Eric Claes and Emilie Van Daele present a critical and constructive reflection on the possibility of relating the spiritual roots of a moderate version of restorative justice to the institutions and volunteers working in contemporary secular society. They illustrate how a tradition or outlook on morality and justice can be set free from its religious past and re-shaped into a secular engagement without losing its content or dynamic. A coherent framework is developed in which voluntary work is grounded in active, participative citizenship, while at the same time responding to the spiritual aspirations of restorative justice. Volunteers play a crucial role in the secular version of moderate restorative justice since it is through them that civil society is deployed.

Mary Hancock's contribution 'Short-Term Mission Voluntarism and the Post-Secular Imaginary' is based on ethnographic research in Southern California, conducted between 2009 and 2012, involving three Christian short-term mission (STM) agencies engaged with non-Christians in the context of international projects that mixed service, evangelism and tourism. She argues that STM's effects, while partially explicable in terms of the social capital that it may (or may not) engender at home and in mission fields, also include challenges to secular norms and institutions in a post-secular environment. Her research shows that, although the paradigm of social capital may suggest ways to explain the functions and social effects of norms, practices and institutions that it brings about, STM, especially as carried out among non-Christian communities, provides (1) experiential contexts for imagining a world in which divinity is considered as being immanently and sensorially present and (2) the communication tools for enacting that world. It may thus rework the categorical boundaries between secular and religious practices and spaces at home as well as on mission sites. As such, STM can be understood as an artifact of an emergent post-secular imaginary, a characterization that signals the limits of the secularization thesis and the recognition of the significance of plural religiosities, spiritual orientations and faith commitments in social action and institutions. In the midst of post-secular realities, Mary Hancock reintroduces the idea of spirituality as a means to connect inner worlds and motivations with material and political realities.

In the fourth and final section of this anthology, 'Politics of Religion and Volunteering', we study how religion and the relationships between religion and volunteering have the capacity to bring about political or social change. Religiously inspired volunteering can be used deliberately to bring about change or unintended social consequences for society can arise from religiously motivated volunteering. To analyse this capacity for bringing about political change, a causal model of a unitary actor to account for how religion affects volunteering is not sufficient: More account has to be taken of the contexts in which religious followers and volunteers live and work and this leads to more pragmatically articulated models that take their lead from how religion is 'expressed' and 'performed' in different settings. The contributions of this section illustrate these realities in some particular contexts.

In his contribution 'Religion and Social Solidarity: A Pragmatist Approach' Paul Lichterman presents findings from an ethnographic case study of a small civic group consisting of congregational leaders, housing and homeless advocates, to explore how people enact religious identities in everyday settings. Rather than focusing on individual religious actors, he studies 'group styles' in particular settings. Lichterman observes that even though many of the participants in the case study were clergy or religious leaders, they exposed their religious identity in varied ways, even ignoring it at certain times and in certain circumstances. The 'group style' that coordinated the setting was characterized by the fluidity of the boundaries between the religious and the secular, inviting participants to relate to their religiosity in a highly personalized way, to claim or not to claim their religious identities in the group setting. As a result, rather than considering the group as religious—as would be the case in the unitary actor model—Lichterman concludes that it is very difficult to make generalisations about the religious or non-religious character of the setting as a whole, and the presence or absence of religious identities and motives in the individuals who interact in these group settings. As a consequence, in such a post-Toquevillian or pragmatist approach, the relation between religion and civic action is variable, depending on how individuals relate to religion in specific settings, and more specifically, on whether the shared group style enables or disables the performance of religion for civic ends.

The Charismatic/Pentecostal (C/P) movement has emerged in Beirut mainly because of its capacity to mobilize new believers towards greater participation in their emergent groups within a tribalized and fragmented post-war society and city. In his contribution 'Your Prayer Moves God': On the Relation Between Voluntarism, the Emergent Charismatic Movement in Beirut and Social Capital", Oleg Dik demonstrates how the volunteering of C/P believers is rooted in the benefits and religious culture of emerging C/P communities. Dik's qualitative research, conducted in Beirut between November 2009 and April 2011, focuses on participatory observation and interviews with volunteers in the C/P movement. In this research the interplay between individuals, the larger sociopolitical context and the concrete social setting in which the volunteers are active are studied to show how religious volunteering shapes social solidarity. C/P groups without institutional ties subvert the established religious and political landscape by volunteering outside of the established religious welfare organizations and create novel, trans-sectarian possibilities for volunteering. The effect of religious volunteering on social solidarity is not static, but hinges mainly on the religious culture within which the volunteering is embedded, the larger sociopolitical context and the concrete setting and encounters of volunteers. This contribution leads to a fuller understanding of how religiously motivated volunteering works in post-war societies with weak state institutions.

In his contribution 'The Role of Voluntary Faith-Based Organizations in Political Transformation in Post-Revolution Egypt', Mustafa Khalil uses participant observation and interviews to investigate the role faith-based organizations played before, during and after the 2011 revolution in Egypt that toppled the then president Mubarak. He presents three case studies of Mosques in Cairo, the first without specific political affiliation, the second connected to the radical Salafi movement and the third under the influence of the Muslim Brotherhood. The revolution worked as a catalyst for the emergence of a strong, collective and civic commitment, embodying the desire to change political realities beyond the already existing volunteering that targeted poverty reduction. Some faith-based organizations could become a platform for political change and were used as such because of their connections with organized political and religious movements. This contribution offers early research on the role of faith-based organizations in a context of changing political and revolutionary realities.

The efforts to promote and expand volunteering are particularly significant in Israel. Here the field of volunteering becomes a space through which the privileged social strata of Ashkenazi (European) Jews try to reconsolidate the group's hegemonic status that has been eroded during the period of neoliberal transformation.

In his contribution 'Going Back to Our Values': Restoring Symbolic Hegemony Through Promoting 'Volunteering' In Israel', Itamar Y. Shachar presents the results of extensive ethnographic fieldwork in following the efforts to promote volunteering as pursued by the board and staff members of a prominent NGO in Israel called 'Good Spirit'. The Ashkenazi staff of the organization regained a sense of managerial control over the national space through successfully promoting a liberally inspired construction of volunteering. This construction is universalised through its representation as a professional, apolitical and consensual realm, while its symbols and rituals can be seen as a new version of the civil religion that naturalized Ashkenazi hegemony in the past. These strategies of legitimization and universalisation obscure and 'whiten' the exclusionary character of this managerial activity, and bypass challenges—sometimes even phrased in religious terms—posed to this project by subjugated groups. This contribution illustrates the usefulness of examining why, how and by whom volunteering is constructed and being used.

In the final contribution of this anthology, 'Volunteering in Religious Communities: What does it Bring to Society? Calculating Social Yield', Welmoet Boender studies the initiative of Oikos, a Dutch ecumenical civil society organization that has elaborated a methodology to measure the social value and importance of religious organizations in which volunteers are involved in terms of social yield. In a secular society, this offers the possibility of discussing the value of religious organizations in the public realm. By investigating some published text cases in the Netherlands, it allows her to critically discuss the very idea of measuring the social yield: For though it allows religious organizations to gain appreciation, this approach does not pay full tribute to their goals and practices, such as convivial labour or the fact that volunteering does not aim at economic gain. It also allows her to study to what extent such social yield will provoke public and state reactions: There does not seem to be a direct relationship in this case as is illustrated in the differences in public reaction towards Christian, immigrant and Muslim religious organizations.

We wish our readers a fruitful interdisciplinary journey through the varied contributions and hope they will spark in them new ideas on the relations between religion, volunteering and rapidly changing societies.

References

Beaumont, J., & Baker, C. (Eds.). (2011). *Postsecular cities: Space, theory and practice*. London: Continuum.

Beckford, J. (2012). Public religions and the postsecular: Critical reflections. *Journal for the Scientific Study of Religion, 51*(1), 1–19.

Breckman, W. (2005). Democracy between disenchantment and political theology: French post-Marxism and the return of religion. *New German Critique, 94*, 72–105.

Brugger, W. (2009). From hostility through recognition to identification: State-church models and their relationship to freedom of religion. In H. Joas & K. Wiegand (Eds.), *Secularization and the world religions* (pp. 160–180). Liverpool: Liverpool University Press.

Casanova, J. (1994). *Public religions in the modern world*. Chicago: University of Chicago Press.

Casanova, J. (2009). The religious situation in Europe. In H. Joas & K. Wiegand (Eds.), *Secularization and the world religions* (pp. 206–228). Liverpool: Liverpool University Press.

Chapman, R., & Hamalainen, L. (2011). Understanding faith-based engagement and volunteering. In J. Beaumont & C. Baker (Eds.), *Postsecular cities: Space, theory and practice* (pp. 184–200). London: Continuum.

Cnaan, R. A., Handy, F., & Wadsworth, M. (1996). Defining who is a volunteer: Conceptual and empirical considerations. *Nonprofit and Voluntary Sector Quarterly, 25*(3), 364–383.

Cnaan, R. A., Wineburg, R. J., & Boddie, S. C. (1999). *The newer deal: Social work and religion in partnership.* New York: Columbia University Press.

de Hart, J., & Dekker, P. (2013). Religion, spirituality and civic participation. In J. de Hart, P. Dekker, & L. Halman (Eds.), *Religion and civil society in Europe* (pp. 169–188). New York: Springer.

de Hart, J., Dekker, P., & Halman, L. (2013). Introduction: European diversity and divergences. In J. de Hart, P. Dekker, & L. Halman (Eds.), *Religion and civil society in Europe* (pp. 1–12). New York: Springer.

de Vries, H., & Sullivan, L. (Eds.). (2006). *Political theologies. Public religions in a post-secular world.* New York: Fordham University Press.

Dekker, P., & Halman, L. (2003). Volunteering and values. An introduction. In P. Dekker & L. Halman (Eds.), *The values of volunteering. Cross-cultural perspectives* (pp. 1–17). New York: Kluwer Academic.

Dinham, A., & Lowndes, W. (2009). Faith and the public realm. In A. Dinham, R. Furbey, & V. Lowndes (Eds.), *Faith in the public realm. Controversies, policies and practices* (pp. 1–19). Bristol: Policy Press.

Eliasoph, N. (1997). "Close to home": The work of avoiding politics. *Theory and Society, 26*(5), 605–647.

Eliasoph, N. (2013). *The politics of volunteering.* Cambridge: Polity.

Geertz, C. (1966). Religion as a cultural system. In M. Banton (Ed.), *Anthropological approaches to the study of religion.* London: Tavistock Publications.

Gillespie, M. A. (2008). *The theological origins of modernity.* Chicago: The University of Chicago Press.

Goss, K. (2010). Civil society and civil engagement: Towards a multi-level theory of policy feedbacks. *Journal of Civil Society (Special Issue: Volunteering and social activism), 6*(2), 119–143.

Grönlund, H. (2011). Identity and volunteering intertwined: Reflections on the values of young adults. *Voluntas: International Journal of Voluntary and Nonprofit Organizations, 22*(4), 852–874.

Habermas, J. (2006). Religion in the public sphere. *European Journal of Philosophy, 14*(1), 1–25.

Handy, F., Cnaan, R. A., Brudney, J., Ascoli, U., & Meijs, L. (2000). Public perception of "who is a volunteer": An examination of the net-cost approach from a cross-cultural perspective. *Voluntas: International Journal of Voluntary and Nonprofit Organizations, 11*(1), 45–65.

Haski-Leventhal, D., Meijs, L. C. P. M., & Hustinx, L. (2010). The third party model: Enhancing volunteering through governments, corporations and educational institutes. *Journal of Social Policy, 39*(1), 139–158.

Heelas, P., & Woodhead, L. (2001). Homeless minds today? In P. L. Berger, L. Woodhead, P. Heelas, & D. Martin (Eds.), *Peter Berger and the study of religion* (pp. 43–72). New York: Routledge.

Hustinx, L. (2003). *Reflexive modernity and styles of volunteering. The case of the Flemish Red Cross volunteers* (Diss.) Leuven: Faculteit Sociale Wetenschappen, Katholieke Universiteit Leuven.

Hustinx, L. (2010). Institutionally individualized volunteering: Towards a late modern reconstruction. *Journal of Civil Soicety, 6*(2), 165–179.

Hustinx, L., Cnaan, R. A., & Handy, F. (2010). Navigating theories of volunteering: A hybrid map for a complex phenomenon. *Journal for the Theory of Social Behaviour, 40*(4), 410–434.

Hustinx, L. and Meijs, L.C.P.M. (2011) Re-embedding volunteering: in search of a new collective ground. *Voluntary Sector Review, 2*(1), 5–21.

1 Religion and Volunteering

Jacobsson, K. (2014). Elementary forms of religious life in animal rights activism. *Culture Unbound.* vol. 5, 305–326.

Janoski, T. (2010). The dynamic process of volunteering in civil society: A group and multi-level approach. *Journal of Civil Society (Special Issue: Volunteering and social activism), 6*(2), 99–118.

Joas, H. (2009). Society, state and religion: Their relationship from the perspective of the world religions: An introduction. In H. Joas & K. Wiegand (Eds.), *Secularization and the world religions* (pp. 1–22). Liverpool: Liverpool University Press.

Kong, L. (2010). Global shifts, theoretical shifts: Changing geographies of religion. *Progress of Human Geography, 34*(6), 755–776.

Lam, P.-Y. (2002). As the flocks gather: How religion affects voluntary association participation. *Journal for the Scientific Study of Religion, 41*(3), 405–422.

Lilla, M. (2007). *The stillborn God: Religion, politics, and the modern west.* New York: Alfred Knopf.

Lim, C., & MacGregor, C. A. (2012). Religion and volunteering in context: Disentangling the contextual effects of religion on voluntary behavior. *American Sociological Review, 77*(5), 747–779.

Lyons, M., Wijkström, F., & Clary, G. (1998). Comparative studies of volunteering: What is being studied? *Voluntary Action, 1*(1), 45–54.

Musick, M., & Wilson, J. (2008). *Volunteers. A social profile.* Bloomington: Indiana University Press.

O'Reagan, A. (2009). *Imaging the voluntary actor: Interpreting narratives of intent and meaning. European civil society series.* Baden-Baden: Nomos.

Pick, D., Holmes, K., & Bruecknar, M. (2011). Governmentalities of volunteering: A study of regional Western Australia. *Voluntas: International Journal of Voluntary and Nonprofit Organizations, 22*(3), 390–408.

Putnam, R. D. (1995). Bowling alone: America's declining social capital. *Journal of Democracy, 6*(1), 65–78.

Ruiter, S., & De Graaf, N. (2006). National context, religiosity, and volunteering: Results from 53 countries. *American Sociological Review, 7*(2), 191–210.

Schwadel, P. (2005). Individual, congregational, and denominational effects on church members' civic participation. *Journal of the Scientific Study of Religion, 44*(2), 159–171.

Svennungsson, J. (2004). *Guds återkomst. En studie av gudsbegreppet inom postmodern filosofi* (Diss.). Göteborg: Glänta Production.

Turner, B. (2011). *Religion and modern society. Citizenship, secularization and the state.* Cambridge: Cambridge University Press.

van Tienen, M., Scheepers, P., Reitsma, J., & Schilderman, H. (2011). The role of religiosity for formal and informal volunteering in the Netherlands. *Voluntas: International Journal of Voluntary and Nonprofit Organizations, 22*(3), 365–389.

Verba, S., Schlozman, K. L., & Brady, H. E. (1995). *Voice and equality: Civic voluntarism in American politics.* Cambridge: Harvard University Press.

Vermeer, P., & Scheepers, P. (2011). Religious socialization and non-religious volunteering: A Dutch panel study. *Voluntas: International Journal of Voluntary and Nonprofit Organizations, 23*(4), 940–958.

von Essen, J. (2008). *Om det ideella arbetets betydelse—en studie om människors livsåskådningar* (Diss.). Uppsala: Teologiska institutionen, Uppsala Universitet.

Wilson, B. (1985). Secularization: The inherited model. In P. E. Hammond (Ed.), *The sacred in a secular age. Toward revision in the scientific study of religion* (pp. 9–20). Berkeley: University of California Press.

Wilson, J. (2012). Volunteerism research: A review essay. *Nonprofit and Voluntary Sector Quarterly, 41*(2), 176–212.

Wuthnow, R. (1991). *Acts of compassion. Caring for others and helping ourselves.* Princeton: Princeton University Press.

Wuthnow, R. (1996). *Sharing the journey.* New York: Free Press.

Wuthnow, R. (2002). Reassembling the civic church. The changing role of congregations in American civil society. In R. Madsen, W. M. Sullivan, A. Swidler, & S. M. Tipton (Eds.), *Meaning and modernity. Religion, polity and self* (pp. 163–180). Berkeley: University of California Press.

Wuthnow, R. (2004). *Saving America? Faith-based services and the future of civil society.* Princeton: Princeton University Press.

Yeung, A. B. (2004). An intricate triangle. *Nonprofit and Voluntary Sector Quarterly, 33*(3), 410–422.

Yinger, M. (1970). *The scientific study of religion.* New York: Macmillan.

Part I
Theologies of Religion and Volunteering

Chapter 2
Christian Calling and Volunteering

Jacques Haers and Johan von Essen

Introduction

It may come as a surprise that the word "volunteering" does not appear in well-known and reliable Christian theological dictionaries such as Jean-Yves Lacoste's *Dictionnaire critique de théologie* (Lacoste 2007). Of course, "volunteering" is a recent word: It originated in a military context and "volunteer" charitable organizations seriously took off only in the nineteenth century. Nevertheless, research, as in this volume (Hustinx et al.), points to a positive relation between individual religiosity and altruistic motivations to volunteer: This could be explained by individuals participating in religious communities that further prosocial behaviour (Wuthnow 1991) or by values and convictions about neighbourly love as found in religious belief (Bennett in this volume). In this contribution, we will argue that the absence of the word "volunteering" in the theological dictionaries does not come as a surprise. It reflects a tension between neighbourly love—which, in the Christian tradition, represents the idea nearest to volunteering—and the modern, secularized understanding of the concept of "volunteering". This tension concerns the role and possibility of free will, a key issue both in secularized modernity, where it is considered a core feature of the autonomous subject, and in Christian theology, where free will is understood relationally and where, therefore, the idea of a fully autonomous and independent free will is criticized. We will explore, from a Christian theological viewpoint that takes into account some of the many Christian traditions—in our case the Lutheran and Ignatian traditions—how free will and neighbourly love as understood by Christians relate to one another and determine a Christian approach to volunteering that, to a certain extent, is at odds with the modern understanding of volunteering. We will provide some idea of how the Christian understanding of

---

J. Haers (✉)
University Centre Saint-Ignatius Antwerp, Antwerp, Belgium
e-mail: jacques.haers@ucsia.be

J. von Essen
Institute for Civil Society Studies, Ersta Sköndal University College, Stockholm, Sweden
e-mail: johan.vonessen@esh.se

L. Hustinx et al. (eds.), *Religion and Volunteering,* Nonprofit and Civil Society Studies, 23
DOI 10.1007/978-3-319-04585-6_2, © Springer International Publishing Switzerland 2015

free will and its role in understanding neighbourly love, from the perspective of a relationship with God and in response to a calling from God, are different from the secularized take on the free will of autonomous human beings that originated with the modern western world and that is characteristic for most of our contemporary understanding of volunteering. As a consequence, we will also highlight the existence of specifically Christian perspectives on volunteering.

Volunteering refers to a complex social phenomenon that can best be understood as a social construct (Hustinx et al. 2010; Wilson 2000). Therefore, it is dependent on its contexts: Definitions of volunteering will vary between different welfare regimes, cultures and historical periods (Dekker and Halman 2003). Nevertheless, in most of the academic discussions and in widely accepted perceptions of volunteering, some common features surface: Volunteering concerns (a) unpaid activities (which is not the same as unrewarded activities as volunteers draw some reward and appreciation from their commitments) that are (b) performed out of free will and (c) for the benefit of others beyond friendship and kinship ties. Moreover, volunteering is often carried out (d) in an organizational context. These common elements appear in a content analysis study of 200 definitions of volunteering (Cnaan and Amrofell 1994; Cnaan et al. 1996) and have been used in cross-national quantitative studies to assess what people perceive when they design activities as volunteering (Handy et al. 2000; Meijs et al. 2003). Qualitative in-depth studies targeting the phenomenology of volunteering confirm these findings (von Essen 2008; O'Reagan 2009).

In our contribution, we focus on the second of these common features: free will. We approach the idea of volunteering through the nearest concept that Christian traditions have to offer, neighbourly love. Theologians cannot but agree that the understanding of free will is crucial in articulating the differences between various Christian traditions, such as Lutheranism and Roman Catholicism: A long history of fierce debates and disagreements on the issue testify to this. Beyond these interdenominational differences, the idea of free will is also crucial to understand the tensions between secularized modernity and Christianity, even if some of the roots of secularized modernity are, from an historical perspective, to be found in theological debates about the relations between God, human beings and nature (see, for instance, Gillespie 2008, p. 12; Sigurdson 2009, p. 120). Therefore, one would expect that an in-depth analysis of the idea of free will is necessary for clarifying the relationship between volunteering, as understood in a modern, secularized environment, and religious faith and commitment.

Surprisingly, only scant attention has been devoted in the academic literature to this aspect of volunteering as constituted of freely chosen actions. There is a lively debate concerning the altruistic character of volunteering (see Haski-Leventhal (2009) for a recent overview of this debate) and there is also an effort to assess the degree of volunteering by the use of a net-cost approach (Handy et al. 2000). Both these research perspectives concern the outlook of human beings as "homines oeconomici" and touch upon volunteering as nonpaid work. The understanding of what "free will" is, although it carries an important role in volunteer work and in the motivations for volunteering, has often been assumed as "known" and remains academically understudied. As a consequence, the moral character of volunteering (see Story 1992) is poorly discussed. Academic research has paid even less attention to the contrasting understandings that secularized western actors and religious actors may have of volunteering and free will, precisely because of the reference of the latter to their faith. However, in a Christian perspective on volunteering, free will is a core issue, and Christian theologians cannot but approach free will and volunteering from the perspective of human beings in their relationship to God.

It is to an analysis of the idea of "free will", particularly from a diversified Christian viewpoint, that we want to invite the readers of this contribution: We hope, in doing this, to also deepen our understanding of the complex dimensions of volunteering. In this book, other authors will focus on non-Christian religions (see the contributions of Roos and Fazlhashemi). We will, therefore, not present a comparative interreligious study here.

Basic Structural Features of Neighbourly Love

If volunteering displays the above-mentioned common features and aims to benefit others, really different others, then one of the Christian ideas closest to it is the love of neighbour, the call to "love one's neighbour as oneself" (Matthew 22: 39). We will present the common basic structural features of the idea of neighbourly love in Christian thought although there exists a variety of interpretations and traditions on the matter. A brief analysis of the iconic parable of the good Samaritan (Luke 10: 29–37)[1] helps us to grasp the idea narratively:

> [29]But wanting to justify himself, he asked Jesus, "And who is my neighbour?" [30]Jesus replied, "A man was going down from Jerusalem to Jericho, and fell into the hands of robbers, who stripped him, beat him, and went away, leaving him half dead. [31]Now by chance a priest was going down that road; and when he saw him, he passed by on the other side. [32]So likewise a Levite, when he came to the place and saw him, passed by on the other side. [33]But a Samaritan while traveling came near him; and when he saw him, he was moved with pity. [34]He went to him and bandaged his wounds, having poured oil and wine on them. Then he put him on his own animal, brought him to an inn, and took care of him. [35]The next day he took out two denarii, gave them to the innkeeper, and said, 'Take care of him; and when I come back, I will repay you whatever more you spend.' [36]Which of these three, do you think, was a neighbour to the man who fell into the hands of the robbers?" [37]He said, "The one who showed him mercy." Jesus said to him, "Go and do likewise."

Those listening to Jesus may have been shocked. Of course, they knew about the importance of neighbourly love: Luke (10: 25–28) presents the parable of the good Samaritan as part of Jesus' answer to the question of a lawyer—the "he" in the initial verse of the story—about what should be done to inherit life. In the parallel texts of Mark (12: 28–34) and Matthew (22: 34–40), this question is phrased in terms of the search for the most important of the commandments. Jesus teases the answer out of the lawyer: "You shall love the Lord your God with all your heart, and with all your soul, and with all your strength, and with all your mind; and your neighbour as yourself." To Jesus, the parable illustrates how the two most important commandments of what Christians have come to call the First Testament, Deuteronomy

---

[1] Biblical passages are quoted from the New Revised Standard Version.

6: 4–5 ("you shall love the Lord your God...") and Leviticus 19: 18 ("you shall love your neighbour as yourself"), are intimately connected: The love of neighbour springs from God's love for creation. The commitment to others, therefore, is an expression of the faith in God and commitment to God, as God commits to human beings in God's creation. Those listening to Jesus knew about these commandments: They were a crucial part of their tradition.

None of this is very shocking thus far. The surprise lies in the fact that both the priest and the Levite—persons with a leadership status and who in the Jewish culture of that time were expected to proclaim and put into practice the commandments of the Law—pass by the wounded man. A Samaritan, who was not a part of the faith community and who belonged to a group frowned upon, is the unexpected person who, out of pity, takes care of the wounded man. That comes as a first surprise: Not the priest, not the Levite, but a despicable Samaritan shows mercy. Moreover, and here comes a second surprise, Jesus asks a twisted question that provokes his hearers: Who of those who walk along the road "was a neighbour to the man who fell into the hand of the robbers"? This is unexpected: We expect the wounded man to be called "neighbour", not the Samaritan. By asking who is a neighbour to the wounded man, Jesus seems to invite his hearers, and the readers of the parable, to hear a call: "Can I be, as the good Samaritan, moved by pity, a neighbour to my fellow human being?" and, in the context of our contribution, we are tempted to add here: "and volunteer to help him and take care of him?" The parable is a call to become neighbours: Our response to the challenge that is set before us reveals our free decision and our humanity. In the process it is clear that the wounded man becomes a neighbour, when we respond to the call to become a neighbour. Being or becoming a neighbour, therefore, to Christians means taking responsibility for others out of compassion—not the easy, emotional compassion, but the tough, demanding compassion that answers the call to commitment. That is why the Roman Catholic Jesuit theologian Jon Sobrino (1992) speaks about the principle of compassion and the Lutheran theologian Dietrich Bonhoeffer (1989) claims that grace (in this case the call to take care of others) is costly and demanding. Compassion is a "principle" as it does not depend merely on the autonomous decisions of individuals but reflects the structure of reality itself, one that calls on individuals to commit: The freely made decision is in answer to the compassionate structure of reality.

Discernment

Each of the three persons walking along the road took a decision, to ignore or to care for the wounded man. All three of them had seen him, all three were challenged and each one made up his mind. One would expect the Levite and the priest to take care of the wounded man. But they were free to do otherwise and they did otherwise. The Samaritan, who was not really expected to take care, does take care, in a consistent and even somewhat extravagant way. He is the real neighbour, i.e. he reflects the fitting relationship with God and answers God's call to love. In a Christian perspective, ideas such as neighbourly love and free will are always understood in terms of the relationship to God. Christian decision processes—some Christian traditions, like the Ignatian spiritual tradition,[2] use the expression "discernment"[3]—involve free will, but a free will that is always embedded in the relationship to God, as revealed in the life of Jesus of Nazareth, the Christ who, in the eyes of Christians, embodies decisively in his life and words both human and divine love. From a Christian point of view, human beings are centres of decision-making in which free will plays a crucial role.[4] The use of free will involves a heuristic endeavour in which account is taken of God's call as it appears in realities that challenge us and in texts that reflect the Christian tradition in Jesus Christ, inspiring people to follow Jesus Christ, to act as he did, albeit in new circumstances. In the Christian perspective, there is always the question as to which spirits or inner movements are moving us when using our free will to reach decisions: Are we moving in line with God's call as we perceive it and as supported by tradition or are we moving against that call? In terms of the technical notion of discernment: Are we in consolation or in desolation? In their volunteer commitments, Christians will gauge how they use their free will and how it relates to their relationship with God: Free will is never merely that of an autonomous, unrelated and unconnected human being; it has a relational context—with God, with other human beings, with nature and with the world. Such processes of discernment are not easy, they require self-knowledge, the willingness to listen to others, the humility to accept that mistakes can be made and the awareness that sometimes one will go against the direction of the discernment because of inner resistances or desires. It is not surprising, therefore, that free will decisions are considered by Christians to have a distinct spiritual and relational character.

It will be clear from what has been said that the idea of "free will", from a Christian perspective, does not refer to human subjects fully on their own, with a capacity to decide for themselves without taking others into account, in particular, wounded and excluded others—including also an awareness that is growing today, of created beings different from human beings—nor without taking into account their relationship with the one they consider to be the other. Although the creativity of human beings as centres of decision-making is certainly not denied, processes of free will always involve relationships that belong to the very core of a definition of free will. If volunteering is a decision of the free will, then, for Christians, this volunteering will be embedded in the call that emerges from their relationships with the (broken) world and with God. Their volunteering, therefore, will always be the answer to a call, which in their eyes provides them with the relationships necessary to exercise this free will. The extent to which this call leaves them space to move against it provides for never-ending discussions in the history of theology and of various Christian traditions, discussions that have been subsumed under the theological area of the tension between "grace" and "nature".

---

[2] Meaning the tradition starting with Ignatius of Loyola, in the sixteenth century. It will be used further on in the article to illustrate the Roman Catholic approach to free will.

[3] The idea and practice of spiritual discernment represents a long and solid tradition in Christianity. See, for example: (Ruiz Jurado 1994; Guillet et al. 1957).

[4] The early theology of Origen of Alexandria (ca. 185–254) illustrates this point. See, Crouzel (1989).

Creation, Incarnation and the Kingdom of God

In their desire to understand what is going on in processes of discernment, Christians attempt to articulate intellectually—theologically, they would say—their relationships with God. Various types of relationships can be distinguished, of which we will discuss three: creation, incarnation and the vision of the Kingdom of God. We will also consider how various traditions in Christianity have variously evaluated the impact of God in the processes of decision-making: How can the collaboration of God and human beings be understood and what does this mean for our understanding of free will? Does God's grace—God's free, loving commitment and action—leave human nature free to decide and act? Does creative human nature allow for the work of God's grace in the world?

The faith in God as Creator of the universe invites Christians to reflect on the idea of creation. Theologians have often discussed whether or not creation refers to a temporal beginning of the universe, but all agree in saying that creation certainly means that the world as we know it cannot be disconnected from its Creator, even if this world seems to work according to its own laws and dynamics that can be studied as if there were no Creator involved. Christians are also sensitive to the fact that the world as creation is an interconnected whole, of which human beings, even if they may occupy a special place, are a part. There is no otherness that is not relational otherness, i.e. otherness that would allow an escape from mutual responsibility. This awareness of the underlying interconnectedness of all things and beings created, however different from one another these beings may be, points to a fundamental and crucial interrelationship of all in God. From this perspective of creation, human free will cannot be disconnected from the call to interconnectedness and interdependence that shapes all existence. Committing to this interconnectedness, assuming responsibilities amidst interrelatedness is, therefore, a challenge to human free will and shapes the willingness to volunteer. Volunteering is, in this perspective, committing to the interconnected world as creation, particularly there where the sense of interconnectedness is broken. Not surprisingly, Christians often want to engage in the struggle against poverty and exclusion or in the attempts to build a more sustainable world. Indeed, neighbourliness reflects this deep creational challenge to caring interconnectedness.

The incarnation points to God's own self-commitment in Jesus of Nazareth, the Christ. To Christians, the mystery of human life is opened up in the life, actions and words of Jesus of Nazareth as a gift from God and a full commitment of God to our world. To Christians it is imperative, therefore, to know the life of Jesus and to connect to it, to recognize in it the deep calls that constitute human life. Jesus teaches—God in Jesus teaches—by living human life to the full and in all its consequences. It is, so to say, a call that comes from the inside and reveals what it means to be a human being, not some external force imposed on human beings. Following Jesus Christ, therefore, is not in the first place following a set of rules that he would have put on the agenda, but, rather, coming to know him so that this knowledge transforms us by leading us into deeper human life and a commitment to creation and fellow human beings. The narrative structure of the Gospels lures its readers into this process of assimilation, in which they recognize both who God is in Jesus of Nazareth and what a human being is: God's reality and the deepest essence of human life are revealed together. A story about Jesus' life that may help us to better understand the meaning of the incarnation can be found in Mark 7:24–30:

> [24]From there he set out and went away to the region of Tyre. He entered a house and did not want anyone to know he was there. Yet he could not escape notice, [25]but a woman whose little daughter had an unclean spirit immediately heard about him, and she came and bowed down at his feet. [26]Now the woman was a Gentile, of Syro-Phoenician origin. She begged him to cast the demon out of her daughter. [27]He said to her, "Let the children be fed first, for it is not fair to take the children's food and throw it to the dogs." [28]But she answered him, "Sir, even the dogs under the table eat the children's crumbs." [29]Then he said to her, "For saying that, you may go—the demon has left your daughter." [30]So she went home, found the child lying on the bed, and the demon gone.

We avoid a full exegetical discussion here, which would draw on the place of this passage in the overall gospel of Mark and on the existing parallel text in Matthew's gospel (15: 21–28), to concentrate on its narrative power. Initially, there is a clear refusal of Jesus to engage—we are tempted to say: to volunteer—into helping the Syro-Phoenician woman: She is an "other", not part of Jesus' own faith community, a Gentile. Jesus resists the call that arises from her and rebukes her harshly. The response of the woman, turning Jesus' analogy against him, changes the situation: Jesus recognizes that her faith, i.e. in her God—the one whom Jesus called his Father—challenges him. God is already committed to this woman and that is the call that moves out towards Jesus and to which he responds by caring. As a consequence, God is recognized in an even more profound way: The child is healed from its demon. Incarnation can be understood from this text: being drawn into a commitment to the world, out of an encounter with God and so that this encounter with God can be deepened. In his diary (1971), an important Flemish mystic, Egied van Broeckhoven, a Jesuit worker and priest, describes how in his contacts with fellow workers, whose lives he wanted to share by sharing their working conditions, friendships deepened and how this allowed the self-revelation of God to unfold in a profound way. Commitment to the world and to fellow human beings and the self-revelation of God work hand in hand. So, volunteering from a Christian perspective is an answer to a call addressed to us by God in the midst of reality, a call we follow and that allows us to discover more deeply who Godself is. Volunteering, then, is also, in the eyes of Christians, the search for a God who is recognized in the call directed at them by their fellow human beings and in whose work they participate by engaging in the care for these fellow human beings.

The vision of the Kingdom of God, presented by Jesus in images of natural growth, banquets and judgement—as well as articulated in his actual life—provides us with a third approach to Christian perceptions of the relationships between human beings and God. The Kingdom offers a vision of the ultimate reconciled and fulfilled future for the whole of creation, a future that human beings, as part of this broken and fallen world—i.e. a world that has moved away from its rootedness in the relation to God—cannot bring about but will receive as a gift from God. It is a promise that invites these human beings to already commit fully to this promise in their actions: Inspired and strengthened by the life of Jesus of Nazareth, who embodies the Kingdom, human beings attempt to act to realise the Kingdom, in view of the Kingdom. The relationship with God in Jesus, therefore, focuses Christians on the future community of the Kingdom even if they have difficulty imagining it in the twisted, unjust and harsh present world: The Kingdom lies within reach only because it is God's gift on which human beings can rely. Volunteering, from a Christian perspective, therefore, aims at a future that lies beyond human reach but that nevertheless, as a promise within the relationship with God, works as a powerful attractor that empowers human beings to change and transform the twisted world of which they are a part. Christian volunteering, ultimately, focuses towards this vision of a healed world and fulfilled community of solidarity and care, in response to all exclusions and injustices in the contemporary world. Volunteering is thus a response to immediate needs from the perspective of God's promise of the Kingdom: It arises out of the faith and trust in God's promise as the natural thing to do.

Creation, incarnation, the vision of the Kingdom of God: These three key elements of the Christian faith unwrap features of the relationships between God and human beings that are crucial in a Christian understanding of neighbourly love and of volunteering. The commitment of Christians as volunteers receives strength from their faith in a God who creates the world, who commits fully to the world in the life of Jesus of Nazareth and who guarantees a vision of the future for the world. In that perspective, God could be said to be the first volunteer: God chooses to create and to bind Godself to the created world; God chooses to enter into a difficult and risky, concrete relationship with a troubled world by sharing the life of this world; God chooses to commit Godself in the promise of the Kingdom of God. Even if Christians never articulated God's actions in terms of volunteering—they prefer to speak about "love"—the four main features of volunteering as given at the outset of this contribution seem to be met: unpaid, out of free will, for the benefit of others and with structural features. When Christians become volunteers, their volunteering should be understood in the context of their relationships with the God-volunteer and this determines their understanding of free will, making it explicit. The free will of a Christian is not the free will of a human being who would have the capacity to isolate him- or herself from the rest of the world, so as to take a fully autonomous decision about what to do. Christian free will results from relations that articulate a complex call: the call that arises out of the fact of belonging to an interdependent, networked world (creation); the call that becomes visible in the face of fellow human beings, particularly those who suffer (incarnation) and the call of the vision of a reconciled community for a broken world. This call can be understood as an "imperative of belonging" that shapes human free will.

Two Theological Perspectives

The understanding of the "imperative" character originating out of the relationship with God, conditioning human free will, has proven to be a tricky and contentious issue for Christians: How do God and human beings relate to one another, within the foundational relationship of creation upon which all Christians seem to agree. Thomas Aquinas spoke about a "relatio quaedam", a very special relationship, as God has a priority in it: God founds the very relationship in which God and human beings interact.[5] But should the relationship between God and human beings then be understood as a competitive reality, where human freedom has to be asserted over against God's oppression? Should priority be given to God's action, given the vulnerable, mediocre, egoistic and sinful character of human beings, who are not capable of doing good of their own accord? Or should one be careful not to over-stress this superiority of God, so as not to damage the creative and good resources of human beings who can do good, at least some good, out of themselves and will be measured and judged on the basis of the good they do? Or should one avoid to think in such competitive terms and rather emphasizes the complex and delicate balance between God's actions and the actions of human beings? These questions constitute the framework for discussions that arose and continue to arise throughout the history of Christianity and that also, to a large extent, explain some of the differences between various Christian traditions.

The attempts to understand the relationship between God and human beings (or between the God and the human being in Jesus the Christ) have shaped the history of Christian theology right from its beginnings. They are a constant feature of Christian history, usually spoken about, amongst theologians, as the tensions between "nature" and "grace".[6] How do God and human beings cooperate or compete? How free are human beings, when they are totally dependent upon God? And how free is God in God's relationship to human beings? Free will has been a core debate in the history of Christian theology, internally and in the debate with modernity. Indeed, modern secularization tends to understand human free will as in opposition to, or independent of, God's will, as modern people feel the need to escape the domination of a despotic God so as to unfold their own creativity, capacities and potentialities. From an historical point of view, this emergence of the autonomous human being—autonomy seen in opposition to dependence upon God and the social structures and institutions that claim to authoritatively transmit the divine will and order—lies at the core of modernity. This struggle becomes fully visible when medieval political theology came to an end in the seventeenth century and politics became separated from theology, as was the case in the thought of Thomas Hobbes, for example (Lilla 2007).

We will now briefly analyse two different and, at that time, competing Christian approaches to free will, which contrast with the emerging modern understanding of free will seen as indicating the autonomous human being. Martin Luther (1483–1546) and Ignatius Loyola (1491–1556) both struggled with the new modern

---

[5] See, for an analysis of Thomas Aquinas' understanding of the foundational relationship of creation; Sertillanges (1949).

[6] Theological discussions of "nature and grace", to which also belong in-depth analyses of anthropology and of the sinful condition of human beings, usually harbour substantial chapters on ancient, modern and contemporary history. For an introduction—from a Roman Catholic point of view—see, for example: (Haight 1991).

understandings of human freedom and emphasized, although in different ways, the importance of the relationship with God in the understanding of human freedom. Their understanding of free will, when applied to today's views on volunteering, connects with the refusal to make profit—in volunteering, Christian volunteers are not seeking gain or merit but responding to God's call—and, more fundamentally, relativizes the autonomy of the volunteer as a human being to situate this human being in the context of God's call to participate in God's loving commitment to this world.

The Lutheran Perspective

First we concentrate on the writings of Luther concerning the question of free will and continue by discussing how he formulates the Christian calling to neighbourly love in relation to his view on the conditions for salvation. This means that we will not primarily take into consideration the theological tradition as it developed after Luther in Lutheran orthodoxy and was practiced in Lutheran Churches. Our aim is to demonstrate how the Christian perspective on volunteering and free will as described above arises from the theological position of Luther, in which God is omnipotent and has priority over human beings and nature, and in which the outlook of human beings and the restrained will follow from this ontic ordering.

Luther's position on the question of the free will and human autonomy in relation to God is developed in *On the Bondage of the Will*. This text from 1525 is his answer to Erasmus in their debate over free will. The importance of this issue and the hot-tempered tone of the text is due to the fact that Luther's central theological insight is at stake here, namely that human beings are justified and saved by nothing other than grace received in faith (*Sola Gratia*). If Luther were to have admitted that human beings enjoy a free will that leaves them autonomous in relation to God, there would have been a possibility for human beings to save themselves by their own works, for instance by doing good deeds out of neighbourly love. In his answer to Erasmus, Luther wanted to refute precisely such human capacity for self-salvation.

In the beginning of *On the Bondage of the Will,* Luther maintains that it is "... plain evidence that free choice is a pure fiction" (Luther 1989, p. 176). This assertion sets the theme and the tone for the whole text. Firmly rooted in the Bible, Luther argues against the idea of free will and that human beings are capable of making free choices. He makes it clear that this applies to all human beings, regardless of whether they are excellent and righteous: Free choice is ungodly and wicked; it deserves the wrath of God. This means that the condition of the free will is not dependent on a certain higher faculty that could be more refined in some persons than in others. Instead, original sin "...leaves free choice with no capacity to do anything but sin and be damned" (Luther 1989, p. 203). According to Luther, we encounter here a fundamental aspect of the human condition: Human beings are totally dependent on God. What human beings perceive as free choices is an illusion

2   Christian Calling and Volunteering   33

since they are never indifferent in their choices but choose what they are motivated to choose (Gillespie 2008, p. 154). From this follows an anthropology where human beings do not possess a free will, and when human beings attempt to make use of what they perceive as being their free choice, they, in fact, wage war against God's grace (Luther 1989, p. 181).

It is this antagonism between human beings and God which derives from the notion of human autonomy that makes it so important for Luther to both condemn and reject the idea of free will. First, the idea of human autonomy challenges the omnipotence of God as understood in Luther's nominalist theology and ontology. According to this theological standpoint, there is an insuperable break between the omnipotent God and human beings. Hence there is no natural theology that can bridge between human beings and God by the use of human reason or good will. Secondly, human autonomy precludes the idea of salvation solely as an act of God given through grace. Indeed, if human beings were to enjoy a free will and autonomy, there would be the possibility for them to earn righteousness on the basis of their own merits. Human beings, then, would see responsibility for their salvation fall on their own shoulders. This is why Luther states that there is nothing good and that there are no virtues left in human beings. Instead they are unrighteous and ignorant of God. By declaring that human ignorance of God betokens cruelty, lack of mercy towards neighbour and love of self, Luther argues that the idea of free will does not lead to good deeds and neighbourly love, but to the contrary, namely to selfishness (Luther 1989, p. 187). Actually, there is no room for human autonomy since human beings are slaves either to God or to the devil: There is nothing outside Christ but Satan. Therefore, there does not exist a position from where human beings could know or do the good that would make them righteous; they cannot even follow God's law on the basis of their own capacities.

This is Luther's conception of the free will in a nutshell. In *The Freedom of a Christian,* a treatise Luther wrote to Pope Leo X in 1520 to make his theological position clear as a response to the threat of being excommunicated, he discussed the Christian calling to neighbourly love. Already at the beginning of this treatise, he declared that a "Christian is a perfectly free lord of all, subject to none" and, at the same time, "a perfectly dutiful servant of all, subject of all" (Luther 1989, p. 596). The subsequent text revolves around this apparently contradictory anthropology.

But this contradiction is resolved as Luther declares that human nature is twofold and presupposes an anthropological divide between the free inner human being and the outer human being, subjugated to the corporeal reality of the world. Luther has to keep these two aspects apart since he argues that external signs as "sacred robes" or "sacred duties" belong to the outer being and do not help the soul since they exert no influence on the righteousness and the freedom of the soul. Instead, something far different is required, the Word of God. The word of God, for Luther, refers to the Gospels. When this Gospel becomes a living reality in human beings through faith (*Sola Fide*), they are saved. This is why Luther can say that "Christ is the end of the Law", that "everyone who has faith may be justified" and that human beings are free from the law. If it were possible for human beings to be justified by anything else, by their own good deeds for example, they would not need the Word and consequently neither would they need faith (Luther 1989, p. 597). Christian liberty means that human beings are totally independent of law and deeds for their salvation since they are totally dependent on faith and the word of God for their salvation. Hence, freedom for Luther differs from the modern understanding of freedom as referring to an autonomous person: Freedom to Luther presupposes total dependence on God in order to be independent of the world and one's own merits to earn salvation.

Luther depicts the process of the Word of God becoming a reality in human beings as their soul unites with Christ as a bride unites with her bridegroom (Luther 1989, p. 603). When this union is completed, the soul consents to God's will and it clings to God's promises and does not doubt that God is just and provides all things well. When human beings are obedient by faith alone, God becomes the reality in them and as a consequence they are free to act without striving for righteousness because nothing can do them any harm. To understand the importance of God becoming a reality in human beings, Gillespie points to Luther's dependence on the Stoic belief that happiness and freedom is to be found in union with the divine logos (Gillespie 2008, p. 158). This does not mean that human individuality becomes dissolved; on the contrary, when God becomes the will of the individual, this individual is free to act without fear of condemnation and is also empowered to act in accordance with the will of God. When God has become a reality in human beings they become free actors in the world. Paradoxically, by describing human beings as totally dependent on God, Luther defends human freedom and emphasizes human actions as genuinely caring for the sake of the neighbour.

However, Luther has to take the commandment of doing good works into consideration. First of all, the law is needed to remind human beings of the will of God and of their fundamental incapacity to fulfil it. As a consequence, they are driven to despair and have to seek their righteousness in faith in the grace of God. Hence, the law makes human beings aware of their sins and brings them to understand that they can do nothing else but trust the grace of God. Secondly, when God's commandment of neighbourly love becomes a reality in human beings, they become free to live only for others and not for themselves. Then human beings may freely serve and benefit others, considering nothing except the need and the advantage of their neighbours without hope for reward. It is worth citing Luther when he points out the rule for the life of Christians: "…we should devote all our works to the welfare of others, since each has such abundant riches in his faith that all his other works and his whole life are a surplus with which he can by voluntary benevolence serve and do good to his neighbour" (Luther 1989, p. 618). As Christians and obedient to God, human beings are free to be servants to all since it is not through doing effort for merits or to earn righteousness but through faith that human beings acquire an abundance of good things in Christ. Hence, the anthropology of Luther is totally relational. Human beings do not lean on themselves; when they try to save themselves, they will be unfree since they are threatened by the wrath of God and unable to do good for the sake of their neighbour. At the end Luther concludes: "…a Christian lives not in himself but in

Christ and in his neighbour" and "He lives in Christ through faith, in his neighbour through love" (Luther 1989, p. 623).

The reason for Luther's understanding of the conditions of human freedom lies in his premodern religious outlook where righteousness and a benign God are what ultimately concern human beings. Without a benign God, human beings cannot exist in a world where everything depends on God's will. Here we can recall Luther's position concerning free will in *On the bondage of the will*. According to Luther, free choice is an illusion because humans cannot choose indifferently, only God can; they are always motivated by their ultimate concern (cf. Gillespie 2008, p. 154). This may today seem a strange outlook on the human condition, belonging to times long past, but it is worth noticing that in research on the meaning of volunteering, volunteers claim that being unpaid is a precondition for being free to act. If their efforts were to be paid, they would be part of the necessity of earning one's living or for benefit (von Essen 2008). Hence, in contemporary society also human beings perceive that they are freer to act as volunteers when their volunteering is "put outside" what they find as a necessary condition, namely the material benefits of employment.

A view of reality where everything depends on God's will certainly differs from an outlook in which material needs are a necessity. But within these two views of the human condition it seems that freedom to act demands the same. For an action to be free and a concern for the other to be sincere it has to be placed outside of what is needed for human beings. Therefore, the differences between how Luther describes neighbourly love in his premodern and religious anthropology and how volunteering is described and perceived in contemporary society does not seem to be that crucial after all.

The Ignatian Perspective

Several Jesuits, members of the religious order of which Ignatius of Loyola (for the writings of Ignatius of Loyola, as used in this article, see Saint Ignatius of Loyola 1996) became the first general superior, participated in the council of Trent (1545–1563), in which the council fathers attempted to clarify the Roman Catholic understanding of free will and justification in answer to the challenges of the Reformation, of which Martin Luther was a leading figure. In a recent book on the Council of Trent, John W. O'Malley (2013) describes the tensions as follows: "For all Trent's insistence on the determining role of grace in justification (…), it seems clear that what to a considerable extent prevailed in post-Trent Catholicism was a persuasion that doing one's best was a prerequisite for God to give his grace. Catholics in their own view and in the view of their enemies stood for 'good works'." The council fathers at Trent attempted to strike a delicate balance between human efforts in the process of salvation and the total dependence on God's grace for salvation, a balance which not all Roman Catholics were capable of understanding. The Jesuits, however, well versed in Ignatian spirituality and thought, enjoyed a privileged position to understand.

Ignatius of Loyola attempts to walk the tightrope of human free will as something emerging in the balance between God's grace and actions and human decisions and actions. Human free will, to Ignatius, is not the enemy of God's will, entering into competition with it as the expression of a human and selfish autonomy that wants to be free of God's interference; human free will blossoms when intimately connected to God's commitment to creation. Therefore, Ignatius' attitude towards modernity is complex: He and his fellow Jesuits recognize and promote human creativity and its expressions but would always want to elaborate them in the perspective of a positive "indifference" that considers human creativity in its relationship with God's creative presence in creation. The idea of indifference appears in one of the key texts of his Spiritual Exercises (# 23), the so-called "Principle and Foundation". It gives us a good insight in Ignatius' perspective on the world and human life in it: "The human person is created to praise, reverence and serve God our Lord, and by doing so to save his or her soul. The other things on the face of the earth are created for human beings in order to help them pursue the end for which they are created. It follows from this that one must use other created things in so far as they help towards one's end, and free oneself from them in so far as they are obstacles to one's end. To do this we need to make ourselves indifferent to all created things, provided the matter is subject to our free choice and there is no prohibition. Thus as far as we are concerned, we should not want health more than illness, wealth more than poverty, fame more than disgrace, a long life more than a short one, and similarly for all the rest, but we should desire and choose only what helps us more towards the end for which we are created." At the core of human life stands the relationship to God and the promotion of this relationship constitutes what is at stake in human life and towards which human creativity works. But human creativity and action stand in the perspective of their relationship to God: That is the meaning of "indifference", which refers to the capacity to see the whole world and all that happens in its relationship with God.

If we want to understand what this human creativity in the perspective of the relationship to God means with regard to human free will, there is a difficult but illuminating phrase attributed to Ignatius: "Let your first rule of action be to trust in God as if success depended entirely on yourself and not on him: but use all your efforts as if God alone did everything, and yourself nothing."[7] There is no suspicion with regard to human activity and creativity here, on the contrary: The best is asked from every human being, and in that best human beings serve and reveal God's own efforts, if and when that human commitment lies in line with God's own commit-

---

[7] Thoughts of St. Ignatius Loyola for Every Day of the Year. From the Scintillae Ignatianae compiled by Gabriel Hevenesi, S.J. Translated by A.G. McDougall, New York: Fordham University Press, 2006, p. 15 (the quote for 2 January). The original Latin text runs as follows: "Haec prima sit agendorum regula: Sic Deo fide, quasi rerum successus omnis a te, nihil a Deo penderet: ita tamen iis operam omnem admove, quasi tu nihil, Deus Omnia solus sit facturus" (see: Hevenesi, Gabriel, Scintillae Ignatianae, sive Sancti Ignatii de Loyola, Societatis Iesu Fundatoris apophtegmata sacra, per singulos anni dies distribute, Et ulteriori consideration proposita. Viennae, Typis Joannis Georgii Schlegel, 1705).

ment. Indeed, here free will does not enter into competition with God's graceful work in the world; on the contrary, as mentioned in one of the other key meditations presented in the Spiritual Exercises, the so-called "Contemplation for attaining love" (## 230–237), Ignatius does not tire of telling the person involved in the exercises to feel the call that arises from the admiration for God's work: "To bring to memory the gifts received…To see how God dwells in creatures…To consider how God works and labours on my behalf in all created things on the face of the earth…" so as to "be able to love and serve His Divine Majesty in everything". The human commitment to the created world arises from and reflects the commitment of the Creator to creation. Ignatius' way of answering this call is to exercise the following of Jesus Christ into the world by narratively connecting with his life.

In the process of the Spiritual Exercises, then, Ignatius of Loyola introduces people existentially to the dynamics required to decide in the midst of such complex interactions between God and human beings. They are invited to reflect upon their own lives as situated within God's creation and as broken by suffering and sin; they are also invited to take Jesus of Nazareth, the Christ, in whom divine and human natures coincide, as their example and to contemplate the meaning of his life, death and resurrection for theirs, so as to follow him in his commitment to the world. This requires an affective and narrative bond with God in Jesus of Nazareth, in which Christians are called to discover how God, through the movements of their emotions and their heart, provides guidance to which they may or may not respond. Consolation arises when Christians are drawn nearer to God in movements of faith, hope and love; desolation comes about when Christians move away from God and feel lack of faith, despair, etc.:

> I use the word "consolation" when any interior movement is produced in the soul that leads her to become inflamed with the love of her Creator and Lord, and when, as a consequence, there is no created thing on the face of the earth that we can love in itself, but we love it only in the Creator of all things. Similarly, I use the word "consolation" when one sheds tears that lead to love of one's Lord, whether these arise from grief over one's sins, or over the Passion of Christ Our Lord, or over other things expressly directed towards His service and praise. Lastly, I give the name "consolation" to every increase of hope, faith and charity, to all interior happiness that calls and attracts a person towards heavenly things and to the soul's salvation, leaving the soul quiet and at peace in her Creator and Lord. (…) "Desolation" is the name I give to everything contrary to what is (consolation) (…). (Spiritual Exercises, ## 316–317)

Through discerning these movements, Christians are called upon to decide in which direction to move in their lives, even if they are called to follow Christ on the road of the cross. In this process of discernment, human beings are not left alone: God stands on their side and lies at the heart of their commitments, as they discover in the movements of deep consolation. It is through God's commitment that human beings are able to follow Jesus Christ.

At the heart of Ignatian spirituality thus lies this process of discernment which articulates the relationship between God and human beings: the attempt to find out how God's commitment to creation and human action in the world relate to one another. Also, when one researches the issue of volunteering from an Ignatian perspective, account will have to be taken of the process of discernment, in which

God's grace and human free will interact creatively. The Ignatian writings, apart from the Spiritual Exercises, articulate how this process of discernment shapes reality: In Ignatius' Autobiography, the reader discovers how Ignatius of Loyola himself grew in the capacity to discern; in the Constitutions of the Society of Jesus, founded after a common process of discernment between the first companions, Ignatius of Loyola lays down the rules that will help to build and structure a community and indicates the service this community may render in the world, by taking account of vulnerable fellow human beings so as to discover God's presence in their and our lives. In the many letters written by Ignatius of Loyola, there also appear the first contours of a worldwide network: Community building and institutionalization at the service of the poor and excluded are part and parcel of the Ignatian endeavour and define its understanding of the meaning of the Church.

All of these constitute characteristics of what one could call an Ignatian approach to volunteering, of which the Jesuit Volunteer Corps provides a good example.[8] This movement builds on four main principles: spirituality and spiritual growth, simple living, community amongst the volunteers and with those people whom the volunteers serve and social justice. The emphasis on spirituality corresponds, here, to the emphasis given in most of the definitions of volunteering to human free will. The free will cannot be considered as separate from the relationship with God as a necessary condition to the use of this free will. Ignatius of Loyola also emphasized that a human being cannot simply be autonomous, but that human autonomy exists only in a relational perspective: the relation with God, with fellow human beings and with creation as a whole.

Those who situate themselves in line with Ignatian spirituality are volunteers who enter the world precisely, there where it hurts or where it stands at its limits and frontiers. In doing so, they follow the God who commits lovingly to the world in Jesus Christ. In this sense, volunteering—the mission to respond to God's call as it emerges in our world—belongs to the core of what it means to be a Christian.

Conclusions

The reality of volunteering in a secular modern perspective takes for granted the free will of human beings as their capacity to decide for themselves independently of a relationship to God or to fellow human beings. Christians such as Martin Luther and Ignatius of Loyola situate volunteering in the relationship with a God who calls to us through creation and through fellow human beings in a process that human beings cannot fully control and that defines them in their very being. Volunteering, in such Christian perspective, where God calls us to become neighbours in a loving commitment towards fellow human beings, particularly those who suffer, contains a community building aspect: In the service to others and with others, a community is being built that takes to heart the very commitment of Godself in building the

---

[8] See, http://www.jesuitvolunteers.org/.

Kingdom community. Being a volunteer, then, is not a mere subjective decision but also means following the compassionate pulse of creation as a whole and, in that, God's loving commitment to the world.

Volunteering in this sense does not only not expect a reward (although, of course, that reward may come in various ways, of which the consolations of belonging to a community of concern and solidarity (Álvarez de los Mozos 2002; chapter of von Essen) is one) but also often leads to "strange", "extravagant" or "excessive" logics, as exemplified in the parable of the workers of the eleventh hour: The payment for services rendered is not calculated in terms of the hours of work provided (Matthew 20: 1–16). The justice that is aimed at is the justice of loving and compassionate relationships and this moves into the logic of forgiveness (see, e.g. the parable of the prodigal son, Luke 15: 11–31).

Volunteering comes as natural to these Christians, in that it concerns unpaid activities, activities that are not mercantilized, originating in the relationship with God which transforms the faithful insofar as they follow Christ and, thus, also God's love and commitment towards human beings and creation. When these Christians volunteer, they move into the footsteps left by a volunteering God in the life of Jesus Christ. The activities of volunteers are performed out of free will, understood from a Christian perspective on free will: Here autonomy cannot be disconnected from heteronomy, from a complex and difficult historical relationship with God and, therefore, also with the rest of creation, for the benefit of others (even in a universal sense, as it is participation in God's love stretching out to the whole world), and embedded in organized community contexts. The creative interaction between autonomy and heteronomy is what defines these Christian modes of volunteering and traditions may differ in how they gauge the tension between autonomy and heteronomy. Some secularized Christians might not even share the Christian perspective as we analysed it here and hold on to a more secularized take on free will. Understood in the Christian theological sense we proposed, however, volunteering cannot be seen merely in the perspective of the autonomous, secularized free will: It receives its real meaning from the relationship with God. This allows us to pose two critical questions with which to end this contribution: Would it not be interesting to introduce the word "volunteering" in theological dictionaries? Can the Christian emphasis on heteronomy constitute an invitation to researchers to research more profoundly the role played by free will in volunteering?

References

Álvarez de los Mozos, P. (2002). *Comunidades de solidaridad*. Bilbao: Ediciones Mensajero.
Bonhoeffer, D. (1989). *Nachfolge* (edited by M. Kuske & I. Tödt) (Dietrich Bonhoeffer Werke, 4). München: Chr. Kaiser Verlag.
Cnaan, R. A., & Amrofell, L. (1994). Mapping volunteer activity. *Nonprofit and Voluntary Sector Quarterly, 23*(4), 335–351.
Cnaan, R. A., Handy, F., & Wadsworth, M. (1996). Defining who is a volunteer: Conceptual and empirical considerations. *Nonprofit and Voluntary Sector Quarterly, 25*(3), 364–383.
Crouzel, H. (1989). *Origen* (transl. from French: A.S. Worrall). Edinburgh: T. & T. Clark.

Dekker, P., & Halman, L. (2003). Volunteering and values: An introduction. In P. Dekker & L. Halman (Eds.), *The values of volunteering: Cross-cultural perspectives.* New York: Kluwer Academic.

Gillespie, M. A. (2008). *The theological origins of modernity.* Chicago: The University of Chicago Press.

Guillet, J., Bardy, G., Vandenbroucke, F., Pegon, J., & Martin, H. (1957). *Discernement des esprits. In Dictionnaire de spiritualité ascétique et mystique, doctrine et histoire* (Vol. 3, pp. 1222–1291). Paris: Beauchesne.

Haight, R. (1991). Sin and grace. In F. Schüssler Fiorenza & J. P. Galvin (Eds.), *Systematic theology: Roman Catholic perspectives* (Vol. II, pp. 75–141). Minneapolis: Fortress Press.

Handy, F., Cnaan, R. A., Brudney, J., Ascoli, U., & Meijs, L. (2000). Public perception of "who is a volunteer": An examination of the net-cost approach from a cross-cultural perspective. *Voluntas: International Journal of Voluntary and Nonprofit Organizations, 11*(1), 45–65.

Haski-Leventhal, D. (2009). Altruism and volunteerism: The perceptions of altruism in four disciplines and their impact on the study of volunteerism. *Journal for the Theory of Social Behaviour, 39*(3), 271–299.

Hustinx, L., Cnaan, R. A., & Handy, F. (2010). Navigating theories of volunteering: A hybrid map for a complex phenomenon. *Journal for the Theory of Social Behaviour, 40*(4), 410–434.

Lacoste, J.-Y. (Ed.). (2007). *Dictionnaire critique de théologie* (3rd ed.). Paris: Quadrige.

Lilla, M. (2007). *The stillborn God: Religion, politics, and the modern west.* New York: Alfred Knopf.

Luther, M. (1989). *Martin Luther's basic theological writings* (edited by T. F. Lull, foreword by J. Pelikan). Minneapolis: Fortress.

Meijs, L., et al. (2003). All in the eyes of the beholder: Perceptions of volunteering across eight countries. In P. Dekker & L. Halman (Eds.), *The values of volunteering: Cross-cultural perspectives* (pp. 19–34). New York: Kluwer Academic.

O'Malley, J. W. (2013). *Trent: What happened at the council* (p. 254). Cambridge: The Belknap Press of Harvard University Press.

O'Reagan, A. (2009). *Imaging the voluntary actor: Interpreting narratives of intent and meaning. European civil society series.* Baden-Baden: Nomos.

Ruiz Jurado, M. (1994). *El discernimiento espiritual: Teología, historia, práctica.* Madrid: BAC.

Saint Ignatius of Loyola. (1996). *Personal writings: Reminiscences, spiritual diary, select letters, including the text of 'The spiritual exercises'* (transl. with introductions and notes: J. A. Munitiz & P. Endean). London: Penguin Books.

Sertillanges, A.-D. (1949). *L'idée de creation et ses retentissements en philosophie.* Paris: Aubier.

Sigurdson, O. (2009). *Det postsekulära tillståndet: Religion, modernitet, politik.* Munkedal: Glänta Produktion.

Sobrino, J. (1992). *El principio misericordia. Bajar de la cruz a los pueblos crucificados* (Presencia teológica, 67). Santander: Sal Terrae.

Story, D. (1992). Volunteerism: The "self-regarding" and "other-regarding" aspects of the human spirit. *Nonprofit and Voluntary Sector Quarterly, 21*(3), 3–18.

van Broeckhoven, E. (1971). *Dagboek van de vriendschap* (uitgegeven door G. Neefs). Brugge: Emmäus, Desclée de Brouwer. English translation: van Broeckhoven, E. (1977). *A friend to all men: The diary of a worker priest.* Denville: Dimension Books.

von Essen, J. (2008). *Om det ideella arbetets betydelse: En studie om människors livsåskådningar* (Diss.). Uppsala: Acta Universitatis Upsaliensis.

Wilson, J. (2000). Volunteering. *Annual Review of Sociology, 26,* 215–240.

Wuthnow, R. (1991). *Acts of compassion: Caring for others and helping our selves.* Princeton: Princeton University Press.

Chapter 3
If I Am Only for Myself, Who Am I?

Volunteering and Righteousness in Judaism

Lena Roos

Introduction

When I was asked to contribute to this anthology with an article on religion and volunteering in Jewish tradition, I had to devote some time to pondering what such an article might focus on. Both terms seemed problematic from a traditional Jewish point of view.

Let us start with "religion". When we take as our point of departure such pairs as "religion and volunteering", "religion and politics", "religion and sexuality", etc., then our primary assumption is that these two things are separate and can be related to one another. Sexuality, politics and volunteering are NOT part of what we define as religion, although we recognize that religion can be a value system and a set of traditions that can influence groups and individuals into assuming views concerning, for instance, what proper sexuality is, what political values a just society should be based upon and what the value of volunteering might be. When we use such pairs, we conceive of religion as something quite narrow, largely connected with faith, ritual behaviour and perceptions of the supernatural. In other words, a definition that fits most neatly with mainstream Protestant Christianity in a modern, secularized society. It is then fitting to recognize that with respect to the bulk of the history of humankind, this is not a suitable definition of the concept religion. A far more common view has been to understand religion (or related terms referring to this phenomenon that is so hard to define) as a much more broad term, referring not only to ideas about supernatural and ritual practices but also a set of values and prescribed behaviours for every facet of life, both of the individual and of the group.[1] This is definitely the case with the majority of forms of Judaism that have emerged throughout history.

---

[1] The difficulties concerning the use of the term religion is a long-standing debate within the field of Religious Studies, see for instance most recently Schalk (2013).

L. Roos (✉)
Department of Theology, Uppsala University, Uppsala, Sweden
e-mail: lena.roos@teol.uu.se

L. Hustinx et al. (eds.), *Religion and Volunteering,* Nonprofit and Civil Society Studies, 41
DOI 10.1007/978-3-319-04585-6_3, © Springer International Publishing Switzerland 2015

With this broader definition of religion, the term "volunteering" also becomes problematic. A minimal definition of volunteering would be to do something voluntarily, without being paid for it. Many of the things that in modern scholarship are treated under the heading "volunteering", such as, for instance, caring for the poor and sick, would in Jewish tradition fall under the heading of *mitzvah* meaning "commandment". This means that, from a Biblical point of view, it is not something that you are doing voluntarily, out of the goodness of your heart, but rather something you are commanded to do, on a par with keeping the Sabbath and circumcising your male children. Already in the Talmud, however, the term *mitzvah* rather means "good deed", something that earns merit, and not just a commandment that should be kept by all, which makes it more compatible with the discourse on "volunteering" (Rothkoff 2007a).

Judaism as a religious tradition also presents its difficulties when compared to other religions. Being Jewish is not determined by beliefs or behaviour but by lineage (or conversion). Where you locate yourself on the diverse map of Jewish identities, however, is determined by your adherence to prescribed practices. This means that it is not your religion that moves you to fulfill the commandments, fulfilling the commandments is the most important part of your religion. It can perhaps be compared to different ways of understanding parenting. One way of understanding parenting is that you care for your children because it is your duty as a parent. Another way of seeing it is that it is caring for your children that makes you a parent, rather than just the biological or legal status.

From an outsider's point of view, living your life according to traditional Jewish law may seem daunting, with its attention to minute details in life: what to eat, how to dress, how to interact with other people, when to work and when to rest, how to have sex, how to comply with the ritual life and compulsory prayers, etc. An insider's point of view can be different: All those things provide opportunities for a person to recall his or her Jewish identity as belonging to the Jewish people and being in a covenant with God. Once again returning to the analogy of parenthood: The everyday duties of parenting can be onerous but they also serve to remind us of the joy and privilege of being a parent.

In spite of this, there are of course similarities between voluntary work for the needy in Jewish and non-Jewish traditions. As a minority, Jews have always been influenced by their non-Jewish surroundings. For instance, in the Middle Ages, much charity work was done by various charitable societies that collected contributions from fellow Jews, in a similar way to comparable societies in the Christian world. Likewise, middle-class Jewish women in the nineteenth century dedicated their time to charitable organizations just like their non-Jewish counterparts (Berman et al. 2007). Still, there are some particular characteristics in Jewish tradition which are visible in religious volunteerism today.

The title of this chapter comes from a longer quote, attributed to the first century rabbi Hillel. "If I am not for myself, who will be for me? If I am [only] for myself, who am I? If not now, when?" (Mishnah Avot 1: 14). It is found in one of the most well-known and beloved texts in Jewish tradition, *PirqeAvot, The sayings of the fathers*. It seems to express the necessity of combining caring for one's own needs

3 If I Am Only for Myself, Who Am I?

and caring for the needs of others, and that this duty is incumbent upon each and every individual, in each generation.

In this chapter, I discuss three important commandments in Jewish tradition that all deal with caring for the needs of others: caring for the poor, the dead and the sick. I will discuss their textual background, how they have developed in rabbinic and medieval times and how they have translated into what might be understood as religious volunteerism in the Israel of the twenty-first century. I will focus in particular on voluntary work initiated and performed by members of Israel's ultraorthodox (Haredi) community. The situation in Israel differs from that of diaspora Jewish communities in the rest of the world in two important aspects: (1) The state of Israel is the only country in the world where the Jews are a majority. It is therefore interesting to analyse how values and structures concerning charity and voluntary work that have been formed in a minority situation have developed in Israel. (2) Israel is the country in the world with the highest percentage of Haredi Jews in the population. The discussion on these particular voluntary organizations cannot therefore be transferred directly to Jewish diaspora communities that form a small minority in their countries and contain a much smaller percentage of Haredi Jews.

Volunteerism in Israel

When you sit at a regular Jerusalem bus stop, you can let your eyes wander over a number of notices for organizations seeking *mitnadvim*, volunteers. According to the umbrella website Volunteering in Israel, there are 24,000 volunteer organizations in Israel (http://www.ivolunteer.org.il/eng/).

In his article "Reflections on the voluntary non-profit sector in Israel. An international perspective", Ralph M. Kramer distinguishes three major international trends during the decades after World War II:

- An increase in the number and type of voluntary non-profit organizations (VN-POs)
- That governments use them to a higher degree, which leads to a mutual dependency
- A fading of the boundaries between the public and private sectors (Kramer 1994, p. 255)

All three trends are visible in Israel, and increasingly so since the publication of Kramer's article.

Kramer identifies three characteristics where VNPOs in Israel differ from those in most other countries:

1. Unlike in other countries, the formation of VNPOs in Israel predates the formation of the state. Many such organizations were founded already during the British mandate, as part of preparing for the creation of a Jewish state. Since such organizations were founded by different Jewish groups with different visions

of the future state, it also helps explain the continued presence of two separate streams of volunteerism in Israel: one (orthodox/ultraorthodox) religious and another secular. At the beginning of the existence of the state, volunteerism decreased momentarily, as many people felt that these responsibilities should now be assumed by the state. Soon, however, voluntary activities were on the rise again (Jaffe 1991, p. 196). This long-term perspective means that some of the VNPOs provide more stability in their services than the state. The policy-making process in Israel on matters of welfare and health generally lacks long-term planning, partly due to the political situation with a rapid succession of unstable governments and a multitude of political parties and alliances, some of short duration (Yishai 1990, p. 226). Many voluntary organizations, however, are short-lived; almost 60 % last less than 10 years. If they make it past the 10-year mark, however, they can show impressive longevity (*Israel's third sector at a glance* 2007).

2. There is a characteristic blurring of the boundaries between public and private, state and society and religion and state, where the state is involved in every aspect of society and religious groups exercise great influence over government, national as well as local.

3. Unlike VNPOs in Europe, those in Israel depend to a large extent on economic contributions from abroad and are therefore not as dependent on contributions from their own government. Still, a particular tactic often employed by Israeli VNPOs is to "create facts on the ground", meaning that they initiate projects which they later expect the government to help finance (Kramer 1994, p. 257 f.).

The third sector in Israel is large. During the 1980s, when volunteerism grew in many countries with diverse welfare systems and political cultures, this happened in Israel as well (Kramer 1994, p. 255). A study published in 1985 showed that the expenditure of VNPOs corresponded to almost 8 % of gross national product (GNP), which was twice as much as, for instance, in the USA or the UK. VNPOs provided more than half of the social services (Kramer 1994, p. 255). A study of non-profit and nongovernmental organizations from 2002 shows that the third sector had been growing continuously since the 1990s, its expenditure in 2002 corresponding to 13.3 % of Israel's gross domestic product (GDP) (*Israel's third sector at a glance* 2007).

In a survey done in 2006, 16 % of the respondents were at that moment volunteering and 28 % had done so in the past. The average amount of time given was 11 h per week (Bar-Ilan and Azoulay 2012, p. 1148). The rates of volunteering increased by 40 % between 1996 and 2006 (*Israel's third sector at a glance* 2007). A new survey from 2008 showed that nearly half of the adult population (48 %) "participated in volunteer-related activities, both formal and informal". The most important motive for volunteering was, according to the respondents, that "volunteering makes for a better society" (85.1 %). The statement "Volunteering corresponds to my religious beliefs" (Haski-Leventhal et al. 2011) was agreed by 39.6%.

Of particular interest for this study is that the religious Israelis, and in particular the Haredi community, stand out in the statistics with a much higher rate of voluntary activity, as well as monetary donations to VNPOs, than the rest of the Israeli public. This is also noteworthy because it goes against another demographic characteristic that the rich tend to volunteer more than the less affluent (*Israel's third sector at a glance* 2007). This pattern is also known from other contexts (Hustinx et al. 2010, p. 422). The Haredi community, however, has a high percentage of poor families (see below) yet are the ones that volunteer the most among Jewish Israelis. This seems to indicate that Haredi religious identity is an important factor that contributes to the willingness to volunteer.

This contradiction is also substantiated by another recent study of the founders of non-profit organizations in Israel. It shows that there are two distinct groups among the founders: The founders of nonreligious organizations tend to have a level of education and income that was significantly higher than those of the founders of religious organizations (Ben-Nun 2010).

The Haredi Community in Israel

Religion in Israel is anything but a private matter. Religious parties influence government policies, all matters of family law are administered by religious authorities and paid for by the taxpayers and religious institutions, holy sites and places of religious education are maintained and operated, at least in part, with taxpayers' money (Jaffe 1991, p. 201). This also means that the particular lifestyle cherished by the Haredi population would not be possible, were it not for state subsidies and exemptions.

The Haredi community makes up 6–10 % of the population. It is however, growing as a proportion of the Jewish population due to its birth rates (on average 7.7 children per family, compared to 2.6 for the Israeli population as a whole).

The Haredi community life centers around the yeshiva, the institute for religious learning. All adult men belong to a yeshiva and are ideally required to spend as much of their time there as possible, preventing them from working in regular jobs as well as from serving in the army. The ideal for members of the Haredi community is to live their entire life within their community with as little contact with the non-Haredi world as possible, since it is perceived as having a negative influence (Stadler et al. 2011, p. 140 f.). The Haredi women receive a more secular education and do not have access to the yeshivot, thus usually being the principal breadwinners of the Haredi families.

Although members of the Haredi community see themselves as the continuation of an unbroken Jewish tradition, in reality the idea that all men should study full time for the better part of their adult lives is something unique in Jewish history. That has been a privilege granted only to a select few in earlier epochs (Stadler 2009, p. 39).

Among non-Haredi Israelis, there has been a growing animosity against the Haredi community. They have been seen as parasites because they do not serve in the army nor participate in the labour market, which makes them dependent on subsidies from the state (Stadler 2009).

The animosity is mutual as Haredis feel hostile towards non-Haredis. Nurit Stadler, an Israeli sociologist who has conducted 10 years of fieldwork among

Haredi yeshiva students, describes the Haredi's view of themselves in relation to the non-Haredi Jewish world thus:

> Haredi members regard anyone who accepts the legitimacy of modern culture as being essentially anti-Jewish and therefore a potentially contaminating influence. Haredim [Hebrew plural for members of the Haredi community] rationalize their scriptural choices by seeing themselves as the elite whose piety will save all Jews (Stadler 2009, p. 9).

There are numerous volunteering associations in the Haredi community specializing in various kinds of charitable work: helping the poor, orphans, widows, sick, disabled, etc. (Stadler et al. 2005, p. 634). As stated above, the members of the Haredi community rank well above other Israelis in their tendency to volunteer.

Sociologist Richard Shure has pointed to three factors that tend to enhance volunteering:

1. Individual and group norms
2. Sense of empathy
3. Guiding universal principles (Shure 1991)

All three would seem to fit with the Haredi example. Their lifestyle is to a great extent determined by group norms. The fact that in many cases they are both recipients and providers of the voluntary services would serve to strengthen the sense of empathy with the people being helped through the voluntary service. The strong religious identity of the group would provide the guiding universal principles that would be conducive to volunteering.

Various scholars have, during the last decade, pointed to what seem to be radical changes in attitudes within the Haredi community. This is seen, for instance, in an increased interest in doing military service or working in regular jobs, using new technology like computers and DVDs, and participation in voluntary organizations that would entail contacts with the non-Haredi public (Stadler 2009, p. 50 f.). The examples I will discuss can be seen as signs of these changes.

Caring for the Poor

I remember a sermon I heard in a Jerusalem synagogue in 2001. The country was suffering from the economic effects of the Al-Aqsa intifada, the Palestinian uprising. Tourism had plummeted due to the unstable security situation. Some countries had started to recommend their citizens not to visit the region. The Israeli newspapers were reporting an increase in the number of Israeli children under the statistical poverty line. In this liberal, progressive synagogue, some of the members had decided that they needed to get involved in the fight against poverty, and they started by investigating what was already being done. I recall how the rabbi told us of his surprise when he discovered that the work towards alleviating poverty in Israel was totally dominated by Haredi organizations. His explanation: The ultraorthodox had kept the traditional Jewish community structure which existed everywhere in the diaspora prior to the formation of the state of Israel, where the

3 If I Am Only for Myself, Who Am I? 47

community as a whole was responsible for caring for their needy. The present lack of more progressive or secular Jews in this field, he explained, was because: "We somehow expected the state to take care of that."

The Hebrew Bible stresses in many passages the responsibility to provide for the poor, for instance: "The poor will never cease from the land. For this reason God commands you: 'You shall surely open your hand to your brother, to the poor and the needy in your land'" (Deut. 15: 11). Among those that are frequently mentioned as in need of aid are the orphans, widows and strangers (Deut. 14: 29; 16: 11, 14; 26: 12, 13).

The Hebrew Bible also institutes a system designed to prevent exaggerated differences between rich and poor, the sabbatical year. Every 7th year, the land shall rest and no crops shall be planted. During that year all debts are also cancelled (Lev. 25: 2–6; Deut. 15: 1–6). Every 50th year is a jubilee year when slaves shall be freed and all land shall return to its original owners (Lev. 25: 10).

The Hebrew word that comes closest to charity is *tsedakah*. Its connotations are, however, different from the word charity. Charity comes from the Latin word *caritas*, meaning "love". Charity in Christian tradition has meant voluntary acts done on behalf of the needy out of love. *Tsedakah* on the other hand comes from the root צדק meaning "to be correct". This means that charity in Jewish tradition is understood as "the correct thing to do", "justice". The word is also related to words like *tsaddik* "righteous one", meaning that to be righteous is to do what is right, amongst other things, to give to the needy what is needed. Righteousness in Jewish tradition does not therefore merely require one to refrain from doing what is evil but also to do what is good and required and to constantly pursue justice (Jacobs and Szubin 2007; Levitats 2007, p. 569; Friedman 2003).

Tsedakah is seen as something that benefits the needy, the giver, and ultimately the whole (Jewish) world. It is said to be as important as all of the other commandments put together (Babylonian Talmud, BT Baba Batra 9a). It causes the giver's sons to become wise, wealthy and learned (Babylonian Talmud, BT Baba Batra 9a). It atones for sin and hastens redemption (Baba Batra 9a and 10a).

During the Middle Ages, the forms that charity took in the Jewish communities became more set:

1. Every community collected money in a charity box (*kuppah*).
2. The needy also received other gifts, for instance clothing and food, the latter often through a soup kitchen (*tamchui*).
3. There was an association for burial, the *chevra kaddisha* (more on that below).
4. There was an association for visiting and caring for the sick, *bikkur cholim* (more on that below) (Ben-Sasson and Levitats 2007, p. 572).

In the so-called Genizah documents, found in a repository in the old synagogue in Cairo, reflecting Jewish life around the Mediterranean between the tenth and thirteenth centuries, charity plays a prominent part. Collecting charity was the privilege of the leader of the community, and being able to do so was a sign of good leadership. The collection of charity was done in a ritual setting, accompanied by the taking out of the Torah scrolls from the tabernacle in the synagogue and the reading of special prayers. It also served to reinforce hierarchies within the community since the size of each donation was announced publicly (Frenkel 2009, p. 361).

Back to the present and the organizations fighting poverty in Israel today. Poverty is a problem that has grown in Israel during the past decades, partly in the wake of the deterioration of the economy during the first decade of the twenty-first century.

The 1970s was the golden age of the Israeli welfare state when new social security programs where launched and benefits increased. The expansion ended in the 1980s (Rosenhek 2011, pp. 71, 76). Starting in the year 2000, Israel went through a radical transformation of its welfare system resulting in drastic cuts, for instance in children's allowances, income support and old age pensions. From 2000 to 2003 the rate of poor families (with a net income of 50 % or less of the national median net income) rose from 17.6 to 19.3 %. Among large families (four or more children) it rose from an already high 41.8 to 48.9 % (Silber and Sorin 2006, p. 253 ff.). The changes in the welfare system should not only be connected to a strained economy but also to the increased influence of neoliberal ideologies that support individualism, privatization, deregulation and reduced government spending (Rosenhek 2011, p. 76).

A comparison between the new non-profit organizations that were registered between 1996 and 2005 shows that the section dealing with welfare and health has grown, compared to earlier periods, as a response to the harsh economic conditions and the decreased commitment on behalf of the government in this area (*Israel's third sector at a glance* 2007).

This means that if Haredi organizations bear a large share of the work against poverty in Israel, the Haredi community also constitutes a large proportion of the recipients of various form of aid, since Haredi families are most likely to be among the bulk of those large families that have such a high rate of poverty. This means that the Haredi voluntary work among the poor is to a large extent directed towards members of their own community.

Caring for the Dead

Haredi volunteers do not merely care for the living though. An area where members of the Haredi community come into contact with the non-Haredi Israeli world is in the care for the dead.

One of the most well-known Israeli, religious volunteer organizations is called ZAKA. It comprises about 1500 volunteers, most of them Haredi men, who assist in the rescue and recovery of victims of sudden death, for instance in terror attacks and natural disasters.[2] The abbreviation stands for *zihui qorbanot ason* ("identification of victims of disaster"), and whereas regular emergency teams focus on aiding the wounded, ZAKA members also painstakingly gather all scattered body parts,

---

[2] According to their webpage, ZAKA also has a "minorities unit" that is formed by members of non-Jewish groups, "especially the Druses of the north and the Bedouins in the south", that can assist in performing the same services for members of their groups.

3 If I Am Only for Myself, Who Am I?

including blood, in order to give the victims a proper Jewish burial. The members themselves talk about their work as *chesed shel emet* ("true kindness") since they regard the service they provide a true kindness in the sense that the victims they assist in burial will never be able to repay them nor even express gratitude (www.zaka.org.il, Hebrew, www.zaka.us or www.zaka.org.uk, English).

The members of ZAKA are trained not only in the ritual aspects of their work but also in the scientific aspects of identification of bodies and body parts, for instance through finger prints, dental records and DNA.

ZAKA functions in Israel but has occasionally sent delegations to other countries where Jews have been killed in terror attacks. ZAKA also organizes volunteer lawyers who assist bereaved families in matters relating to "honouring the dead", for instance legal action in order to prevent autopsies or dealing with bureaucracy and legal authorities in order to shorten the time until the funeral.

One would expect the service provided by ZAKA to be problematic for its volunteers for three main reasons:

- *Haredi seclusion:* Members of the Haredi community generally prefer to have minimal contact with the non-Haredi public. Unlike most Haredi volunteering organizations, ZAKA do not focus on the members of the community.
- *Torah studies:* Haredi men are expected to spend their time exclusively on Torah studies, and any interruption of their sacred studies is considered to be a sin (Stadler et al. 2005, p. 627). Members of ZAKA, however, must be ready to abandon their studies at any time, for instance if there is a terror attack that demands their service (Stadler 2006, p. 847).
- *Purity/impurity:* From a traditional Jewish point of view, any contact with a dead body renders a person ritually impure (Heilman 2001, p. 25).

When the organization was first founded in 1995, many religious leaders of the Haredi community condemned ZAKA as a sin, claiming that the fact that the volunteers interacted with persons and organizations outside of their own group was a threat to the Haredi community (Stadler et al. 2005, p. 624). Over time, however, this has changed.

Scholars have explained the willingness to volunteer for ZAKA and the now benign attitude of the Haredi leadership in ways that should probably be seen as complimentary:

- ZAKA has been seen by non-Haredi Israelis as "good" Haredis, which has improved the status and image of the group in the eyes of other Israelis. Stadler has therefore interpreted the involvement in ZAKA as another type of "national service" in the eyes of the Israeli public and of the volunteers themselves, and as something that compensates for their refusal to participate in the mandatory military service. Some of the volunteers also express this idea themselves (Stadler et al. 2005, p. 637).
- The representatives of ZAKA themselves, however, rather cite religious reasons for their service, talking about showing care for all human beings as well as expressing Jewish solidarity (Stadler et al. 2005, p. 635).

- The work in ZAKA can be understood as a way of constructing a form of pious masculinity, which differs from the ideal of the pious Torah scholar and resembles ideas associated with the courageous soldier among the non-Haredi public (Aran et al. 2008).

The development of ZAKA could be seen as an extension of another field where the Haredi community holds an exclusive position in Israel: that of burials. The intricate demands of Jewish law when it comes to the handling of corpses require a high level of expertise. This area has therefore become an exclusively Haredi domain in Israel where they have established traditional communal burial societies that handle the burials of all Jewish Israeli citizens (Stadler et al. 2005, p. 628). The task to escort the dead to their graves is considered as a great *mitzvah* (meritorious deed), so great that it even warrants the interruption of Torah studies (Stadler et al. 2005, p. 632). These two services taken together have elevated the Haredi community in Israel to an exclusive position as specialists on death.

One important aspect of Jewish burial traditions is that the body is to be buried as intactly as possible, which explains the labour ZAKA dedicates to collecting and identifying fragments of bodies at sites of terror attacks and disasters (Stadler 2006, p. 841).

In interviews, ZAKA volunteers stressed three religious interpretations of their service:

1. A comparison between dead bodies in a terror scene and a burning Torah scroll
2. The commandment concerning respect for the dead (*kvod ha-met*)
3. The concept of "true kindness" (*chesed shel emet*) (Stadler 2006, p. 844)

The informants explain the gathering of the body parts through the logic of the sacrificial system of the Temple (Stadler 2006, p. 847). Stadler does not comment further on this but it is possible that this should be connected to another feature of Israeli religious discourse on the victims of terrorism: that they are martyrs, claiming for instance that they have died *al qiddush ha-Shem*, for the sanctification of God. Concerning Jewish martyrs there is a long-standing tradition, going back to the Middle Ages and the persecutions of the Jews during the First Crusade, to portray the death of the martyr in sacrificial terms (Roos 2006).

In the Middle Ages the association responsible for burial was the most influential one in the Jewish community, so much so that the generic name *chevra kaddisha* ("holy society") in time came to refer exclusively to this association. (Ben-Sasson and Levitats 2007, p. 572). During the High Middle Ages there were generally several different associations in a community, each responsible for the burial of its own members. In the sixteenth century we find sources that mention associations responsible for the burial of all Jews in the community (Rabinowitz and Goldberg 2007, p. 81 f.).

The most important task of the *chevra kaddisha* was to prepare corpses for burial according to the appropriate laws and making sure the body of the dead was treated with proper respect. Membership in the *chevra kaddisha* was considered to be an honour. Women were not allowed to be members, nor bachelors, that is, not until

3 If I Am Only for Myself, Who Am I? 51

the modern era, and then only in progressive branches of Judaism (Rabinowitz and Goldberg 2007, p. 82).

The service of the *chevra kaddisha* is sometimes referred to as *gemilut chasadim* "the bestowal of kindness". This is the most general of Jewish virtues towards others since it encompasses all forms of kind deeds done on behalf of a fellow human being. In the Mishnah it is mentioned as one of the three pillars of Judaism that serve to uphold the world, beside Torah and prayer (MishnaAvot 2: 1). *Gemilut chasadim* is a broader term than *tsedakah*:

- *Tsedakah* can only be given with money or other material things, *gemilut chasadim* can also be services.
- *Tsedakah* can only be given to the poor, *gemilut chasadim* to poor or rich.
- *Tsedakah* can only be given to the living, *gemilut chasadim* to the living or the dead. (Babylonian Talmud, Sukkah 49b).

Already the eleventh-century commentator Rashi denotes the paying of respect to the dead as the only truly altruistic *gemilut chasadim*, since the giver cannot hope that the recipient might one day do him a kindness in return (Levitats and Rabinowits 2007, p. 428).

Recruitment to ZAKA has some similarities to recruitment to a *chevra kaddisha*. The volunteers must be married. It is a position of honour and the recruitment is selective. Not everyone is perceived to "have what it takes" (Stadler et al. 2005, p. 630).

ZAKA is guided by rabbis who instruct the volunteers on the ritual aspects of their work but who also make decisions on matters of Jewish law when that is required. For instance, as regards working on the Sabbath, at first the rabbis only allowed the assistance to survivors, not the removal of bodies. Since then the position of ZAKA has changed and they now also remove bodies on the Sabbath, citing *kvod hamet* ("the honour of the dead") as an overriding principle that allows this (Stadler et al. 2005, p. 631).

Stadler also connects the development of ZAKA to another trend that is visible in the Haredi community. The community, which traditionally has been largely anti- or at least a-Zionist, is becoming more nationalistic and more inclined towards contributing to the state of Israel, as can be seen, for example, in a growing tendency to do military service and work in regular jobs (Stadler 2006, p. 840; Stadler et al. 2008).

Caring for the Sick

One final area where Haredi volunteers are also active is in the care for the sick and the example we will discuss is the organization Yad Sarah. Yad Sarah ("Sarah's hand") is the largest non-profit organization in Israel, organizing more than 6,000 volunteers, both Haredi and non-Haredi. It provides a wide range of services, one of its main goals being to care for sick and elderly in their homes rather than in institutions (www.yadsarah.org; Mann 1997).

Yad Sarah was founded in the 1970s, originally in order to loan medical equipment to persons and families who needed them, for instance vaporizers, crutches and wheelchairs. In the foundation narrative of the organization, it all started when the founder Uri Lupolianski had to borrow a vaporizer from a neighbour for his sick child. Realizing the scarcity of vaporizers, he bought a couple in order to be able to loan them to other families. From there the services expanded.

Yad Sarah has grown during the beginning of the twenty-first century in response to the reduction in the support for the needy provided by the state. Reports have indicated that during the past decade every other Israeli family has been helped by the organization (Stadler et al. 2011, p. 149).

The duty to visit the sick, *bikkur cholim*, was one of the traditional duties incumbent upon the Jewish community as a whole. God himself visited Abraham when he was recovering from circumcision and all Jews are commanded to follow this example (Rothkoff 2007b). According to the Talmud, this was one of the good deeds that produced rewards in this world, and even more so in the world to come (Babylonian Talmud Shab. 127a). Merely visiting was not considered enough to fulfill this *mitzvah*; one should also try to meet the material needs of the sick person (Rothkoff 2007b).

In the webpage of Yad Sarah, however, there are no references to *halacha, mitzvot* or to Jewish traditions generally concerning the responsibility for caring for the sick. Instead, terms like "mutual social responsibility" and "warm humanity" are used in their vision statement. The organization was not named after the matriarch Sarah, wife of Abraham, but rather after the founder's grandmother who died in the holocaust ("Yad" can mean either "hand" or "memorial". Yad Sarah may therefore also be translated as "Sarah's memorial"). The fact that the public image of the organization is so much less religious and less connected to Jewish tradition than ZAKA should probably be ascribed to the fact that they employ many non-Haredi volunteers and also provide long-term services to many non-Haredi, nonreligious and even non-Jewish families.

Its founder Uri Lupoliansky, however, does connect the services to Jewish charitable traditions:

Judaism teaches us to respect and care for every human being, created in the image of God. But the Jewish concept of chesed goes beyond that: We should actively seek out ways to help. (Coopersmith and Simmons 2003)

One of the most fundamental ideas of a vibrant Jewish community involves the idea of voluntarism on all levels. It is the spirit of the dedicated volunteer that has bound the Jewish community together through the centuries...In Jerusalem, the Yad Sarah organization, which supplies every level of service to people with special needs, represents one of the shining examples of voluntarism. (Article in The Jewish News Weekly, 30 May, 2003, quoted in Stadler et al. 2011, p. 150 f.)

Yad Sarah has expanded into the international arena, developing aid programs and courses in Angola, Cameroon, Jordan, South Korea and China. They also sent aid to the survivors of hurricane Katrina in New Orleans in 2005 (Stadler et al. 2011, p. 152).

3 If I Am Only for Myself, Who Am I?

Whereas ZAKA is an exclusively male organization, Yad Sarah also organizes women volunteers and is therefore an important source of contact with the non-Haredi world for Haredi women. Yad Sarah is yet another example of how members of the ultraorthodox Jewish community break their seclusion and begin to interact with secular Israelis, in a way which is still perceived as acceptable according to the value system of their community.

Fundamentalist Influence in Modern Societies

Stepping back and viewing these three types of voluntary work, we can note a shift towards a greater interaction with the non-Haredi public. Whereas many of the organizations that work to alleviate poverty mainly work within the Haredi community, the work of ZAKA and Yad Sarah benefits all Israelis, Haredi as well as non-Haredi. Through voluntary work in organizations like Yad Sarah and ZAKA, the members of the Haredi community have increased their contacts with non-Haredi Israelis. Such volunteer organizations have also served to improve the image of the Haredi community in the eyes of non-Haredi Israelis and, in part, to counter accusations of parasitism.

It is interesting to note that in this development, the Haredi community in Israel have increased their influence in Israeli society in a way which much resembles developments in other contemporary fundamentalist and/or militant religious movements, for instance the Hizballah in Lebanon, Hamas in Palestine and the Hindunationalist movement in India (usually referred to as *hindutva*, "Hinduness"). These movements have stepped in and provided basic social services such as health, welfare and education in situations where the state has failed to provide adequately for its citizens. This increased influence has in turn paved the way for increased political influence resulting, for instance, in Atal Bihari Vajpayee, leader of the Hindunationalist party BJP having been elected prime minister three times and in Hamas winning the Palestinian parliamentary elections in 2006 (Knudsen 2005; Flanigan 2006). Similar strategies have been employed by organizations like the Muslim Brotherhood in Egypt and the orthodox religious party Shas in Israel, both of them eventually gaining major political influence. Shas became the third largest party in the parliamentary elections of 2006 and the Muslim Brotherhood's candidate Mohamed Morsi was elected president in 2012 (Davis and Robinson 2009).

The relationship between charitable organizations and religiously motivated fundamentalist/militant groups can be understood in different ways:

1. Charitable work and fundamentalist/militant movements can be seen as two ways of addressing the shortcomings of a given society, for instance in providing for the needs of a minority.
2. Charitable work can be a way of gaining wider acceptance among groups that would otherwise not support a fundamentalist/militant cause but who become dependent on the services they provide (Flanigan 2006).

In this connection we can note that in 1994 Yad Sarah was awarded the Israel Prize, the highest civilian honour given in Israel and that in 2003 its founder, Uri Lupolianski, was elected the first Haredi mayor of Jerusalem. In Jerusalem, relations between the Haredi and the non-Haredi population have been notoriously tense. The Haredis make up a growing proportion of Jerusalem's population, about one third in 2005 (Erlanger 2005). Jerusalem is also one of the two cities (with Tel Aviv) that have the highest concentration of non-profit organizations (*Israel's third sector at a glance* 2007). The election of a Haredi mayor would probably not have been possible without the increased Haredi influence in Israeli society and their improved image, partly as the result of these voluntary organizations.

Conclusions

The extent of the voluntary services offered by Israeli Haredis in three areas: Caring for the poor, the dead and the sick provides clear examples of how premodern Jewish traditions of volunteerism have translated into new forms in the present. It represents a religiously anchored response to the failure of the secular Israeli state in providing its citizens with basic services. At the same time, this voluntary work has increased contacts between the Haredi community and the non-Haredi public, and improved the image of the Haredis in the eyes of many non-Haredi Israelis. Also at the same time, the work of these voluntary organizations have extended the influence of the Haredi community on Israeli society as a whole and its work could be compared to that done by other fundamentalist religious movements, which, over time, has paved the way for increased political influence as well.

Utilitarian analyses of volunteerism often stress the benefits for the volunteer: What rewards can he or she expect from this apparently altruistic act: from individuals, from society and from God (Haski-Leventhal 2009, p. 274). This perspective can help in understanding the tendency among Haredis to volunteer. The short- and long-term rewards expected are clear. There is a tradition of reciprocal help within the Haredi community, so the giver of help may someday be the receiver of help from a voluntary organization. Voluntary work enhances the status of the volunteers within Haredi society. In addition to this, the work of these volunteers benefits the image of the Haredi community among non-Haredi Israelis, which in turn could also provide rewards for the whole of the Haredi community. Finally, there is a theological understanding that a pious life, for instance by fulfilling the commandments of caring for the poor, the sick and the dead, will provide rewards in this world as well as in the world to come.

Another key to understanding Haredi volunteerism is provided by the discipline of social psychology which has related volunteering to community: Volunteering strengthens a sense of community, and a strong sense of community is also a factor that tends to increase the likelihood of a high index of voluntary work

3 If I Am Only for Myself, Who Am I?

in a group (Haski-Leventhal 2009, p. 279). The Haredi community is characterized by the marked presence of reciprocal services. Members of the community help each other and feel a responsibility for one another. Since charitable work is seen as a sign of piety, the community also provides a framework that awards status to a person who engages in such work. The extension of its charitable services outside the Haredi community, as seen in the examples above, can also be understood as a way of expanding the community. Instead of primarily caring for members of the Haredi community and avoiding contacts with non-Haredis, this new tendency can be seen as a way of including all of the Israeli population in the perceived responsibility of the Haredis. This blurring of the boundaries between Haredis and non-Haredis can also be seen in the growing involvement of Haredis in politics, the labour market, the military services and other aspects of Israeli civic society. It is possible that these are signs of a gradual shift in strategy on the part of the Haredi leadership. Instead of closing the community to external influences, there is a greater acceptance of contacts with non-Haredi Israelis, which may be based on a strategy of trying to steer Israeli society as a whole more towards Haredi ideals, such as, for instance, keeping the Sabbath or observing separation between the sexes. Such a strategy would be logical since the Haredi portion of the population is growing.

One final aspect that needs to be taken into account is the question of volunteering and identity. Research has shown that religious affiliation tends to increase the tendency to volunteer. Religious affiliation strengthens the feeling of community and that very community reinforces the value of volunteering and of charitable works (Haski-Leventhal 2009, p. 283). In accordance with what I argued in the beginning of this chapter, performing charitable acts is seen as an integral part of Haredi religious identity. Performing such acts therefore confirms one as belonging to the Haredi community. You do not do what is right because you are Haredi. Doing what is right is what makes you Haredi. Confirming the value of such acts by awarding status to those who perform them also ensures that this value continues to be upheld.

References

Aran, G., Stadler, N., & Ben-Ari, E. (2008). Fundamentalism and the masculine body: The case of Jewish ultra-orthodox men in Israel. *Religion, 38,* 25–53.

Bar-Ilan, J., & Azoulay, R. (2012). Map of nonprofit organization websites in Israel. *Journal of the American Society for Information Science and Technology, 63*(6), 1142–1167.

Ben-Nun, R. (2010, March). The demographic composition of the founders of nonprofit organizations. Israeli Center for Third-Sector Research, 34.

Ben-Sasson, H. H., & Isaac Levitats, I. (2007). Charity. In M. Berenbaum & F. Skolnik (Eds.), *Encyclopaedia Judaica* (2nd ed., Vol. 4, pp. 569–575). Detroit: Macmillan Reference USA.

Berman, M. M., Einhorn, D. S., & Zibbell, C. (2007). Philanthropy. In M. Berenbaum & F. Skolnik (Eds.), *Encyclopaedia Judaica* (Vol. 6, pp. 38–47). Detroit: Macmillan Reference USA.

Coopersmith, N., & Simmons, S. (2003, December 20). Mayor with the golden touch. http://www.aish.com/jw/j/Mayor-with-the-Golden-Touch.html. Accessed 2 June 2013.

Davis, N. J., & Robinson, R. V. (2009). Overcoming movement obstacles by the religiously orthodox: The Muslim Brotherhood in Egypt, Shas in Israel, Comunione e Liberazione in Italy, and the Salvation Army in the United States. *American Journal of Sociology, 114*(5), 1301–1349.

Erlanger, S. (2005, July 16). An ultra-orthodox mayor in an unorthodox city. *The New York Times*. Accessed 2 June 2013.

Flanigan, S. T. (2006). Charity as resistance: Connections between charity, contentious politics, and terror. *Studies in Conflict & Terrorism, 29*(7), 641–655.

Frenkel, M. (2009). Charity in Jewish society in the medieval Mediterranean world. Charity and giving in the monotheistic religions. In M. Frenkel & Y. Lev (Eds.), *Studien zur Geschichte und Kultur des islamischen Orients* (Vol. 22, pp. 343–364). Berlin: Walter de Gruyter.

Friedman, B. D. (2003). Two concepts of charity and their relationship to social work practice. *Journal of Religion & Spirituality in Social Work: Social Thought, 21*(1), 3–19.

Haski-Leventhal, D. (2009). Altruism and volunteerism: The perceptions of altruism in four disciplines and their impact on the study of volunteerism. *Journal for the Study of Social Behavior, 39*(3), 271–299.

Haski-Leventhal, D., Yogev-Keren, H., & Katz, H. (2011, June). Philanthropy in Israel 2008: Patterns of volunteering, donations and organ donation. Israeli Center for Third-Sector Research, 38.

Heilman, S. C. (2001). *When a Jew dies. The ethnography of a bereaved son*. Berkeley: University of California Press.

Hustinx, L., Cnaan, R. A., & Handy, F. (2010). Navigating theories of volunteering: A hybrid map for a complex phenomenon. *Journal for the Theory of Social Behaviour, 40*(4), 410–434.

Jacobs, L., & Szubin, Z. H. (2007). Righteousness. In M. Berenbaum & F. Skolnik (Eds.), *Encyclopaedia Judaica* (Vol. 17, pp. 307–309). Detroit: Macmillan Reference USA.

Jaffe, E. D. (1991). State, religion, and the third sector. In R. Wuthnow (Ed.), *Between states and markets. The voluntary sector in comparative perspective* (pp. 189–216). Princeton: Princeton University Press.

Knudsen, A. (2005). Crescent and sword: The Hamas enigma. *Third World Quarterly, 26*(8), 1373–1388.

Kramer, R. M. (1994). Reflection on the voluntary nonprofit sector in Israel. *Journal of Jewish Communal Service, 70*, 253–263.

Levitats, I., & Rabinowitz, L. I. (2007). Gemilut chasadim. In M. Berenbaum & F. Skolnik (Eds.), *Encyclopaedia Judaica* (Vol. 7, pp. 427–428). Detroit: Macmillan Reference USA.

Mann, K. J. (1997). The home as a framework for health care. *Disability and Rehabilitation, 19*(4), 128–129.

Rabinowitz, L. I., & Goldberg, S. A. (2007). Chevra kaddisha. In M. Berenbaum & F. Skolnik (Eds.), *Encyclopaedia Judaica* (Vol. 9, pp. 81–82). Detroit: Macmillan Reference USA.

Rosenhek, Z. (2011). Dynamics of inclusion and exclusion in the Israeli welfare state: State-building and political economy. In G. Ben-Porat & B.-S. Turner (Eds.), *The contradictions of Israeli citizenship: Land, religion and state* (pp. 63–86). London: Routledge.

Rothkoff, A. (2007a). Mitzvah. In M. Berenbaum & F. Skolnik (Eds.), *Encyclopaedia Judaica* (Vol. 14, p. 372). Detroit: Macmillan Reference USA.

Rothkoff, A. (2007b). Sick, visiting the. In M. Berenbaum & F. Skolnik (Eds.), *Encyclopaedia Judaica* (Vol. 18, pp. 543–544). Detroit: Macmillan Reference USA.

Schalk, P. (Ed.). (2013). *Religion in Asien. Studien zur Anwendbarkeit des Religionsbegriffs* (Historia religionum) (Vol. 32). Uppsala: Acta Universitatis Upsaliensis.

Shure, R. (1991). Volunteering: Continuing expansion of the definition and a practical application of altruistic motivation. *Journal of Volunteer Administration, 9*(4), 36–41.

Silber, J., & Sorin, M. (2006). Poverty in Israel: Taking a multi-dimensional approach. In M. Petmesidou & C. Papatheodorou (Eds.), *Poverty & social deprivation in the Mediterranean. Trends, policies & welfare prospects in the new millennium. CROP International studies in poverty research*. London: Zed books.

Stadler, N. (2006). Terror, corpse symbolism, and taboo violation: The Haredi disaster victim identification team in Israel (Zaka). *Journal of the Royal Anthropological Institute, 12*, 837–858.

Stadler, N. (2009). *Yeshiva fundamentalism: Piety, gender, and resistance in the ultra-orthodox world*. New York: New York University Press.

Stadler, N., Ben-Ari, E., & Mesterman, E. (2005). Terror, aid and organization: The Haredi disaster victim identification teams (ZAKA) in Israel. *Anthropological Quarterly, 78*(3), 619–651.

Stadler, N., Lomsky-Feder, E., & Ben-Ari, E. (2008). Fundamentalism's encounters with citizenship: The Haredim in Israel. *Citizenship Studies, 12*(3), 215–231.

Stadler, N., Lomsky-Feder, E., & Ben-Ari, E. (2011). Fundamentalist citizenships: The Haredi challenge. In G. Ben-Porat & B.-S. Turner (Eds.), *The contradictions of Israeli citizenship: Land, religion and state* (pp. 135–157). London: Routledge.

The Israeli third sector at a glance. (2007). The Israeli Center for Third-Sector Research, Ben-Gurion University of the Negev.

Volunteering in Israel. http://www.ivolunteer.org.il/eng/. Accessed 21 May 2013.

Yad Sarah. www.yadsarah.org. Accessed 2 June 2013.

Yishai, Y. (1990). State and welfare groups: Competition or cooperation? Some observations on the Israeli scene. *Nonprofit and Voluntary Sector Quarterly, 19*(3), 215–235.

Chapter 4
Philanthropic Virtue

Mohammad Fazlhashemi

Introduction: Compassion in Muslim Theology

Both the charitable and the philanthropic motives can be traced to the Muslim moral philosophy concerning compassion. A compassionate person shows pity and tenderness of heart towards his fellow beings and first and foremost towards the weak and fragile members of the society. Compassion is a virtue that is emphasized through interaction with other people. It is thus not limited to clean living, abstinence, the performance of certain rituals, saying prayers or something similar. Rather, it is an honourable action that is brought out through active deeds towards other people.

Viewed from the reward-oriented perspective, charitable deeds control what happens to a person after death, in a future life. Charity is rewarded with a place in Paradise or other forms of reward. According to this perspective, a charitable act takes place in a deontological, ethical perspective where the principal value of the act lies in its being founded on a duty that in turn is based on a religious norm. The act can therefore be viewed as a kind of bargaining on the part of the doer, when the person who performs an act will be rewarded in some way or other.

An idea formulated by the Muslim philosopher Ibn Rushd, Averroës (1126–1198) opposed this conception. He played down the reward perspective in favour of the intrinsic value of the ethical norm. When people act on the basis of ethical norms, they contribute to the creation of a better world. Averroës thereby went against the reward imperative and emphasized intrinsic value of the ethical norm, which does not necessarily need to be based on religious norms. He said that ethical principles not only exist to determine the fate of people in what happens after death, but also have significance here and now. We know nothing of what happens after we die, but we know that these norms are very important as regards the life we live in the

---

Some parts of this article are historical overviews based on the author's previous research. These parts focus on examples and the development within the Shiite tradition in Iran.

M. Fazlhashemi (✉)
Department of Theology, Studies in Faith and Ideologies, Systematic Theology and Studies in World Views, Uppsala University, Uppsala, Sweden
e-mail: mohammad.fazlhashemi@teol.uu.se

L. Hustinx et al. (eds.), *Religion and Volunteering,* Nonprofit and Civil Society Studies, DOI 10.1007/978-3-319-04585-6_4, © Springer International Publishing Switzerland 2015

present. When people break ethical norms, this affects not only our own lives but the whole of society. And conversely, when we act on the basis of ethical norms, we contribute to the creation of a better world, Averroës said.

The philanthropic perspective is assumed to safeguard society's best interests and also protects humanity from cynicism, profit, egocentric consumerism, narcissistic self-absorption and last but not least discrimination on the grounds of financial standing, social status, ethnicity or other discriminatory factors.

In the Islamic theological tradition of ideas, however, compassion is not only represented as a human virtue. It is to an even greater degree a divine quality. This is not least made clear by the phrase with which every chapter, *sura*, of the Qur'an begins. With the exception of the 9th*sura*, every chapter of the Qur'an begins with the phrase: "In the name of God the Beneficent, *ar-rahman*, and the Merciful, *ar-rahim*". Both qualities can also be found among the 99 names that are used in Islam to refer to God.

The purpose of the recurring reminders about God's compassion in the Qur'an seems to be to emphasize that which is most divine about God. Compassion is, however, not only described as a prominent quality of God but also as a human virtue that can bring out the most magnificent aspects of the person who has accepted the virtue. Compassion is also represented as a virtue that every human being can adopt if they want to live up to their human self or even the divine qualities they bear within themselves. This reasoning takes its starting point in the conceptions of the double nature of human beings that has its origins in the characterization of man that is found in the Qur'an:

> Indeed We created man in the best form. Then We reversed him to the lowest of the low. Except those who believe and do good deeds, for whom there is never-ending recompense. (Qur'an, 95: 4–6).

The Islamic notion of man's double nature has its roots far back in history. It can be traced back to ancient Indian, Chinese, Persian and Greek world-views. It is also an established conception in the Abrahamic philosophical tradition that differentiates between man's earthly/material and spiritual sides. According to this tradition, man's spiritual nature derives from God, since God breathed His own spirit into man and created him in His own image. One side of man is the one we are considered to have in common with all other living creatures, i.e. man's material side. We thus share this side with, for example, animals and other living creatures and in this respect we are controlled by our instincts, our urges and our desires. That part of human nature that sets us apart from other creatures is the thinking, sensible, spiritual dimension.

Compassion is considered to be founded on this part of man's nature. This virtue allows us to rise above our material, earthly, animal side and unite with the divine. The relationship between the material and spiritual sides of human beings is characterized by a continuous struggle. A person who manages to acquire this virtue is regarded as having achieved an inner freedom which allows them to no longer be ruled by their own desires, instincts and material needs. Through compassion, man can counteract his material side, which will in turn lead to the spiritual aspects, fill-

4 Philanthropic Virtue

ing the vacuum that occurs when the material aspects are driven back. Compassion allows man's spiritual side to grow and master the material side.

In the Islamic theological tradition, compassion is also described as a virtue that helps us as social beings to avoid putting ourselves in a dysfunctional or destructive position in our interaction with our fellow beings. The idea is that people must not focus on themselves, personal gain or group interests in their social relations. Compassion is consequently represented as an important basis for people's involvement in philanthropic activities, meaning the kind of volunteer work that is done without any thought of receiving something in return from the targets of the intervention or reward from a higher power.

Fundamental Respect for Human Beings

In the Muslim theological tradition concerning both charity and philanthropic volunteer work, personal experience of hardship and suffering has a central place. This experience is considered to increase an individual's degree of motivation to participate in both charitable and philanthropic activity. Personal experience of hardship increases the will to help people who find themselves in a similar situation. We can of course find out about these people's plight from various information channels but personal experience is considered to increase our awareness nonetheless. The starting point is that we feel greater affinity in a reality where we are present ourselves than in a world that we observe from a distance.

It is on the basis of this perspective that we view the month-long fast during Ramadan in the Islamic world. Suffering thirst, hunger and tiredness in conjunction with the fast is represented as a privation that we should undergo in order to gain personal experience of hardship and suffering, to be able in turn to understand the situation of distressed people and thereby become more willing to help them.

Charity, philanthropy and willingness to participate in volunteer work take their starting point in a virtue, compassion, through which people as individuals show empathy and solidarity with each other. Unselfish aid work, however, is not intended to remain an individual virtue. In addition to the individual relationships, compassion must form the foundation for building a functioning social network in society. Compassion seems to be used here as a basis for a mind-set of equality through which the very weakest in society will be given help to rise to the same level as other members of society. Viewed from this perspective, it is a virtue that constitutes a foundation for active measures that help people who find themselves in a kind of "situational inequality", meaning that they have involuntarily come up against various problems that have put them in an unequal position in relation to their fellow men.

On the basis of this perspective, it is interesting to note which people qualify for help according to the Qur'anic basis for this collective compassion. It is primarily those who are closest to a person, their immediate circle of people, who are included in this social care program. This circle consists of parents, family members and close relatives but is not limited to only those who have some sort of family relationship through blood ties. People who live in physical proximity and are part of the people's social network are also included. Neighbours in particular are an important group. Common to all these people is that they have, for various reasons, ended up in difficulties (Qur'an, 2: 83, 4: 36). In the next step, the circle is widened to encompass all vulnerable people who find themselves outside what society regards as a normal, equal level. These include orphans, people who can be categorized as distressed, the needy, heavily indebted people, etc. Common to all these groups is that they have, in one way or another, found themselves unable to pay their debts or are going through some crisis in their lives (Qur'an, 9: 60, 17: 26).

Social Safety Net

The discussions about the creation of a social safety net connect to a debate that goes far back in Islamic history. It was already going on during the formative phase of Islamic theology and philosophy in the eighth and ninth centuries (according to the Christian calendar) or the third and fourth centuries of the Islamic calendar. It was a time when rational-minded Muslim theologians and philosophers tried to emphasize rational arguments for the most central conceptions within the Islamic philosophical tradition alongside the strictly religious arguments. Their debate was not only limited to ontological and epistemological conceptions but was just as much linked to issues that concerned social life.

In their discussions of the Qur'an's exhortations to be compassionate, Muslim theologians and philosophers tried to use rational arguments. They said that such exhortations should not only be interpreted as something that concerned life after death. According to these thinkers, the imposed actions would lead to the creation of a better world and people would therefore benefit from them already in this life. The debate also concerned the question of whether compassion should be regarded as a virtue, a religious duty for the pious and the virtuous to devote themselves to, or if it was fundamentally based on a rational argument about creating a social safety net, the purpose of which was to help one's fellow men who were enduring hardship in their life. This was an idea that in its turn had its origins in the notion that helping one's fellow men who found themselves in difficulties can also be regarded as a desire that people would wish to be treated in the same way in times of trouble.

The discussions about philanthropic and social aspects of compassion follow from these ideas. Philanthropic activities include a particular emphasis on taking care of the distressed and the weak in the lowest stratum of society.

Another group who are mentioned explicitly as people qualifying for collective compassion are those termed *Ibn as-sabil*—literally son of the road/wayfarer (Qur'an, 2: 177, 8: 41, 30: 38, 59: 7).[1] The term is used to refer to a stranger who

---

[1] See for example following verses: "It is not righteousness that you turn your faces toward the east and the west [in prayer], righteousness is rather one who believe in God, and the Last Day, and the

finds himself far from home, more precisely someone who, because of their circumstances, has insufficient means to survive. In a broader perspective, this also includes people who for various reasons cannot return home, e.g. refugees seeking sanctuary/asylum from political, religious or some other form of persecution.

Other groups mentioned include prisoners and slaves. The rules relating to these last groups take their starting point in the local conditions prevailing during pre-modern times and concern the efforts that should be made when fellow believers or people belonging to the same tribe or clan were captured during the recurring conflicts between different tribes and clans. The same applied to the slave trade since redemption of slaves was considered a compassionate and God-pleasing deed. These groups were a natural part of the social context in pre-modern times. What unites them with the other named groups is that they were classified as distressed and afflicted people who needed help from others.

As the legal discussion continues today, further categories have come to be included among those who should be included in social care programs, for example mentally handicapped people and minors who have no guardian or trustee, divorced women and widows who have no source of income, etc.

The conceptions concerning caring for the distressed are not unique to the Islamic theological tradition. According to French islamologist Louis Massignon (1883–1962), these conceptions can be traced to the Semitic and Abrahamic religious philosophical tradition. Referring to exhortations to take care of strangers and the oppressed in the Biblical tradition—for example Exodus 22:21, Leviticus 19:33 and Deuteronomy 27:19—Massignon considers the notion of compassion founded on respect for man's inner person to exist in all three Abrahamic religions. In the Muslim civilization, this philosophical tradition was given a functioning social and political form (Sandgren 2007, pp. 125–126).

Created of One Essence

In conclusion, we might say that compassion was intended as a virtue, the principal purpose of which was to safeguard fundamental respect for human beings. This applies in particular in circumstances where people find themselves in a weak and fragile position. The question is how the debates have run as regards living up to this virtue and all the ideas and conceptions associated with them.

One question that has dominated the discussions about compassion and philanthropic interventions in the Muslim context is that of who should have borne responsibility for ensuring that the needy and distressed would be taken care of from pre-modern times until the debates going on today.

The exhortations for everyone to do their utmost to live up to the recommendations associated with the virtue of compassion are an inseparable part of everyday

---

angels, and the Book, and the prophets, and give away wealth out of love for Him to the kindred, and the orphans, and the poor, and the wayfarer, and the needy, and for the emancipation of those in bondage and the slaves..." (Qur'an, 2: 177).

religiosity. People are constantly reminded of life's fragility and that it is every human being's duty to show compassion towards their fellow men. The thirteenth-century Persian poet Sa'di of Shiraz (1184–1283/1291) believed that humankind's kinship constitutes a foundation for volunteer efforts and that people must involve themselves in the work of helping the distressed. In his collection of poems and prose *Golistan* (The Rose Garden), he expresses this through the following poem:

> The Children of Adam are limbs of each other,
> Having been created of one essence.
> When the calamity of time afflicts one limb
> The other limbs cannot remain at rest.
> If thou hast no sympathy for the troubles of others,
> Thou art unworthy to be called by the name of a man

The view of man that permeates Sa'di's poetry stands out as the complete opposite of the individual-centred, modern view of man. The latter puts a focus on the individual and his/her individual needs. Volunteer work, both as an individual and collective philanthropic activity, loses its meaning in a view of mankind in which society consists of people who in their turn disintegrate into individuals with very disparate needs and where the individuals are constantly busy realizing their individual ideals and asserting their right to realize their egocentric targets. This view of mankind also differs from the social model in which support and help for the distressed is passed from the individual to a state or municipal level through the taxes that the working population pay. Philanthropic volunteer work does not necessarily need to mean abandoning our individual objectives in life or rejecting state and municipal responsibility in favour of non-profit-making charitable activities.

This is work that has its origins in a mind-set of equality, a social structure and a view of mankind that presumes that human beings will live in community and coexistence with each other and that they show consideration to each other and, not least, that they show consideration for the weaker individuals in society and the world around.

Institutionalisation

The social care issues that compassion included were, however, too extensive to be able to be dealt with at the level of the individual. The scale of the different measures that would be implemented meant that it was felt that the task would be too much for single individuals. Without depriving the individual of the opportunity to act on his/her own micro level, good soil was laid down for making demands for the establishment of social structures and interventions from society to realize the objectives of creating a social safety net. This in turn laid the foundation for the growing institutionalization of social care and coordination of voluntary work in this respect. In addition to action on an individual basis as a volunteer, the individual was also to assist in the work of creating structures. This would be done with the help of the religious tax that every Muslim has to pay, among other things, at

4 Philanthropic Virtue

the end of Ramadan, *zakat al-fitr*. This task is specifically intended for aid to weak and distressed people.

Another important question, however, was who would take on the role/responsibility for organizing or monitoring the creation of the social safety net's institutionalization. The modern welfare state and its pretension to take on this responsibility were conspicuous by their absence.

The regulations concerning Islam's religious taxes made the ruling powers during the history of Islam get involved with various initiatives in this area but they were as a rule far from sufficient. This responsibility did not sit comfortably with the powers of the day. From the tenth century, the major Islamic empire, the Abbasids, had become more and more unstable. The rulers were all too occupied with the problems of holding on to their power, i.e. staying on the throne. This meant defending themselves against all external and internal threats directed against their positions of power. Caring for the weak and the vulnerable in society consequently was not a priority on the agenda of the earthly rulers. It was also a resource-intensive measure that was based on a mind-set of equality and caring. This way of thinking ran counter to the ruling powers' authoritarian form of government that was based on the unquestioning allegiance of their subjects in exchange for protection by the earthly rulers. Issues of social care and taking care of the weak were seen as an area of jurisdiction that could just as well be shifted to other principals who might consider involving themselves in charitable activities.

One group who were more than willing to take on this role were the scholars, the religious leaders. They felt that it lay within their field of responsibility to ensure that this central virtue was realized both at the personal/individual level and, most importantly of all, on a social plane. The scholars justified their commitment with a number of motives. On the one hand, they referred to strict religious arguments, claiming that the scriptures laid this responsibility upon the scholars. On the other hand, they claimed that, considering the significant needs within society, substantial social structures and their associated institutions were needed that could deal with these societal matters. Without institutionalization, there was a great risk that the work of creating a social safety net would be left to fate, or as the scholars put it, there was a risk that these issues would lie fallow.

It did not, however, go without saying that the scholars would view these issues as a self-evident part of their jurisdiction. We find fairly different perceptions of the matter at different times in Islamic history and in different branches of Islam. A number of other factors had also played a crucial role in this context; these are historical, social and economic circumstances and different interpretations of the Islamic scriptures.

In both the main branches of Islam, Sunni and Shia, the scholars involved themselves in the issues of social care. They did so, however, for different reasons. In the larger of the two groups, the Sunnis, it was viewed as a kind of distribution of work between the earthly leaders and the scholars as religious/spiritual leaders. Seen from this perspective, the earthly leaders were accepted as legitimate rulers since they had succeeded in usurping earthly power. Things were quite different in the Shiite branch. The Shiite scholars also believed that social care issues were part of their jurisdiction but unlike the Sunni scholars, the Shiite scholars belonged to a vulnerable and often persecuted minority who, moreover, considered that the earthly powers were not legitimate. They took on the social care issues but refused to recognize the legitimacy of earthly rulers. Some went so far as to lay claim to the earthly power and considered challenging its representatives in order to take over this power for themselves.

The scholars' involvement in this question meant that a virtue had been institutionalized. They created institutions and structures to deal with the issues of social care. This was generally done on condition that there was no civil society with associated institutions to provide the social safety net. Even if the scholars mainly viewed their involvement from a religious perspective, the purpose of which was to maintain a central virtue in society, they were forced to involve themselves in the institutionalization of care activities. This required, among other things, systematizing routines and organizing the collection of donated real estate that ended up in the so-called waqf system.[2] In conjunction with this, volunteer efforts to help with the collection and administration of contributions and donations were of great importance.

Collections were to begin with local administration, but in some Muslim countries, for example Persia during the Safavid era (1501–1736), the work was centralized. Centralization of the collection of financial contributions and taxes meant that the scholars achieved economic independence that not only gave them financial muscle and the resources to carry on resource-intensive social activities, but also rendered them independent of the earthly powers. These increased financial resources and the economic independence opened up new possibilities for the scholars. They did not limit their efforts to helping the weak and the distressed in society financially, but began to act increasingly as public representatives who looked after these people's legal interests. People who considered themselves to be subjected to injustice by the ruling powers turned to the scholars for assistance. Their role developed into that of defender of legal security, an authority to turn to when one wished to make a complaint against the ruling power (Zargarinejad 1995, p. 120).

This development meant that compassion was not limited to financial aid for the distressed and the financially weak individuals and groups in society. Efforts to combat legal insecurity and provide support for people subjected to injustice or arbitrariness within the legal field, or what in today's terminology would be termed social activism, became just as self-evident a part of a spectrum of activities that went under the heading of compassion. The scholars' support of the socially vulnerable, the financially weak and those who were heading for a showdown with the ruling powers gave them even greater grass-roots support. Their increased popularity led in turn to more people paying their religious taxes to the scholars or donating

---

[2] The basis of the waqf system was that a person could donate real estate, wells, schools, hospitals, agricultural land, etc. for charitable purposes during their lifetime. A donation meant that the property was withdrawn from the market and could not be sold, pledged, inherited or confiscated by the state. It belonged to the waqf institution that acted as a foundation to manage the property and ensure that it was used or that income from it was used for various charitable purposes.

4 Philanthropic Virtue

property for social care in the so-called waqf system that was being increasingly developed in Muslim countries.

Sociopolitical Factors

The group that distinguished itself as regards their involvement in issues of social care was the scholars. They found support for their role in, amongst other things, the prophet's tradition which pointed to the scholars as a group with a defined task. This applies first and foremost to the following pronouncement from prophet Muhammad: "The scholars are the heirs of the prophets and my congregation's scholars are like the prophets of Israel." (Fazlhashemi 2011, p. 104)

Based on this prophetic pronouncement, they considered that leading the congregation was one of the scholars' tasks. But despite the prophetic pronouncement and several other arguments that all underlined the scholars' tasks, there has never, not even today, been any consensus regarding the scholars' area of responsibility. There are groups that believe that the scholars' area of responsibility is limited to the spiritual area and to helping people in general to find their way around all the religious sources and traditions. Opposing this are those who believe that the scholars' responsibility includes both spiritual and earthly leadership. Here again, we find no consensus regarding the extent of the scholars' jurisdiction. All groups, however, agreed that the scholars should, in one way or another, take responsibility for the social care issues. The only detail that has caused any problems and where opinions have diverged was whether the scholars themselves should deal with the issue or whether they should monitor or delegate responsibility to others. In general, they agreed that they should act as administrators of the social safety net (Fazlhashemi 2011, p. 105).

The scholars' social involvement, and the organization of the volunteer work associated with it, has, however, been affected by political and social circumstances. For a long time, there has been an unwritten but de facto division of work between the earthly rulers and the religious institutions, where the latter were responsible for the social work and the voluntary activities associated with it.

The winds of change began to blow in the nineteenth century, as the central powers in the principal Muslim states of the time, i.e. the Ottoman Empire and the Persia of the Qajars, were becoming progressively weaker. This weakness had its origins mainly in internal circumstances such as political incompetence, widespread corruption, absence of legal security and a weakened economy. To this must be added the European colonial powers' challenge to the Muslim states both on the battlefield and in the political and financial arenas. The different factors had contributed to increased social, political and economic problems. There was a greater need for efforts that would safeguard society's social safety net.

The weakening of the central powers in Muslim countries and the increased social and financial problems opened up the field for the scholars and the religious institutions to play a greater role in the earthly area. This was most evident in Persia.[3]

---

[3] The country officially changed its name to Iran in the 1930s.

The scholars believed that the unsatisfactory situation in the country demanded their involvement. They wanted to assist their sorely tried compatriots. Their involvement was not, however, limited to issues of social care but also came to include political questions. Many of them involved themselves in the efforts to bring about a paradigm shift in the country, that is to say, a transition from autocracy to a constitutional form of government. The scholars found inspiration in the constitutional form of government that had its roots in the modern European form of government. They held high hopes that a transition to a constitutional form of government would lead to major political, social and economic improvements in the country. Among other things, it would work to counter the country's economic destitution, strengthen legal security, combat corruption and, last but not least, it would break the influence of foreign countries over the earthly powers, which in their vocabulary they had termed colonialism (Mahallati Gharavi 1995, p. 475). Here again, they justified their involvement in political questions by pointing to the need to create a social safety net to take care of the weak and the distressed. They believed that a transition to a constitutional form of government would give the social care issues a significant boost (Khalkhali 1995, p. 232, pp. 318–319).

One of the scholars who had been working actively for the introduction of constitutional government since the 1890s was Ayatollah Seyyed Mohammad Tabatabai. In one of his pronouncements, he justified his support for a constitutional form of government as follows:

> We have not seen for ourselves those countries that are led by constitutional governments. But from what we have heard and what people who have been in those countries tell us, a constitutional government leads to security and development. For this reason we wish to take action to establish constitutional government in this country. (Kermani 1992, p. 339; Kasravi 1977, pp. 85–86)

Tabatabai somewhat ironically writes that his ambitions to establish a constitutional form of government worked against the scholars' jurisdiction because in a country with legal security and in a sound economic position, fewer and fewer people would join them. But he had nothing against going down in history as the person who worked to establish a parliamentary, constitutional system and a constitutional state where social care issues did not lie fallow (Kasravi 1977, p. 76).

The scholars' efforts regarding social care issues were dependent on the financial contributions they could bring in through taxes, grants and donations. Alongside the religious taxes, the merchants were one of the biggest contributors. As their revenues shrank, the religious institutions' coffers also began to run dry. This was to some degree due to the general economic decline that had resulted from the mismanagement of the economy by the earthly powers. Another and more important reason was their clumsy handling of the awarding of concessions to foreign businessmen that excluded the domestic businessmen.

In the early 1890s, the English major G.F. Talbot was granted a monopoly on purchasing, processing and selling tobacco in Persia. Over the following 2 years, this concession gave rise to widespread opposition against the king and against what was perceived as foreign influence over the country's economy. The measure

4 Philanthropic Virtue 69

caused great indignation among the merchants who were effectively excluded from the tobacco trade in the domestic market.

The merchants were driven by fears that the foreign tobacco company threatened their financial interests. Their appeals to the royal court had been in vain and they therefore turned to the Shiite scholars. The highest Shiite scholar of the time, Ayatollah Mirza Shirazi (1814–1896), wrote to the king complaining about his frivolous awarding of concessions to foreign states and companies. He demanded that the tobacco concession be annulled but the reply from the king's envoy was that the agreement with the English was binding and impossible to cancel. The highest spiritual leader's reply to this was that, if the state was unable to do so, then he would personally and with God's help annul the concession. This was followed by a serious demonstration of power on the part of the highest Shiite scholar.

The Ayatollah issued a fatwa through which he forbade the faithful to use tobacco. The fatwa was very concise but its symbolic value was all the greater. In the fatwa, the Ayatollah wrote that all use of tobacco was to be considered an act of war against Islam. In practice, the fatwa meant that the Ayatollah imposed a religious prohibition on tobacco. In addition to boycotting tobacco products, the fatwa gave rise to a series of extensive protests against the king and the foreign companies. The bazaars, which were the hub of the economy, were closed by general strikes and mass protest rallies were organized. In 1892, the king gave way and annulled the concession.

The Ayatollah's actions in the tobacco affair and the debates that followed showed how the religious leaders and the institutions advanced their positions as the central powers continued to weaken. The religious authorities not only spoke of the need to safeguard Islam but also touched upon other areas such as safeguarding the nation, the kingdom's sovereignty, independence from foreign powers and the public's interests and, last but not least, the necessity to protect the weak members of society. The scholars reserved the right to have opinions regarding the actions of the earthly powers and to curtail their authority. Their successful action against the royal family and the foreign companies made the scholars aware of the potentially enormous power that they had. These events marked the beginning of a series of other manoeuvres on the part of the scholars through which they advanced their positions still further. At the same time, it is interesting to note that, despite the Ayatollah's demonstration of his great power through the fatwa, he did not wish to proceed further. Despite his opposition to the king, he did not wish to go as far as to demand his abdication and that the scholars should take over his power while waiting for the secret imam. When the king had conceded to the Ayatollah's exhortation, albeit extremely unwillingly, and annulled the agreement with the English, the matter was closed (Kermani 1992, pp. 20–28).

The nineteenth century was also the era of constitutionalism. Increasing numbers of scholars fell in behind the demand for a transition from autocracy to a constitutional form of government. The main motive was that a transition to a constitutional form of government would enable issues of social care to be handled better. Their reasoning was that the constitutional form of government was not the most ideal form, but it was definitely second best and since it presented better possibilities to deal with the social care, they were prepared to support such a transition. A constitutional form of government would also mean the final demise of autocracy in the country and, last but not least, it would mean the end of foreign influence over the state.

Earthly Power Ambitions

The transition from autocracy to constitutional government took place in Persia in 1906, but instead of better conditions and the realization of all the hopes that had been tied to the constitutional form of government, the country was thrown into political chaos. The power struggle between different political factions intent on filling the vacuum after the abolition of autocracy led to anarchy and political disarray. The economic situation worsened and the weak and vulnerable saw their circumstances deteriorate still further. The chaos frightened a large group of scholars who chose to withdraw their support for constitutional government. The final turning point came during the inter-war years, when the autocratic ruler of the time, King Reza Shah, inspired by Turkish dictator Ataturk, implemented a de-islamification campaign that clamped down on everything that had to do with Islam and focused in particular on its representatives. The campaign made Islam out to be an obstacle to modernisation of the political, economic, social and cultural areas. The religious leaders were now even more sceptical towards the constitutional form of government. In fact, there was not much left of the political reforms associated with the constitutional form of government (Fazlhashemi 2011, pp. 153–160).

We see the same trend in other countries. In Egypt, great hopes were pinned to the transition to constitutional government in the early 1920s. There, it was England as a colonial power that dashed all hopes by its refusal to relinquish its hold on the country. In the late 1920s, the first demands began to be voiced for the establishment of an Islamic form of government. In Iran, the demand was first voiced in the mid-1940s. It did not, however, meet with any great sympathy since support for political Islam was still weak. Support grew all the stronger in the 1960s and 1970s. The most important reason for this was the actions of the government which had suppressed all forms of political opposition.

The religious leaders accused the earthly powers of betraying the distressed when, at the same time, they and their immediate family were rolling in money, from, for example, the enormous oil revenues that were flowing into most Muslim countries. The oil revenues were spent on weapons and lives of luxury for those in power and their immediate families. The destitution of society's weak and distressed was one of the most important aspects that the religious leaders focused on in their criticism of the people in power.

It was in conjunction with this that a group of scholars put forward their demand for a transition to Islamic government. The religious leaders were, however, far from unanimous on this point. Most of them supported the demand for action in the social area and caring for the distressed but they did not wish to go so far as to support the demand for a political takeover of power. Their interpretations of the scriptures and the regulations concerning compassion on the social plane were based on it being the scholars' responsibility to ensure that this virtue was realized in society. They also added that the task of scholars was to see to it that this task really was carried out and that this important issue did not lie fallow. This did not, however, mean that scholars would assume political power or that they themselves would intervene personally. They could just as easily delegate or transfer the task to the legal entities or institutions that were well equipped for the task.

From the early 1960s, demands to take over political power as an important prerequisite to be able to deal with the social care issues became increasingly vociferous. The most important component of the scholars' opposition to the earthly leadership was the fact that the earthly powers had reneged on their commitments. Not only had they submitted to foreign powers and mismanaged the economy. What was even more serious was that they were implementing a deliberate anti-Islam policy.

The generally unsatisfactory conditions involving widespread corruption, skewed finances and lack of an adequate social safety net for the distressed were taken as further evidence that the powers that were had not fulfilled their earthly duties. These circumstances were, in the final analysis, considered as disqualifying them as earthly leaders in Muslim countries (Fazlhashemi 2011, pp. 172–202).

Compassion in the Fight Against Religious Oppression

Endeavours to introduce an Islamic form of government had borne fruit in several Muslim countries. In Iran, a social revolution in 1979 led to the deposition of the despotic Shah. In Turkey, an Islamic party has won three general elections since 2002. In Tunisia, where the popular uprising in the wake of the Arab spring have led to old dictator being forced from power, an Islamic Party has won the electorate's mandate to rule the country. In all these countries, commitment to social issues to aid society's distressed and organize volunteer efforts in this respect have been anchored in the political context.

The form of government that has endured longest is the Iranian example. It is based on a specific and rather unusual political doctrine that goes by the name of the rule of the scholars. The many changes that took place in the country once the scholars had come to power include the establishment of a number of governmental and quasi-governmental institutions with the specific task of dealing with the issue of social care and organizing volunteer work. These institutions took stock of the country's households to identify the weak and the distressed. A large group of people among the country's weak and distressed have since then been enveloped by a social safety net that aids vulnerable groups in different ways, for example in the form of social security allowances. Alongside these governmental and quasi-governmental institutions, individual scholars and non-profit-making organizations run their own activities that involve volunteers in their work with financially weak families and other groups of citizens in need of extensive assistance.

72   M. Fazlhashemi

Despite all the endeavours to meet the needs of the distressed, the debates concerning social care and a social safety net and the need for volunteer activities have not ceased; on the contrary, the debate has intensified and the religious leaders have been severely criticized for not having been able to create sufficient protection for society's neediest. Another problem was that the new political system proved to be extremely authoritarian and developed into a totalitarian form of government that showed no compassion at all towards political opponents or citizens who, in one way or another, deviated from the ethical, social, cultural and political norms that the state had set up. During the past three decades, prominent religious leaders have demanded that the powers that be live up to the compassionate norms. Their demands have not been limited to caring for society's financially weak individuals but have come to an increasing extent to encompass legal security and worthy, humane treatment of dissidents and political opponents. An illustrative example of the involvement of religious leaders in this respect is the events that followed the controversial presidential election of 2009. The popular protests against election rigging were brutally beaten down, causing vociferous protests from several high-ranking religious leaders, including Ayatollah Hussein Ali Montazeri (1922–2009). He condemned the assaults on the protesters and people who had been imprisoned, the collective sham trials, the coercion of confessions in front of TV cameras, etc., as actions which were in glaring contrast to compassion.[4] In one of his pronouncements, he compared the sham trials after the presidential election in Iran with Soviet dictator Stalin's and Iraqi dictator Saddam Hussein's show trials and insisted that such sham trials and confessions obtained under coercion ran counter to Islamic beliefs.[5] Ayatollah Montazeri went so far as to say, with the support of his religious authority, that the regime in power in Iran lacked religious/Muslim legitimacy.[6] In his view, the right to demonstrate and express one's opinions was to be regarded as a civil right and underlined the fact that respect for human rights and fundamental civil liberties is an important aspect of compassion in Islam.

A Question of Personal Responsibility

Discussions concerning social care, caring for those in need of protection and the distressed, as well as volunteer work in the Muslim context, have been able to be linked to an ethical question or a religious obligation through the virtue of compassion. On the personal plane, the discussions have concerned both ethical questions and conceptions that volunteer efforts will be rewarded in one way or another. Another side of the debate has been the discussions about the role of religion in society

---

[4] He refers, amongst others, to the following sources: Wasail al-shia, (Shiite jurisprudence's handed down sources), vol. 18, pp. 497–498 and Daim al-islam, (The pillars of Islam), vol. 2, p. 466.

[5] www.amontazeri.com/farsi/ (topic 217, posted on 4 Aug 2009) and www.amontazeri.com/farsi/ (topic 223, posted on 22 Sep 2009).

[6] www.amontazeri.com/farsi/ (topic 219, posted on 26 Aug 2009).

4 Philanthropic Virtue

and the attitudes of religious institutions to earthly questions and politics. Central to the discussions has been the question of whether compassion is to be regarded as a personal virtue or is to function as a societal virtue and, first and foremost, whether the representatives of the religious institutions are to play an active role when it comes to designing a social safety net and organizing volunteer efforts. It is important to note that the discussions about compassion have not been carried on in a social or historical vacuum, but have very much been coloured by social and political circumstances. Under certain historical and social conditions, the discussions about compassion have also come to encompass such questions as legal security and respect for fundamental civil liberties.

It can be seen that some kind of consensus has existed on personal responsibility. Every individual must strive to fulfil this virtue. The dividing lines have been drawn regarding the issue of realizing it on the societal plane. As the somewhat abbreviated historical account above shows, the scholars' entry into the social and political arena was motivated by the lack of institutions and players dealing with social care and the defence of legal security. In modern times, safeguarding the various aspects of this virtue has been used as an excuse to justify arrogating political power. In a modern welfare state and community founded on the rule of law, where an independent judicial system guarantees legal security and social authorities take care of weak and vulnerable people, there should not be any scope for religious leaders to intervene in these areas because realization of the public aspects of the virtue of compassion is a matter for the state and the judicial and social authorities. What remains, then, is personal responsibility, which is a matter for the individual. In this respect, volunteer work becomes a question for the individual who can justify his or her decision to participate in volunteer work for both religious and ethical reasons.

As regards the scholars and their role, the Shiite Ayatollah Akhund Khorasani (1837–1911) distinguished himself through the vision that he sketched at the beginning of the last century. He was a devoted advocate of the constitutional form of government but warned the scholars against involving themselves in politics because he did not consider this to be compatible with their responsibilities. On the one hand, he spoke about personal responsibility and based on this he reserved the right for the scholars to act as warning voices in society with the right to criticize politicians and statesmen who were not fulfilling their obligations. As individuals, the scholars were to watch, scrutinize and criticize the government and combat corruption and oppression. He compared this role to that of salt. The scholars would be the salt of the earth. In the same way as salt prevents decay, the scholars would counteract autocratic attitudes and the decay of power. They would act as defenders of compassion when the earthly powers committed transgressions against legal security and sound a note of warning when social care was neglected (Kadivar 2006, pp. 16–17).

Akhund Khorasani's point of departure was not any conception of the scholars' special standing in society. He saw no difference between the scholars and other people in the public sphere. Like everyone else, the scholars were to pursue the struggle against social injustice as individuals, a role that he described as the salt of the earth (Kadivar 2006, p. 19).

References

Bernström, M. K. (1998). *Koranensbudskap (Qur'an)*. Stockholm: Proprius.

Fazlhashemi, M. (2011). *Troellerförnuftipolitiskislam*. Stockholm: Norstedts.

Jafarian, R. (2000). *Safaviyyedararse-ye din, farhangvasiyasat* (Vol. 1). Qom: Pajoheshkade-ye Hawzehvadaneshgah.

Kadivar, M. (2006). *Siyasatnameh-ye Khorasani*. Teheran: Kavir.

Kasravi, A. (1977). *Tarikh-e mashroute-ye Iran* (14th ed.). Teheran: Amir kabir.

Kermani, N. al-E. (1992). *Tarikhe bidarye iranian* (Vol. 1, 3rd ed.). Teheran: Entesharat-e bonyad-e farhang-e Iran.

Khalkhali, E. al-ulama. (1995). Bayan-esaltanat-e mashroteh va favayedha. In G. H. Zargarinejad (Ed.), *Rasa il mmashrotiyyat. 18 resaleh dar bare-yemashrotiyyat*. Teheran: Kavir.

Khonsari Esfahani, M. B. (1978). *Rawdat al-jannat fi ahwal al-ulama wa al-sadat* (Vol. 5). Teheran: Eslamiyyeh.

Mahallati Gharavi, S. M. E. (1995). Morad az saltanat-e mashroute. In G. H. Zargarinejad (Ed.), *Rasailmashrotiyyat. 18 resalehdar bare-ye mashrotiyyat*. Teheran: Kavir.

Montazeri, H. A. (2006). *Resale-ye huquq*. Qom: Arghavan-e danesh.

Montazeri, H. A. (2008). *Eslam din-e fetrat* (3rd ed.). Teheran: Vasef.

Montazeri, H. A. (2009). *Hokumat-e dini va hoquqe ensan*, (Religiöst styre och människans rättigheter) (2nd ed.). Teheran: Sarai.

Nordberg, M. (1988). *Profetens folk. Stat, samhälle och kultur i islam under tusen år*. Stockholm: Tiden.

Qur'an, English translation by S.V. Mir Ahmed Ali. New York: TahrikeTarsile Qur'an.

Sadi, A. M. M. al-din bin Abdullah Shirazi. (2007). In M. A. Foroghi (Ed.), *Golistan*. Teheran: Behzad.

Samia, M. (1999). In M. Dabir Siyaqi Seyyed (Ed.), *Tazkirat al-Muluk*. Teheran: Amir Kabir.

Sandgren, J. (2007). *Banbrytare I, Pierre Teilhard de Chardin & Louis Massignon*. Skellefteå: Artos.

Zargarinejad, G. H. (1995). *Rasailmashrotiyyat. 18 resalehdar bare-ye mashrotiyyat*. Teheran: Kavir.

References from Internet

Message Ayatollah Montazeri objected to the official trails (in Farsi), see www.amontazeri.com/, topic 217, posted on 4 Aug 2009, accessed and printed on 20 November 2010.

www.amontazeri.com/ (in Farsi) (topic 219, posted on 26 Aug 2009), accessed and printed on 20 November 2010.

www.amontazeri.com/ (in Farsi) (topic 223, posted on 22 Sep 2009), accessed and printed on 20 November 2010.

Part II
Religion as a Determinant of Volunteering

Chapter 5
Religiosity and Formal Volunteering in Global Perspective

Matthew R. Bennett

Introduction

Volunteering is a central element of civic engagement and is often considered an important part of social life. Such involvement has been studied extensively and a wide body of literature documents its predictors (Wilson 2000; Musick and Wilson 2008). The focus of this chapter is on the comparative study of volunteering, examining religiosity as an individual and contextual level explanation for this behaviour. As such, this research builds on previous studies and tests a number of religious explanations for the likelihood of volunteering among a diverse sample of 165,625 people from all major religious traditions living in 113 countries. At the individual level this study asks if religious affiliation and religious service attendance are associated with a greater likelihood of volunteering. This research also investigates two relatively novel religious explanations of volunteering: First, at the contextual level, it asks if the religious diversity of a society is associated with a greater likelihood of volunteering; and secondly, it tests whether belonging to a religious minority group within a country increases the likelihood of volunteering. Towards this aim, this research also takes into account a number of individual and contextual factors that have been linked to volunteering, such as background, demographics and the democratic and economic climate of a country.

The comparative study of volunteering has been relatively slow to evolve. Progress in this area has been hampered due to a dearth of comparable material and the limited scale of the data. Similarly, the role played by the geographical context in which people live has also received limited attention (Wilson 2000). Another limitation of previous research is that relatively little is known about volunteering outside of the western world, let alone the factors that influence it in such countries. The extent of volunteering in developing countries is unclear as official statistics regarding voluntary behaviour are limited or non-existent and often contradictory in these

---

M. R. Bennett (✉)
Department of Sociology, University of Oxford, Oxford, England
e-mail: matthew.bennett@nuffield.ox.ac.uk

L. Hustinx et al. (eds.), *Religion and Volunteering,* Nonprofit and Civil Society Studies, 77
DOI 10.1007/978-3-319-04585-6_5, © Springer International Publishing Switzerland 2015

societies (cf. Govaart et al. 2001). Musick and Wilson (2008) stress the importance of the comparative study of volunteering:

> ... the comparative study of voluntarism, now flourishing, is a relatively underdeveloped area of scholarly investigation in the field of philanthropy. Progress in this area has been slowed by: the difficulty of gathering comparable data; wide cultural variations in the understanding of the volunteer role; and lack of theoretical development. Recent work has altered this picture quite dramatically. A number of cross-national surveys using standardized definitions of volunteer work and other socio-demographic variables make comparisons easier. (Musick and Wilson 2008, p. 368)

A unique feature of the data used in this study is that it contains an unusually large sample of countries, allowing the testing of prior theories against a more representative sample of the world's religious traditions. This allows researchers to explore whether previous explanations associated with religion applied to single nation or comparative studies with a smaller number of countries can be generalized to a larger number of religions. The study uses data that is more representative of all the world's major religious traditions, such as Islam, Orthodox Christianity, Hinduism, Judaism and Buddhism, as well as Catholic and Protestant Christian denominations that have typically been the focus of prior studies. Though these religions clearly vary widely in terms of their doctrine and the religious practices, this research asks if there is something about being affiliated with a religion or attending a religious service that is common to all religions in terms of the effects on volunteering. Ruiter and De Graaf (2006) highlight the importance of such a study in the conclusion of their earlier work:

> Keep in mind though that only 7% of the data population is non-Christian and that questions pertaining to religion in the World Values Surveys might be better applicable to Christians than to non-Christians. Therefore, we cannot make strong claims with respect to non-Christian countries. (Ruiter and De Graaf 2006, p. 207)

However, while the research design and potential contributions of this study come with many positives, the earlier comments of Musick and Wilson highlight a number of caveats and reasons to remain cautious. How do different survey designs or question wordings (and even orderings) affect survey responses? How can western concepts of "volunteering" be applied to non-western contexts and how translatable are these terms cross-culturally? These and other issues will be discussed in more detail throughout the study as they arise.

In what follows I discuss the relevant individual and contextual level religious explanations of volunteering, before describing the data and methods used for this study. After testing the hypotheses, I finally discuss the results and the implications for future research.

Religion as an Individual Level Explanation of Volunteering

Religious Affiliation and Service Attendance

A vast body of literature demonstrates the importance of individual religiosity as a robust and consistent predictor of volunteering nationally and cross-nationally

5 Religiosity and Formal Volunteering in Global Perspective

(Musick and Wilson 2008; Putnam and Campbell 2010; Ruiter and De Graaf 2006; Wilson 2000; Wuthnow 1991, 2004). The positive association between religion and volunteering is attributed to two explanations: religious norms and social networks (Bekkers and Schuyt 2008; Curtis et al. 2001; Lam 2002; Ruiter and De Graaf 2006; Watt 1991; Wilson and Musick 1997; Wuthnow 1991). On the one hand, religious norms associated with religious doctrine and religious texts stress the importance of helping others and those in need. People with a religious affiliation are more likely to internalize these norms, thus increasing the likelihood of their being prosocial, or in the current case, of them volunteering. On the other hand, religious networks stress the role of social connections between religious people. According to this argument, religious service attendance increases the connectedness of religious people, and as religious organizations are more likely to engage in and encourage volunteering (Ruiter and De Graaf 2006, p. 191), service attendance increases the likelihood of being asked and hearing about opportunities to volunteer.

Previous research has found that Protestants volunteer more than affiliates of other religions (Lam 2002; Ruiter and De Graaf 2006; Wuthnow 1991; Wilson 2000; Musick and Wilson 2008). This has been attributed to a number factors such as that the Protestant church is not hierarchically organized and typically subdivides itself into smaller parishes, which is better suited to social sanctioning (Dekker and De Hart 2001), but also that it does more to encourage the pursuit of social responsibility among its members relative to other religions (Lam 2002). However, the literature has thus far been built on data capturing religious traditions in western or developed countries, where comparisons and descriptions are made explicitly between Christian denominations, while non-Christian religions get combined into a single "other" category. The data used in this research provides researchers with an interesting opportunity to describe patterns of volunteering across religious traditions and to assess how the explanations associated with norms and networks might be applicable and generalized to each, despite a wide range of differences in doctrine and religious participation. Such a project is not without its problems. Measuring the objective level of religiosity in a comparative study is problematic. For example, for both Hindus and Buddhists, worship is considered a relatively more individual rather than communal act. Hindus and Buddhists often worship in home-made shrines, where the former make personal offerings to the deities. Whether collective service attendance has the same universal validity across countries and faiths is hard to garner. However, given the importance put on social relations it assumes that religious service attendance does increase the knowledge of, and opportunities for, individuals to volunteer. Qualitative differences in doctrinal and collective worship aside, this research tests the generalizability of previous research. Accordingly, it can be hypothesized that people who report a religious affiliation are more likely to volunteer compared to unaffiliated respondents (H1), and people who attend religious services are more likely to volunteer than non-attenders (H2a).

As mentioned earlier, studies have suggested that volunteering is not driven by church membership per se but rather service attendance (Ruiter and De Graaf 2006; Watt 1991; Wilson and Musick 1997). As service attendance increases the connectedness of religious people and thus the likelihood that they hear about and are asked to volunteer, service attendance should moderate the initial effect of religious affiliation. Accordingly, it can be hypothesized that the initial differences between religious members and non-members in the likelihood of volunteering will diminish controlling for service attendance (H2b).

Religion as a Contextual Level Explanation of Volunteering

Previous work has made substantive progress in theorizing why aspects of religious context may influence volunteering. For example, Ruiter and De Graaf (2006) hypothesized that the level of religious devoutness in a country is associated with the likelihood that individuals volunteer. The authors argue that a greater proportion of religious service attenders in a country provide an additional "boost" within a country, over and above the individual-level effect of service attendance, thus affecting the likelihood that both the religious and non-religious will volunteer. This is regarded as a network extension to the role of service attendance as a country with a higher proportion of service attenders increases the likelihood that these individuals will be part of a given social network, thus increasing the likelihood of being asked or hearing about volunteering for everyone. Similarly, the possibility of having more service attenders in one's network potentially increases the exposure to religious norms of altruism and stewardship. Ruiter and De Graaf (2006) did find that the average devoutness of a country influences volunteering and also that there is a spillover effect whereby the non-religious are more likely to volunteer in religious countries as they may be more likely to have religious people in their networks, relative to the non-religious in a secular country, thus increasing the opportunities of the non-religious to get involved in volunteering in a devout country.

The findings have received some criticism due to influential country cases that influence the relationship (Van der Meer et al. 2010). Lim and MacGregor (2012) explicitly test the mechanisms involved in the religious spillover effect and highlight the incorrect ecological inferences that can be made when using religious network data at the individual level to make inferences about the measurement of religious context at both country and county level—a common practice in this area of research. The authors also argue that contradictory theoretical mechanisms could produce similar aggregate findings. Lim and MacGregor (2012) use network data and find that having religious friends does increase the likelihood of volunteering for the non-religious, but that this relationship cannot be inferred empirically from county or country level data. In fact, at the country level, the authors find a curvilinear relationship between country devoutness and volunteering at the contextual level (i.e. a greater probability of volunteering in secular and devout countries and lower likelihoods in countries with relatively moderate levels of religiosity), while they find a negative relationship between devoutness and volunteering at the county level (i.e. the likelihood of volunteering decreases with devoutness at the contextual county level). However, it should also be noted that the data used by Lim and Macgregor only captures self-reported, "strong-tie" network data and cannot test the notion that religious "weak-ties" may also increase the likelihood that the non-religious will volunteer.

Given the above, the current research is cautious about any theoretical claims that highlight possible mechanisms that explain the link between the contextual-level measures of religion and volunteering. This chapter considers these issues and tests two relatively novel religious contextual explanations that have been found to influence volunteering among smaller geographical units and does so by using independent measures of context that do not rely upon aggregating data from the individual to the country level. As such, while testing the causal mechanism at a lower level of analysis is beyond the scope of this chapter, the explanations have been tested at a lower level of analysis in previous studies. While these prior studies do, then, lend support to the current research, the cautions outlined by Lim and MacGregor must be acknowledged. With this in mind, this research now begins discussing the two novel religious explanations in the comparative literature of volunteering.

Religious Diversity

Borgonovi (2008) argues that the religious diversity of a context is associated with an increased likelihood of volunteering. The author extends the Rational Choice approach applied by some scholars in the Sociology of Religion who claim that religious diversity increases the level of religious commitment (Finke and Stark 1988, 1992; Iannaccone 1998). According to this perspective, the demand for religion is constant in a population, but an increase in religious competition between religious groups requires them to produce a better quality religious product to encourage more participation in their particular religious group. Religious group survival in a diverse religious context is somewhat dependent on increased efforts by the religious leadership and members alike, including volunteering efforts of members to sustain the group. Competition creates incentives among church leaders and congregation members alike to both raise money and request extra-religious goods such as volunteering to sustain the organization (Stark and Finke 2000). As all religious groups seek to optimize their product, there will be a higher likelihood of volunteering. Similarly, religious groups are more likely to be smaller in a diverse religious context, making it easier to monitor and sanction fellow members and thus decreasing the occurrence of free-riding while increasing the likelihood that members will respond to social pressures to fully commit to and take part in the activities of the religious group, including volunteering. Borgonovi (2008) did find that religious diversity in a sample of US counties is associated with a greater likelihood of religious volunteering, but found no significant association with secular volunteering. This theory, however, has yet to be tested at the country level. Accordingly, it can be hypothesized that religious diversity is associated with a greater likelihood of volunteering (H3).

Religious Minority Group Affiliation

Borgonovi (2008) has derived testable hypotheses regarding the impact of belonging to a religious denomination that represents the minority group in a population. Again, Borgonovi (2008) borrows from research in the Sociology of Religion that finds that belonging to a religious minority group is associated with increased commitment to that group by its members (Iannaccone 1991; Stark 1992; Stark and McCann 1993) and more religious giving (Perl and Olson 2000; Zaleski and Zech 1995). Group solidarity and the sense of in-group bias should be stronger among members of a group that represent a minority group (Tajfel 1979; Tajfel and Turner 1979). If the majority of prosocial behaviour happens via religious membership, and more specifically, by regular service attenders, then it is reasonable to assume that minorities are more likely to be prosocial for their religious causes. Accordingly, it can be hypothesized that belonging to a religious minority group in a country is associated with a greater likelihood of volunteering (H4).

Data and Methods

The hypotheses are tested using pooled data from the 2007 and 2008 waves of the Gallup World Poll (GWP) (Gallup Inc. 2010, 2011). Data at the individual level was gathered via phone or face-to-face interviews in the main language of each country, based on nationally representative samples. The data capture self-reported demographics, attitudes and behaviours of respondents, including formal volunteering. The GWP is a useful data source as it not only contains an unusually large sample of countries, but also contains a standardized set of questions across all countries. Cases with complete information for the dependent and independent variables were selected, accounting for 165,625 individuals across 113 countries. The analyses were restricted to respondents aged 18–90 years.

The dependent variable is dichotomous and accounts for the instance of volunteering. Since the data is clustered, where individuals are nested in countries, it makes multilevel logistic regression the most appropriate method for analysing the data (Snijders and Bosker 1999). The data contains two levels: Level one is the lowest level and accounts for individual respondents, level two accounts for countries. All continuous variables are mean-centered in the analyses.

Dependent Variable

The question of interest gauges whether the respondent reported any unpaid volunteering for an organization in the past month ("Have you done any of the following in the past month? How about volunteered your time to an organization?"). The

5 Religiosity and Formal Volunteering in Global Perspective

outcome measure takes the value 1 if the respondent reported "yes" for that question, and 0 to respondents who reported "no". Descriptive statistics for this outcome measure are displayed in Table 5.1. Table 5.3 in the Appendix displays the average volunteer rate per country. The dichotomous outcome measures account for the instance of volunteering.

There do, however, remain a number of caveats that must be carefully considered in this research. The wording of the question of the dependent variable is problematic as it only gauges formal organizational volunteering, and it does not differentiate between specific types of volunteering or whether the volunteering is done for religious or secular causes. An "organization" may be an ambiguous term, and responses will depend on what is interpreted as an organization by the respondent; for example, whether a charity or religious group counts as organizations. Given the scope of the GWP, what counts as volunteering, culturally or historically, when a respondent is surveyed is problematic, and is even more so when definitions vary between countries or when the concept is not translatable.

Sociopolitical factors between countries may influence the findings. For example, in some countries volunteering for third sector parties has been normalized as taboo, made illegal by governments or is associated with a high degree of bureaucratic red tape inhibiting mobilization and involvement (Govaart et al. 2001). A wide range of other voluntary outlets may also exist, and these may under- or over-represent the level of different forms of volunteering that occurs in a society. As such, unorganized and unofficial grassroot volunteering may be more prevalent in such a society and volunteering may be narrower in scope, geared towards kinship and family networks (Govaart et al. 2001). In such a case, the measure of volunteering used in this study may capture a low degree of formal volunteering as occurring in that country, but may under-represent an actually thriving network of informal voluntary behaviour. Given the cross-national scope of the GWP these factors may bias responses between countries.

These caveats may also result in discrepancies between national and cross-national datasets. The question may also be sensitive to positive response bias given that for many countries in the GWP volunteering and other prosocial behaviours are socially desirable activities (Govaart et al. 2001). As such, people may overestimate how much they volunteer if such deeds are honored and esteemed. Not having a list of volunteer activities and organizations to choose from may affect recall rates—it may lead to under-biased estimates because respondents are not primed about relevant activities that they may have participated in (Rooney et al. 2004).

All of these issues raise concerns about the quality and comparability of data. While the descriptive results of country rates of volunteering are of interest, this study is concerned with the underlying explanations associated with the likelihood of volunteering. The robustness of these individual-level associations are therefore (a) compared to the findings of Ruiter and De Graaf (2006) in the first instance because the data used in their study is from the World Values Survey/European Values Survey, both of which are widely used in the social sciences and (b) subse-

Table 5.1 Descriptive statistics for dependent and independent variables

	Obs	Mean/ proportion	Std. Dev.	Min.	Max.
Dependent variable					
Formal volunteering	165625	0.22	0.42	0	1
Individual-level variables					
Female (ref. male)	165625	0.54	0.50	0	1
Age	165625	40.78	16.46	18	90
Age-squared	165625	1933.77	1534.18	324	8100
Education					
≤8 years	165625	0.28	0.45	0	1
9–15 years	165625	0.43	0.49	0	1
≥16 years	165625	0.11	0.32	0	1
Unknown	165625	0.18	0.38	0	1
Marital status					
Single	165625	0.27	0.44	0	1
Married	165625	0.54	0.50	0	1
Separated/divorced	165625	0.05	0.22	0	1
Widowed	165625	0.07	0.25	0	1
Cohabiting	165625	0.05	0.22	0	1
Unknown	165625	0.02	0.14	0	1
Religious membership					
Catholic	165625	0.33	0.47	0	1
Protestant	165625	0.18	0.39	0	1
Orthodox	165625	0.05	0.23	0	1
Muslim	165625	0.24	0.43	0	1
Hindu	165625	0.04	0.20	0	1
Buddhist	165625	0.07	0.25	0	1
Jewish	165625	0.01	0.10	0	1
Other	165625	0.02	0.14	0	1
None	165625	0.05	0.22	0	1
Service attendance	165625	0.53	0.50	0	1
Religious minority	165625	0.26	0.44	0	1
Country-level variables					
Economic development	165625	8.62	1.30	5.87	11.21
Democracy	165625	8.71	3.48	1	13
National devoutness	165625	0.52	0.21	0.10	0.88
Religious diversity	165625	0.41	0.23	0.00	0.86

quently restricted to the available country list used by Ruiter and De Graaf (2006). The findings of the current results do not substantively change between these sample specifications. Furthermore, the aggregate rates of volunteering could be easily verified with the expansion of other existing datasets using standardized questions and definitions. Until then, or indeed until governmental or independent statistics agencies collect official statistics on third sector behaviour in developing countries, the GWP may provide the best data available for comparatively testing

5 Religiosity and Formal Volunteering in Global Perspective

individual and contextual explanations of volunteering across such a wide representation of countries.

Independent Variables

Basic descriptive statistics for all independent variables are displayed in Table 5.1. Firstly, the discussion focuses on the religious variables of substantive interest. At the individual level, religious affiliation was measured by the question asking respondents which religion they belonged to, and where nine categories were created: Protestant, Catholic, Orthodox, Muslim, Hindu, Buddhist, Jewish, other and non-religious. Service attendance was measured with the question "Have you attended a place of worship or religious service within the past seven days?", where "yes" was coded as 1 and "no" coded 0. A distinction is made between respondents who belong to a religious minority group by including a dummy variable coded 1 if the respondent belongs to a religious group that is not the largest religious group in their country. This variable is thus technically a cross-level interaction as it is calculated using individual-level religious affiliation and the distribution of other religious groups in the country.

At the contextual level, religious diversity is measured using the Fractionalization Index (Alesina et al. 2003). This measure is calculated as the inverse of the Herfindahl Index and ranges from 0–1, where scores of 1 indicate the highest level of religious diversity.

This study also controls for other factors associated with volunteering. At the individual level, controls were included for demographic variables measuring the gender, age, educational level and marital status of respondents. Gender takes the value 1 if the respondent is female and 0 if male. Cross-nationally, females are less likely to engage in formal volunteering (Lim and MacGregor 2012; Ruiter and De Graaf 2006). Age is a continuous variable that ranges from 18–90. The relationship between age and volunteering in comparative research has been found to be positive and curvilinear (Ruiter and De Graaf 2006). All else being equal, the middle-aged are more likely to be integrated in work networks and have more family responsibilities relative to the young and old. A quadratic term for age is also included to account for this curvilinear relationship. Marital status is included as a set of dummy variables that take the value 1 for each category: married, cohabiting, separated/divorced, widowed, single and "unknown". Cross-nationally, married people do volunteer more (Lim and MacGregor 2012; Ruiter and De Graaf 2006). Education level is included as a set of dummy variables coded 1 for each education level: completed elementary education or less (up to 8 years of basic education); secondary education—3-year tertiary/secondary education and some education beyond secondary education (9–15 years of education); completed 4 years of education beyond high school and/or received a 4-year college degree and "unknown" education level. A higher level of education is associated with a greater likelihood of volunteering (Lim and MacGregor 2012; Ruiter and De Graaf 2006).

The study also takes into account contextual-level controls hypothesized to be associated with volunteering. National devoutness is included along with its quadratic term to account for the curvilinear findings of Lim and MacGregor (2012), and is measured by averaging service attendance within each country. High values indicate that the country is relatively devout and low values indicate that the country is relatively secular. Economic development is included as real gross domestic product (GDP) per capita in purchasing power parity for 2007 (in 1000's of constant 2005 international dollars), obtained from the World Bank (2007). National economic development is hypothesized to have a positive effect on rates of volunteering for two reasons. Firstly, it can lead to occupational development resulting in more diverse interest groups in which people can volunteer (Curtis et al. 2001; Halman 2003; Salamon et al. 1999). Secondly, affluent countries would provide people with more resources necessary to participate. Alternatively, Putnam (2000) argues that economic development also increases the likelihood that people use technology, including television and the Internet, and women are also more likely to be active in the labour market in such countries. Putnam (2000) also argues that much of this is due to cohort replacement—younger cohorts are less likely to be engaged in prosocial behaviour. Parboteeah et al. (2004) found a positive effect, but Curtis et al. (2001) and Lim and MacGregor (2012) found no effect. Ruiter and De Graaf (2006) found a significant positive effect for voluntary membership, but no relationship for general volunteering. Norris (2002, p. 157) confirms a correlation between GDP purchasing power parity (PPP) and volunteering across 46 countries. Musick and Wilson (2008) used the World Bank categorization of wealth, dividing countries into low, lower middle, upper middle and high gross national income. Only advocacy volunteering was found to be related, and only in low-income countries.

The level of democracy is included as the Gastil Index (Freedom House 2007). The scores are summed for "political rights" and "civil liberties" and the scale is reversed. Scores range from 1–13, where a value of 13 represents the highest level of democracy. It is assumed that the level of democracy of a country provides the foundations of civil society and therefore the infrastructure necessary for voluntary organizations to flourish (freedom of speech, the right to assemble, free association, etc.). It may be that in democratic societies there is more of an expectation to contribute towards charitable causes or public projects. Volunteering will be limited in countries that lack a democratic foundation. Halman (2003) and Parboteeah et al. (2004) both found significant positive effects for their measures of democracy (years of continuous democracy and political rights, and degree of liberal democracy, respectively), however, both studies are hampered by small country samples and limited variation between countries. Ruiter and de Graaf (2006) find that democracy is negatively related to volunteering for both general volunteering and voluntary memberships, but is significant only in the former analysis. Musick and Wilson (2008) find a negative association—more volunteering in less free coun-

5 Religiosity and Formal Volunteering in Global Perspective

tries. Lim and MacGregor (2012) find no relationship between level of democracy and volunteering.

Results

Table 5.2 displays the results predicting formal volunteering. Initially, a null model with random intercepts was estimated, which demonstrated that the probability of formal volunteering varies across countries (not displayed). Model 1 includes individual level controls for sex, age, age-squared, highest level of education, marital status and dummy variables representing the religious affiliation of a respondent. Hypothesis 1 states that religious affiliates will be more likely to volunteer than people with no religious affiliation. As such, respondents with no religious affiliation serve as the reference category so that the results can be interpreted with respect to how much respondents from each religious affiliation deviate from people with no religious affiliation. The results suggest that religious respondents are more likely to volunteer compared to the unaffiliated, supporting hypothesis 1. Protestants also have the highest predicted probability of volunteering (0.28), relative to Catholics (0.25), Orthodox Christians (0.25), Muslims (0.27), Jewish (0.35), Hindus (0.24), Buddhists (0.26) and others (0.27).

All but one of the control variables are influential in predicting volunteering and confirm the associations with volunteering in previous cross-national studies using different data (cf. Ruiter and De Graaf 2006). Females are associated with a lower likelihood of formal volunteering compared to males. Age has a curvilinear relationship with volunteering: In other words, the likelihood of volunteering increases with age but then drops off in later life. The likelihood of volunteering increases with education level and respondents with an "unknown" education level are also more likely to volunteer compared to those with the fewest years of education. Married people are more likely to volunteer relative to the separated/divorced, the widowed and cohabiters. There is no significant difference between married and single respondents or those with an "unknown" marital status.

Model 2 includes the effect of service attendance and suggests that attending a religious service in the past week is associated with an increased likelihood of volunteering. People who attend a religious service are nearly twice (1.87 times, exp (0.625)) as likely to volunteer relative to those who do not attend a religious service, thus confirming hypothesis 2a. The estimates associated with each religious affiliation in model 1 have changed, controlling for religious service attendance, decreasing considerably in size, thereby supporting hypothesis 2b. This suggests that the difference between the religious and the non-religious is to a certain extent due to service attendance. Respondents reporting a Hindu or Jewish religious affiliation are now no different from the non-religious in their likelihood of volunteering. This finding may suggest that, on average, communal religious worship drives volunteering among members of these two affiliations. This could mean that opportunities to volunteer among Hindus and Jews are more available through networks attached to

Table 5.2 Multilevel logistic regression results predicting the likelihood of formal volunteering in the past month

	Model 1	Model 2	Model 3
Individual-level variables			
Female	−0.146***	−0.157***	−0.156***
	(0.013)	(0.013)	(0.013)
Education (ref. ≤8 years)			
Education (9–15 years)	0.377***	0.371***	0.371***
	(0.017)	(0.017)	(0.017)
Education (≥16 years)	0.657***	0.645***	0.645***
	(0.023)	(0.023)	(0.024)
Unknown education	0.246***	0.254***	0.253***
	(0.027)	(0.027)	(0.027)
Age	0.030***	0.029***	0.029***
	(0.002)	(0.002)	(0.002)
Age squared	−0.000***	−0.000***	−0.000***
	(0.000)	(0.000)	(0.000)
Marital status (ref. married)			
Single	0.012	0.020	0.020
	(0.017)	(0.017)	(0.017)
Separated/divorced	−0.098***	−0.067*	−0.067*
	(0.028)	(0.028)	(0.028)
Widowed	−0.150***	−0.148***	−0.149***
	(0.029)	(0.029)	(0.029)
Cohabiting	−0.097**	−0.055+	−0.054+
	(0.030)	(0.031)	(0.031)
Unknown marital status	−0.056	−0.032	−0.022
	(0.079)	(0.080)	(0.079)
Non-religious (ref.)			
Catholic	0.320***	0.126***	0.160***
	(0.037)	(0.038)	(0.039)
Protestant	0.436***	0.228***	0.249***
	(0.038)	(0.038)	(0.039)
Orthodox	0.315***	0.166**	0.183***
	(0.055)	(0.055)	(0.055)
Muslim	0.345***	0.127**	0.161***
	(0.044)	(0.044)	(0.045)
Hindu	0.196**	0.018	0.053
	(0.070)	(0.070)	(0.070)
Buddhist	0.342***	0.244***	0.260***
	(0.048)	(0.049)	(0.049)
Jewish	0.297*	0.175	0.220+
	(0.119)	(0.121)	(0.120)
Other	0.413***	0.292***	0.284***
	(0.054)	(0.054)	(0.054)
Service attendance		0.625***	0.623***
		(0.014)	(0.014)
Country-level variables			
Economic development			−0.029
			(0.074)
Democracy			0.007

5 Religiosity and Formal Volunteering in Global Perspective

Table 5.2 (continued)

	Model 1	Model 2	Model 3
			(0.016)
National devoutness			−5.524***
			(1.164)
National devoutness sq.			5.292***
			(1.218)
Religious diversity			0.709***
			(0.200)
Member of minority religion			0.055***
			(0.016)
Intercept	−1.832***	−1.991***	−1.980***
	(0.066)	(0.065)	(0.067)
Level 1 units	165625	165625	165625
Level 2 units	113	113	113
Log Likelihood	−83656.147	−82656.152	−82630.846
AIC	167354	165356	165322
BIC	167565	165577	165622

*+p<0.10 *p<0.05 **p<0.01 ***p<0.001*

organized religion. It might suggest that Hindus and Jews who do not attend communal services are reporting their religious affiliation in terms of a cultural identity as opposed to a purely religious identity; however, this is a hypothesis beyond the scope of the current research. The estimates for the other individual level controls are largely unchanged with the exception of cohabiters, who are now no different from married people in their likelihood of volunteering.

Model 3 includes all contextual level variables.[1] The level of religious diversity of a society is associated with an increased likelihood of volunteering. The odds of volunteering in a society range from 1.37 (exp (0.317)) to 3.00 (exp (1.101)) for the least diverse and most diverse countries respectively.[2] This confirms hypothesis 3. Figure 5.1 displays this relationship in terms of predicted probabilities. The parameters of the individual-level variables remain unchanged.

Belonging to a religious minority group in a country is associated with an increased likelihood of volunteering. People who belong to a religious minority are 1.06 times (exp (0.055)) more likely to volunteer relative to those who belong to the religious majority in a country. This finding supports hypothesis 4. The contextual level controls measuring economic development and level of democracy are not associated with volunteering. As demonstrated by Lim and MacGregor (2012), the national level of devoutness is associated with a curvilinear relationship with volunteering, where volunteering is more likely in relatively secular and devout countries, challenging the network arguments of Ruiter and De Graaf (2006).

---

[1] Analyses were also conducted for each contextual-level parameter separately to assess their robustness but there were no substantial differences from those reported in the full model.

[2] Calculated based on a normally assumed distribution where 95% of all coefficients are between ± 1.96 times the standard deviation: 0.709 ± 1.96*(0.200), resulting in a range of 0.317 to 1.101.

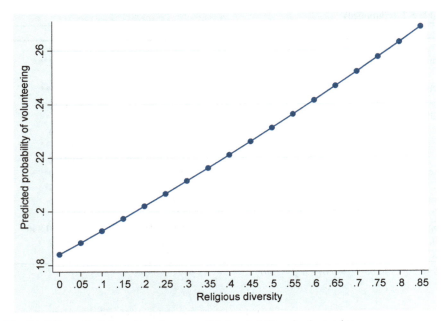

Fig. 5.1 Effect of religious diversity on predicted probability of volunteering

Summary and Conclusions

This research demonstrates that religion plays an important role as an individual and contextual level predictor of volunteering across 113 countries that are representative of the world's major religious traditions. It tested the generalizability of established explanations of volunteering (religious affiliation and service attendance) and also applied two relatively novel explanations to the comparative study of volunteering (religious diversity and minority group membership). The main motivation behind examining the role of religiosity at the individual level was to understand whether religious norms and networks are also applicable to non-Christian religious traditions as explanations in the likelihood of volunteering.

The research found that the religiously affiliated were more likely to volunteer than the unaffiliated. These findings suggest that although religious traditions vary widely in terms of their traditions and doctrine, the norms of altruism and stewardship common to all major religious traditions influence the likelihood of volunteering for all of them. People with Protestant affiliations were also more likely to volunteer compared to other religious groups. A subsequent model demonstrated that religious service attendance accounted for a significant degree of the association between the religiously affiliated and non-affiliated. This finding is also consistent with previous studies highlighting the role of networks and that the initial associations for religious affiliates may be explained by service attendance. This finding supports the notion that while religious traditions are qualitatively unique in terms of the role, format and function of service attendance and communal worship, there is something similar between all religions when their congregations worship together collectively in terms of the influence it has on volunteering. Here religious networks are likely to increase the opportunities of hearing about and being asked, and even pressured to volunteer by members of their religious affiliation.

Interestingly, when controlling for service attendance, respondents with a Hindu and Jewish affiliation were no more likely to volunteer than the unaffiliated. This finding suggests that, on average, communal worship drives volunteering among members of these two affiliations. This could mean that services solely drive volunteering among Hindus and Jews as the opportunities to volunteer increase through networks attached to organized religion. It might also suggest that Hindus and Jews who do not attend communal services are reporting their religious affiliation in terms of a cultural identity as opposed to a purely religious identity.

The research also suggests that religion at the contextual level influences the likelihood of volunteering. There is evidence to suggest that increased religious diversity in a society is associated with higher levels of volunteering. This supports the findings of Borgonovi (2008) in US counties, albeit at the country level in the current study. An important conclusion is that it tests the generalizability of this explanation from the county level to the country level. A point of departure between this study and Borgonovi's is that the latter was able to distinguish between volunteering for a religious cause and volunteering for a secular cause, in which only the measure of religious volunteering was significantly associated with religious diversity. This raises the question as to whether the GWP measure actually captures a high proportion of religious volunteering. Future work should focus on this distinction and whether religious diversity encourages all forms of volunteering—cross-nationally and in European contexts—especially as the religious marketplace in the USA can be considered a relatively unusual case study.

Belonging to a religious minority group in a country was associated with a greater likelihood of volunteering. The inclusion of this indicator was motivated by the work of Borgonovi (2008) and the work in social identity theory (Tajfel 1979; Tajfel and Turner 1979) arguing that the strength of commitment and group solidarity amongst members of a minority religion should be greater. It follows that members of a religious minority group are more sensitive to group norms, especially the mobilization of collective in-group causes such as volunteering. An interesting question for future research is whether volunteering behaviour by minority groups is less likely to spillover into other forms of volunteering for non-minority groups.

These findings raise some important questions. The fact that religious affiliates and service attenders are more likely to volunteer than the non-religious and those who do not attend services means that the process of secularization could be detrimental to the future of volunteering. In the short term, it may mean that the religious do more volunteering to compensate for the lack of secular involvement or indeed do so to maintain the interests of their group. It is uncertain what this means for the long-term future of volunteering. On the one hand, secularization may fizzle out religious involvement in volunteering. On the other hand, internal and external migration may counteract this process to some degree. The data suggests that individuals are more likely to volunteer in more religiously heterogeneous countries. As migration rates increase and countries become more diverse, there may be an increase in volunteering. This may counteract the process of secularization to some degree in terms of sustained levels of volunteering. Furthermore, these migrants may well consist of the minority religion in a country or local area, which may encourage them to volunteer more as shown in this research. Future research should explore the consequences of these findings. For example, while religious heterogeneity and belonging to a religious minority group may increase the likelihood of volunteering, it may do so to a greater extent for causes relevant to the religious in-group. This may result in homogenous in-group interactions and limited out-group interactions and have further implications for civil society. In sum, the findings suggest that individual and contextual aspects of religion are likely to remain important characteristics of volunteering for the foreseeable future.

Other non-religious institutional processes are clearly important and merit further investigation, as demonstrated by the earlier work of Lim and MacGregor (2012) and replicated here. The authors found that national religious devoutness was associated with an increased likelihood of volunteering but so too was a low level of devoutness, which challenges the network spillover arguments posited by Ruiter and De Graaf (2006). The authors argued that a higher proportion of religious adherents in a society would increase the likelihood of volunteering for everyone in a society because there is a greater probability that a service attender will be in your network and thus diffuse information about volunteering opportunities or indeed ask people to get involved in efforts they take part in. However, this mechanism is challenged in secular societies as there are fewer religious people in a network who can diffuse information, yet the likelihood of volunteering is high in these countries as well. This could suggest that non-religious people mobilize to compensate for the lack of religious people that would otherwise be volunteering. Lim and Macgregor (2012) note that countries with low devoutness levels are relatively more democratic and developed whereas the opposite is true for more devout countries. However, the secular countries included in the data have more established welfare states and this could suggest that the welfare state "crowds in" participation in these countries, which is why involvement in volunteering is also more likely (see Van Oorschot and Arts 2005 for a discussion of this, albeit for a limited sample of 23 European countries). On the one hand, the crowding-out hypothesis argues that state provision of social services and obligations makes citizens less likely to participate in formal and informal collective outcomes such as volunteering. In other words, citizens volunteer less in a society where the state provides substitutes in the form visible social welfare commitments. On the other hand, the crowding-in hypothesis argues that a developed welfare state increases the civic participation and volunteering of citizens due to increased normative and structural opportunities to do so from state support. Complete information on all forms of welfare expenditure, such as public healthcare, education, pensions and unemployment is unavailable for such a diverse group of countries in the GWP. This is clearly an interesting area of future research but is ultimately beyond the scope of this chapter.

While this chapter uses a unique data set that captures an unusually large sample of countries, it is not without its limitations. Comparative survey programs are likely to face problems in terms of recall and social desirability, as well as the difficulty of translating a question accurately into the language and cultural context of such a broad range of countries. Furthermore, the survey design will elicit different responses across datasets that may be the result of the wording of a question, interview method or the order of questions within an interview. For example, asking a number of related questions on civic engagement or prosocial behaviour may prime respondents to remember other types. However, the lack of priming may make the responses less culturally biased between countries. All of these issues in the current data as well as the methodological approaches between survey data sets make it hard to ascertain and validate the "true" rates of volunteering.

Interestingly, the majority of the other individual level variables were associated with voluntarism as they were in previous studies using different data albeit with fewer countries (c.f. Ruiter and De Graaf 2006). Females volunteer less than males, age is curvilinear (increasing with age but declining in later life), the higher educated volunteer more and married and single people volunteer more than the separated/divorced and widowed. While discrepancies may exist between data sets in national estimates of volunteering, the association between these individual characteristics and volunteering in the GWP appear to be consistent and robust within the World Values Survey. These are the relationships and explanations that have motivated this study. Furthermore, subsequent analyses also restricted the number of countries to those available in Ruiter and De Graaf (2008), the results of which were not substantially different from those presented. Until survey programs and government agencies agree on standardized measures of volunteering that can be consistently used between countries and data sources, and the countries included can be significantly expanded, the uncertainty of estimates and individual and contextual level associations will continue. Until these improvements, the GWP may provide the best data available for comparatively testing individual and contextual explanations of formal volunteering across such a wide representation of countries.

To conclude, this research demonstrates that religion is an important individual and contextual explanation of volunteering. It finds patterns common to all religious traditions in terms of religious affiliation and service attendance. The growing literature in this area of investigation also helped test two relatively novel contextual level hypotheses regarding the role of religious diversity and belonging to a minority religion in a country. Hopefully, it will be useful to comparative researchers and encourage more theory development and investigation in this area of the literature.

94 M. R. Bennett

Appendix

Table 5.3 Mean percentage of volunteers in the past month per country

Country	Volunteers %	Country	Volunteers %	Country	Volunteers %
Central African Rep.	48.34	South Korea	26.95	South Africa	18.36
Sierra Leone	45.50	Malaysia	26.56	Kazakhstan	18.17
New Zealand	44.27	Belize	26.36	Georgia	17.30
Sri Lanka	43.47	Cameroon	26.00	Armenia	16.93
Guinea	41.95	Mongolia	25.68	El Salvador	16.21
USA	41.89	Denmark	24.48	Namibia	16.04
Angola	41.05	Trinidad & Tobago	24.25	Ethiopia	15.80
Netherlands	40.74	Belarus	24.22	Ecuador	15.68
Haiti	40.60	Botswana	24.17	Argentina	15.38
Liberia	40.28	Nepal	24.15	India	15.30
Norway	39.97	Japan	24.13	Chile	15.22
Uzbekistan	39.03	Rwanda	23.77	Burkina Faso	15.08
Canada	38.11	Indonesia	23.73	Spain	14.91
Ireland	37.85	Mali	23.66	Sweden	14.67
Australia	37.64	Moldova	23.28	Burundi	14.65
Tajikistan	36.39	Tanzania	23.06	Pakistan	14.31
Nigeria	36.04	Nicaragua	22.66	Lebanon	14.14
Philippines	34.50	Malta	22.57	Iraq	13.99
Honduras	33.79	Kenya	22.56	Singapore	13.92
Ghana	33.73	Peru	22.51	Venezuela	13.63
Djibouti	33.01	Ukraine	21.55	Madagascar	13.50
Laos	32.79	Costa Rica	21.43	Bangladesh	13.35
Guyana	32.74	Benin	21.41	Hong Kong	13.31
Azerbaijan	31.71	Bolivia	21.19	Niger	13.21
Kyrgyzstan	31.65	Russia	20.81	Iran	12.80
Austria	31.35	Uganda	20.60	Uruguay	12.80
Zambia	29.20	Thailand	20.55	Egypt	11.17
Chad	29.19	Panama	20.36	Mexico	10.67
Dominican Rep.	28.99	Mauritania	20.35	Portugal	10.61
Senegal	28.94	Italy	20.25	Lithuania	10.20
UK	28.55	Congo Brazzaville	20.10	Saudi Arabia	9.970
Guatemala	28.40	Togo	19.95	Poland	9.83
Finland	28.21	Latvia	19.87	Turkey	9.27
Iceland	28.07	Estonia	19.49	Greece	7.08
Belgium	27.97	Colombia	19.27	Cambodia	6.92
France	27.79	Mozambique	19.20	Hungary	6.51
Luxembourg	27.70	Afghanistan	18.78	Romania	4.63
Czech Rep.	26.98	Israel	18.59	Average	22.45

References

Alesina, A., Devleeschauwer, A., Easterly, W., Kurlat, S., & Wacziarg, R. (2003). Fractionalization. *Journal of Economic Growth, 8*(2), 155–194.

Bekkers, R., & Schuyt, T. (2008). And who is your neighbor? Explaining denominational differences in charitable giving and volunteering in the Netherlands. *Review of Religious Research, 50*(1), 74–96.

Borgonovi, F. (2008). Divided we stand, united we fall: Religious pluralism, giving, and volunteering. *American Sociological Review, 73*(1), 105–128.

Curtis, J. E., Baer, D. E., & Grabb, E. G. (2001). Nations of joiners: Explaining voluntary association membership in democratic societies. *American Sociological Review, 66*(6), 783–805.

Dekker, P., & De Hart, J. (2001). Levensbeschouwing en vrijwilligerswerk. Het belang van netwerken in een seculariserende samenleving. *Tijdschrift voor Humanistiek, 8,* 9–17.

Finke, R., & Stark, R. (1988). Religious economies and sacred canopies—Religious mobilization in American cities, 1906. *American Sociological Review, 53*(1), 41–49.

Finke, R., & Stark, R. (1992). *The churching of America, 1776–1990 : Winners and losers in our religious economy.* New Brunswick: Rutgers University Press.

Freedom House (2007). Freedom in the world country ratings. http://www.freedomhouse.org/sites/default/files/Country%20Status%20and%20Ratings%20By%20Region%2C%201973-2013_0.xls. Accessed 4 June 2011.

Gallup Inc. (2010). The Gallup World Poll 2007 and 2008. Washington, DC.

Gallup Inc. (2011). Gallup worldwide research methodology and codebook. Unpublished document.

Govaart, M.-M., Allen, K., Nederlands Instituut voor Zorg en Welzijn, Verwey-Jonker Instituut, & Community Partnership Consultants. (2001). *Volunteering worldwide.* Utrecht: NIZW.

Halman, L. (2003). Volunteering, democracy, and democratic attitudes. In P. Dekker & L. Halman (Eds.), *The values of volunteering* (pp. 179–198). New York: Kluwer Academic.

Iannaccone, L. R. (1991). The consequences of religious market structure. *Rationality and Society, 3*(2), 156–177.

Iannaccone, L. R. (1998). Introduction to the economics of religion. *Journal of Economic Literature, 36*(3), 1465–1495.

Lam, P. Y. (2002). As the flocks gather: How religion affects voluntary association participation. *Journal for the Scientific Study of Religion, 41*(3), 405–422.

Lim, C., & MacGregor, C. A. (2012). Religion and volunteering in context: Disentangling the contextual effects of religion on voluntary behavior. *American Sociological Review, 77*(5), 747–779. doi:10.1177/0003122412457875.

Musick, M., & Wilson, J. (2008). *Volunteers: A social profile.* Bloomington: Indiana University Press.

Norris, P. (2002). *Democratic Phoenix: Reinventing political activism.* Cambridge: Cambridge University Press.

Parboteeah, K. P., Cullen, J. B., & Lim, L. (2004). Formal volunteering: A cross-national test. *Journal of World Business, 39*(4), 431–441. doi:10.1016/J.Jwb.2004.08.007.

Perl, P., & Olson, D. V. A. (2000). Religious market share and intensity of church involvement in five denominations. *Journal for the Scientific Study of Religion, 39*(1), 12–31. doi:10.1111/0021-8294.00002.

Putnam, R. D. (2000). *Bowling alone: The collapse and revival of American community.* New York: Simon & Schuster.

Putnam, R. D., & Campbell, D. E. (2010). *American grace: How religion divides and unites us* (1st Simon & Schuster hardcover ed.). New York: Simon & Schuster.

Rooney, P., Steinberg, K., & Schervish, P. G. (2004). Methodology is destiny: The effect of survey prompts on reported levels of giving and volunteering. *Nonprofit and Voluntary Sector Quarterly, 33*(4), 628–654. doi:10.1177/0899764004269312.

Ruiter, S., & De Graaf, N. D. (2006). National context, religiosity, and volunteering: Results from 53 countries. *American Sociological Review, 71*(2), 191–210.

Salamon, L., Anheier, H., List, R., Toepler, S., & Sokolowski, S. W. (1999). *Dimensions of the nonprofit sector*. Baltimore: Center for Civil Society Studies.

Snijders, T. A. B., & Bosker, R. J. (1999). *Multilevel analysis : An introduction to basic and advanced multilevel modeling*. London: Sage Publications.

Stark, R. (1992). Do Catholic societies really exist? *Rationality and Society, 4*(3), 261–271.

Stark, R., & Finke, R. (2000). *Acts of faith : Explaining the human side of religion*. Berkeley: University of California Press.

Stark, R., & Mccann, J. C. (1993). Market forces and Catholic commitment + Locating religious vitality in pluralism and competition in regard to the so-called newer paradigm of religious monopolies—exploring the new paradigm. *Journal for the Scientific Study of Religion, 32*(2), 111–124. doi:10.2307/1386791.

Tajfel, H. (1979). Individuals and groups in social psychology. *British Journal of Social and Clinical Psychology, 18*(June), 183–190.

Tajfel, H., & Turner, J. C. (1979). An Integrative Theory of intergroup conflict. In W. G. Austin & S. Worche (Eds.), *The social psychology of intergroup relations* (pp. 33–47). New York: Praeger.

Van der Meer, T., Grotenhuis, M. T., & Pelzer, B. (2010). Influential cases in multilevel modeling: A methodological comment. *American Sociological Review, 75*(1), 173–178. doi:10.1177/0003122409359166.

Van Oorschot, W., & Arts, W. (2005). The social capital of European welfare states: The crowding out hypothesis revisited. *Journal of European Social Policy, 15*(1), 5–26. doi:10.1177/0958928705049159.

Watt, D. H. (1991). United States: Cultural challenges to the voluntary sector. In R. Wuthnow (Ed.), *Between states and markets: The voluntary sector in comparative perspective* (pp. 243–287). Princeton: Princeton University Press.

Wilson, J. (2000). Volunteering. *Annual Review of Sociology, 26*, 215–240. doi:10.1146/Annurev. Soc.26.1.215.

Wilson, J., & Musick, M. (1997). Who cares? Toward an integrated theory of volunteer work. *American Sociological Review, 62*(5), 694–713.

World Bank. (2007). World Development Indicators. GDP per capita, Purchasing Price Parity (constant 2005 international $). http://data.worldbank.org/indicator/NY.GDP.PCAP.PP.KD. Accessed 4 June 2011.

Wuthnow, R. (1991). *Acts of compassion: Caring for others and helping ourselves*. Princeton: Princeton University Press.

Wuthnow, R. (2004). *Saving America? Faith-based services and the future of civil society*. Princeton: Princeton University Press.

Zaleski, P. A., & Zech, C. E. (1995). The effect of religious market competition on church giving. *Review of Social Economy, 53*(3), 350–367.

Chapter 6
A Cross-National Examination of the Motivation to Volunteer

Religious Context, National Value Patterns, and Nonprofit Regimes

Lesley Hustinx, Ronan Van Rossem, Femida Handy and Ram A. Cnaan

Introduction

Motivation to volunteer (MTV) is one of the most frequently researched topics in the field of volunteering research (Handy and Hustinx 2009). Understanding why people volunteer can provide important cues to organizations in their recruitment and retention of volunteers. The literature on why people choose and continue to volunteer is rich but mostly limited to a single country, industry, or organization. Moreover, the dominant approach is a functional one, treating MTV as an expression of preexisting needs and dispositions that precede and drive the act of volunteering. For example, the "Volunteer Functions Inventory" (VFI) developed by Clary and colleagues (Clary et al. 1998; Clary and Snyder 1999), one of the most frequently used instruments for measuring multiple motivational dimensions, assumes that MTV originates from a basic set of universal human needs that can only be met through volunteer activities. Clary and Snyder (1999) pointed out that although different volunteers pursue different goals and that a single volunteer may have multiple important motivations, all reasons for volunteering can be traced back to the universal psychological functions volunteering generally serves.

This prevailing understanding of MTV as originating from inner human drivers explains why few studies have examined how volunteer motivations are shaped by contextual characteristics. However, other social-constructionist perspectives on MTV do exist. Such perspectives consider motivational accounts as a reflection of

---

L. Hustinx (✉)
Department of Sociology, Ghent University, Ghent, Belgium
e-mail: lesley.hustinx@ugent.be

R. Van Rossem
Department of Sociology, Ghent University, Ghent, Belgium

F. Handy · R. A. Cnaan
School of Social Policy and Practice, University of Pennsylvania, Philadelphia, Pennsylvania, USA

R. A. Cnaan
Graduate Institute for Peace, Kyunghee University, Seoul, Korea

L. Hustinx et al. (eds.), *Religion and Volunteering,* Nonprofit and Civil Society Studies,
DOI 10.1007/978-3-319-04585-6_6, © Springer International Publishing Switzerland 2015

a larger set of cultural understandings, that is, the prevailing values and beliefs in a society (Dekker and Halman 2003; Wuthnow 1991). For instance some motivations give expression to a culture of volunteering that emphasizes selfless and compassionate acts and disapproves of self-oriented or egoistic orientations. In this perspective, motives do not precede action, but help to frame and justify our actions by referring to the broader set of cultural understandings. Motives, specifically "motive talk" (Wuthnow 1991), are "constitutive of action, part of a discourse giving meaning to and helping to shape behavior" (Wilson 2000, p. 218).

An essential assumption therefore is that the context influences the use of motives and hence that important differences depending on the societal context may occur. In his classic book Acts of Compassion, Wuthnow (1991) very extensively describes how the unique context of "American individualism" makes volunteers struggle to find a balance between altruistic and utilitarian accounts of their caring activities. As Wuthnow notes, "an adequate language of motivation is thus one of the critical junctures *at which the individual and the society intersect*: being able to explain why is as important to our identity as a culture as it is to our sense of selfhood as individuals" (Wuthnow 1991, p. 50– emphasis added).

A more contextual understanding of MTV further explains changes in the prevalence of certain motivations. In Western European societies, there has been a growing conviction that, due to modernization and secularization, "traditional," religiously inspired and other-oriented volunteering is gradually being replaced by "new," more individualized and self-interested types of involvement. As a result, volunteers, especially from younger generations, are less inclined to provide altruistic reasons for volunteering (Hustinx and Lammertyn 2003).

In this study, we aim to extend our contextual understanding of MTV by examining cross-national differences in the motivations of volunteers. We assess if and how specific societal characteristics are associated with self-reported motivations to volunteer. In particular, we will focus on the role of religion (individual religiosity and religious context), positing a major link with the importance of altruistic MTV. Some of the alternative and competing hypotheses that will be explored within the context of more secular societies are the broader cultural framework, focusing on the dominant value pattern as well as the extent of institutional variations in welfare state regimes and the characteristics of the nonprofit sector.

To examine our hypotheses, we use the second wave of the World Values Surveys (WVS 1990), which includes a series of questions on participation in voluntary work and the main reasons for doing so. For our analysis, we selected 18 countries based on the availability of contextual data for the year 1990. To our knowledge, the 1990 WVS survey is the only cross-national survey that included a question on volunteer motivation. Given that the data was collected more than two decades ago, our study has a major limitation: Our findings do not reflect the motivational accounts of contemporary volunteers or current contextual factors, but rather provide a test for a number of theoretical assumptions. As a result, the main contribution of this study will be to improve our understanding of contextual factors influencing MTV, an approach that is underdeveloped in the current literature.

Literature Review

MTV is a well-researched topic (Wilson 2000). Much of the research has been conducted either at the national level, using representative samples, or at the organizational or sector level, using volunteers both in specific activities and those involved with particular organizations (Musick and Wilson 2008). Regardless of this diversity in the study of MTV, scholars have consistently found MTV to be a complex interplay that includes both altruistic and self-interested accounts (Cnaan and Goldberg-Glen 1991; Wuthnow 1991).

However, existing research indicates that the importance attached to both of these motivational dimensions differs across individuals and groups. For example, it is well established in the literature that the MTV of youth differ from other age-groups (Handy et al. 2010). Gillespie and King (1985) found that a greater proportion of older volunteers reported giving time for altruistic reasons such as to "help others" and "contribute to the community." By contrast, younger volunteers more often expressed MTV in order to acquire training and skills. In a national survey of Canadians, volunteer rates were highest among youth, who also put stronger emphasis on self-interested motivations than other age cohorts. For example, 65 % of 15- to 19-year-olds versus 13 % of those 25 and older reported volunteering to improve their job opportunities (Hall et al. 2006). Among the student population, Winniford et al. (1995) found that American college students said that they volunteered primarily because of altruistic concern for others, although they also stated that they sought to satisfy self-fulfillment and development needs (e.g., affiliation, sense of satisfaction and development of career skills). In addition, Dickinson (1999) reported that in the UK, students who volunteer interpreted it as a conscious attempt to enhance their chances of success in finding postgraduate employment.

In explaining variations in motivational accounts, altruistic reasons for volunteering are primarily connected to religion and religious belief. Altruism is a key value taught by many religions. A sense of selflessness and duty towards the poor is central to all major religions. In essence, it urges religious people to engage in social activities such as volunteering on behalf of others in need (Batson et al. 1993; Cnaan et al. 1993; Ellison 1992; Graham 1990; Wuthnow 1990, 1991; Wymer 1997).

Thus, religious involvement may change the nature or priority of people's motives (Weiss Ozorak 2003; Wilson and Janoski 1995). Its role is educational, sensitizing people to social concerns on which they might not otherwise focus (Weiss Ozorak 2003). There has been some tendency to relate the spirit of altruism to particular religious traditions, most commonly the Judeo–Christian tradition rooted in the Old Testament commandment to "treat your neighbor as yourself" (Leviticus, Chap. 18; in Salamon and Sokolowski 2009). Wuthnow (1991) found a strong relationship between familiarity with the story of the Good Samaritan (Luke 10:30–36) and doing good oneself.[1]

---

[1] It should be noted that Wuthnow more generally referred to "knowing the story" rather than dogmatic knowledge or religious belief.

The opportunity to express religious beliefs and values is thus an important function of volunteering (Wood and Hougland 1990; Wymer 1997), and it also predicts whether volunteers complete their expected period of service (Clary and Miller 1986; Clary and Orenstein 1991). In the USA, expressing religious beliefs or responding to a moral obligation based on religious beliefs is among the top three motives for giving and volunteering (Wymer 1997).

Research on the relationship between religion and volunteering has, however, revealed that it is not religious conviction but rather religious practice that constitutes a key determinant for volunteering. In other words, religious convictions are fostered through active participation in a religious community (Lam 2002; Lim and MacGregor 2012; Ruiter and De Graaf 2006; see also the chapter by Bennett in this book). It is through religious practice that social networks among fellow members of the religious community are built and that information is shared. Active members of religious communities are thus more likely to learn about volunteering opportunities and to be asked to volunteer. Consequently, in research on religion and volunteering, religious attendance is used as a key predictor (Lim and MacGregor 2012).

In this chapter, we do not focus on volunteer behavior but on motivations to volunteer. Nevertheless, we also expect to see some influence of religious attendance: Through social interaction and interpersonal influence among individuals within a "moral community" (Stark and Bainbridge 1996), shared norms and values are strengthened and motivations and discourses are regulated.

Given that the endorsement of altruism is universal among all the world's major religious traditions, we hypothesize:

- H1a: Religious people express a stronger support for altruistic MTV and a weaker support for self-oriented MTV. We expect a positive association with both personal beliefs and service attendance.
- H1b: There is no difference between the various religions with respect to their effect on altruistic MTV.

The (increasing) importance of self-interested MTV, on the other hand, could be explained on the basis of theories of modernization and value change. It has been argued that as a result of processes of advanced modernization, secularization, and individualization, present-day volunteers put increasing emphasis on self-oriented reasons for their involvement, at the expense of altruistic reasons (Hustinx and Lammertyn 2003). From this perspective of social change, "traditional" volunteering was embedded in a religious tradition of benevolence and altruism. Dedication to the common good was a highly esteemed asset to which deviating individual motivations were easily subordinated. By contrast, in a more individualized context, traditional loyalties weaken and the interaction between an individualized biography and volunteer experience intensifies. As volunteering becomes increasingly embedded in self-authored individualized narratives, it becomes a tool for self-actualization or "life(-style) politics" (Bennett 1998). The volunteering field is seen as a "market of possibilities" (Evers 1999) for self-realization and the setting of personal goals.

This shift in motivational accounts can be linked to theories of value change in general, most notably Inglehart's theory on postmaterialist value change (Inglehart 1971, 1997; Inglehart and Welzel 2005). The basic assertion of Inglehart is that among Western populations, a gradual change in values, from materialist to post-materialist, has been occurring through generational replacement. These generational differences can be traced back to different socialization experiences during the formative years. Whereas older cohorts experienced the economic deprivation of wartime as well as the Great Depression and the mutual efforts to rebuild society, younger cohorts were raised in times of economic prosperity and a growing emphasis on individual autonomy and self-expressive values (Inglehart 1997; Inglehart and Welzel 2005).

Not only has the economic well-being of the average citizen increased objectively, but so has their sense of existential security. As a consequence, citizens develop new value priorities (Delhey 2009). Value change is observed as occurring along two axes: from traditional authority to secular rational values, and from survival values to self-expressive values. The younger age cohorts no longer stress values such as economic growth, the fight against rising prices or crime rates, obedience and trust in (religious) hierarchies; rather, they prioritize more secular and self-expressive values such as tolerance, freedom of speech, environmental protection and individual fulfillment. Support for freedom of expression, in addition to tolerance of ethnic or sexual minorities, is found to be stronger and more widespread among the younger age cohorts (Stolle and Hooghe 2005).

While self-expression values are associated with higher levels of individualism, Welzel (2010) notes that disagreement exists about whether these values are of a civic nature or not. Scholars have argued in both directions. On the one hand, individualism is easily equated with more self-oriented attitudes and behavior, hence with egoism. On the other hand, Welzel argues that since self-expression values imply a basic sense of human equality, it enables universal feelings of solidarity. Therefore, Welzel argues for self-expression values as a civic or socially responsible form of modern individualism. Other authors have also argued in favor of a "solidary individualism" (Berking 1996) or "altruistic individualism" (Beck 1997) that can constitute a seemingly contradictory motivational basis for present-day volunteering (Hustinx 2001; Hustinx and Lammertyn 2003).

Using data from the World Values Study, Welzel (2010) found that the association between self-expression values and altruism is mixed. Higher country levels of self-expression were strongly associated with higher levels of altruism. At the individual level, however, the association with egoism/altruism was U-shaped: In the lower range of the self-expression values scale (i.e., respondents that scored weaker on this scale), increasing support for self-expression values was associated with stronger egoism, whereas in the upper range of the scale (i.e., respondents that scored stronger on this scale), increasing support for self-expression values was associated with stronger altruism. While this pattern confirms neither the civic nor the "uncivic" interpretation of self-expression values, Welzel argues that it more clearly supports the civic interpretation because stronger self-expression values are associated with stronger altruism, not egoism, especially at high levels of these values (Welzel 2010, pp. 13–15).

In sum, the emergence of a self-expressive value pattern could be linked to altruistic as well as self-interested reasons for volunteering. According to the "civic" interpretation, both types of motives could be easily combined, while the "uncivic" interpretation considers them as mutually exclusive. We therefore formulate two competing hypotheses:

- H2a: Volunteers with a self-expressive value pattern will put less emphasis on altruistic motivations and more emphasis on self-interested reasons for volunteering.
- H2b: Volunteers with a self-expressive value pattern will put a stronger emphasis on both altruistic motivations and self-interested reasons for volunteering.

Beyond these individual factors, important contextual influences may be at play as well. Ruiter and De Graaf (2006, pp. 193–194) note that the relation between the national religious context and volunteer work is somewhat neglected in the literature. Based on Kelley and De Graaf (1997), they develop arguments to predict a positive impact for the degree of devoutness of a society on volunteer participation. Kelley and De Graaf (1997) found that people who were raised by secular parents in relatively devout countries were more religious than people who grew up with similar parents in more secular countries. The authors explained this through people's exposure to religious culture and their pools of potential friends, teachers, colleagues, and marriage partners who would be predominantly devout. Ruiter and De Graaf (2006) expected this "spillover" effect on nonreligious people for volunteering as well. Moreover, a religious context exerts a socialization effect on secular people as the likelihood of encountering religious people in one's personal social network would be greater while the impact of individual religiosity would be weaker in more devout societies. We further argue that having more religious people in one's network also increases the exposure to religious beliefs and values such as altruism. Hence, we expect a higher likelihood of altruistic motivations to volunteer in a more religious national context.

While Ruiter and De Graaf (2006) found support for the "spillover hypothesis" based on data from the World Values Study, their findings were not reproduced using the Gallup World Poll data that includes a larger number of countries, pointing to higher rates of volunteering in both secular and highly devout societies (Lim and MacGregor 2012, Bennett in this volume). While this shows that the results are sensitive to the countries included in the analysis (Van Der Meer et al. 2010), Lim and MacGregor (2012) further argue that although the average service attendance in a country is commonly used to test the network spillover hypothesis, such a national average is a poor proxy for the influence of religiosity in the personal networks of individuals. They formulate several reasons: Religion is not evenly distributed geographically; homophily among the nonreligious may be higher in religious environments, hence levels of segregation might be higher in devout areas compared to secular ones; recruitment efforts of religious organizations are more likely to be targeted at religious people; and finally, interpersonal influence is based on a shared identity and thus might be more effective when individuals share a religious faith. Furthermore, Lim and MacGregor (2012) indicate that the average service attendance of a country could relate to individual volunteering through mechanisms other than network spillover. In more devout countries, where a national religious culture may influence people's likelihood of volunteering through public discourse and the media, a higher organizational density may exist with more volunteer opportunities. Thus, even while contextual effects are present, other mechanisms than network spillover could exist and it is very difficult to disentangle these different mechanisms. In their own study, using data from the Gallup World Poll, Lim and MacGregor (2012) found evidence for the existence of a national religious culture, rather than a spillover effect.

Taking into account different contextual mechanisms, we can safely assume that secular volunteers in a devout society will express more support for altruistic values compared to their secular counterparts in secular societies. Altruism is a more central part of the prevailing religious culture and could be fostered through the higher likelihood of religious persons being present in the personal networks of individuals (Bellah et al. 1985; Lim and MacGregor 2012; Ruiter and De Graaf 2006; Wuthnow 1991):

- H3: A religious national context will be associated with a stronger emphasis on altruistic MTV

Besides the religious context, we also expect the dominant value pattern to influence MTV. Following Inglehart (Inglehart 1997; Inglehart and Welzel 2005), we expect self-expressive values to prevail in more secular societies. Parallel to the hypotheses of network spillover and national culture in the case of a religious national context, similar mechanisms could apply with respect to the dominant value pattern in a country. As argued above, however, existing perspectives predict an association with altruism or egoism. We therefore formulate two competing hypotheses:

- H4a: A national context in which the dominant value pattern is postmaterialist will be associated with a stronger emphasis on self-interested MTV.
- H4b: A national context in which the dominant value pattern is postmaterialist will be associated with a stronger emphasis on both altruistic and self-interested MTV.

Besides these variables involving cultural context, institutional explanations for motivational differences could be formulated. For this argument, we relied on three cross-national examinations of MTV that looked at differences in the particular welfare regime of a country (Hustinx et al. 2010; Hwang et al. 2005; Ziemek 2006). First, Hwang et al. (2005) compared MTV between Canada and the USA and found Americans more likely to mention altruistic MTV, while Canadians were more likely to emphasize self-interested reasons. To explain these differences, the authors argued that while both countries are liberal democracies, Canada's government provides more extensive social welfare programs (such as universal health care and aid to vulnerable groups) than the US government. Thus, volunteers in the USA see helping the poor and disadvantaged as part of their role as citizens and are more likely to report altruistic MTV than Canadian volunteers who see this role fulfilled by their government (the authors controlled for individual religiosity, for it should be noted that the USA is a far more religious country than Canada). A second study by Ziemek (2006) examined MTV across countries with different levels of economic development, namely, Bangladesh, Ghana, Poland and South Korea. Clustering MTV into three categories, "altruism," "egoism," and "investment in human capital," she tested the differences in MTV through the volunteer's perceived level of public spending. Perceptions of high public spending were found to negatively influence altruistic MTV and positively influence investment motivation.

A more recent study on student volunteers across six countries suggests that MTV is also influenced by regimes, albeit partially (Hustinx et al. 2010). The latter study applied the social origins theory, advanced by Salamon and Anheier (1998) and predicated on Esping-Andersen's (1990) "worlds of welfare capitalism." This theory explains the size and development of the nonprofit sector as an outcome of broadly defined power relations among social classes and social institutions. In brief, social origins theory identifies four different regimes: liberal, social democratic, corporatist, and statist, with corresponding levels of government social welfare spending and nonprofit sector size ranging from high to low. In addition, the social origins theory examines the role nonprofit organizations serve in a society (Salamon and Sokolowski 2003). Depending on the regime, the nonprofits are more likely to provide some of the services that have an instrumental value to society or expressive services that are the actualization of values or preferences, such as the pursuit of artistic expression, preservation of cultural heritage or the natural environment.

At one end, in the liberal model, low government spending on social welfare services is associated with a relatively large nonprofit sector mainly focused on service provision. At the opposite end is the social-democratic model in which high government spending on social welfare results in a limited role for service provision by nonprofits, but a larger role for the expression of political, social, or recreational interests. In addition, corporatist and statist models are both characterized by strong states, in which the state and nonprofits are partners in the corporatist model while the state maintains the upper hand in many social policies in the statist model. In both models, the service role is dominant.

Across these four types of regime, the relationship with volunteering is not linear (Salamon and Sokolowski 2003). There are two regime types in which the amount of volunteering is high. The social-democratic regime has a distinct pattern of high levels of volunteering, but mostly in expressive rather than service roles. In the liberal regime, participation in volunteering is also very high yet mainly located in serviced-oriented sectors that are underserved by public workers. The corporatist regime also produces a much more service-oriented pattern of volunteering, yet with moderate levels of volunteering given the substantial amount of paid staff. Finally, in the statist regime, volunteering is largely underdeveloped.

In addition to the varying rates of volunteering, we suggest that MTV will also differ in different regimes, and that a systematic link can be found between the re-

6 A Cross-National Examination of the Motivation to Volunteer

gimes and the primary MTV. Following Hwang et al. (2005), we hypothesize that volunteers are most likely to report altruistic MTV when they provide services that are underserved by government, that is, when nonprofits fulfill a primary role in the welfare production of a country. Based on social origins theory, this will most likely be the case if a nonprofit regime is characterized by (1) a revenue structure with low government spending; (2) a large nonprofit sector with a small paid workforce and a large unpaid workforce; and (3) service provision as the dominant volunteering type. These characteristics correspond to the liberal regime. In clear contrast are the social-democratic and corporatist regimes, which both heavily rely on government support for the sector. In the former, volunteering is largely expressive in form, while in the latter, a majority of volunteers is involved in service provision but their role is moderate and auxiliary. Hence, we expect altruistic MTV to be the weakest in the social-democratic regime and moderate in the corporatist regime. Finally, the statist regime is characterized by limited growth in both government social spending and nonprofit activity; moreover, nonprofit organizations lack the type of autonomy and resources typical of Western democracies. Nevertheless, existing volunteers mainly provide services that are underserved by government; thus, we predict moderate support for altruistic MTV. Given that the social-democratic regime is the only regime in which the expressive role of volunteering is dominant, we predict that self-interested reasons for volunteering will be the most prevalent in this regime.

In sum, we hypothesize that:

- H5a: Support for altruistic MTV is the weakest in the social-democratic regime, and the strongest in the Liberal regime. Corporatist and statist regimes express moderate support for altruistic MTV.
- H5b: Support for self-interested reasons for volunteering is the strongest in the social-democratic regime.

Data and Methods

Sample

We use data from the 1990 wave of the WVS. To our knowledge, this is the only cross-national survey which includes a question on motivations to volunteer. As already mentioned in the introduction, the data mainly allows for testing theoretical assumptions about contextual influences on self-reported MTV (i.e., a test of cultural vs. institutional explanations), and does not provide an up-to-date empirical picture.

The 1990 wave includes data from 40 countries worldwide. We selected only those countries for which valid measures on all dependent and independent variables were available. More specifically, the countries selected for this study are those countries (1) in which questions on volunteer participation and motivations to volunteer were asked; and (2) that were included in the early wave of the Johns Hopkins Comparative Nonprofit Sector Project. This made data available for the size of the nonprofit sector, the composition of the workforce, dominant functions, and sources of revenue within the national nonprofit regimes, all as close to the year 1990 as possible. As a result, 18 countries were included in the analysis (West and East Germany still counted separately), with a total of 7,186 respondents who indicated a willingness to volunteer at the time of the survey (27.1% of the total sample). Appendix A6.1 provides an overview of the number and proportion of volunteers per country.

Variables

Our key dependent variable is the motivation to volunteer. In the WVS survey, the first question determined whether respondents were currently doing unpaid work for any organization taken from a list of 16 types of organizations. In a subsequent step, for those respondents who indicated that they were doing unpaid work in any of these organizations, their reasons for doing voluntary work was asked using a 5-point Likert-type question format (1 = unimportant, 5 = very important). The 14 reasons for doing voluntary work included statements ranging from "a sense of solidarity with the poor and disadvantaged" to "purely for personal satisfaction," thereby reflecting both "altruistic" and "self-interested" dimensions of the motivation to volunteer. A principal component analysis confirmed that the different MTV clustered into these two dimensions. We treat both measures as summated scales.

Altruistic reasons for volunteering (Cronbach's alpha.81) include seven items: (1) a sense of solidarity with the poor and disadvantaged; (2) compassion for those in need; (3) an opportunity to repay something, give something back; (4) a sense of duty, moral obligation; (5) identifying with people who were suffering; and (6) to help give disadvantaged people hope and dignity. We dropped an item about "religious beliefs" as altruistic MTV as this might have artificially inflated the effects of the religion variables on altruistic MTV.

Self-interested reasons for volunteering (Cronbach's alpha.66) include four items: (1) time on my hands, wanted something worthwhile to do; (2) purely for personal satisfaction; (3) for social reasons, to meet people; and (4) to gain new skills and useful experience.

The independent variables are situated both at the individual and the country level.

Background Characteristics First of all, we account for relevant socio-demographic variables: gender (ref = male), age (continuous), education level (age at which education completed, divided into ten categories ranging from 1 = 12 years of age or earlier; 10 = 21 years of age or older), marital status (ref = married/cohabiting vs. single, divorced/separated/widowed), employment status (ref = working vs.

unemployed, student, housewife/husband, retired, other), and political orientation (10-point scale, 1 = left, 10 = right).

Religiosity Next, we measure individual religiosity by means of three measures. Firstly, we look at religious membership, which is measured by questioning whether people belong to a religious denomination and, if so, which one. The questionnaire included the following options: Roman Catholic (41,8 %), Mainline Protestant (25,2 %), Fundamentalist Protestant (3,6 %), Jew (0,4 %), Muslim (0,1 %), Hindu (0,4 %), Buddhist (0,8 %), other (5,8 %), never (21,6 %), and no answer (0,4 %). We assign respondents to the following five categories: Catholic, other Christian, other (non-Christians), none (nonreligious), and missing. While we acknowledge that these broad categories do great injustice to the existing religious diversity, most religious denominations have too low a number of observations to be considered separately in the analysis.

Secondly, we assess the influence of religious service attendance by asking respondents how often they attended religious services, apart from weddings, funerals and christenings (ranging from more than once a week to never or practically never).

Finally, we consider professed closeness to God as a measure of individual religiosity, by including a question that asked how important God is in the respondent's life, which was assessed on a scale from 1 (not important at all) to 10 (very important).

At the contextual level, we include the mean religious attendance and the mean level of closeness to God in a particular country.

Value Patterns Besides religiosity, we look at individual and collective value patterns. As argued above, while we hypothesize that religiosity is correlated with altruistic MTV, support for postmaterialist values will be associated with self-oriented reasons for volunteering. We use the Inglehart measure of postmaterialism, which was included in the 1990 wave of the WVS. This scale is based on a series of three questions about what the respondent thinks that the aims for his/her country should be for the next 10 years. In each of the questions, the respondents are presented with two choices that represent a materialist value pattern (e.g., "maintaining order in the nation") and with two that represent a postmaterialist one (e.g., "protecting freedom of speech"). The final score on the postmaterialism scale is the count of the number of postmaterialist items over these three questions that were mentioned as first or second choice ("high" priority) from the given group of four goals.

At the country level, we integrate the mean postmaterialism score in the analysis.

Nonprofit Sector Regime A final contextual variable assesses cross-national variation in MTV as a function of institutional variations in the national nonprofit sector regime. As indicated above, Salamon and Anheier's social origins theory is predicated on Esping-Andersen's (1990) "worlds of welfare capitalism"; hence, the different nonprofit regimes are embedded in the broader welfare state regimes. Therefore, we first include a measure of the welfare state regime types based on

Esping-Andersen's seminal work (1990). He identified three models: liberal (Anglo-Saxon), social democratic (Scandinavian), and conservative corporatist (continental Europe). We add an Eastern European type to include these countries in our analysis.

In addition, to assess the influence of the country-specific nonprofit sector regime more exactly, and based on the discussion above, we use four indicators that are available from the Johns Hopkins Comparative Nonprofit Sector Project (CNP; Salamon et al. 1999, 2004) and which were gathered in the early period of the project, so as to match the WVS data of the 1990 wave as closely as possible. The indicators included in our analysis are:

- Percentage of Civil Society Organization (CSO) workforce as share of economically active population
- Percentage of volunteer share of CSO workforce (expressed in full-time equivalents, FTEs)
- Percentage of source of CSO revenue: government (vs. fees and philanthropy)
- Dominant function of the nonprofit sector: service or expressive

Because the CNP estimates the amount of volunteer labor in an aggregated way, generating a count of the total amount of volunteer effort in terms of FTEs, we additionally look at the mean percentage of volunteers in the population based on the WVS survey.

Results

In a first step, we look at the distribution of MTV across countries. Figure 6.1 shows that the motive mix differs depending upon the national context. If we consider a mean score above 3.50 on a scale from 1 to 5 as a measure of the importance of one of the two motivational dimensions, it is only in Austria that both MTVs are (very) important. Altruistic motivations are also important in the USA, East Germany, Great Britain and Northern Ireland, and self-interested reasons for volunteering play an important role in Finland as well. There is also one country, Romania, in which none of the motivations are important (mean score below 2.75 for both motivational dimensions).

When one considers the mean scores for both dimensions we can clearly discern a cluster of Anglo-Saxon countries (USA, Great Britain, and Ireland) that score average to high on altruism and low to average on self-interested benefits. Most other countries present the reversed pattern, with a low to average score on altruism and an average to high score for self-interested reasons for volunteering.

In a second step, we aim to explain variations in MTV by means of a causal analysis. In Table 6.1, we present the results of a set of multilevel linear regression models, with altruistic and self-interested reasons for volunteering as dependent variables. Model 1 includes individual-level predictors only, model 2 contains both

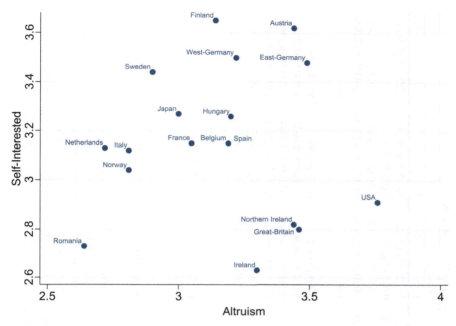

Fig. 6.1 Scatterplot of motivation to volunteer (MTV) by country

individual-level and country-level variables, and model 3 shows the most parsimonious model with only significant individual and country-level variables.

At the individual level, looking at the indicators of individual religiosity, there is no influence of denominational differences. Religious service attendance and the importance of God in one's life, on the other hand, are significantly and positively associated with altruistic MTV, while a more frequent service attendance also weakens the importance attached to self-interested MTV. These findings confirm hypotheses H1a and H1b.

Next, a postmaterialist value pattern does not relate to altruistic MTV and is weakly and negatively associated with self-interested motivations. This disconfirms H2a, but as there is no pronounced relationship between self-expressive values and altruism, it does not support H2b either. In our analysis, we also included political orientation as a measure of broader value orientations. The results show that volunteers who identify themselves as more left wing report more altruistic MTV.

We furthermore observe a number of significant relationships with the socioeconomic background characteristics of volunteers. Female and older volunteers put significantly stronger emphasis on altruistic motivations than male and younger ones, and younger volunteers indicate significantly more frequently that they are motivated by self-interested reasons than older volunteers. Higher educated volunteers express significantly weaker support for both altruistic and self-interested reasons for volunteering in comparison with lower educated ones.

Table 6.1 Multilevel linear regression model for altruistic motivations and self-interested motives for volunteering

b (se)	Altruism			Self-interest		
	1	2	3	1	2	3
Intercept	3.184*** (0.120)	4.124* (1.657)	3.992*** (0.372)	3.682*** (0.122)	3.095** (0.962)	3.259*** (0.414)
Sex (Male)	−0.139*** (0.025)	−0.138*** (0.025)	−0.151*** (0.023)	0.002 (0.025)	0.002 (0.025)	
Age	0.006*** (0.001)	0.006*** (0.001)	0.006*** (0.001)	−0.007*** (0.001)	−0.007*** (0.001)	−0.007*** (0.001)
Education level	−0.028*** (0.005)	−0.028*** (0.005)	−0.028*** (0.005)	−0.035*** (0.005)	−0.035*** (0.005)	−0.034*** (0.005)
Employment status (ref: Working)				***	***	***
Other	−0.011 (0.093)	−0.009 (0.093)		0.068 (0.096)	0.071 (0.096)	0.078 (0.095)
Unemployed	0.091 (0.062)	0.092 (0.062)		0.254*** (0.063)	0.256*** (0.063)	0.264*** (0.063)
Student	−0.011 (0.057)	−0.010 (0.057)		0.211*** (0.058)	0.210*** (0.058)	0.223*** (0.056)
Housewife	0.082 (0.042)	0.085* (0.042)		0.160*** (0.043)	0.163*** (0.043)	0.159*** (0.039)
Retired	0.053 (0.043)	0.053 (0.043)		0.178*** (0.044)	0.179*** (0.044)	0.189*** (0.044)
Income	−0.005 (0.005)	−0.005 (0.005)		−0.021*** (0.005)	−0.020*** (0.005)	−0.021*** (0.005)
Marital status (ref: married, cohabiting)						
Single	0.007 (0.035)	0.009 (0.035)		0.050 (0.035)	0.051 (0.035)	
Divorced, separated, widowed	−0.012 (0.039)	−0.012 (0.039)		0.028 (0.040)	0.029 (0.040)	
Post-materialism	0.013 (0.009)	0.013 (0.009)		−0.015 (0.009)	−0.016 (0.009)	
Political orientation	−0.022** (0.007)	−0.023** (0.007)	−0.025*** (0.006)	0.010 (0.007)	0.010 (0.007)	−0.018* (0.009)
Religion (ref: Catholic)						
Other Christian	−0.024 (0.035)	−0.024 (0.036)		−0.046 (0.036)	−0.048 (0.036)	
Other	−0.026 (0.111)	−0.031 (0.113)		−0.026 (0.112)	−0.020 (0.114)	
None	−0.020 (0.190)	−0.023 (0.199)		−0.038 (0.188)	−0.061 (0.196)	
Missing	0.007 (0.039)	0.003 (0.039)		−0.018 (0.040)	−0.016 (0.040)	
Religious attendance	−0.027*** (0.006)	−0.027*** (0.006)	−0.028*** (0.006)	0.013* (0.006)	0.013 (0.006)	0.011* (0.005)
Importance of god	0.056*** (0.005)	0.056*** (0.005)	0.055*** (0.005)	−0.001 (0.005)	0.000 (0.005)	

Table 6.1 (continued)

b (se)	Altruism			Self-interest		
	1	2	3	1	2	3
Country level vars						
Mean religious service attendance		−0.110 (0.131)			0.042 (0.100)	
Importance of religion		−0.128 (0.129)	−0.213*** (0.047)		−0.110 (0.104)	−0.088** (0.033)
Mean postmaterialism score		0.028 (0.298)			0.361 (0.229)	0.380** (0.111)
CSO workforce		0.012 (0.040)			−0.055 (0.032)	
Revenue from government		−0.012 (0.007)	−0.013* (0.004)		0.002 (0.006)	
Volunteer share of CSO workforce		−0.013 (0.009)	−0.010* (0.004)			
Volunteering in population		0.032* (0.012)	0.031*** (0.007)		0.011 (0.008)	0.013** (0.004)
Expressive work dominant		0.037 (0.331)			0.167 (0.246)	
Welfare state regime (ref: Social-democratic)						
Eastern European		0.481 (0.483)	0.549* (0.185)		0.014 (0.333)	
Not clearly classified		1.289** (0.335)	1.254*** (0.261)		−0.050 (0.300)	
Liberal		0.527 (0.419)	0.570** (0.216)		0.191 (0.276)	
Christian-democratic		0.632 (0.340)	0.693*** (0.197)		0.030 (0.281)	

b regression coefficient; *se* standard deviation; * .05; ** .01; *** .001

Employment status is mainly associated with self-interested reasons for volunteering. In comparison with volunteers who are employed, unemployed volunteers, students, housewives, and retired volunteers are significantly more strongly motivated by self-interested reasons for volunteering. Housewives also value altruistic MTV higher. A higher income scale is negatively associated with both altruistic and self-interested reasons for volunteering. There is no relationship between marital status and MTV.

At the country level, we have included the mean importance of God and the mean religious service attendance as measures of the level of devoutness in a particular national context. The mean importance of God has a negative influence on both altruistic and self-interested reasons for volunteering; the mean religious service attendance does not influence self-reported MTV. Hypothesis H3 could thus not be confirmed. Our analysis further reveals that a national context in which the dominant value pattern is postmaterialist has a positive influence on self-interested MTV, confirming hypothesis H4a and disconfirming H4b.

While these variables measure the influence of the cultural context, our analysis also includes measures of national differences in institutional welfare regimes. As hypothesized in H5a, support for altruistic MTV is the weakest in the social-democratic regimes; however, no differentiation exists among the other regimes. Contrary to H5b, welfare state regimes do not differ in their population's support for self-interested MTV. More specific characteristics of the particular nonprofit regime partially relate to MTV. The revenue structure of the nonprofit sector influences MTV: As predicted, the more government support for the nonprofit sector, the less volunteers express altruistic MTV. The size of the CSO workforce negatively influences self-interested MTV yet is not associated with altruistic MTV. The relative share of volunteers in the CSO workforce (measured in terms of FTEs) relates to altruistic MTV but in the opposite direction of what we hypothesized: the larger the share of volunteers in the CSO workforce, the weaker volunteers' support for altruistic MTV. The proportion of volunteers in the population, on the other hand, has a positive influence on both altruistic and self-interested reasons for volunteering. The dominant function of the nonprofit sector is not related to reported MTV.

Discussion and Conclusion

In this study, we examined whether and how motivations to volunteer are shaped by contextual characteristics. In contrast to prevailing understandings of MTV in terms of inner human drivers, we approached MTV in a social-constructionist way, considering motivational accounts as a reflection of prevailing values and beliefs in society. A more contextual understanding of MTV further allows examination of how changes in the emphasis put on certain motivations are linked to broader social transformations. In the volunteering literature, a shift from altruistic to more self-

6 A Cross-National Examination of the Motivation to Volunteer

Table 6.2 Summary of the findings

Hypotheses	Empirical findings
Individual-level hypotheses	
H1a: Religious people express a stronger support for altruistic MTV and a weaker support for self-oriented MTV. We expect a positive association with both personal beliefs and service attendance	Confirmed
H1b: There is no difference between the various religions with respect to their effect on altruistic MTV	Confirmed
H2a: Volunteers with a self-expressive value pattern will put less emphasis on altruistic motivations and more emphasis on self-interested reasons for volunteering	Disconfirmed
H2b: Volunteers with a self-expressive value pattern will put a stronger emphasis on both altruistic motivations and self-interested reasons for volunteering	Disconfirmed
Country-level hypotheses	
H3: A religious national context will be associated with a stronger emphasis on altruistic MTV	Disconfirmed
H4a: A national context in which the dominant value pattern is postmaterialist will be associated with a stronger emphasis on self-interested MTV	Confirmed
H4b: A national context in which the dominant value pattern is postmaterialist will be associated with a stronger emphasis on both altruistic and self-interested MTV	Disconfirmed
H5a: Support for altruistic MTV is weakest in a social-democratic regime, and strongest in a liberal regime. Corporatist and statist regimes express moderate support for altruistic MTV	Partially confirmed
H5b: Support for self-interested reasons for volunteering is strongest in a social-democratic regime	Disconfirmed

interested or instrumental MTV has been described, which can in turn be linked to broader societal processes of secularization and changes in values.

As a result, in this chapter, we examined the influence of national context on motivations to volunteer using data from the second wave of the WVS 1990, including 18 countries in the analysis and with a total of 7,186 respondents who volunteered. Up to the present, only few studies have endeavored to carry out such a cross-national examination of MTV. On the one hand, we focused on the broader cultural framework, understood in terms of the national religious context and the dominant value pattern. On the other hand, we assessed how institutional variations in terms of welfare state regimes and characteristics of the nonprofit sector affect motivations to volunteer.

Across all countries studied, people who volunteered expressed both altruistic and self-oriented motivations, a finding that is consistent with previous studies. Nevertheless, we observed important variations in the emphasis that was put on both motivational dimensions depending on individual background characteristics and variations in the national context. In Table 6.2, the key hypotheses and corresponding empirical findings are summarized.

First, at the individual level, we assessed the role of religion and religiosity in explaining MTV. As discussed above, altruism is a value that is central to all religions; hence, religious involvement may influence or change people's chief reasons for volunteering. As expected, we did not find any differences between belonging to different religious traditions (however, we noted limited variation in the religious membership in the countries selected for our analysis in which Christian affiliations dominate), but personal closeness to God and religious service attendance increased the importance of altruistic motivations to volunteer. A more frequent service attendance reduced the emphasis put on self-interested MTV. Thus, religious people seem to have internalized other-oriented values, and they acquire these values in places of religious worship and through their stronger integration in religious networks. At the individual level, motivational accounts, and more specifically the emphasis put on altruistic versus self-interested reasons for volunteering, can therefore be related to both religious conviction and practice.

At the country level, we examined the influence of a national religious context, assuming that in a devout society both religious and secular volunteers will express more support for altruistic MTV. This hypothesis was based on both the religious culture and network arguments: In a religious country, altruism will be more central to the general value pattern and it will be more likely that religious people are part of the social network of secular volunteers. Contrary to our expectations, our analysis showed, first, that the mean religious service attendance in a country did not affect reported MTV, and second, that a more religious national context in terms of a larger segment of the population emphasizing the importance of God in their life had a negative influence on both altruistic and self-interested MTV. There are two possible explanations for the negative effect on altruistic MTV: First, when you know that there are a lot of religious people in your environment, you may assume that helping the poor and disadvantaged will be part of their role as citizens; hence, you feel less inclined or obliged yourself to volunteer for altruistic reasons. Another explanation could be that individual religiosity is contained in the private sphere, as something personal; hence, there is little religiously inspired "motive talk." On the other hand, the negative influence on self-interested reasons for volunteering could be explained by the fact that, in a religious context, to "gain" something from volunteering is met with disapproval. In other words, in a more devout country, self-oriented MTV is considered inappropriate and volunteers are less likely to report such motivations. This hampering effect of a high level of religiosity in a country on the support for self-interested MTV could be interpreted as a contextual effect of national religious culture. Surprisingly, however, there is no association between a high level of religiosity in a country and support of volunteers for altruistic reasons. Combined with the lack of influence of mean church attendance, the strong connection that exists between individual religiosity and altruistic MTV is not strengthened at the contextual level. That average church attendance is not associated with support for altruistic MTV suggests that more extended religious networks do not necessarily lead to a greater exposure to religious culture or greater interpersonal influence. This seems to confirm Lim and MacGregor's (2012) argument that such

6 A Cross-National Examination of the Motivation to Volunteer

a national average is a poor proxy for the influence of religiosity in the personal networks of individuals.

While, on the one hand, we expected a strong link between national religious context and altruistic MTV, on the other hand, a postmaterialist value pattern, commonly associated with higher levels of individualism, was linked to self-interested motivations. However, arguments could be made for a positive association between self-expressive values and altruistic MTV as well. In our analysis, we observed effects both at the individual and country level, but these effects go in opposite directions. Individuals with a stronger postmaterialist value pattern put less emphasis on self-interested reasons for volunteering, while countries with a stronger postmaterialist value pattern are more likely to express self-interested motivations. Similar to Welzel (2010), we thus found no conclusive evidence regarding the "civic" or "uncivic" nature of postmaterialist values. Furthermore, Welzel found mixed associations. While Welzel observed that higher country levels of self-expressive values were associated with higher levels of altruism, we found an opposite pattern. Based on our analysis, we may in any case conclude that both at the individual and country level, postmaterialist values do not seem to be at odds with altruistic MTV; they neither stimulate nor hamper support for such other-oriented reasons for volunteering.

Finally, we also looked at variables determined by institutional context as an alternative explanation for cross-national variations in MTV. Here we find partial evidence. As suggested in earlier exploratory studies, we find that when government social spending is high, as in social-democratic welfare regimes, altruistic MTV receives less support. This finding could also be linked to the fact that in a social-democratic regime, the nonprofit sector performs a more expressive role, given that most services are provided by government (Salamon et al. 2004). Our findings also show that the higher a government's share in the revenue structure of the nonprofit sector in a particular country is, the less likely volunteers are to express altruistic motivations. The total size of the nonprofit sector, in terms of the CSO workforce as a share of the economically active population, has a negative influence on self-interested MTV. While we had argued that a larger nonprofit sector would increase the support for altruistic MTV, this is not the case; the presence of a large organizational universe that represents social goals and values, embodied by (un-)paid workers, seems to moderate self-interested accounts of volunteer service. Contrary to our expectations, the dominant function of the nonprofit sector did not have an effect on MTV. Regarding the relative share of volunteers within the CSO workforce, the higher the total amount of volunteer labor, in terms of full-time equivalents, the less emphasis that is put on both altruistic and self-interested reasons for volunteering—a finding for which we do not have an explanation; possibly, this may be too abstract a measure that is not connected to individual volunteers' perceptions of the characteristics of the nonprofit sector. As already noted, the relative share of volunteer labor in the total CSO workforce is an aggregate measure, estimating the total number of hours given by volunteers. This measure creates an abstraction of the actual number of volunteers. Indeed, the effort of several volunteers is necessary to arrive at one FTE. Therefore, we also looked at the mean percentage of volunteers in the population. The higher the percentage of volunteers in the population, the more inclined volunteers are to emphasize altruistic motivations to volunteer. This may point to the embedded nature of volunteering to help others: a more general culture of voluntarism, as we hypothesized.

Although not the focus of our study, our results also revealed the influence of various individual background characteristics on MTV. We observed that female volunteers are more altruistically motivated than their male colleagues, a finding that resonates with earlier research that found women to be more disposed to care and to express stronger altruistic concerns and empathy than men. This is invariably explained in terms of either biology or socialization (Gerstel 2000; Musick and Wilson 2008). Younger volunteers are significantly more motivated by self-interested reasons than older volunteers, which is also consistent with earlier research. For example, as discussed above, young people are more focused on career-related reasons for volunteering, a typical life course effect. Surprisingly, higher educated volunteers express less support for both altruistic and self-interested reasons for volunteering. A possible methodological explanation may be that the self-interested reasons for volunteering measured in the survey do not match the self-oriented MTV of higher educated volunteers. Finally, we could discern a more instrumental use of volunteering by people who are not in a full-time employment position: Unemployed volunteers, students, housewives, and retired volunteers more frequently expressed self-interested reasons for volunteering; thus, for these categories, volunteering may perform functions otherwise served by a paid job, such as to gain new skills or useful experiences, or be undertaken for social reasons.

To conclude, some general insights can be drawn from our findings. Firstly, based on our cross-national analysis, we found evidence for a contextual understanding of the motivation to volunteer. Religious context, national value patterns, and welfare/nonprofit regimes influence the support for altruistic and self-interested reasons for volunteering. It thus makes sense to situate motivational accounts at the intersection between individual and society (cf. Wuthnow 1991), and not just treat them as a matter of inner psychological needs—as dominant theories of MTV claim. The emphasis put on certain types of motivations is clearly influenced by broader cultural and structural patterns. As a result, further cross-cultural examination of volunteer motivations is a fruitful option.

Secondly, the "traditional" beneficial relationship between religion and altruistic motivations holds at the individual level. While studies predicting participation in volunteering have mainly pointed to the importance of active religious networks, the reported reasons for volunteering are influenced by both religious beliefs and practices. Altruistic orientations are fostered through religious teachings and through active participation in a religious community. While we found some evidence for the influence of a religious national context, the evidence was partial and in an unexpected direction: On the one hand, no relationship was found between extensive religious networks and support for altruistic motivations; on the other, strong religious beliefs among the general population were negatively associated with both altruistic and self-interested MTV. In a more devout country, self-interested reasons for volunteering are therefore less culturally accepted, yet surprisingly the expression of altruistic motivations is also hampered. In other words, when there are more religious people in one's environment, there is less religiously inspired "motive talk." Just as traditional volunteering was a "good deed" that lost its sincerity when being "shown off" too much (Beck 1997), it seems that to expose one's "good intentions" too much undermines the credibility of these intentions in a more devout context.

Our multilevel findings on the relation between religion and MTV consequently imply that the process of secularization cannot be linked in a straightforward way to the weakening of altruistic MTV. Although a decline in individual church practice and individual beliefs would decrease the support for altruistic motivations, and increase the approval of self-interested MTV, in a more secular national context the support for altruistic MTV would, on the contrary, be stronger. Furthermore, we found other variables that had a positive effect on altruistic MTV. At the individual level, gender (females), age (older people) and political orientation (left wing) were positively correlated with altruistic MTV. At the country level, the prevalence of a postmaterial value pattern, which stands in opposition to traditional religious beliefs, did not represent a threat to feelings of altruism, and produced mixed findings concerning self-interested MTV. Furthermore, we may carefully conclude that welfare states with lower social spending, a large nonprofit sector with little revenue from government and an active citizenry, in terms of a high rate of volunteering, all stimulate the expression of altruistic motivations. On the other hand, there are also factors that hinder altruistic motivational accounts and stimulate the expression of self-interested MTV. Higher educated people are less likely to support altruistic motivations (yet surprisingly also less frequently mention self-interested MTV). The employment status of volunteers also plays a role: The nonemployed approach their volunteer involvement in a more instrumental way, as a means to acquire skills and experience, and to do something worthwhile. At the contextual level, a "crowding out" effect seems to occur: When government social spending is high, and nonprofit organizations to a large extent depend on government subsidies, volunteers are less inclined to express support for altruistic MTV.

In sum, the assumed transition from altruistic to self-interested motivations, which is claimed to result from processes of secularization and value change cannot therefore be confirmed unambiguously. Religion is not the only and unmistakable source of altruistic inspiration. In a secular context, there are also individual and contextual factors that are positively associated with altruistic MTV. While higher levels of individual religiosity will continue to foster altruism, more secular contexts will also continue to express a mix of altruistic and self-interested motivational accounts.

118 L. Hustinx et al.

Appendix

Table 6.3 The number and proportion of volunteers per country and as a percentage of the total volunteer population in the sample of 18 countries

Country	Number of volunteers	Total sample (100%)	Percentage of volunteers in total sample (%)	Percentage of total volunteer population in all countries (%)
Austria	668	1,460	45.8	9.3
Belgium	759	2,792	27.2	10.6
Britain	317	1,484	21.4	4.4
East Germany	535	1,336	40.0	7.4
Finland	202	588	34.4	2.8
France	228	1,002	22.8	3.2
Hungary	121	999	12.1	1.7
Ireland	263	1,000	26.3	3.7
Italy	467	2,018	23.2	6.5
Japan	127	1,011	12.6	1.8
Netherlands	356	1,017	35.0	5.0
Northern Ireland	78	304	25.7	1.1
Norway	466	1,239	37.6	6.5
Romania	264	1,103	23.9	3.7
Spain	310	4,147	7.5	4.3
Sweden	417	1,047	39.8	5.8
USA	969	1,839	52.7	13.5
West Germany	639	2,101	30.4	8.9
All countries	7,186	26,487	27.1	100.0

References

Batson, C. D., Schoenrade, P., & Ventis, L. (1993). *Religion and the individual*. New York: Oxford University Press.

Beck, U. (1997). Kinder der Freiheit: Wider das Lamento über den Werteverfall [Children of freedom: against loud regrets concerning the collapse in values]. In U. Beck (Ed.), *Kinder der Freiheit* (pp. 9–33). Frankfurt a. M.: Suhrkamp.

Bellah, R. N., Madsen, R., Sullivan, W. M., Swidler, A., & Tipton, S. M. (1985). *Habits of the heart: Individualism and commitment in American life*. Berkeley: University of California Press.

Bennett, W. L. (1998). The uncivic culture: Communication, identity, and the rise of lifestyle politics. *PS: Political Science & Politics, 31*(4), 741–761.

Berking, H. (1996). Solidary individualism: The moral impact of cultural modernisation in late modernity. In S. Lash, B. Szerszynski, & B. Wynne (Eds.), *Risk, environment and modernity: Towards a new ecology* (pp. 189–202). London: Sage.

Clary, E. G., & Miller, J. (1986). Socialization and situational influences on sustained altruism. *Child Development, 57*(6), 1358–1369.

Clary, E. G., & Orenstein, L. (1991). The amount and effectiveness of help: The relationship of motives and abilities to helping behavior. *Personality and Social Psychology Bulletin, 17*(1), 58–64.

Clary, E. G., & Snyder, M. (1999). The motivations to volunteer: Theoretical and practical considerations. *Current Directions in Psychological Science, 8*(5), 156–159.

Clary, E. G., Snyder, M., Ridge, R. D., Copeland, J., Stukas, A. A., Haugen, J., & Miene, P. (1998). Understanding and assessing the motivations of volunteers: A functional approach. *Journal of Personality and Social Psychology, 74*(6), 1516–1530.

Cnaan, R. A., & Goldberg-Glen, R. S. (1991). Measuring motivation to volunteer in human services. *Journal of Applied Behavioral Science, 27*(3), 269–284.

Cnaan, R. A., Kasternakis, A., & Wineburg, R. J. (1993). Religious people, religious congregations, and volunteerism in human services: Is there a link? *Nonprofit and Voluntary Sector Quarterly, 22*(1), 33–51.

Dekker, P., & Halman, L. (2003). Volunteering and values: An introduction. In P. Dekker & L. Halman (Eds.), *The values of volunteering: Cross-cultural perspectives* (pp. 1–18). New York: Kluwer Academic.

Delhey, J. (2009). From materialist to postmaterialist happiness? National affluence and determinants of life satisfaction in cross-national perspective. *World Values Research, 2*(2), 30–54.

Dickinson, M. J. (1999). Do gooders or do betters? An analysis of the motivation of student tutors. *Educational Research, 41*(2), 221–227.

Ellison, C. G. (1992). Are religious people nice people? Evidence from the National Survey of Black Americans. *Social Forces, 71*(2), 411–430.

Esping-Anderson, G. (1990). *The three worlds of welfare capitalism*. Cambridge: Polity.

Evers, A. (1999). Verschiedene Konzeptionalisierungen von Engagement. Ihre Bedeutung für Analyse und Politik [Different conceptualizations of commitment: Their meaning for analysis and politics]. In E. Kistler, H. Noll, & E. Priller (Eds.), *Perspektiven Gesellschaftlichen Zusammenhalts. Empirische Befunde, Praxiserfahrungen, Messkonzepte* (pp. 53–65). Berlin: Sigma.

Gerstel, N. (2000). The third shift: Gender and care work outside the home. *Qualitative Sociology, 23*(4), 467–483.

Gillespie, D., & King, A. E. (1985). Demographic understanding of volunteerism. *Journal of Sociology and Social Welfare, 12*(4), 798–816.

Graham, G. (1990). *The idea of Christian charity*. South Bend: University of Notre Dame Press.

Hall, M., Lasby, D., Gumulka, G., & Tryon, C. (2006). *Caring Canadians, involved Canadians: Highlights from the 2004 Canada survey of giving, volunteering and participating*. Toronto: Statistics Canada.

Handy, F., Cnaan, R. A., Hustinx, L., Kang, C., Brudney, J. L., Haski-Leventhal, D., Holmes, K., Meijs, L. C. P. M., Pessi, A. B., Ranade, B., Yamauchi, N., & Zrinscak, S. (2010). A cross-cultural examination of student volunteering: Is it all about résumé building? *Nonprofit and Voluntary Sector Quarterly, 39*(3), 498–523.

Handy, F., & Hustinx, L. (2009). Review essay: The why and how of volunteering. *Nonprofit Management and Leadership, 19*(4), 549–558.

Hustinx, L. (2001). Individualisation and new styles of youth volunteering: An empirical exploration. *Voluntary Action, 3*(2), 57–76.

Hustinx, L., Handy, F., Cnaan, R. A., Brudney, J. L., Pessi, A. B., & Yamauchi, N. (2010). Social and cultural origins of motivation to volunteer: A comparison of university students in six countries. *International Sociology, 25*(3), 349–382.

Hustinx, L., & Lammertyn, F. (2003). Collective and reflexive styles of volunteering: A sociological modernization perspective. *VOLUNTAS: International Journal of Voluntary and Nonprofit Organizations, 14*(2), 167–187.

Hwang, M., Grabb, E., & Curtis, J. (2005). Why get involved? Reasons for voluntary association activity among Americans and Canadians. *Nonprofit and Voluntary Sector Quarterly, 34*(3), 387–403.

Inglehart, R. (1971). The silent revolution in Europe: Intergenerational change in post-industrial societies. *The American Political Science Review, 65*(4), 991–1017.

Inglehart, R. (1997). *Modernization and postmodernization. Cultural, economic, and political change in 43 societies*. Princeton: Princeton University Press.

Inglehart, R., & Welzel, C. (2005). *Modernization, cultural change, and democracy*. New York: Cambridge University Press.

Kelley, J., & De Graaf, N. D. (1997). National context, parental socialization, and religious belief: Results from 15 nations. *American Sociological Review, 62*(4), 639–659.

Lam, P.-Y. (2002). As the flocks gather: How religion affects voluntary association participation. *Journal for the Scientific Study of Religion, 41*(3), 405–422.

Lim, C., & MacGregor, C. A. (2012). Religion and volunteering in context: Disentangling the contextual effects of religion on voluntary behavior. *American Sociological Review, 77*(5), 747–779.

Musick, M. A., & Wilson, J. (2008). *Volunteers: A social profile.* Indianapolis: Indiana University Press.

Ruiter, S., & De Graaf, N. D. (2006). National context, religiosity, and volunteering: Results from 53 countries. *American Sociological Review, 71*(2), 191–210.

Salamon, L. M., & Anheier, H. K. (1998). Social origins of civil society: Explaining the nonprofit sector cross-nationally. *VOLUNTAS: International Journal of Voluntary and Nonprofit Organizations, 9*(3), 213–248.

Salamon, L. M., Anheier, H. K., List, R., Toepler, S., & Sokolowski, S. W., et al. (1999). *Global civil society: Dimensions of the nonprofit sector.* Baltimore: The Johns Hopkins Center for Civil Society Studies.

Salamon, L. M., & Sokolowski, S. W. (2003). Institutional roots of volunteering: Toward a macro-structural theory of individual voluntary action. In P. Dekker & L. Halman (Eds.), *The values of volunteering: Cross-cultural perspectives* (pp. 71–90). New York: Kluwer Academic.

Salamon, L. M., & Sokolowski, S. W., et al. (2004). *Global civil society: Dimensions of the nonprofit sector* (Vol. 2). Bloomfield: Kumarian Press.

Salamon, L. M., & Sokolowski, S. W. (2009). *Bringing the 'social' and the 'political' to civil society: Social origins of civil society sector in 40 countries.* Paper presented at the 38th Annual Conference of the Association for Research on Nonprofit Organizations and Voluntary Action, Cleveland, OH, November 12–21, 2009.

Stark, R. & Bainbridge, W. (1996). A Theory of Religion. New Brunswick, N.J.: Rutgers University Press.

Stolle, D., & Hooghe, M. (2005). Inaccurate, exceptional, one-sided or irrelevant? The debate about the alleged decline of social capital and civic engagement in Western societies. *British Journal of Political Science, 35*(1), 149–167.

Van Der Meer, T., Grotenhuis, M. T., & Pelzer, B. (2010). Influential cases in multilevel modeling: A methodological comment. *American Sociological Review, 75*(1), 173–178.

Weiss Ozorak, E. (2003). Love of God and neighbor: Religion and volunteer service among college students. *Review of Religious Research, 44*(3), 285–299.

Welzel, C. (2010). How selfish are self-expression values? A civicness test. *Journal of Cross-Cultural Psychology, 41*(2), 152–174.

Wilson, J. (2000). Volunteering. *Annual Review of Sociology, 26,* 215–240.

Wilson, J., & Janoski, T. (1995). The contribution of religion to volunteer work. *Sociology of Religion, 56*(2), 137–153.

Winniford, J. C., Carpenter, D. S., & Grider, C. (1995). An analysis of the traits and motivations of college students involved in service organizations. *Journal of College Student Development, 36*(1), 27–38.

World values survey, 1981–1984 and 1990–1993 [Data file]. World Values Study Group. Ann Arbor, MI: Inter-university Consortium for Political and Social Research [distributor]; 1994 (ICPSR; 6160).

Wood, J. R., & Hougland, J. G. (1990). The role of religion in philanthropy. In J. Van Til & Associates (Eds.), *Critical issues in American philanthropy* (pp. 29–33). San Francisco: Jossey Bass.

Wuthnow, R. (1990). Religion and the voluntary spirit in the United States: Mapping the terrain. In R. Wuthnow, V. A. Hodgkinson, & Associates (Eds.), *Faith and philanthropy in America: Exploring the role of religion in America's voluntary sector* (pp. 3–21). San Francisco: Jossey-Bass.

Wuthnow, R. (1991). *Acts of compassion.* Princeton: Princeton University Press.

Wymer, W. W. (1997). A religious motivation to volunteer? Exploring the linkage between volunteering and religious values. *Journal of Nonprofit and Public Sector Marketing, 5*(3), 3–17.

Ziemek, S. (2006). Economic analysis of volunteers' motivations: A cross-country study. *Journal of Socio-Economics, 35*(3), 532–555.

Chapter 7
Volunteering Among Church Attendees in Australia

Individual and Collective Dimensions

John Bellamy and Rosemary Leonard

Introduction

Christian churches are significant organizations in western society that subscribe to the value of helping others. Churches have long played a role in meeting social and welfare needs, for example through congregations and parishes working in their local communities. Help may be provided through the programmes and agencies of Christian denominations, sometimes acting on their own initiative or, in some contexts, on behalf of governments. Such help may be given through individual church attendees volunteering to take part in the activities of community organizations which may have little or no connection with their church involvement.

One way of conceptualising these relationships between individuals, congregations and the wider community is through a social capital framework. The social capital theorist, Robert Putnam, defined social capital as 'those features of social organization, such as trust, norms and networks, that can improve the efficiency of society by facilitating coordinated actions' (Putnam 1993, p. 167). As significant social institutions, churches have often been viewed as making a positive contribution to social capital. Putnam has observed that faith communities are the single most important repository of social capital in America and has identified the links between religiosity and increased volunteering, giving and civic engagement (Putnam 2002; Putnam and Campbell 2010). Formal volunteering through not-for-profit organizations such as churches has been described as the core of social capital, as people come together in an organised way for the benefit of others (Leonard and Onyx 2004).

J. Bellamy (✉)
Social Policy & Research Unit, Anglicare Sydney, Sydney, Australia
e-mail: jbellamy@anglicare.org.au

Australian Catholic University, Strathfield, Australia

R. Leonard
School of Social Sciences, University of Western Sydney, Penrith, Australia

Ecosystem Sciences, Commonwealth Scientific and Industrial Research
Organisation (CSIRO), Acton ACT, Australia

L. Hustinx et al. (eds.), *Religion and Volunteering,* Nonprofit and Civil Society Studies,
DOI 10.1007/978-3-319-04585-6_7, © Springer International Publishing Switzerland 2015

Although there has been some debate in the literature about the best way to define social capital, all conceptualizations of social capital refer to the advantages that accrue from social networks. Thus, activities that increase opportunities for social networking should increase social capital. This has led researchers to consider the level of participation in activities and organizations as good indicators of within-group social capital, assuming that as people become more involved in a group, their network of relationships will grow and strengthen. As van Staveren and Knorringa (2007) point out, it is the dynamics within and between groups that generate social capital.

A distinction has been drawn in the literature between bonding social capital and bridging social capital (Woolcock and Narayan 2000). Bonding social capital is associated with dense, multiplex networks, long-term reciprocity, thick trust, shared norms and less instrumentality (that is, not specifically developed for personal or group advantage). Bridging social capital is theorised to be associated with large, loose networks with weak ties, relatively strict reciprocity, thin trust, greater risk of norm violation and more instrumentality (Leonard and Onyx 2003).

The focus of this chapter is on bridging social capital as it occurs in relation to Christian congregations. 'Bridging' has been used in different ways in the literature, including:

- The extent of relationships beyond a group. These can include ties that congregations create with social service agencies and the relationships that members of one group can create by participating in other groups (Wuthnow 2004).
- Relationships that cross demographic divides such as class or ethnicity (e.g. Portes 1998).
- Bridges across gaps between networks where there has hitherto been little connection (e.g. Burt 2004), which may occur as a result of geographic distance or organizational structure.
- The capacity to access resources such as information, knowledge and finance from sources external to an organization or community (e.g. Woolcock and Narayan 2000).

This chapter follows Paxton's (1999) description of bridging and bonding social capital as between-group and within-group social capital. In the current chapter, 'bonding' will refer to the social capital that may be developed within a congregation and 'bridging' will refer to the social capital that develops through church attendees interacting with other groups in the wider community, including volunteering. It should be noted that under this definition, denominational organizations would be considered to be outside the congregation, the relationship between them being more typically a form of bridging than bonding. Compared with the bonding between attendees within a congregation, the links between a centralised denominational organization and its congregations would be characterised by far fewer personal relationships than within the congregation itself, more obvious and explicit terms of reciprocity and thin trust. In terms of instrumentality, agency is often the focus between the denominational organization and the congregation, with volunteering and financial giving occurring principally to increase agency. Even the more local situation between a congregation and a school within a parish would carry many of the hallmarks of bridging.

An aspect of bridging that has received little attention in the literature is whether the bridge is formed by an individual, a subset of the group such as a delegation or the majority of the group. Although Burt (1998) has demonstrated the advantages to an individual of bridging, a group might expect a greater advantage if the bridging was more of a group-based activity. This chapter will consider bridging activity both as an activity carried out by individual attendees in volunteering beyond their congregation, and as a group activity which a section of or all the congregation may undertake in the wider community.

This chapter will also consider the relationship between bridging and bonding, which has received at least some attention in the literature. It has been concluded that excessive bonding can restrict the possibilities for bridging (Fukuyama 1995; Granovetter 1973; Molina-Morales and Martínez-Fernández 2010; Portes 1998; Rostila 2010). However, others question the direction of causation where there is strong bonding and little bridging (Crowe 2007; Donoghue and Tranter 2010). For instance, building up the internal resources of a group can be a legitimate strategy, especially when it appears that there are few opportunities to acquire external resources through bridging, as in the case of minority groups experiencing discrimination.

The examination of the impact of bonding upon bridging raises the broader question of what are the motivations that lead individual church attendees to volunteer in the wider community. To what extent does bonding experienced within the congregation itself account for individuals being motivated to volunteer for other community organizations and to what degree is it a function of the individual's own beliefs? The literature on volunteer motivations is large and complex with numerous approaches and typologies. Some examples are Deci and Ryan's (2000) self-determination theory, which focuses on the three core psychological needs of competence, connectedness and autonomy; Edwards' (2005) eight dimensions of motivation among museum volunteers (personal needs, relationship network, self-expression, available time, social needs, purposive needs, free time and personal interest); the Australian Bureau of Statistics' (2001) two motivational categories of helping others or the community and gaining personal satisfaction; Shye's functioning modes of cultural, social, physical or mental wellbeing (Shye 2010).

The Volunteer Functions Inventory (VFI, Clary and Snyder 1999) was selected as the basis for identifying motivations in this research because it has been developed with large samples and used effectively in a wide variety of contexts. The functional approach allows for the possibility that people will have multiple motivations for volunteering. The six motivations identified provide a good range of distinct motivations broadly covering those that appear in most other typologies. The VFI categories are: values, expressing or acting on important values such as humanitarianism; understanding, learning more about the world or using skills; enhancement, growing and developing psychologically; career, gaining career-related experience; social, strengthening social relationships and protective, reducing guilt or addressing personal problems. However, none of these typologies of volunteering specifically cover religious motivations and it was important that survey respondents were able to recognise the types of reasons with which they would be familiar. So in the present research, items used were based on the VFI categories and some items were added to address religious motivations.

Churches and Volunteering in Australia

The present research has been conducted in the context of Christian churches in Australia, in order to identify the nature of bridging between church congregations and the wider community. The research was partly funded by an Australian Research Council (ARC) Linkage Projects grant and was conducted jointly by the University of Western Sydney and NCLS Research. The focus of the research on churches reflects the interests of the partner agency, NCLS Research, a research group supported at the time of the study by the Catholic, Anglican and Uniting Churches.

Most Australians identify with a Christian denomination. In the 2011 national census (Australian Bureau of Statistics 2011), 61% of Australians identified as Christian, 22% had no religion and 9% did not state a religious affiliation. Only 7% identified with a non-Christian religion. Far fewer, however, attend a church regularly. The International Social Survey Programme (ISSP) survey found that 16% of Australian adults claimed to attend church monthly or more often, with 13% claiming to attend every week or nearly every week (ISSP 2009). Church headcounts point to even lower rates of attendance, with an estimated 1.66 million people attending Catholic, Anglican and Protestant churches each week, or 8.8% of the then population of 18.77 million people (Bellamy and Castle 2004).

From a historical perspective, the churches in Australia have been very active both in the establishment of charities for furthering social welfare objectives and in the establishment of schools. The Catholic Church is the largest non-Government provider of school education in Australia. Catholic, Anglican and Uniting Churches as well as the Salvation Army run most of Australia's largest charities. Thus, churches in Australia provide the social organizations necessary to carry out significant volunteer work.

Although many studies have found a positive relationship between a person's religiosity and volunteering (e.g. Shye 2010; Perry et al. 2008), other studies have found a weak relationship or none (Yeung 2004, p. 402). In the Australian context, research has generally found that religion has a positive impact on volunteering; people's religious identity and frequency of attendance at religious services are both related positively to volunteering (Lyons and Nivison-Smith 2006). Furthermore, there is a positive correlation between hours spent on volunteering within congregations and hours volunteering beyond congregations (Leonard and Bellamy 2006, 2010).

One of the reasons for the different outcomes in studies of the relationship between religion and volunteering may be the kind of volunteering that is looked at. Although most churches employ paid staff, many roles are carried out by volunteers.

In Australia, it has been found that around 50% of church attendees have a voluntary role of some kind within the congregation; these roles can include preaching, leading worship, running groups for children and youth and administrative and business roles (Bellamy and Kaldor 2002). Volunteer roles are necessary for the successful operation of church congregations. This kind of volunteering needs to be distinguished from volunteering in community groups or social service organizations outside of the church, which is the subject of this chapter.

A related question for researchers in Australia has been whether the relationship between volunteering and religion is best explained by individual belief and commitment, or whether it is better explained by the activity of congregations in recruiting attendees into volunteer work. Lyons and Nivison-Smith (2006) found that committed belief was the key driver of individual volunteering, not the impact of religious networks. However, other Australian researchers have found that churches are important sites for volunteer recruitment, suggesting the importance of relationships and networks within congregations (Hughes and Black 2002; Evans and Kelley 2004).

The current chapter examines both sides of this question. The advantage of drawing upon a sample of church attendees is that the study has been able to look at the impact of various aspects of congregational life and the theological orientations of church attendees in some detail. Whilst it is not possible in such a sample to examine the relative impact of unbelief or of different faiths, the study has been able to consider the effects of different theological orientations in a nuanced way that would not have been possible in a broader population study.

There are tens of thousands of not-for-profit organizations in Australia, ranging from small arts and craft organizations and local sports clubs through to large social service organizations and charities. Given the range of volunteering activities in the wider community, it is likely that motivations for involvement will vary with the type of activity. In Australia, volunteering for recreation and sporting organizations is the largest domain of volunteering activity, accounting for 37% of volunteers. Volunteering for community and welfare organizations (22%) and education and training organizations (18%) are the next largest domains, apart from volunteering for religious organizations such as churches (22%). Volunteering for social action, social justice or lobby activities are among the smaller categories of volunteering (Australian Bureau of Statistics 2010). These four domains were selected for detailed study because they accounted for the majority of volunteering activity outside of local churches and also covered many of Australia's church-run charities and schools. Examining these domains provided the best approach, within the constraints of the survey, for gaining an appreciation of volunteering by church attendees beyond their local church, with only minimal deviation from what would be the overall picture had it been possible to explore all domains in depth.

A further aspect to consider in relation to volunteer motivations is whether the community organization that is the context for the volunteering is itself a church-run organization or a secular organization. This aspect will also be examined in the current chapter in relation to volunteer motivations as the type of motivation may vary among church attendees depending upon whether the community organization is run by a church, has a Christian heritage or is a purely secular organization.

Research Questions

The discussion suggests at least two sets of research questions for examination. The primary set of questions is to do with the relationship between congregational bonding capital and congregational bridging to the wider community. These primary research questions are:

- Does congregational bonding stimulate individual volunteering in the wider community and, if so, how?
- Does congregational bonding stimulate collective bridging to the wider community and, if so, how?

A secondary set of research questions considers the types of stated personal motivations found among church attendees who volunteer in the community. Answers to these questions extend the understanding of how bridging is occurring between Christian congregations and the broader community. Such questions include:

- While religious motivations play a major role in individuals volunteering within congregations, how important are such motivations when it comes to church attendees volunteering beyond the congregation?
- Are the main stated reasons for volunteering altruistic, instrumental or more intrinsically 'religious'?
- How do these stated motivations vary depending upon the type of volunteering context (e.g. whether the community organisation is church-run or secular)?

Method

Data Collection and Sample

The National Church Life Survey (NCLS) is a major survey of church attendees aged 15 years or over carried out every 5 years, involving all the major Christian denominations in Australia. Attendees at participating congregations complete a four-page survey. In the 2006 NCLS, respondents were asked to indicate if they would be interested in participating in further research by becoming part of a research panel. This chapter draws on data obtained from this research panel of church attendees drawn from across Australia.

Those attendees who indicated their interest in taking part in further research were sent a preliminary questionnaire for a study of social capital. More than 6,000 attendees completed this preliminary questionnaire that identified their demographic and religious profiles. Of these, 3,363 responded to a second, much longer questionnaire. Participants who had provided email addresses were sent emails with a hyperlink to a website containing this main questionnaire. Those without email addresses (about half of the entire panel) were mailed the main questionnaire. An individual code linked the data from the preliminary and main questionnaires for each respondent.

Most respondents to the main questionnaire were religiously committed people, with nine out of ten attending church weekly or more often. Most respondents (79 %) had a voluntary leadership or ministry role at their church for example in administration, children's ministry, music or teaching. The respondents tended to be older than church attendees generally, with 78 % being aged over 50 compared with 59 % of attendees in the NCLS. Just over half of the respondents were female (52 %). Some 45 % of respondents had a university degree and about half were employed (full-time or part-time) or self-employed. Some 8 % of participants were born in a non-English speaking country, which is about the same proportion as found in the NCLS.

Individuals were asked about their experience of their congregation and their own levels of activity at church. Other questions were asked about their perceptions of their congregation. These questions treated the respondent as a key informant and examined the respondent's impression of their congregation's level of bonding. Respondents will differ in their knowledge of their congregation and so some will be better key informants than others. The potential negatives of being in groups cannot be ignored (Abbott 2009), so respondents were also asked about perceptions of congregational divisions and conflicts.

Scale Development

As mentioned in the Introduction, bridging has been defined in the current chapter as between-group social capital and bonding as within-group social capital, where the group is the congregation. Bridging activity can be seen as both an individual activity of attendees volunteering beyond their congregation, and as a group activity which a section of, or all, the congregation undertake together in the wider community.

A number of the key concepts in the study, including bonding, bridging and volunteering activity, have multiple facets and are generally not susceptible to measurement through the use of a single global item. Consequently scales were derived from multiple items by using Exploratory Factor Analysis on one half of the sample and then confirmed on the other half using Confirmatory Factor Analysis in Mplus. All scales achieved a reliability of 0.7 or more as measured by Coefficient H, indicating good scale reliability (Holmes-Smith 2011). Two bridging scales were developed which measure individual volunteering in the wider community and congregational bridging to the wider community. Three sub-scales were developed which measure different aspects of congregational bonding.

Individual Volunteering in the Community Scale Arising out of the factor analysis, a scale of individual volunteering in the wider community was created from the following items:

- Hours of volunteer work carried out in the wider community in the past month
- Number of wider community organizations participated in during the past 2 years
- Number of wider community organizations for which volunteer work was carried out in the past 2 years
- Having been a spokesperson for a wider community organization/group in the past 2 years
- Your advice was sought on a community issue in the past 2 years (excluding surveys)

Congregational Bridging Scale Four items in the survey were scaled to measure the degree of congregational bridging to the wider community. The data is from the viewpoint of the respondent as a key informant of congregational activity; as a further stage in the research, it is intended to add more objective data from the larger National Church Life Survey database to more accurately describe congregational activity in the wider community. Items forming the congregational bridging scale include:

- The congregation has been effectively helping people in the wider community
- Leaders at church keep attendees strongly focused on connecting with people in the wider community
- People at church mostly have similar attitudes to actively engaging in community service
- Involvement of the congregation in other community organizations and events (e.g. community fairs, marches, beautification programmes, Carols by Candlelight)

The first and fourth items focus on the external activity of the congregation while the second and third items focus upon the internal attitudes of the congregation. The third item could potentially register strong agreement where the congregation has mostly negative attitudes to engaging in community service; however, the correlation with the other items showed that respondents interpreted this in terms of positive attitudes to community service.

Congregational Bonding Sub-Scales Previous analysis (Leonard and Bellamy 2013, forthcoming) using Structural Equation Modeling (SEM) identified a single underlying congregational bonding factor, with three primary sub-dimensions, measured by the following sub-scales:

- *Friendships in the congregation*: Including the number of close friends who are part of the congregation, ease of making friendships at the congregation, being satisfied with friendships at church, the sense that the congregation is close-knit and a willingness among attendees to go out of their way to help each other (Standardised pathway coefficient = 0.53).

7 Volunteering Among Church Attendees in Australia

- *Congregational unity*: Since personal relationships can also be divisive, data was collected from respondents about perceived congregational divisions, personal experiences of criticism or excessive demands. The resulting scale also included individual responses about trust in people at church and the outcome of any conflict at church (Standardised pathway coefficient = 0.48).
- *Collective efficacy*: Respondents provided their perceptions regarding the ability of their congregation's leaders to bring people together to make things happen, confidence that the congregation would come together to solve serious problems, willingness of the congregation to try new things, the presence of a clear congregational vision for its mission and confidence that the congregation would achieve its vision (Standardised pathway coefficient = 0.83).

Level of Church Involvement The level of church involvement was not found to be part of the underlying bonding factor (Leonard and Bellamy 2013, forthcoming). A separate Level of Church Involvement scale was developed comprising frequency of attending services, number of years at the congregation, number of roles in the congregation, involvement in special projects, having a leadership role or being a spokesperson for the congregation.

Motivations for Volunteering in Four Domains and Three Organizational Types

Participants were asked about motivations in four specific domains of volunteering activity, apart from volunteering within a church. The four domains were:

- Schools
- Recreation, sport or leisure organizations/groups
- Community service, care or welfare activities
- Social action, social justice or lobby groups/activities

For each domain, three types of organizations were distinguished:

- Organizations associated with a local church
- Other religious organizations
- Secular organizations

For each of the four domains, there were six questions regarding the stated reasons for volunteering based on Clary and Snyder's VFI (1999) and two specifically religious reasons for volunteering. It should be noted that, given the need to cover four domains and the constraints of the survey meant that single items rather than the full VFI scales were used to measure each function. The single items were:

- To meet the needs of others or to make the world a better place (reflecting VFI values function)
- To use my skills or to gain more knowledge (reflecting VFI understanding function)

- To grow more as a person through volunteer activities (reflecting VFI enhancement function)
- To gain career-related experience (reflecting VFI career function)
- To meet new people or to spend time with people I know (reflecting VFI social function)
- To address my own personal needs or problems (reflecting VFI protective function)
- As part of living out my Christian values or living out my faith
- As part of God's mission to the world

For each of these motivations, respondents could indicate that it was the main reason, a very important reason, of some importance or not a reason for me.

To assess the relationship among the religious and VFI items, Exploratory Factor Analyses were conducted for each domain. In each domain, the pattern was the same:

- The Religious Motivation Factor consisting of the two religious items and the values function item
- The Personal Motivation Factor consisting of the other five VFI items

Each factor was confirmed using SEM and two scales for each domain were formed with Coef. $H > 0.7$ indicating strong reliability (Holmes-Smith 2011).

Demographics and Religious Orientation

The survey contained several standard demographic measures including Age, Gender, Highest Education Level and Country of Birth.

Respondents were asked to identify the Denomination of their congregation. They were also asked whether they personally identified with any of several theological streams. Catholicism and Anglo-Catholicism are major theological streams in the Australian context, with Evangelicalism and Pentecostalism being two other major streams. In contrast to these theologically conservative streams, Liberalism is another significant stream. These streams tend to cut across denominational boundaries and are often influential in many denominations.

Analysis

1. Volunteering as an individual in the community was analysed using correlations and a regression analysis with the individual volunteering scale as the dependent variable and age, gender, education, denomination, theological orientation, levels of congregational involvement and congregational bonding as the independent variables.

2. Congregational bridging to the community was analysed using correlations and a regression analysis with the congregational bridging scale as the dependent variable and age, gender, education, denomination, theological orientation, levels of congregational involvement and congregational bonding as the independent variables.
3. Reasons for volunteering in the wider community by type of organization (local church, other religious, secular) was assessed through four repeated measures linear models, one for each domain (school, sport/ recreation, welfare, social action) with the two composite volunteer motivations (Religious and Personal) as dependent variables and type of organization as the independent variable.

Findings

Correlates of Individual Volunteering and Congregational Bridging

It was noted in the Method section that most respondents in this sample have a voluntary role of some kind within their congregation. In addition to this, the vast majority (96%) had participated in the activities of at least one wider community organization outside of their local church in the past couple of years, while 82% indicated that they had undertaken other types of volunteer work apart from volunteer roles in their congregation.

Among various demographic characteristics, a person's highest education level ($r=0.10$; $p<0.001$) and being born overseas in a non-English-speaking country ($r=-0.07$; $p<0.01$) are weakly but significantly correlated with the Individual Volunteering in the Community scale used in this research.

The church attendees in this sample come from a wide range of theological and denominational backgrounds. Table 7.1 shows that self-identified theological orientation and the denomination of the respondent's congregation are weakly related or unrelated to both individual volunteering levels and congregational bridging to the wider community. An exception to this finding is being involved with the Uniting Church, which is positively and significantly correlated with individual volunteering. However, being involved with other Protestant denominations (as a single grouping) was negatively but weakly correlated with individual volunteering levels.

Whilst Table 7.1 shows that very little individual volunteering behaviour in the wider community is explained by theological and denominational background, Table 7.2 shows that friendships, unity and collective efficacy—all of which are central to bonding social capital—are also either weakly related or unrelated to individual volunteering in the community. The negative correlation with bonding as unity suggests that situations of congregational disunity may also be a catalyst for some attendees choosing to increase their volunteer involvement with other organizations.

Table 7.1 Bivariate correlations of individual volunteering and congregational bridging with individual theological orientation and denomination (r)

	Individual volunteering in the wider community	Congregational bridging to the wider community
Respondent's theological orientation		
Catholic/Anglo-Catholic	ns	ns
Evangelical	ns	ns
Reformed	ns	−0.06*
Charismatic	ns	ns
Pentecostal	ns	0.06*
Liberal	ns	−0.07**
Denomination of respondent's congregation		
Anglican	ns	−0.06*
Catholic	ns	ns
Uniting	0.10***	ns
Other Protestant	−0.07**	ns

*$p < 0.05$; **$p < 0.01$; ***$p < 0.001$

Table 7.2 Bivariate correlations of bridging, bonding and congregational involvement (r)

	Individual volunteering in the wider community	Congregational bridging to the wider community
Congregational bonding—collective efficacy	ns	0.61***
Congregational bonding—unity	−0.12***	0.26***
Congregational bonding—friendships	0.08**	0.41***
Involvement level in the congregation	0.44***	ns

**$p < 0.01$; ***$p < 0.001$

It could also be that with increasing unity in the congregation, individual focus and satisfaction are more firmly found in the congregation itself, meaning that volunteering outside the congregation becomes a less attractive option. This interpretation, however, is tempered by the much stronger positive correlation between an individual's involvement level in the congregation, which includes both volunteering at church and frequency of attendance, and individual volunteering in the community. This suggests that attendees who are highly involved in their local congregations are not doing so at the expense of volunteering in other community organizations; rather a church involvement may well motivate attendees to also volunteer elsewhere.

However, Table 7.2 also shows that the picture is very different when it comes to congregational-level bridging to the wider community. Here all congregational bonding measures are correlated positively and strongly or moderately with congregational bridging to the wider community. The strongest association is between bonding as collective efficacy, or the sense that together we can achieve things, and congregational bridging. A moderate correlation also exists with bonding in the form of friendships.

7 Volunteering Among Church Attendees in Australia

Table 7.3 Predictors of congregational bridging to the community

Source	B	Std error	Beta	t	Sig.
Congregational bonding—collective efficacy	3.69	0.19	0.54	18.96	<0.0005
Congregational bonding—friendships	1.02	0.21	0.14	4.96	<0.0005
Denomination—Uniting Church	0.42	0.14	0.11	3.05	0.002
Involvement level in the congregation	−0.39	0.14	−0.07	−2.81	0.005
Reformed faith	−0.25	0.11	−0.05	−2.24	0.025
Evangelical faith	−0.17	0.08	−0.06	−2.08	0.038
Traditionalist faith	−0.16	0.08	−0.05	−1.89	0.059
Catholic/Anglo-Catholic faith	0.18	0.11	0.06	1.69	0.092
Fundamentalist faith	0.30	0.19	0.04	1.55	0.121
Pentecostal faith	−0.19	0.13	−0.04	−1.51	0.130
Highest educational qualification	0.06	0.04	0.03	1.47	0.141
Denomination—other Protestant	0.18	0.12	0.06	1.47	0.141
New Age faith	−0.38	0.29	−0.03	−1.32	0.186
Denomination—Anglican	0.10	0.10	0.03	1.00	0.320
15-year age bracket	−0.03	0.03	−0.02	−0.83	0.409
Gender (male)	−0.05	0.06	−0.02	−0.77	0.444
Liberal faith	−0.08	0.11	−0.02	−0.72	0.473
Congregational bonding—unity	0.06	0.17	0.01	0.37	0.711
Growth in the Christian faith	0.03	0.10	0.01	0.33	0.743
Country of birth (NESB)	0.02	0.05	0.01	0.33	0.744
Moderate faith	0.01	0.10	0.00	0.13	0.901
Charismatic faith	0.00	0.11	0.00	0.03	0.977
Adj R^2=0.383					

Reference categories: Denomination—Catholic, Faith type—don't identify with such descriptions

Predictors of Congregational Bridging to the Community

Regression analysis was carried out to identify the key predictors of congregational bridging, the results of which are shown in Table 7.3. Table 7.3 highlights the importance of congregational bonding in predicting congregational bridging. Collective efficacy in particular predicts a large part of the variance in congregational bridging (Beta=0.54), with some 38 % of the variance in congregational bridging being predicted overall. The strength of friendships within congregations (Beta=0.14) and being involved in the Uniting Church (Beta=0.11) also made positive contributions to the model, whilst involvement level in the congregation and having an Evangelical or Reformed faith made smaller negative contributions.

Predictors of Individual Volunteering

In keeping with previous Australian research (Leonard and Bellamy 2010; Lyons and Nivison-Smith 2006), Table 7.4 shows that an individual's congregational involvement level, which includes both volunteering at church and frequency of attendance, was the most significant predictor of individual volunteering in the community (Beta=0.38). It is notable that aspects of congregational bonding generally do not feature in the model, with the exception of bonding as unity, which makes a small negative contribution (Beta=−0.06). This relative lack of contribution by congregational bonding provides some support for Lyons and Nivison-Smith's (2006) position that there are church attendees who are committed to volunteer across a range of contexts, irrespective of the impact of the social networks within their congregations.

Demographics, such as highest education level and increasing age, also make an independent, positive contribution to the model, while being born in a non-English-speaking country makes a small negative contribution (Beta=−0.06). These results highlight the positive effects of education in providing both vision and skills for volunteer work, while the positive contribution of increasing age is consistent with the greater likelihood of volunteering among middle aged and older people in Australia (Australian Bureau of Statistics 2010). The negative contribution of country of birth may reflect barriers to do with English language literacy and relative opportunity for wider community participation among migrant groups.

Furthermore, Table 7.4 shows that personal beliefs also have a small independent impact, with particular theological orientations being present in the model—a traditional approach to faith making a positive contribution to predicting individual volunteering (Beta=0.06) and a Charismatic theological orientation making a negative contribution (Beta=−0.07).

Motivations for Volunteering

Motivations to volunteer beyond the congregation were explored for four domains; schools, sport, recreation or leisure organizations, community service or welfare organizations and social action, justice or lobby groups. Participants were able to respond for any or all the domains and, in the past 2 years, 82 % had volunteered in at least one domain and 11 % had volunteered in all four.

In these four domains, altruistic reasons and religious reasons were the most commonly stated reasons for their volunteering activity. Table 7.5 shows that for each of the four volunteering domains investigated, 'meeting the needs of others', was the most frequently stated reason for volunteering. This was closely followed by 'living out Christian values or faith' and volunteering 'as part of God's mission to the world. Reasons to do with personal growth and the use of skills were the next most common reasons across the four volunteering domains. The least frequently reported reasons were those to do with the meeting of personal needs through volunteering, such as career enhancement and addressing one's own personal problems or needs.

As described in the Method section, these eight motivations factored into two clear strong factors: a Religious Motivations factor which included the religious motivations and meeting the needs of others and a Personal Motivations factor which included the other listed motivations. These two factors were then used to ex-

7 Volunteering Among Church Attendees in Australia

Table 7.4 Predictors of individual volunteering in the community

Source	B	Std error	Beta	t	Sig.
Involvement level in the congregation	1.49	0.11	0.38	13.23	<0.0005
Highest education level	0.11	0.03	0.09	3.45	0.001
Charismatic faith	−0.23	0.09	−0.07	−2.62	0.009
Country of birth (NESB)	−0.10	0.04	−0.06	−2.40	0.017
Age group (15 year)	0.06	0.03	0.06	2.25	0.024
Congregational bonding—unity	−0.28	0.14	−0.06	−2.03	0.043
Traditionalist faith	0.14	0.07	0.06	2.01	0.045
Catholic/Anglo-Catholic faith	0.17	0.09	0.08	1.93	0.054
Evangelical faith	−0.12	0.07	−0.06	−0.190	0.059
Denomination—Uniting Church	0.17	0.11	0.06	1.49	0.137
Reformed faith	−0.13	0.09	−0.04	−1.41	0.160
Moderate faith	−0.10	0.08	−0.03	−1.25	0.213
Cong. bonding—collective efficacy	−0.19	0.16	−0.04	−1.16	0.246
Denomination—Anglican	−0.09	0.08	−0.04	−1.07	0.284
Denomination—other Protestant	−0.08	0.10	−0.04	−0.79	0.432
New Age faith	−0.10	0.24	−0.01	−0.40	0.688
Gender (male)	0.02	0.05	0.01	0.38	0.704
Growth in the Christian faith	0.03	0.08	0.01	0.35	0.730
Pentecostal faith	−0.03	0.11	−0.01	−0.29	0.772
Fundamentalist faith	−0.03	0.15	−0.01	−0.22	0.829
Liberal faith	0.01	0.09	0.00	0.07	0.942
Congregational bonding—friendships	0.01	0.17	0.00	0.05	0.962
Adj $R^2 = 0.173$					

Reference categories: Denomination—Catholic, Faith type—don't identify with such descriptions

Table 7.5 Stated reasons for doing volunteer work in four domains

	Domain of volunteer work (mean scores 0–1)			
Reason given	Schools (n=871)	Sport, leisure or recreation activities (n=1230)	Community service or welfare activities (n=1554)	Social action, social justice or lobby groups (n=808)
Meet the needs of others	0.65	0.67	0.77	0.80
Live out Christian values or faith	0.63	0.57	0.69	0.71
As part of God's mission to the world	0.60	0.53	0.64	0.67
Use skills or gain knowledge	0.44	0.49	0.45	0.41
Grow as a person	0.37	0.43	0.46	0.38
Meet new people or spend time with friends	0.31	0.45	0.39	0.31
Gain career-related experience	0.15	0.12	0.11	0.10
Address personal needs or problems	0.10	0.17	0.13	0.14
Another reason	0.29	0.20	0.15	0.13

Table 7.6 Motivations for doing volunteer work by type of organization

Reason given	Type of organization (mean scores 0–1)		
	As part of a local church	Another religious organization	A secular organization
School			
Religious motivation	0.63	0.60	0.61
Personal motivation	0.30	0.32	0.28
Sport, leisure or recreation organization			
Religious motivation	0.68	0.70	0.43
Personal motivation	0.38	0.37	0.36
Community service or welfare organization			
Religious motivation	0.71	0.72	0.53
Personal motivation	0.25	0.25	0.26
Social action, justice or lobby group			
Religious motivation	0.74	0.80	0.55
Personal motivation	0.35	0.27	0.29

plore how motivation varied with the type of organization in which the volunteering occurred: the local church, a denominational agency or other religious organization or a non-religious (secular) organization.

Table 7.6 shows the means for the two motivation scales for each domain by type of organization. First, as expected from the table of the separate motivations, religious motivations are stronger than personal motivations for all domains. (F values: school = 607.9, sport/recreation = 424.6, community service = 2,392.9, social action = 1,005.7. All F values were significant at $p < 0.0005$.)

For type of organization, however, there was a difference between the school domain and the other three domains. For schools, there were no substantial variations in motivation based on the type of organization (For the effect of organization $F = 0.6$ NS and for the interaction with the motivation scales $F = 1.4$ NS). However, religious reasons for volunteering were less likely to be given when the organization was a secular sport, recreation or leisure organization, a secular community service or welfare organization or a secular social action, justice or lobby group. (F values for the interaction of type of organisation and motivation scales: sport/recreation = 83.6; community service = 68.3; social action = 36.1. All F values were significant at $p < 0.0005$.)

The overall picture here is that, no matter the domain for the volunteering, church attendees say that they mostly volunteer out of love for God and love of neighbour rather than for reasons of personal interest. Further, although religious reasons still remained prominent for doing volunteer work even within secular organizations, it appears that for some church attendees the connection between their volunteer work and their faith was less clear when the volunteering was done for a secular organization or group other than a school. While it is unclear why the religious motivation remains strong for volunteering in schools irrespective of the type of organization, part of the reason is likely to be the teaching of religious instruction by volunteers in public schools in Australia.

Discussion

Individual Volunteering in the Community

Based on respondents' reports of their volunteering activities, the level of involvement of the attendees in their congregations emerged as the strongest predictor of individual volunteering in the community. This finding is in keeping with previous Australian research and echoes the findings of Putnam and Campbell's study of religion in the USA (2010). They found that religiosity was influential on various forms of civic engagement such as volunteering, not through the beliefs and values of the churches, but rather through the impact of religious social networks within churches. In this respect, they identified close friendships at church, the frequency of discussing religion with family and friends and involvement in small Bible study groups as being key drivers of various forms of civic engagement (Putnam and Campbell 2010, p. 472). However, the findings of the current study suggest that the situation in Australia may be different to that of the USA. It is notable that congregational bonding expressed as friendships did not emerge in this study as a predictor of individual volunteering in the community. Further, the attendee's involvement in small groups was not strongly correlated with individual volunteering in the community ($r=0.11$; $p<0.001$). The lack of strong, positive associations between various aspects of congregational bonding and individual volunteering weakens the notion that religious social networks are key drivers of such activity in Australia. The different patterns between Australia and the USA may be explained by the relatively lower levels of church attendance in Australia, leading to a stronger correlation between believing and belonging. By comparison, Putnam and Campbell refer to the 'imperfect correlation' in the USA, both with significant numbers of believers outside the churches and non-believers within the churches (Putnam and Campbell 2010, p. 473).

Collective Efficacy and Congregational Bridging

An important distinction emerges in the current study between respondents' reports of their individual activity (individual volunteering in the community) and their perceptions of collective involvement by the congregation as a whole (congregational bridging to the community). Whilst religious beliefs and outlook appear to be important to individual volunteering, it is the social dimension that appears to play a stronger role in congregational-level activity. Both individual volunteering and congregational activity have the potential to contribute in positive ways to the social capital of the community. But the way in which each is to be promoted appears to differ greatly, given the very different sets of predictor variables.

The findings about the importance of collective efficacy give an important clue about how congregations can stimulate volunteering, by raising questions about the focus of a congregation: Does it have goals and does it achieve them? Collective efficacy and similar concepts such as collective agency or collective action have been canvassed in the social capital literature (Onyx and Bullen 2000; Leonard and Onyx 2003; Sampson 2006; Staveren and Knorringa 2007) providing a dynamic quality missing from conventional thinking about social capital. More recently Williams and Guerra (2011) noted the importance of collective efficacy and argued that social networks are a necessary precursor for collective mobilisation for the common good. However, rather than a simple causal relationship, it is possible that collective efficacy and congregational bridging work in a positive cycle in which they enhance each other.

The importance of personal friendships is widely acknowledged in church life, and is seen as necessary and expected in the light of Christian teaching to love one another. However the finding that collective efficacy is a stronger factor than the level of friendships in predicting congregational bridging suggests that the achievement of goals and the pursuit of a vision are key ingredients to a richer congregational life and the production of social capital, apart from how attendees treat one another. The current research brings direction and achievement back into the spotlight. Implicit in these findings is the suggestion that congregations should not shy away from the change that would be required in pursuing a vision but should embrace it as part of building social capital both in the wider community and potentially within the congregation.

Previous analysis of the National Church Life Survey data of Anglican and Protestant church attendees in Australia has also pointed to the importance of congregations having a vision for the growth of the church and its members, which is both clearly understood and owned by the congregation itself. This facet of congregational life, which forms part of collective efficacy, has been found previously to not only predict church attendance growth but is strongly linked to attendees' own sense of belonging to the congregation (Kaldor et al. 1997, p. 141). Commitment to a vision was found to be one of the most important predictors of a sense of belonging to a congregation, along with other aspects of collective efficacy such as a belief that the leaders are capable of achieving goals and that they place a great emphasis on helping attendees to discover their own gifts and skills. The current research elaborates these previous findings by showing the framing of a vision to be part of a greater collective efficacy that needs to be fostered. It means chiefly that congregations need to believe that together they can achieve things and that they can trust both their leaders and each other in pursuing such a vision. In this respect, the link between having a sense of belonging to a church and commitment to a vision becomes clearer. The current research suggests a new focus for the development and understanding of social capital within congregations; the dominance of collective efficacy suggests a dynamic concept whereby a congregation is goal-oriented but not at the expense of relationships among the members of the congregation.

The Relationship Between Bonding and Bridging

The current study sheds light on the relationship between bonding and bridging capital, as identified in the context of church congregations. The research shows that the relationship between bonding and bridging is not a simple one and how some studies point to a negative relationship between the two while others point to a positive relationship. The current study shows the relationship to be more nuanced than first thought. Bonding and bridging are quite strongly related where it is congregational bridging activity that is in question. Even then, it is particular aspects of bonding that appear to be more important within church congregations, particularly aspects of collective agency and the strength of friendship networks.

In this respect, the current study complements other studies which find that interactions inside church groups help to explain ties beyond the groups. For instance, based on a 3-year study of Protestant-based volunteering and advocacy projects in the USA, Paul Lichterman (2005) found that bridges can be successfully built where group customs allow for ongoing reflection and critical discussion about the group's place in the wider community. He found that the nature of a group's own togetherness will shape the kind of togetherness it will seek to create in the wider community. Bartkowski and Regis (2003) explored how the abundance of bonding capital within congregations can lead to both compassion towards, and judgment of, those outside the congregation and to coordinated service action or the withholding of such action. Cnaan et al. (2002) showed how congregations work both independently and together to provide social services for individuals and neighbourhoods, complementing Government welfare services in the USA.

Religious and Personal Motivations to Volunteer

The results of the current study have shown that in a sample of church attendees, the religious motivation of individuals plays an important role in their volunteering activity in the wider community. Although differences in theological orientation can play some role, it was broader altruistic reasons and religious reasons, such as living out one's faith and values, or being part of fulfilling God's mission in the world, which emerged as important for attendees engaging in a variety of volunteering activity in the wider community. More self-oriented motivations, such as seeing volunteering as a way of dealing with personal problems, using personal skills, or for career enhancement, were less likely to be reported among this sample of Australian church attendees than elsewhere (e.g. Hustinx and Lammertyn 2003).

However, it is noted that the nature of the sample, which is skewed towards more committed and older church attendees, will have an influence on these results. The over-representation of older attendees means that this sample would be less likely to cite career enhancement as a reason for volunteering. Similarly, the high rating for religious motivations across all types of volunteering activity may reflect the high levels of commitment among this sample of church attendees. Nevertheless it needs to be recognised that church attendance in Australia is engaged in by a committed minority of the population for largely intrinsic reasons; it is far less likely now than in previous times that people would attend church for reasons of social desirability, status or other extrinsic reasons.

Attendees' reasons for volunteering are consistent with Putnam and Campbell's (2010, pp. 463–465) finding about the importance of altruism as a motivation for church-goers and Clary and Snyder's (1999) 'values' motivation. The eight motivations suggested to respondents grouped into two factors; religious reasons and meeting the needs of others grouped together and career enhancement, social and protective functions grouped together in a pattern similar to the two dimensions identified for Australia generally (Australian Bureau of Statistics 2001). However, they do not sit comfortably with conceptualising volunteering in terms of Self-Determination Theory (Deci and Ryan 2000), which focuses on individual competence, connection and autonomy. Although volunteering, as a demonstration of shared Christian values, may be a source of connection with others, social connection was not found to be as strong a reason for volunteering among this sample of attendees.

The prominence of religious reasons for volunteering across a range of volunteering domains outside church life, along with the assumed importance of such reasons for volunteering within church life, points to a common set of motivations both for bridging and bonding activity. This provides further evidence of the connection between bridging and bonding social capital in church life, at least in terms of its expression as volunteering activity. Although motivations were only studied in four domains, they covered the most common avenues for volunteering in Australia (Australian Bureau of Statistics 2010). Further, despite the differences among the domains, (e.g. sport vs. social action) there was a uniformity to the pattern of motivations which suggests that it is likely to be replicated in other domains that were not examined, such as the arts or health services. However, there may be exceptions, such as volunteering for professional associations, which might strongly relate to career motivations.

Respondents reported that religious reasons for doing volunteer work were still prominent even when volunteering for secular organizations. However, it appeared that, for some attendees, the connection between their volunteer work and their faith was less clear when the volunteering was done for a secular organization or group. By comparison, social services provided by religious organizations might have other religious functions and characteristics which are attractive to those who wish to volunteer as an exercise of their faith. Examples of where a religiously run social service may differ from the secular equivalent would include the presence of prayer and Bible reading and the greater likelihood of meeting other religious people, religious conversation and shared meanings, values and culture.

Conclusion

Bringing these findings together, we find support for the importance of a religious outlook and committed belief in the recruitment of volunteers from within churches but add in the importance of the collective efficacy of the congregation. Such collective efficacy has the potential to develop the public activities of the congregation in the wider community. Those activities offer opportunities for volunteering and provide an ideal pathway for recruiting volunteers from the churchgoers who are already volunteering within the congregation and thus have a demonstrable belief in the value of such work.

7 Volunteering Among Church Attendees in Australia 141

These insights are presented from the perspective of those church congregations wishing to increase their social capital and contribution to the community. How well such activities are received by a highly secularised Australian society would depend upon their perceived community benefit. While on the one hand, many Australians are cautious about religious belief that is fervent and passionately held, on the other hand, the welfare and advocacy work of church-based agencies is widely respected. There is already a degree of trust in such church-based agencies and this is reflected in levels of donor support and the awarding of Government contracts; church-based charities are among the largest charitable organizations in Australia. It is within this atmosphere of goodwill that church congregations are able to make a contribution.

The current research is significant in view of the importance of churches, both to the education and welfare sectors in Australia and the importance of volunteering particularly to not-for-profit organizations and charities. The research is also theoretically significant in establishing the relationship between bonding and bridging social capital through collective efficacy.

Future research could investigate whether these insights prove useful to secular organizations, the importance of collective efficacy for example, which may be aided by, but not require, a shared religious faith. Nor does it appear to require a homogeneous group. Leonard and Bellamy (2013, forthcoming) found only a very weak relationship between bonding and a preference for a homogeneous group. A shared commitment to any cause may be a sufficient catalyst for collective efficacy but whether it is actualised in bridging might depend on the group's goals.

Acknowledgments The research which is the focus of this chapter was funded through an Australian Research Council (ARC) Linkage Projects grant. The research was conducted jointly by the University of Western Sydney and NCLS Research, a research group sponsored by Anglicare Diocese of Sydney, Uniting Mission & Education (Synod of NSW & the ACT), the Australian Catholic Bishops Conference and the Australian Catholic University.

References

Abbott, S. (2009). Social capital and health: The problematic roles of social networks and social surveys. *Health Sociology Review, 18*(3), 297–306.

Australian Bureau of Statistics. (2001). *Voluntary work Australia 2000* (ABS Cat No. 4441.0). Canberra: ABS.

Australian Bureau of Statistics. (2010). *Voluntary work Australia* (ABS Cat No. 4441.0). Canberra: ABS.

Australian Bureau of Statistics. (2011). *Reflecting a nation: Stories from the 2011 census, 2012–2013* (ABS Cat No. 2071.0). Canberra: ABS.

Bartkowski, J. P., & Regis, H. A. (2003). *Charitable choices: Religion, race and poverty in the post-welfare era*. New York: New York University Press.

Bellamy, J., & Castle, K. (2004). *2001 church attendance estimates (NCLS Occasional Paper 3)*. Sydney: NCLS Research.

Bellamy, J., & Kaldor, P. (2002). *National Church Life Survey initial impressions 2001*. Adelaide: Openbook.

Burt, R. (1998). The gender of social capital. *Rationality and Society, 10*(1), 5–42.

Burt, R. S. (2004). Structural holes and good ideas. *American Journal of Sociology, 110*(2), 349–399.

Clary, E. G., & Snyder, M. (1999). The motivations to volunteer: Theoretical and practical considerations. *Current Directions in Psychological Science, 8*(5), 156–159.

Cnaan, R. A., Boddie, S. C., Handy, F., Yancey, G., & Schneider, R. (2002). *The invisible caring hand: American congregations and the provision of welfare.* New York: New York University Press.

Crowe, J. A. (2007). In search of a happy medium: How the structure of interorganizational networks influence community economic development strategies. *Social Networks, 29*(4), 469–488.

Deci, E., & Ryan, R. (2000). The 'what' and 'why' of goal pursuits: Human needs and self-determination of behavior. *Psychological Inquiry, 11*(4), 227–268.

Donoghue, J., & Tranter, B. (2010). Citizenship, civic engagement and property ownership. *Australian Journal of Social Issues, 45*(4), 493–508.

Edwards, D. (2005). 'It's mostly about me': Reasons why volunteers contribute their time to museums and art museums. *Tourism Review International, 9*, 21–31.

Evans, M., & Kelley, J. (2004). *Australian economy and society 2002: Religion, morality and public policy in international perspective 1984–2002.* Sydney: Federation Press.

Fukuyama, F. (1995). *Trust: The social virtues and the creation of prosperity.* New York: Free Press.

Granovetter, M. S. (1973). The strength of weak ties. *American Journal of Sociology, 78*(6), 1360–1380.

Holmes-Smith, P. (2011). *Structural equation modeling: From fundamentals to advanced topics.* Melbourne: SREAMS.

Hughes, P., & Black, A. (2002). The impact of various personal and social characteristics on volunteering. *Australian Journal of Volunteering, 7*(2), 59–69.

Hustinx, L., & Lammertyn, F. (2003). Collective and reflexive styles of volunteering: A sociological and modernization perspective. *Voluntas: International Journal of Voluntary and Nonprofit Organizations, 14*(2), 167–187.

ISSP. (2009). *International Social Science Project.* Canberra: Australian National University.

Kaldor, P., Bellamy, J., & Powell, R. (1997). *Shaping a future. Characteristics of vital congregations.* Adelaide: Openbook.

Leonard, R., & Bellamy, J. (2006). Volunteering within and beyond the congregation: A survey of volunteering among Christian church attendees. *Australian Journal of Volunteering, 11*(2), 16–24.

Leonard, R., & Bellamy, J. (2010). The relationship between bonding and bridging social capital among Christian denominations across Australia. *Nonprofit Management and Leadership, 20*(4), 445–460.

Leonard, R., & Bellamy, J. (2013 forthcoming). Dimensions of bonding social capital in Christian congregations across Australia. *Voluntas: International Journal of Voluntary and Nonprofit Organizations.*

Leonard, R., & Onyx, J. (2003). Networking through loose and strong ties: An Australian qualitative study. *Voluntas: International Journal of Voluntary and Nonprofit Organizations, 14*(2), 191–205.

Leonard, R., & Onyx, J. (2004). *Social capital and community building.* London: Janus.

Lichterman, P. (2005). *Elusive togetherness: Church groups trying to bridge America's divisions.* Princeton: Princeton University Press.

Lyons, M., & Nivison-Smith, I. (2006). The relationship between religion and volunteering in Australia. *Australian Journal of Volunteering, 11*(2), 25–37.

Molina-Morales, F. X., & Martínez-Fernández, M. T. (2010). Social networks: Effects of social capital on firm innovation. *Journal of Small Business Management Accounting Research, 48*(2), 258–279.

Onyx, J., & Bullen, P. (2000). Measuring social capital in five communities. *Journal of Applied Behavioral Science, 36*(1), 23–42.

7 Volunteering Among Church Attendees in Australia

Paxton, P. (1999). Is social capital declining in the United States? A multiple indicator assessment. *American Journal of Sociology, 105,* 88–127.

Perry, J., Coursey, D., Brudney, J., & Littlepage, L. (May–June 2008). What drives morally committed citizens? *Public Administration Review, 68*(3), 445–458.

Portes, A. (1998). Social capital: Its origins and applications in modern sociology. *Annual Review of Sociology, 24,* 1–24.

Putnam, R. (1993). *Making democracy work: Civic traditions in modern Italy.* Princeton: Princeton University Press.

Putnam, R. (2002). *Democracies in flux. The evolution of social capital in contemporary societies.* Oxford: Oxford University Press.

Putnam, R., & Campbell, D. E. (2010). *American grace: How religion divides and unites us.* New York: Simon & Schuster.

Rostila, M. (2010). The facets of social capital. *Journal for the Theory of Social Behavior, 41*(3), 308–326.

Sampson, R. J. (2006). Collective efficacy theory: Lessons learned and directions for future inquiry. In F. Cullen, J. P. Wright, & K. R. Blevins (Eds.), *Taking stock: The status of criminological theory.* New Brunswick: Transaction.

Shye, S. (2010). The motivation to volunteer: A systemic quality of life theory. *Social Indicators Research, 98,* 183–200. doi:10.1007/s11205-009-9545-3.

van Staveren, I., & Knorringa, P. (2007). Unpacking social capital in economic development: How social relations matter. *Review of Social Economy, 65*(1), 1–9.

Williams, K., & Guerra, N. (2011). Perceptions of collective efficacy and bullying perpetration in schools. *Social Problems, 58*(1), 126–143.

Woolcock, M., & Narayan, D. (2000). Social capital: Implications for development theory, research and policy. *World Bank Research Observer, 15*(2), 225–249.

Wuthnow, R. (2004). *Saving America? Faith based services and the future of civil society.* Princeton: Princeton University Press.

Yeung, A. B. (2004). An intricate triangle—religiosity, volunteering and social capital: The European perspective, the case of Finland. *Nonprofit and Voluntary Sector Quarterly, 33*(3), 401–422.

Part III
Religion and Volunteering in a (Post-) Secular Context

Chapter 8
Lost and Found in Secularization

A Religious Perspective on the Meaning of Volunteering

Johan von Essen

Introduction

Secularization and the return of religion are two recurrent themes in the general discussion about religion in contemporary society that are also of immediate interest for the topic of this book. Secularization is a highly contested and ambiguous term. There are neither conceptual nor empirically sound arguments for understanding secularization as the fading away of religion as a consequence of modernization. Nevertheless, modernity has entailed a diminished and more peripheral role for religious faith and institutions, especially in Europe (Casanova 2009; Norris and Inglehart 2011).[1] The second theme, the return of religion, is also highly debated and involves an increasing interest in the significance and role of religion for politics and culture in society (see Joas 2009 for an overview). These two themes are seemingly contradictory but only when seeing modernization as a zero-sum game with religion and secularity as two communicating vessels.

However, the two themes can be combined as two interrelated aspects of a certain perspective on modernization. I use the concept of post-secularity to capture and discuss this perspective with respect to the role of religion in society today. Basically, the idea is that secularization implies that religious institutions lose their hegemonic status and that their relation to other organizations therefore becomes horizontal instead of vertical. Furthermore, it implies that affiliations to churches or religious communities are no longer coercive and that faith is not inherited as a matter of course, but results from an individual's own conscious choice. According to these processes religion becomes one phenomenon among others in society and this also makes it more visible, so that it becomes possible to discuss its significance for politics, culture, philosophy, etc. (Bäckström et al. 2011; Sigurdson 2009). One

---

[1] I restrict my discussion to the European situation and its Christian heritage. This is solely due to the character of my empirical data and involves no essential claims on religion as such.

J. von Essen (✉)
Institute for Civil Society Studies, Ersta Sköndal University College, Stockholm, Sweden
e-mail: johan.vonessen@esh.se

L. Hustinx et al. (eds.), *Religion and Volunteering*, Nonprofit and Civil Society Studies,
DOI 10.1007/978-3-319-04585-6_8, © Springer International Publishing Switzerland 2015

could say that secularization leads to the return of religion as a more visible element of society (Bergdahl 2010).

I use the concept of post-secularity to refer to a changed perspective on the role of religion in society and not to a (new) more religious historical period. The post-secular condition is a situation where attention is paid to the importance and presence of religious communities in an increasingly secularized society. Hence, the concept is about a changed attitude of the secular state, and in academic and political debates in the public sphere, with respect to the continued existence of different manifestations of religion and its influence on society (Joas 2004; de Vries 2006).

The fact that the hegemonic Christian church has pervaded European societies since late antiquity, both formally by law and politics and informally in the mentalities and practices of individuals, is an obvious argument for the need of a post-secular perspective in order to fully understand contemporary society. This historical fact would suggest that religious practices and theology and their imprint on society cannot disappear overnight. One aim for academic research is therefore to unpack traces of theology or religiosity in contemporary and allegedly secular practices and ideas. That would imply the undertaking of a religious genealogy of contemporary secular society.

There are several examples of genealogies of this kind. Theologians, philosophers and cultural historians have been able to show that liberal politics, modern philosophy and modernity as such cannot be fully separated from religion (Christianity), but depend on a religious and theological heritage (Breckman 2005; Gillespie 2008; Gray 2007; Lilla 2007; de Vries 2006 just to mention a few). These are examples of intertextual research that study the emergence and formulations of political and philosophical standpoints and demonstrate their dependence on theology. An important conclusion is that religion and modern secular ideologies cannot easily be divided into separate categories.

The Altruistic Volunteer and the 'Problem of Goodness'

In contrast to these studies of how traces of religion can be found in formal ideologies, I will use theology to interpret world-views in people's ordinary talk in everyday life, and hence my interest is on a less formalized level. My aim is to use a religious perspective to enhance understanding of the world-views of individuals. This approach takes as its point of departure the premise that with a religious perspective one can shed some light on the meaning of social practices found in everyday life, inside as well as outside formal religious contexts. This means that religious discourses do not always require conscious deliberation, yet can structure how individuals talk about their lives (Wuthnow 2011).

In accordance with the overarching theme for this anthology, I explore how volunteers perceive the meaning of volunteering, applying a theological framework. A religious perspective ought to be able to contribute to our understanding of the meaning of volunteering because of the long tradition of benevolence as a religious

8 Lost and Found in Secularization

(here Christian) virtue and of religious charity organizations (see chapter of Haers and von Essen). From a historical perspective, volunteering can be said to have one of its precursors in the Christian calling of neighbourly love and in Christian charity organizations.

What I am especially interested in is how volunteers deal with the 'problem of goodness'. By this I refer to the tension they perceive between doing good for the sake of the other, being altruistic, while at the same time receiving 'payment' in the form of gratitude and fulfilment as a consequence of caring for their neighbours by volunteering. To give alms as a public gesture of piety is condemned in the New Testament; instead Jesus urges for a division so that the good deeds will not be used as a merit before God (Matthew 6:1–4). Hannah Arendt also refers to this passage when she discusses the conditions of goodness (Arendt 1958). Hence, the experience that good deeds comprise gratitude and are therefore often valued as a moral worth, undermining the altruistic intention, is not a particular Swedish or Lutheran or even Christian predicament. It emerges and finds different solutions in various religions and world-views. However, since my empirical data is Swedish, I will describe and discuss how this problem is handled by using Lutheran theology.

That good deeds comprise morally desirable outcomes is a problem in a religious context. However, this is not necessarily a problem as such; it depends on which philosophical anthropology one prefers. Taking the economic man as an anthropological point of departure, the dilemma dissolves and the alleged altruistic motives of the volunteers can be interpreted as either naive altruism or as a camouflage for a cynical egoism. In order to go beyond these alternatives and take the utterances of the volunteers at face value, I will approach the meaning of volunteering from a religious perspective as an alternative approach to secular interpretations.

This is an explorative study. My aim is not to prove the influence of religion on contemporary secular culture. My presumption is that, by using a theological framework, it is possible to deepen the understanding of how volunteers deal with the moral dilemma that emerges in the tension between the intention to be altruistic and finding oneself rewarded by volunteering. If the theological framework can do justice to the utterances of the volunteers, it will be an argument for the reasonableness of my interpretative approach. This chapter, in accordance with the post-secular perspective, is an attempt to bridge the divide between religiosity and secularism by using religious themes to understand how people make sense of their volunteer efforts.

Volunteering and Altruism: A Disputed Relationship

Lack of remuneration is a core dimension in the concept of volunteering (Cnaan et al. 1996; Musick and Wilson 2008). As unpaid efforts for the benefit of others, volunteering can be understood as a form of giving. Therefore, volunteering is often perceived, but also critically discussed, as an example of altruism (Haski-Leventhal 2009) and is easily conceived of as something opposed to egoism, since altruism and egoism are often treated as dichotomous concepts. This dichotomy of motives is sometimes incorporated in volunteer research; for instance, to see whether they are correlated to different behaviour patterns among volunteers (e.g. Mesch et al. 1998; Rehberg 2005). As related to the concepts of altruism or egoism, volunteering is also perceived as a normative concept connected to the ongoing discussion in philosophical anthropology about the nature of man (cf. Clohesy 2000; Nagel 1970). Further, it is this normative dimension that makes volunteering a religious virtue (Musick and Wilson 2008; see chapter of Haers and von Essen in this volume). According to Haski-Leventhal (2009), the dominant perspective in theories and studies of volunteering in the social sciences is dependent, however, upon a 'perception of human beings as rational and economical'. Hence, altruism becomes a problematic phenomenon that has to be scientifically explained away. In studies of volunteering, scholars try to bridge the gap between the altruistic character of volunteering, not least their motives, and the theoretical approach to human beings as fundamentally egocentric.

If, on the other hand, we treat volunteering as altruistic behaviour, the altruistic–egoistic dichotomy causes problems, since there are several studies that report how volunteers benefit from their efforts (for an overview see Haski-Leventhal 2009). In these studies, it is evident that volunteers often experience satisfaction and self-fulfilment as a result of their work. This is also reflected in the study this chapter is based upon (von Essen 2008; see Hvenmark and von Essen 2013 for similar results); the volunteers often stated that they felt satisfied or self-fulfilled and also mentioned that they made new friends, gained better self-esteem and gained experiences that could enhance their CVs. The good feelings, trust, profitable relations and learning experiences they received from their efforts were very important to them and they were eager to stress how rewarded they felt as volunteers, since the rewards were a marker of the importance of their efforts. Volunteering thus does not seem to be all that altruistic after all. The only thing they unanimously excluded and firmly rejected as a possible reward for their volunteering was money.

Of course, it is a well-known fact from other studies that volunteers report that they have both altruistic and egoistic motives for their work (Yeung 2004); and by perceiving altruism as a continuum, there is an alternative to the dichotomous relation between altruism and egoism (Krebs and Van-Hesteren 1994). However, to be content with pointing out this psychological ambivalence or to discuss altruism as a continuum does not theoretically resolve the 'problem of goodness'. Neither does it justice to how the volunteers talked about their volunteer efforts. They did not confine themselves just to noting their altruistic motives and accepting that they were rewarded. On the contrary, in the interviews, they tried to handle the tensions they perceived between their altruistic aim to help and all the good things they received as consequences of their helping.

So, how can we understand the altruistic motives of the volunteers when their efforts obviously bring rewards that are important to them? One, perhaps cynical, interpretation is that volunteering is best understood as calculated rational behaviour, implying that volunteers have egoistic motives after all, some of them overt and others concealed because volunteering is expected to follow a norm of altruism.

8 Lost and Found in Secularization 151

Their altruistic motives could then be understood as a kind of camouflage adjusting to overarching norms. Such an assumption would, however, imply a 'third-person perspective' and to presuppose the economic man as an anthropological point of departure in search of objective causes for volunteering. Since I am studying how volunteers handle the meaning of volunteering by taking their own perspective as a point of departure, such an explanation would become a kind of category mistake.

Religion and Volunteering

There is an interest among academics in the relation between religiosity and volunteering, and more precisely, whether religiosity fosters volunteering. For obvious reasons, there are two main perspectives and research agendas on this topic. Firstly, and preferably among social scientists, there are studies of volunteering as civil society activism, from which perspective religion becomes just one of many predictors of volunteering. Secondly, there is a theological interest in the practical consequences of faith and religiosity. In this perspective, volunteering is treated as an outcome of faith, since faith is expected to have an impact on civility and compassion (see chapters of Haers and von Essen; Roos; Fazlhashemi in this volume).

In studies coming from the first of these perspectives, religion is treated in many cases as a 'black box'. These studies are often quantitative, where different forms or aspects of religiosity occur as independent variables in statistical analyses that tend to give proof of a positive correlation between religiosity and volunteering, albeit with variations according to different aspects of faith and religious practice. A frequent underlying assumption is that affiliation to religious organizations fosters volunteering and/or that religion generates altruistic values. There is also the conviction that internalized beliefs and values matter most when considering religion and that these values are best tapped by survey questions (Wuthnow 2011). In consequence, quantitative surveys are preferred in studies of religious values. Below follows a brief review of some of the findings in quantitative research concerning religion and volunteering in Sweden.

In a study of young volunteers in the Church of Sweden, there was a positive correlation between volunteering over a longer period and traditional religious belief (Bromander 1999). A study of volunteering among Swedish youth also showed that religious individuals were more inclined to volunteer than non-religious ones. There were, however, no differences regarding inclination to volunteer between youths with a traditional religiosity and youths with a late-modern religiosity (von Essen and Grosse 2012). Finally, the most recent national study on volunteering in Sweden shows that individuals attending church on a regular basis were more inclined to volunteer than the population as a whole (Svedberg et al. 2010).

Swedish-organized volunteering has been remarkably stable and extensive in an international perspective during the last two decades (Svedberg et al. 2010), and about half of the Swedish adult population volunteer on a regular basis. At the same time, Sweden is a highly secularized country (understood as low church attendance and little consciously held religious belief), hence religiosity is not a major explanation for this extensive volunteering in spite of the positive effect on volunteering suggested above. One can therefore call into question whether overt religiosity really is an important factor for understanding the overall amount, shape and role of volunteering in contemporary Sweden.

Method and Material

Considering the long hegemony of Christian churches, practices and theology in Europe, it seems odd that, apart from overt religiosity as a cause for volunteering, the role of religion in volunteering has so seldom attracted attention. The theological ideas that permeate culture and influence society are too seldom explored, understood and given explanatory power (see Alexander and Smith 1993 for a similar argument). In order to go beyond the relation between overt, formal religiosity and volunteering I interpreted how volunteers talk about why they volunteer and what their efforts mean to them with the help of a theological framework. Consequently, I am not studying their speech as an expression of causes, but as a justification after-the-fact to render actions meaningful (Mills 1940; Wuthnow 1991) and to describe the actors' identity (Arendt 1958; Taylor 1985).

This chapter is based on 40 interviews with volunteers in four traditional Swedish volunteer organizations, none of them religious. The interviews were conducted within a broader research project concerning volunteers' perception of volunteering as a social phenomenon and what their efforts mean to them as individuals (von Essen 2008). The original research project was thus not to study religious aspects of volunteering as such, but had a more general interest in the conceptual and existential meaning of volunteering.

Conceptually, I searched for commonly held themes that constitute the meaning of volunteering and found five such themes, according to which volunteering is unpaid, beneficial to others, a free choice, a personal engagement and enacted in some sort of a community. I then used interviewee statements to illustrate these themes. By using single volunteers and their concrete stories as examples of the commonly held themes, I was able to describe and discuss the abstract themes that were the results of my analysis (see Bellah et al. 1985; Wuthnow 1991 for a similar technique). The original research project also included an existential perspective and questions about what volunteering meant to the volunteers as persons and its role in their everyday life. These questions generated material demonstrating how experiences of volunteering influence how people formulate and handle meaningfulness and moral issues. In this chapter, I discuss some aspects of my findings.

Since the original project aimed at uncovering the meaning of volunteering from the volunteer perspective, the approach to their statements was phenomenological (cf. Yeung 2004). That is to say, I was primarily interested in the life-world of the volunteers and how they perceive and understand it. Using a phenomenological approach, I searched for themes beneath the surface of the individual descriptions

8 Lost and Found in Secularization

that capture a common understanding of the meaning of volunteering (Polkinghorne 1983). The phenomenological approach is also valid for what I want to discuss in this chapter. Since I am interested in their opinions on volunteering and what it means to them from a first-person perspective, I take their utterances at face value. I do not pass judgment on whether their utterances are false or true, for that would demand a third-person perspective. I am solely interested in how the interviewed volunteers express what they perceive as the meaning of their voluntary work.

Twelve of these 40 interviewees were involved in environmental issues as members of the Swedish Society for Nature Conservation and 12 as members of Friends of the Earth Sweden. Ten persons were volunteer soccer coaches and recreation leaders for the Älvsjö AIK Soccer Club, and six persons were involved in social action, mainly within the Red Cross. These organizations are open, democratic and based on individual membership. In that sense they have a traditional form and are typical for how organizations in Swedish civil society are structured by the popular movement tradition (Hvenmark 2008). The selection is due to the original project's aim to include both ideologically oriented organizations and apolitical organizations oriented towards service production, as well as to study whether the perceived meaning of volunteering differed between voice- and service-oriented organizations. As a further aim was to study whether changes occurring in time affected the meaning of volunteering, organizations established in different time periods and with individuals from different age groups were also included; but since the original project was not concerned about religion and volunteering as such, there was no need to select a religious organization. Religiosity or belief in God was mentioned by almost none of the interviewees as a motive for doing volunteer work. From their perspective, volunteering appears to be a strictly secular matter. To interpret their utterances with the help of a theological framework does not imply that they were unaware of being religious, however, and I do not argue that they believe in God after all. As Ann Swidler (2001) has pointed out, to describe available cultural resources we have to deal both with what people believe and what they disbelieve.

The age distribution among the interviewees ranged from 19 to 66, 15 of them men and 25 women. Age and gender were equally divided between the organizations. Among the volunteers interviewed, there were both core activists with a long history of volunteering and newcomers, but the largest group (17 persons) had been active for between 4 and 10 years. During the research period, two persons were unemployed and the others employed or students. Twenty-three of the volunteers had an academic or postgraduate degree. None of them deviated conspicuously from a middle-class life trajectory. All in all, these volunteers were in accordance with the overall Swedish socioeconomic pattern of volunteers that persists in the national surveys of volunteering in Sweden (Svedberg et al. 2010). An analysis of the interviews did not show profound or important differences with respect to age, gender, education, organization, etc., but rather a commonly held perception of the meaning of volunteering.

The material that emerged from the interviews was interpreted by customary hermeneutical methods. Phenomenological and hermeneutical methods supplement

Empirical Accounts

each other, the first describing patterns or themes and the other interpreting the meaning of those themes (Polkinghorne 1983). Paul Ricœur (1975/1991) among others has criticized descriptive phenomenology for its alleged objectivity. I concur with this critique and consequently do not restrict myself to a phenomenological description.

Empirical Accounts

In this section, I will present how the volunteers articulate the dynamic between volunteering for the benefit of someone or something and being rewarded for their efforts. Their understanding of this dynamic involves how they perceive the meaning of volunteering. Then I will briefly sketch some relevant aspects of Lutheran theology to finally be able to discuss how the volunteers try to deal with the 'problem of goodness'.

Unpaid

That volunteering is unpaid was the most unanimous and most articulated of the five themes I found in the interviews. The volunteers unanimously excluded and firmly rejected money as a possible reward for their volunteering. The reason for this was that money made their voluntary efforts instrumental, which would render them meaningless. The volunteers maintained that their efforts were meaningful only if they were to the benefit of someone or something and if they were expressions of their own wishes, personal values and, in the end, themselves as persons. They had to be sincere to find their volunteering meaningful. Therefore, the meaning of volunteering would disappear if financially remunerated.

At the same time, the interviewees were volunteering in their spare time and most of them were employed and paid for carrying out their ordinary occupation. Of course, they did not think that being paid as employees was wrong or problematic; it was when they considered themselves as volunteers that money became a problem. They perceived employment and getting paid as both a natural and necessary condition for managing their everyday life. One woman described her gainful employment as a condition for managing her life as follows:

On the job there are certain things that have to be done…. One is there for the money, and you want the money to be able to survive.

To earn one's living is for most people a precondition to manage life and is, as for this woman, perceived as a necessity and not entirely as an act of free choice. Many interviewees referred to the need to earn one's living when they declared that or explained why volunteering gave them something else than gainful employment. Another woman made this point by differentiating between the 'inner satisfaction' she got from volunteering and the money she got from her ordinary work. She, like

8 Lost and Found in Secularization

many others, talked about the sincere self and the ordinary person as merely different aspects of herself. One man expressed this contrast between the necessities of ordinary life and the meaningfulness of volunteering as follows:

> Well, it [volunteering] makes my life more meaningful...I must say. I think it encompasses something more than everyday life. Everyday life is like food and that kind of stuff, it is important; it is necessary for everyone of course.

Furthermore, money was the paradigmatic example of instrumentality. There were of course other instrumental motives and rewards as well, such as enhancing a CV or gaining an employment. However, unlike money, other instrumental or external rewards could be accepted if received under certain conditions.

Freedom

According to the volunteers, freedom was another condition for the meaningfulness of volunteering. When asked if there were ideologies, duties or virtues that the volunteers considered as compelling and which demanded that they should do volunteer work, most of them answered that their voluntary efforts stemmed from free will and that they would volunteer as long as they were enjoying it. A man expressed this opinion by saying:

> ...I've never seen volunteering as a duty, but rather as something I've really wanted to do.

This seems an unexpected opinion from dedicated people aiming at the good of the environment or their neighbours. Not even direct demands when confronted with the needs of fellow men or urgent threats to nature made them talk about their volunteering as compelled or necessary. By referring to themselves and their emotions instead of virtues, obligations, ideologies or even the needs of 'the other', they made their volunteering into an expression of their authenticity. By saying that they were volunteering only as long as they 'felt like it' or were enjoying it, they assured that it was their own free choice. Freedom was also a reason for the volunteers to reject money as a possible reward for their volunteering since a monetary reward would have turned their voluntary commitment into gainful employment and a means to earn their living. Of course, they did admit that the everyday volunteering reality was sometimes characterized by promises and commitments and hence not totally free; but they maintained that in the end their volunteer efforts were of their own free will.

The demands of sincerity and freedom are a key to understanding how the volunteers handled the relation between their altruistic motives and the rewards of their volunteer efforts. To be rewarded (thus in a sense coerced) would threaten the freedom of their inner self, instrumentalize their efforts and hence deprive them of meaning. The volunteers perceived themselves as authentic if they were sincere and if their efforts stemmed from free will and authenticity was a condition for finding their volunteer work meaningful.

Rewards as Unexpected By-products

In my interviews with the volunteers, I challenged their altruistic motives, reminding them about all the good things they received through their volunteering. One man who got an apartment lease through his volunteering talked as follows about the true character of volunteering:

> ... to work, to fight for something, without anything being that clear, that this is what I will gain from it. There's nothing to say this is what you will get. Sure, I got // ... // an apartment. One does get things. One can feel better about one's self, one can make friends, but there is nothing that can be guaranteed. The only thing that is guaranteed is that you are fighting for whatever it is you're fighting for.

As illustrated by this quotation, confronted with my objections to their alleged altruism, they rejected an instrumental interpretation of their volunteering. Instead, a recurrent theme emerged that is contradictory to both the continuum perspective of altruism and the either-or logic that follows from the egoist–altruist dichotomy (cf. Jeppsson Grassman 1997). The volunteers were not troubled because of what they received, nor did they feel that it challenged their altruistic motives, as long as the rewards were not expected or calculated. So long as their intention was to give, without expecting anything in return, they had no problem receiving material and immaterial goods (except for money). Therefore, as long as the rewards of volunteering were interpreted as unexpected by-products, they were not in conflict with the altruistic character of volunteering and with their authenticity (cf. Wuthnow 1991).

This dynamic between the right (non-calculating) intention and being rewarded is reflected in the following, where a man, volunteering in his son's football club, talks about his commitment:

> Well, it's unpaid labour...you know, one performs, to be sure one does, one has a mission... that one is supposed to do, and one does that and you are not getting paid for it. For some people this may sound odd that...but I am getting paid in a sense...partly I get to spend more time with my son. I can see that he is enjoying himself, how he is developing, and I can see all the other kids in the team, how they are developing. So that is, like, payment in itself. Or one never thinks about payment...if one thinks in that way, one should not do volunteering.

The fragmentary character of his answer suggests that he finds this dynamic complex and contradictory. It is hard to explain and he imagines that is difficult to understand for some people, probably people without experience of volunteering. In the end he declares that one should not become involved in volunteering if calculating in terms of payment. This theme is also elaborated upon by a woman who explains that she would be alienated, in her expression '*on her own*', if she did it for her own sake; instead her satisfaction is to see that she can bring joy to the children she is helping. A calculating relationship to volunteering is incompatible with being rewarded, not only because it would be improper to expect payment from volunteering but also because to calculate would also preclude the unexpected rewards the volunteers receive. Authenticity is a precondition to be able to receive the rewards of volunteering.

8 Lost and Found in Secularization

As illustrated, this insistence on a non-calculating intention cannot be explained by the idea that the volunteers are consciously cynical, adapting to a conventional norm of altruism by concealing their instrumental motives. Rather it has to do with the meaning of volunteering. This dynamic between motives and meaning is displayed in the case of one man, volunteering in the Red Cross, who described what volunteering meant to him. He was anxious to emphasize the importance of altruistic motives for volunteering and that it was aimed at helping people in need. But at the same time he said:

> ...it is almost contradictory. As a consequence it has...I feel some sense of well-being, but that is not my aim. However, that is the result if one follows the process to the end. It will end up in a sense of well-being for myself.

He has to be authentic and his efforts have to meet the needs of others to be meaningful, but in turn it will give him satisfaction; being altruistic ends up being rewarded.

To be rewarded, according to the volunteers, demands from them that they are authentic. If not they would not be able to receive the relationships, fulfilment and self-esteem that their volunteering gives them. The way the volunteers described and discussed the dynamic between the motives and meaning of volunteering can be understood in accordance with the distinction between internal and external values (MacIntyre 1981). External values are arbitrary and connected to a practice, such as wages for a job done, whereas internal values are integral parts of the practice itself, such as the joy engendered by the actual doing.

To the Benefit of the Other in the Realm of Freedom

It became obvious that the differentiation between the 'inner' sincere self and the ordinary person made it possible for the volunteers to maintain that they were authentic in their volunteering while at the same time employed and being paid. Hence, the volunteers were, in a way, parts of two social settings with different ethical styles (Tipton 2002). This divide is crucial since it made it possible for them to care for others without expecting anything in return, and without the expectation that they should be thoroughly altruistic also in their everyday life. That would have been a naïve and unrealistic moral demand.

As employees and in ordinary life, their actions were driven by social commitments and their motives were often calculative. As employees they received external values (money) for their efforts. As volunteers, on the other hand, they strived for authenticity and they received internal values for their efforts. Some of them did admit, however, that they received rewards—employment, networks or a better CV—that could be understood as external values, but categorized some of these rewards as internal values. For instance, they talked about relationships as something internal to the practice. Rewards categorized as external values such as employment or an apartment lease could be accepted as unexpected by-products without depriving their efforts of meaning.

This did not cause them problems as long as these two settings were separated. The problem arose when they were mixed or the border was blurred. External values such as gaining cash and other arbitrary rewards threatened the meaning of volunteering since it threw suspicion on their authenticity, while having non-calculating motives as an employee was considered stupid or naïve.

When talking about what they received from their efforts, the volunteers most often talked about values internal to the practice of volunteering. Most important of the internal values was the satisfaction they felt when they could help someone. If the voluntary work did not include 'the other', it would lose its meaning. A man engaged in an environmental organization expressed this perception as follows:

> If it's not to the benefit of others then it's not really volunteer work. Then it's more of a hobby.... I definitely think it should be beneficial....

This means that the intention to be beneficial to someone is not only a motive but also has conceptual significance. If their efforts did not have any effect and would therefore not be to the benefit of someone, the interviewees would find their volunteering meaningless. To be needed and to be able to meet the needs of someone was obviously at the heart of what made their efforts meaningful. Calculating motives, then, would jeopardize the internal values of volunteering since their help had to be given for the sake of the receiver, not in order to receiving gratitude. Gratitude would otherwise become some sort of payment for their efforts and therefore render them meaningless. The internal values that made volunteering meaningful presupposed that the volunteers did not expect anything in return (see also Jeppsson Grassman 1997; Johansson 1998; Wuthnow 1991). I will try to demonstrate that these themes that I have discussed and illustrated together make up a coherent structure that becomes visible when it is understood within the framework of Lutheran theology.

The Lutheran Doctrine of the Calling

At the heart of Lutheran theology is man's total dependence on God for her salvation and consequently man's independence from earthly conditions when it comes to her relation to God, since it is solely through the grace of God that man is saved (*Sola Gratia*). However, Luther did not disregard that man is simultaneously living in society and therefore dependent on earthly conditions for her everyday life. This theological approach obviously creates a duality. In *The Freedom of a Christian* from 1520, Luther makes an anthropological divide between the inner and the outer man (Luther 1989, see chapter by Haers and von Essen for a fuller account of this aspect of Lutheran theology). This divide is theologically motivated and makes it possible for Luther to assert that the inner man is free in the sense that nothing in the secular outer world can determine her relation to God and at the same time that man is everybody's servant. Since man is not dependent on her merits in relation to God, she is free to be her neighbour's servant. Hence, the freedom of man is central

8 Lost and Found in Secularization

for Luther, and it is to maintain that freedom that Luther declares that she is totally dependent on God. According to Luther, freedom does not imply that man is autonomous and self-determinant in the contemporary use of the term; that would be an anachronistic interpretation. Luther could not conceive man without God; rather, he implied that nothing but God's grace through his word (Logos) could define man's relation to God.

Historically, this can be regarded as the foundation of, and prelude to, the emergence of modern subjectivity, and has resulted in an anthropological divide between the outer and the inner man where the inner man is free regardless of outer conditions, and where religiosity is located in the sincere inner man (Borowitz 1984; Sigurdson 2009). As noted above, a similar anthropological divide was also found in the interviews and made it possible for the volunteers to maintain their authenticity as volunteers when they simultaneously worked as employees and were financially rewarded.

According to Luther, man is not made righteous in the eyes of God by his deeds, but liberated by God's grace to respond to the calling (*vocatio*) to serve. At the core of Lutheran theology then lies man's responsibility to her neighbour, not her own righteousness. Man will not be righteous in the eyes of God if she responds to the calling with the calculating motive to deserve, or earn, righteousness through her deeds. Therefore, man's righteousness can be described as an unexpected gift. Of course, this goes back to the thesis that man cannot earn salvation through merits but solely by the grace of God (*sola Gratia*). This doctrine has become a cornerstone in Lutheran theology and of preaching in Lutheran churches (see, e.g. Confessio Augustana article 20 in Grane 1959).

This one-sided emphasis on the grace of God for the salvation of man is often said to differentiate Lutheran theology historically from Catholic soteriology, since the Catholic Church accepted a more synergic-oriented thesis: that the will of man and the grace of God cooperate in man's salvation (Schneewind 1998). It is, however, important not to simplify this difference between Lutheran and Catholic theology, since man's total dependence on the grace of God can be found already in the Bible and in the writings of Augustine. Thus, Luther was working in an already established theological tradition that can be found outside Lutheran theology as well.

According to Luther, there are two uses of the law. The first use of law is to 'bridle the wicked', that is, to regulate everyday life and the worldly societal order. The second use of the law, however, is to convince man of her profound sinfulness. Luther argued that when man answers to the law in its second use and tries to become righteous through deeds, she will realize that she is profoundly sinful, more interested in her own salvation than in the good of her fellow man and that the needs of fellow men always will transcend what she can achieve. Therefore, in despair over her self-interest and the fact that she cannot respond to God's calling, man will stop trying to save herself since the needs of her fellow men are endless. As a result, she can only be redeemed by the grace of God, that is, by relying solely on her belief in God (*Sola Fide;* see chapter by Haers and von Essen, also Schervish and Whitaker 2010). Trusting solely in the grace of God, man will be free and able

160   J. von Essen

to respond to God's calling and serve her fellow man and live in peace with herself
and with God. So, when man answers God's calling to serve her fellow man for that
sake alone, she will then become righteous, or be rewarded, to use an improper but
contemporary terminology.

A Religious Perspective on Volunteering

I have tried to capture how the volunteers articulate the dynamic between the meaning of volunteering and the motives of action by interpreting their utterances with
the help of some central aspects of Lutheran theology. First, the volunteers distinguish between the sincere self and the ordinary person, similar to the anthropological division of Luther. In both cases the division manages to separate and defend
the pure sincere self from the necessary realities of worldly, everyday life. For both
Luther and the volunteers this division is crucial in order to avoid a cynical interpretation of man's relation towards God and respectively 'the other'.

If the volunteers had calculating motives when helping their neighbours, their
actions would not be meaningful as volunteering since they would not transcend
themselves and include another person. The help has to be given solely as a response to the need of the neighbour and not for own satisfaction. Yet by authenti-
cally meeting the neighbour's need, they would nevertheless gain 'inner' satisfaction, since it is the internal value, to be able to help, that makes their volunteer
efforts meaningful. The satisfaction that comes from being beneficial to someone
cannot be earned by one's merits or good deeds; instead it has to be an unexpected
by-product. Luther's doctrine of salvation through the grace of God makes this
dynamic intelligible. A calculating motive would turn their satisfaction into some
sort of payment for their volunteering efforts or their good deeds. Then their volunteering would be for their own benefit and not for the good of another person, and
in consequence, meaningless.

Freedom is obviously as central for the volunteers as it is for Luther. This is perhaps surprising considering the fundamental differences between the pre-modern
times of Luther and contemporary Sweden. The volunteers maintained that volunteering must be unpaid in order to be free since it made them independent of
the necessity to earn their living. This is similar to how Luther presupposes man's
total dependence on God in order to be independent of the world. In order to maintain their freedom, the interviewees categorized volunteering as a social setting
separate from their ordinary life and from the straitjacket of gainful employment,
whereas Luther solved the problem of freedom by uniting man with God through
Christ. In these two solutions, the fundamental difference between contemporary
society and the pre-modern time of Luther becomes evident. To be autonomous is a
precondition for freedom for the volunteers, whereas the anthropology of Luther is
totally relational. Hence, it is not freedom as such that differentiates between secular volunteering and Luther's teaching of the calling. It is rather about how freedom
is established, as personal autonomy or in dependence on, and confidence in, God.

8 Lost and Found in Secularization

There is, finally, another aspect of this difference between the volunteering perspective and Luther's doctrine on the calling: The volunteers do not (ostensibly) believe in God. Consequently, they do not refer to God when they depict their volunteering and explain what gives them the inspiration to carry on, and they also do not see their efforts as being required of them, as in Luther's second use of the law. In contrast to Lutheran theology, they argue that they would volunteer as long as it was joyful and gave them pleasure. This means that they cannot refer to something outside themselves and their emotions to make their efforts meaningful. This is an important difference and in this respect the volunteers express immanent world-views, where they refer to the autonomous self and not to the heteronomous self, which relies on the grace of God to make sense of their efforts.

I argue that by using a theological framework in the interpretation of the interviews, it is possible to understand some recurrent themes about the tension the volunteers perceived between their aim of being altruistic, while at the same time receiving gratitude and fulfilment as a consequence of caring for their neighbours. Hence, to study how volunteers perceive the meaning of volunteering by the help of a theological framework can deepen the interpretation and go beyond economic or psychological anthropologies that are reductive and deterministic to the obvious fact that individuals have both altruistic and egoistic motives. It can do justice to moral and existential issues, here 'the problem of goodness', that would otherwise run the risk of being treated as a kind of camouflage adjusting to dominant norms or simply as anomalies. Thus it seems as if the Lutheran scheme fits and can offer an alternative to an interpretation of the motives to volunteering, leading to a dichotomous choice between a naive altruism and a cynical egoism.

Finding Religiosity Lost in Secularization

This chapter is to be considered as a contribution to an alternative perspective on the relation between religiosity and volunteering as compared with the more frequent interest in religiosity as a cause for volunteering. Hitherto, I have made no claims for any historical influence of Lutheran theology on contemporary Swedish society. However, this question lurks beneath the surface and I will finally address this issue and sketch an argument for the plausibility of such an influence. My point of departure is the assumption of Norris and Inglehart (2011) that world-views, originally linked with religious traditions, still shape cultures, even in secular societies and among secular citizens. In doing this, I concur with the approach of Lars Trägårdh (2014) when he argues that the impact of Lutheranism is one of many factors that explains the social contract and the welfare state in contemporary Sweden. To be clear, what I have called the 'problem of goodness' is, as such, not particular Lutheran. This interplay between giving and receiving seems to be a universal dynamic that people can recognize notwithstanding their cultural or religious heritage. What I have tried to unfold is how volunteers in a society with a Lutheran tradition try to handle this problem.

162   J. von Essen

There is theoretically oriented research that is concerned with the question of how culture is preserved through history, used in everyday life and dependent on contexts (see, e.g. DiMaggio 1997; Somers 2007; Swidler 1986, 2001; Thelen 1999 and Lichterman in this volume). This research is of course necessary as a theoretical backdrop for the plausibility of a Lutheran influence and to challenge the idea of Sweden as a straightforward secular society by arguing that religion (principally Lutheranism) is best understood as an ingrained inheritance in the Swedish society of today.

Embedded Religion

Religion is a part of culture, and this holds true for the very secularized country of Sweden as well (Pettersson 2009). Until the mid-1900s, Sweden was a rather monolithic society where, among other dominant institutions, the Lutheran Evangelical Church of Sweden and the free churches exerted great influence. It was only as recently in 1969 that a new education policy abolished Christendom as a confessional school subject and replaced it with the non-confessional study of religions. In the shift between the 1960s and the 1970s, the number of non-religious funerals began to increase while church weddings, baptisms and confirmations began to decrease (Hagevi 2009). The Church of Sweden lasted as a state church until the new millennium when it was finally formally separated from the state, although still remaining as one of the major Swedish civil society organizations.

Both institutional and individual secularization on a broad scale thus appeared surprisingly late in Sweden. Yet in spite of secularization, in 2011, 69% of the Swedish population were still formally members of the now non-state Lutheran Church (www.svenskakyrkan.se). Individuals become members either by being baptized into the Church of Sweden or by applying for membership. This implies an annual membership fee, the amount of which varies between parishes but on average is 1% of taxable income. Members can then use the services of the church for free. In spite of secularization, there is evidence that church buildings and the social efforts of the Church of Sweden are still important to the Swedish population (Bromander 2005; Bäckström and Bromander 1995).

So the situation is contradictory. Sweden is, on the one hand, a highly secularized country where not more than about 10% of the population is religious in the traditional sense, that is, believe in a personal God and attend church on a regular basis (Hamberg 2001). On the other hand, Swedish society has been formed for centuries, and is still characterized by, its heritage as a 'monolithic society'. Together with the popular mass movement tradition, an extensive welfare regime and other powerful institutions, it was long dominated by a hegemonic Protestant theology, in which the former state church and the free churches held a strong position. That the Swedish population still trusts the Church of Sweden and the free churches in spite of being so evidently secularized can probably be explained by this heritage. Today, Sweden seems to be a good example of the vicarious practice of religion, where the former

8 Lost and Found in Secularization

state church operates on behalf of a population that very seldom attends religious services (Davie 2001).

In a secularized country with a long religious tradition such as Sweden, religion is still held as a set of beliefs, values and attitudes by only a small part of the population, but it is used outside faith and religious institutions as a kind of cultural resource to express, interpret and make sense of actions to others and to ourselves (cf. Williams 2003). Since the religious institutions such as churches and congregations have lost their monopoly over the ideas propagated through religion, it has now become just one public phenomenon among others that can be used outside these institutions and their active participants. As a public phenomenon, the meanings and uses of religion are open to interpretation (Turner 2011). Religious symbols, for instance a crucifix or a Christmas crèche, have their origin in and derive their meaning from religious institutions and practices but are used today without signifying a personal belief and therefore have a secular meaning as well. Their secular meaning is dependent, however, on their formal religious origin. In this way, religion is an active and visible part of culture even in a secularized country such as Sweden.

So far, I have discussed such explicit aspects of religiosity as symbols, rites and expressions. But religion, in Sweden not least Evangelical Lutheranism, has permeated the culture and contributed to the shaping of the society on a more fundamental level. The paradigmatic example of religion as an invisible presence in culture is of course the thesis that a Protestant ethic contributed to the shaping of the spirit of capitalism (Weber 1978). Another example is the French *Laïcité* that was moulded by its counterpart, the Catholic Church (Hervieu-Léger 2001). Since religion permeates and is still forming culture on this fundamental level, theologians have argued that there are no distinct borders between what is religious and what is secular culture (cf. Martinsson 2007; Sigurdson 2009). This is true not least of Swedish society, which has been so monolithic for such a long time. This means that what were originally religious themes are now embedded in language and used in secular culture that is often unaware of its source (see Gillespie 2008 for a similar argument). This is obvious when it comes to existential and moral matters, as contemporary literature, movies and art illustrate (Miles 1996; Sigurdson 2003), but also in popular culture (Turner 2011) and political discourse (Mendieta and Van Antwerpen 2011; Sigurdson 2009).

It is obvious that the teaching of Luther cannot by itself explain how contemporary Swedish society is influenced. It is rather a question of how the Evangelical Lutheran Church of Sweden (not least reinforced by the pietistic revival during the eighteenth century) and the Lutheran free churches have maintained this scheme in their theology, teaching and practices over the years. There is no explicit reference to a Lutheran heritage in the interviews. However, considering how religion is embedded in Swedish society, I think it would be worthwhile to take the question of a Lutheran influence seriously and study whether this can be traced in Swedish society of today in terms of worldviews, conceptions of the interplay of man and society, morals, etc.

The hypothesis that religious or confessional traditions have an explanatory value for the shaping of societal values is supported by findings that indicate that the highest level of intrinsic support for democracy is found in 'Protestant Europe' (Welzel 2009). Furthermore, the Lutheran anthropological divide between the exterior man in worldly society and the inner sincere man in relation to God seems to be a promising perspective for understanding the specifically Swedish form of individualism that has been labelled 'statist individualism' since it is a form that does not presuppose an antagonism between an exterior societal order and the inner free self (see Trägårdh 2007, 2014).

Concluding Remarks

Grace Davie is one of the scholars who argue that we have to consider the scope of European secularization with some moderation, pointing to the fact that '...the faith communities of modern Europe are crucial players in civil society.' In civil society there are movements that are overtly religious, movements with a secular agenda but with a substantial religious constituency and movements (for instance the Green movement) that can be analysed as if they were religions (Davie 2001, see also Jacobsson 2014). As a consequence, I would add that religion, or theology, can sometimes be used to interpret how volunteers perceive the meaning of volunteering.

This means that we have to complement a more traditional—or perhaps modern—perception of religiosity as consciously held confessions or identities with a post-secular perspective in which there are no clear boundaries between religion and secular society. Danièle Hervieu-Léger (2001) argues that in the course of time, religion has permeated society and culture beyond its original but eroding institutions and that secularization therefore has its limits. In this perspective, the increasing secularization of society would be transformed from being perceived as a threat to volunteering into an opportunity where religiosity as one belief among others becomes more accessible to a wider, secular public through the erosion of religious institutions (see Hagevi 2009 for a similar argument). Furthermore, the study of how religiosity is used when people try to understand the meaning of their commitment and when volunteering can be understood as a form of religiosity would call for a more qualitative approach to volunteering. Such a research agenda would combine cultural sociology and theology to expose theological themes and understand their function in contemporary culture and society (cf. Madsen 2002). By 'bringing theology back in', we can deepen our understanding of how people understand and make sense of their life-worlds and how institutions are shaped. Lastly, this perspective would contribute to the contemporary, post-secular theological debate that has opened up for the mutual influence of, on the one hand, secular society and, on the other, religiosity and theology.

8 Lost and Found in Secularization

References

Alexander, J. C., & Smith, P. (1993). The discourse of American civil society. A new proposal for cultural studies. *Theory and Society, 22*(2), 151–207.

Arendt, H. (1958). *Människans villkor. Via Activa.* Göteborg: Daidalos [orig. ed. 1958 The human condition. The University of Chicago].

Bäckström, A., & Bromander, J. (1995). *Kyrkobyggnaden och det offentliga rummet. En undersökning av kyrkobyggnadens roll i det svenska samhället.* Uppsala: Svenska kyrkans centralstyrelse.

Bäckström, A., Davie, G., Edgardh, N., & Pettersson, P. (Eds.). (2011). *Welfare and Religion in 21st century Europe (Volume Two): Gendered, Religious and Social Change.* Aldershot: Ashgate.

Bellah, R., et al. (1985). *Habits of the heart. Individualism and commitment in American life.* Berkeley: University of California Press.

Bergdahl, L. (2010). *Seeing otherwise. Renegotiating democracy as questions for education* (Diss.). Stockholm: Stockholm University.

Borowitz, E. B. (1984). The autonomous self and the commanding community. *Theological Studies, 45,* 34–56.

Breckman, W. (2005). Democracy between disenchantment and political theology: French postmarxism and the return of religion. *New German Critique, 94,* 72–105.

Bromander, J. (1999). *Av fri vilja-på fri tid. Mitt i församlingen 1999:1.* Uppsala: Svenska kyrkans församlingsnämnd.

Bromander, J. (2005). *Medlem i Svenska kyrkan. En studie kring samtid och framtid.* Stockholm: Verbum.

Casanova, J. (2009). The religious situation in Europe. In H. Joas & K. Wiegand (Eds.), *Secularization and the world religions* (pp. 206–228). Liverpool: Liverpool University Press.

Clohesy, W. (2000). Altruism and the endurance of the good. *Voluntas: International Journal of Voluntary and Nonprofit Organizations, 11*(3), 237–253.

Cnaan, R. A., Handy, F., & Wadsworth, M. (1996). Defining who is a volunteer: Conceptual and empirical considerations. *Nonprofit and Voluntary Sector Quarterly, 25*(3), 364–383.

Davie, G. (2001). The persistence of institutional religion in modern Europe. In L. Woodhead, P. Heelas, & D. Martin (Eds.), *Peter Berger and the study of religion* (pp. 101–111). New York: Routledge.

de Vries, H. (2006). Introduction: Before, around, and beyond the theologico-political. In H. de Vries & L. Sullivan (Eds.), *Political theologies. Public religions in a post-secular world* (pp. 1–88). New York: Fordham University Press.

DiMaggio, P. J. (1997). Culture and cognition. *Annual Revue of Sociology, 23,* 263–287.

Gillespie, M. A. (2008). *The theological origins of modernity.* Chicago: The University of Chicago Press.

Grane, L. (1959). *Confessio Augustana. Orientering i den lutherska reformationens grundtankar.* Stockholm: Diakonistyrelsens Bokförlag.

Gray, J. (2007). *Black mass: Apocalyptic religion and the death of Utopia.* London: Allen Lane.

Hagevi, M. (2009). Efter sekulariseringen: Förändrade religiösa värden mellan generationer. *Socialvetenskaplig Tidskrift, 16*(3–4), 279–299.

Hamberg, E. (2001). Kristen tro och praxis i dagens Sverige. In C. R. Bråkenhielm (Ed.), *Världsbild och mening. En empirisk studie av livsåskådningar i dagens Sverige* (pp. 33–65). Nora: Nya Doxa.

Haski-Leventhal, D. (2009). Altruism and volunteerism: The perceptions of altruism in four disciplines and their impact on the study of volunteerism. *Journal for the Theory of Social Behaviour, 39*(3), 271–299.

Hervieu-Léger, D. (2001). The twofold limit of the notion of secularization. In L. Woodhead, P. Heelas, & D. Martin (Eds.), *Peter Berger and the study of religion* (pp. 112–125). New York: Routledge.

166 J. von Essen

Hvenmark, J. (2008). *Reconsidering membership. A study of individual members 'formal affiliation with democratic governed federations* (Diss.). Stockholm: Handelshögskolan i Stockholm, EFI.

Hvenmark, J., & von Essen, J. (2013). *Corporate volunteering. Engaging people for a greater cause or just another business case in the brave new world of capitalism?* Paper presented at ARNOVA's 42nd annual conference, Hartford, CT, 21–23 Nov 2013.

Jacobsson, K. (2014). Elementary forms of religious life in animal rights activism. *Culture Unbound, 6,* 305–326.

Jeppsson Grassman, E. (1997). *För andra och för mig. Det frivilliga arbetets innebörder.* Stockholm: Sköndalsinstitutets (skriftserie, nr. 8. Ersta Sköndal University College).

Joas, H. (2004). *Braucht der Mensch Religion? Über Erfahrungen der Selbsttranszendenz.* Freiburg im Breisgau: Herder.

Joas, H. (2009). Society, state and religion: Their relationship from the perspective of the world religions: An introduction. In H. Joas & K. Wiegand (Eds.), *Secularization and the world religions* (pp. 1–22). Liverpool: Liverpool University Press.

Johansson, G. (1998). *Det lilla extra. Om frivilligcentralen i Tyresö.* Stockholm: Sköndalsinstitutets (skriftserie nr. 11. Ersta Sköndal University College).

Krebs, D., & Hesteren, F. (1994). The developments of altruism: Toward an integrative model. *Developmental Review, 14,* 103–158.

Lilla, M. (2007). *The stillborn god: Religion, politics, and the modern west.* New York: Alfred Knopf.

Luther, M. (1989). *Martin Luther's basic theological writings* (Edited by T. F. Lull, Foreword by J. Pelikan). Minneapolis: Fortress.

MacIntyre, A. (1981). *After virtue, a study in moral theory.* London: Duckworth.

Madsen, R. (2002). Comparative cosmopolis. Discovering different paths to moral integration in the modern ecumene. In R. Madsen, W. S. Sullivan, A. Swidler, & S. M. Tipton (Eds.), *Meaning and modernity. Religion, polity and self* (pp. 105–123). Berkeley: University of California Press.

Martinsson, M. (2007). Skrift, tradition och auktoritet. In M. Martinson, O. Sigurdson, & J. Svenungsson (Eds.), *Systematisk teologi. En introduktion.* Stockholm: Verbum.

Mendieta, E., & Van Antwerpen, J. (Eds.). (2011). *The power of religion in the public sphere.* New York: Columbia University Press.

Mesch, D., Tschirhart, M., Perry, J., & Lee, G. (1998). Altruists or egoists? Retention in stipended service. *Nonprofit Management & Leadership, 9*(1), 4–21.

Miles, M. (1996). *Seeing and believing. Religion and values in the movies.* Boston: Beacon Press.

Mills, W. (1940). Situated actions and vocabularies of motive. *American Sociological Review, 5*(6), 904–913.

Musick, M., & Wilson, J. (2008). *Volunteers. A social profile.* Bloomington: Indiana University Press.

Nagel, T. (1970). *The possibility of altruism.* Oxford: Clarendon Press.

Norris, P., & Inglehart, R. (2011). *Sacred and secular. Religion and politics worldwide* (2nd ed.). Cambridge: Cambridge University Press.

Pettersson, T. (2009). Religion och samhällspraktik. En jämförande analys av det sekulariserade Sverige. *Socialvetenskaplig Tidkskrift, 16*(3–4), 233–264.

Polkinghorne, D. (1983). *Methodology for the human sciences. Systems of inquiry.* Albany: State University of New York Press.

Rehberg, W. (2005). Altruistic individualists: Motivations for international volunteering among young adults in Switzerland. *Voluntas: International Journal of Voluntary and Nonprofit Organizations, 16*(2), 109–122.

Ricoeur, P. (1975/1991). Phenomenology and hermeneutics. *From text to action. Essays in hermeneutics, II.* Evanston: Northwestern University Press. [orig. Nous 9 (1975) Indiana University].

Schervish, P., & Whitaker, K. (2010). *Wealth and the will of God. Discerning the use of riches in the service of ultimate purpose.* Bloomington: Indiana University Press.

Schneewind, J. (1998). *The invention of autonomy. A history of modern moral philosophy.* Cambridge: Cambridge University Press.

8 Lost and Found in Secularization 167

Sigurdson, O. (2003). *Världen är en främmande plats. Essäer om religionens återkomst.* Örebro: Cordia.

Sigurdson, O. (2009). *Det postsekulära tillståndet: Religion, modernitet, politik.* Munkedal: Glänta Produktion.

Somers, M. (2007). *Genealogies of Citinzenship. Markets, Statelessness, and the Right to Have Rights.* Cambridge: Cambridge University Press.

Svedberg, L., Jegermalm, M., & von Essen, J. (2010). *Svenskarnas engagemang är större än någonsin: Insatser i och utanför föreningslivet.* Stockholm: Ersta Sköndal University College.

Swidler, A. (1986). Culture in action: Symbols and strategies. *American Sociological Review, 51*(2), 273–286.

Swidler, A. (2001). *Talk of love. How culture matters.* Chicago: University of Chicago Press.

Taylor, C. (1985). *Philosophical papers, vol 1, human agency and language.* Cambridge: Cambridge University Press.

Thelen, K. (1999). Historical institutionalism in comparative politics. *Annual Review of Political Science, 2,* 369–404.

Tipton, S. M. (2002). Social differentation and moral pluralism. In R. Madsen, W. M. Sullivan, A. Swidler, & S. M. Tipton (Eds.), *Meaning and modernity. Religion, polity and self* (pp. 15–40). Berkeley: University of California Press.

Trägårdh, L. (2007). The "civil society" debate in Sweden: The welfare state challenged. In L. Trägårdh (Ed.), *State and civil society in Northern Europé. The Swedish model reconsidered* (pp. 9–36). New York: Berghahn Books.

Trägårdh, L. (2014). Statist individualism: The Swedish theory of love and its Lutheran imprint. In J. Halldorf & F. Wenell (Eds.), *Between the state and eucharist. Free church theology in with William T. Cavanaugh.* Eugene: Pickwick Publications.

Turner, B. (2011). *Religion and modern society. Citizenship, secularization and the state.* Cambridge: Cambridge University Press.

von Essen, J. (2008). *Om det ideella arbetets betydelse: En studie om människors livsåskådningar* (Diss.). Uppsala: Acta Universitatis Upsaliensis.

von Essen, J., & Grosse, J. (2012). Senmodernitetens religiositet och ideella engagemang. In M. Lövheim & J. Bromander (Eds.), *Religion som resurs? Existentiella frågor och värderingar i unga svenskars liv* (pp. 157–182). Skellefteå: Artos.

Weber, M. (1978). *Den protestantiska etiken och kapitalismens anda.* Lund: Argos.

Welzel, C. (2009). Democratization in the human development perspective. In Y. Esmer, H.-D. Klingeman, & B. Puranen (Eds.), *Religion, democratic values and political conflict. Festschrift in honor of Thorleif Pettersson* (pp. 149–180) (Acta Universitatis Upsaliensis no 23). Uppsala: Uppsala University.

Willliams, R. (2003). The language of God in the city of man. Religious discourse and public politics in America. In C. Smidt (Ed.), *Religion as social capital. Producing the common good* (pp. 171–189). Waco: Baylor University Press.

Wuthnow, R. (1991). *Acts of compassion. Caring for others and helping our selves.* Princeton: Princeton University Press.

Wuthnow, R. (2011). Taking talk seriously: Religious discourse as social practice. *Journal for the Scientific Study of Religion, 50*(1), 1–21.

Yeung, A. B. (2004). The octagon model of volunteer motivation: Results of a phenomenological analysis. *Voluntas: International Journal of Voluntary & Nonprofit Organizations, 15*(1), 21–46.

Chapter 9
Making Church Happen

Architectural Methods for Transforming the Parish Churches of Flanders into Civic Collectives

Roel De Ridder and Sylvain De Bleeckere

Introduction

Only quite recently, since the late 1990s, politicians and 'ordinary people' began questioning the future of parish churches in Flanders. The reasons are manifold; the most important, at least when seen from the standpoint of the church buildings themselves and their use, being the lack of Catholic priests in mostly Catholic Flanders. There are only 881 priests (paid for by the federal government) for the 1787 (Van Lierde 2012) parish churches that are still being used for Mass. Apart from that, the general maintenance cost of church buildings are increasing fast (Sellam 2009), while the attendance numbers are decreasing at the same rate: Only 5.4% of Flemings attend church at least once a month (Havermans and Hooghe 2011). The Belgian parish churches, however, rely on a (Napoleonic) system of 'fabric committees': public legal bodies of elected volunteers that take care of the temporal goods belonging to the parish. However, though one member must be the local priest or someone appointed by the bishop, the fabric committees operate more or less independently from the Church hierarchy. The deficits arising from this particular type of church council are being taken care of by local government. The municipalities do not discriminate between the buildings they themselves own (mostly pre-Napoleonic churches) and those owned by the fabric committees (mostly post-Napoleonic churches). The fact that the municipalities pay the fabric committees large amounts of money and that the celebrants are paid by the Belgian federal Department of Justice has raised many eyebrows in parliament, especially after recent scandals in the Belgian Catholic Church. Consequently, the problem of the near-empty church buildings is seen as a financial problem, both by politicians and common citizens.

R. De Ridder (✉)
Arck, Hasselt University, Diepenbeek, Belgium
e-mail: roel.deridder@gmail.com

Faculty of Architecture, KU Leuven, Brussels & Ghent, Belgium

S. De Bleeckere
ArcK, Hasselt University, Diepenbeek, Belgium
e-mail: sylvain.debleeckere@uhasselt.be

L. Hustinx et al. (eds.), *Religion and Volunteering,* Nonprofit and Civil Society Studies, DOI 10.1007/978-3-319-04585-6_9, © Springer International Publishing Switzerland 2015

Similarly, the church buildings themselves are seen as (expensive) commodities, as luxury items for a decreasing group of Catholics. This kind of simple, rational, even opportunist view—however opposed it is to the church buildings' past embeddedness in the social life of local communities—stands only for one way of thinking; needless to say that such a plain financial interpretation of the problem is massively reductionist. On the other hand, when they are listed as monuments by the Flemish agency for heritage (which is the case for about 40 % of parish churches in Flanders), church buildings are seen as valuable examples of national heritage, for all citizens to enjoy and marvel at.

Secularization is a term often coined within the Flemish discourse on the future of parish churches, which of course is not hard to understand. Parish churches used to be at the centre of local community life; on a weekly basis (at least), they used to gather almost all citizens. In 1967, 52 % of Flemings still went to church (Hooghe et al. 2006). Church buildings nourished civic engagement and volunteering, whereas today the church community and its volunteers are both a fast-ageing and shrinking group. While this does not mean that people automatically turn away from all things church related, their direct relationship with the church building did change however.

Secularization is a complex process. Many sociologists attempt to understand and describe it; some more critically than others. What they all share is that they accept 'the still defensible core of the theory of secularization', that is, 'the thesis of the differentiation of the religious and secular spheres' (Achterberg et al. 2009). Religiosity is undeniably in decline, but that does not mean that non-believers are automatically against religion, or that religion is completely disappearing from public life. Achterberg et al.'s 2009 analysis even shows 'that an increasing public significance of religion is not a temporary anomaly, but that it is systematically connected with the decline of religiosity'.

A very useful concept to describe the persisting interest in religion and church buildings is Grace Davie's 'vicarious religion', which, she emphasizes, takes place in 'societies in which well-funded state churches operate on behalf of the population which rarely, if ever, attend religious services' (Davie 2001, p. 106). In Davie's 2001 text on the persistence of institutional religion in modern Europe, she explicitly links vicarious religion and a general appreciation for religious institutions to a sustained public care for church buildings. Thus, the ongoing commitment to religious buildings still has religious significance. There is a general willingness to contribute to the Church, through the parish churches for example, even when most individuals do not 'believe'. Moreover, as Davie (2001, p. 108) states, there is 'a conviction that religious buildings are in some sense public property and belong to everyone, regardless of formal church membership, attendance or even belief'. Regarding the many Flemish parish churches, the observations of both Achterberg et al. and Davie might suggest that the future of these buildings should not be measured and decided solely by the level of Mass attendance.

In federal Belgium, the Dutch- and French-speaking communities, just like the respective regions of Flanders and Wallonia, are autonomous as far as most cultural matters and matters tied to a particular geographical area (*grondgebonden materie*)

9 Making Church Happen

are concerned; culture is a responsibility of the communities, whereas most territorial-related matters (including national heritage) are the responsibility of the regions. It is therefore superfluous to add that the parish churches find themselves in very complex circumstances, especially in the Brussels capital region where the Dutch and the French meet. Moreover, because the church buildings and the celebrants of the recognized faiths are being subsidized by the different governments, the Church–state separation in Belgium and Flanders is a 'moderate separation' (De Pooter 2003); De Pooter also coins the terms 'positive neutrality' or 'benevolent neutrality' to label the unique Belgian state of affairs. All this complicates the situation for politicians and others and makes it hard to deal with the whole picture. This chapter attempts to take a look beyond the 'traditional' situating of the parish church as a strictly sacred building, a luxury item or a 'heritage church'. Simultaneously, it tries to see what opportunities the moderate Church–state separation, typical of Belgium and Flanders, holds for the future of the buildings. The fabric committees, especially, will be scrutinized for their potential as key local actors with respect to future plans for the parish churches. The unique Flemish or Belgian situation, however complex, might be better recognized as a possible advantage than as yet another complicating factor. At the same time, this chapter's focus on the buildings themselves and the social capital surrounding them might well be transposed to other countries.

The Belgian situation, nonetheless, is not characterized by (financial) advantages only. Compared to Catholic Church communities in the Netherlands for example, Flemish communities are rather passive (Draulans and Witte 1999). Unlike their 'colleagues' in the Netherlands, they are not the owners of the church building, since the municipalities and the fabric committees are. As a result, the Flemish communities never had to fight for their buildings (except in some very rare cases) and they never had to pay for their upkeep themselves (as, again, is the case in the Netherlands), except indirectly as taxpayers. Now that Flanders is entering a time of extreme uncertainty as to the church buildings due to the recent political questions, it is not very likely that Flemish local communities will suddenly and spontaneously establish foundations to save their parish churches, however desirable it might be if the local communities did claim their parish churches, since parish churches are essentially meant to be public buildings. It is even more unlikely that this general passivity (with, of course, some important exceptions) will spontaneously turn into organic bottom-up processes resulting in the communal use of the buildings.[1] If community use is the wanted outcome—and a recent note by the Flemish Minister for Administrative Affairs, Local and Provincial Government (Bourgeois 2011) does point in that direction—then some guidance or a certain protocol will be needed.

Before introducing the research problem, the text will take a closer look at a concrete case study conducted by the authors in the village of Schulen, Flanders. By investigating a concrete example of a parish church and its relation to the local

---

[1] Interesting examples of church revitalization are Bruges's Magdalena church and Ghent's Macharius church: Both churches now attract a broader, spiritually interested crowd, looking for meaning, yet still starting from the Catholic tradition.

172 R. De Ridder and S. De Bleeckere

community, the research problem can be situated more precisely within the unique Flemish situation.

Case Study: Schulen's Parish Church and its Uncertain Future[2]

Schulen is a village of 3,000 inhabitants in the west of the Flemish province of Limburg. Since the 1970s, it is part of the municipality of Herk-de-Stad. Schulen's parish church is situated near one of the village's two main roads; it is a traditional 1930s building, built as a broad cross-shaped hall with a pitched roof. It was put up to replace a late-gothic parish church that was in bad shape by the mid-1930s and which was no longer large enough to accommodate the congregation. The rather bulky new church was erected right across the street; the old one was partly demolished, yet its nave bricks were used for the foundations of the new church—the municipality of Herk-de-Stad still keeps old pictures of school children carrying the bricks across the road. The old church tower, which is still standing, is now one of Schulen's rare listed monuments. Unlike more modern church buildings built in the same era, Schulen's new Saint John's has all the features of a nineteenth century church: a high bell tower, a clear separation between the choir and the nave, stained-glass windows (one window came straight from the old church) and a collection of old sculptures. In the late 1930s, the Royal Commission for Monuments and Landscapes insisted on the new church being built with clear neo-gothic characteristics. Moreover in Limburg, the Catholic mission was very alive in the first half of the twentieth century, something that had a lot to do with (foreign) workers coming to Limburg's mining facilities and the Church 'saving' them from socialism and communism. The ecclesiastical and civil authorities worked together to ensure a powerful position for the Church in Limburg, which resulted in a strong Christian sociopolitical group in Limburg. Schulen's parish church, which is partly a late product of the nineteenth century Roman Catholic restoration movement, is, however, primarily a church akin to many others. It is not an exceptional building from a buildings conservation expert's point of view (although it certainly is exceptional for some locals); it is not listed as a monument either.

---

[2] This section is based on research in the archives, more precisely the Rijksarchief in Hasselt (home of Schulen's parish archive), the Hasselt city archive (in which the archive of Joseph Deré, the architect of Schulen's parish church, can be found), the provincial archive in Hasselt and the provincial centre for cultural heritage (PCCE, in Hasselt as well). The Schulen case study was part of a doctoral study on the future of Flanders' parish churches; the PhD defence took place in February 2013 in Hasselt, Belgium. For a more thorough discussion on the empirical research, we refer to Roel De Ridder's PhD thesis: *Kerkgebouw genereert publiek: Een actuele strategie voor de architectuurtheoretische herdefiniëring en de toegepaste herwaardering van de Vlaamse parochiekerk (The Public Performance of the Church Building: a new strategy for the architectural theoretical redefinition and the applied revaluation of Flanders' parish churches)*.

Today, Schulen's parish church has become far too large for just the weekly Mass. About 20–40 faithful (mostly elderly) parishioners attend the church, which can seat 450, on Saturday evenings. There is no Mass on Sunday mornings, since the diocese of Hasselt (Limburg's capital) is not equipped with enough celebrants to provide for all its parish churches. Nevertheless, the church building itself is kept in a fine condition. Neglect of the building is not the problem here as an enthusiastic fabric committee looks after it. Belgium may be blessed with Napoleonic rules, the members of Schulen's church committee, year after year, feel reluctant to ask for money. They make their own calculations and conclude that the municipality has to pay close to 1,000 EUR per parishioner per year to keep the building clean, wind- and waterproof, heated during Mass and supplied with electricity. Although the average amount of money which the municipalities have to spend on their parish churches goes up year by year, this still does not represent much more than 1 % of the municipal budget (Delbeke 2007). It does not, however, prevent the absolute figures from being impressive: The Flemish municipalities spend approximately 32,000 EUR per church every year (Sellam 2009).

Schulen's fabric committee is particularly pessimistic about the future these days, especially since the Flemish Minister for Administrative Affairs, Local and Provincial Government (who also has the final say on fabric and buildings conservation) has asked all fabric committees, central church councils (usually, there is one central church council of elected volunteers per municipality) and municipalities to collectively discuss the future of all the Flemish parish churches (Bourgeois 2011). According to the Minister, and as included in the official memorandum, local associations must be invited as well to represent local social and cultural needs. The Minister expects a clear view on the situation for each municipality: Which church buildings will remain church buildings? Which churches will be partly converted to new uses? Which churches will be reused, and which ones will be demolished? Nobody knows exactly what will happen next, but it is very likely that the more centrally positioned and/or monumental churches will be spared, and this is also the line of reasoning of the dioceses. Schulen's church building is neither of these things despite its quite large size. The local fabric committee's fear for the future is therefore far from irrational. (Fig. 9.1).

Looking at Schulen, it quickly becomes apparent that the members of the fabric committee and the local associations that are connected one way or another to the church building are all ageing. The people that truly care for Schulen's parish church and do not feel reluctant to show this are older: The single most active of them, the fabric committee's treasurer, is 60 years old, a youngster in the others' opinion. When the people who show they care are taken ill or pass away, there is, on the face of it, no one to follow in their footsteps. The absence of youth in the church building on Saturday evenings, as well as the lack of youth in the (traditional) associations, is a major concern for those active in Schulen's social life. In Schulen, and according to those who openly care for Saint John's, the church building is of no concern to younger generations. Along with the small group of middle-aged and elderly men and women, some even remember the church being built in 1938, a significant body of knowledge of the parish church and its embeddedness in the local community is slowly but surely fading away.

Fig. 9.1 Saint John's church in Schulen. (Photograph by Mine Dalemans)

This chapter therefore attempts to examine whether parish churches have the potential to stay, or again become places of public significance. By involving the local community, it also investigates how church buildings and their future can be dealt with in a democratic way. Central to this challenge is finding a stable middle–ground between top–down directives and a centralized line of reasoning on the one hand (which might result in the loss of local knowledge) and an all too idealistic hope for spontaneous grass-roots processes on the other (which, save for some exceptions, are not going to happen). Sociologists often elaborate on the positive effects of church going, such as increased social capital and increased volunteering (Billiet 1998; Hooghe 2000; Elchardus et al. 2001; Bevers et al. 2011). It is hoped that this chapter will contribute to the debate on whether the current, sometimes rather implicit, attention for the inherited religious meaning of church buildings (as indicated by Davie 2001, Achterberg et al. 2009 and by the existing, more general interest in heritage as well) has positive effects too. Since, even in a secular context, the meanings of the church building are still connected to religion, a renewed interest in the church building might be awakened by this legacy. Moreover, a reappropriation of empty churches may possibly stimulate commitment: civic, religious and other. (Fig. 9.2).

Throughout the next three sections, the interface between architecture and the contemporary social sciences will be examined theoretically in an attempt to contribute to a new approach to both discuss and actually tackle the problem of emptying parish churches in Flanders. This new approach seeks to build on the existing and specifically local civic engagement. The next-to-last section discusses the research conducted by the authors in Schulen's parish church; this research puts to the test the findings of the theoretical sections, and Schulen's Saint John's will be used as the case by means of which theory will be discussed and exemplified.

Fig. 9.2 The interior of Saint John's church. (Photograph by Franky Larouselle)

The Architectural Discourse

Two very different strands of (academic) knowledge regarding (old) buildings and their present significance will be discussed here. The first one is the national heritage discourse, which is the 'typical' discourse on church buildings in Flanders; the second one is a contemporary, mostly Anglo-Saxon and explicitly social view on architecture, which goes under the name of spatial agency.

To a significant extent, the current national heritage discourse consists of experts, mostly art historians, attributing 'values' to old buildings—an act that remains largely unquestioned. Predominantly, the heritage values—such as the 'historical', the 'architectural', the 'contextual' or the 'rarity' value—refer merely to the material aspects of the building. Only very rarely is it clear where these values come from exactly or how they are being established; the experts' explanations of the values are rather vague as they are based on quite general historic and hermeneutic constructions; phrases such as 'of universal value' are not shunned in this discourse. The material values always end up being hierarchically superior to the more social values (see for example Smith 2006).[3] Moreover, within this national heritage discourse, there is a rather false attention to 'social values': From time to time, 'socio-cultural values' are taken into account, but more often than not they only stand for the church being built on a pilgrimage site, the presence of certain de-

---

[3] For the argument concerning the superiority of material values and the questioning of the effectiveness of value assessments in general, see Roel De Ridder's PhD thesis.

votional elements or the church building's name referring to a local saint. It is only very rarely that the 'socio-cultural value' does point towards the church building's social activity and its role within (local) civil society.

For the Flemish administration as well, the heritage values of the church building, as Minister Bourgeois points out in his statement (2011), are of more value than its religious character, since the values allegedly matter to all Flemings. The fact that it is precisely the religious character that might contribute to social capital and volunteering seems to be of less importance. The listed status of a building, which is typically the result of the experts attributing heritage value to it, does indeed ensure the continued existence of the building, but the fact that a building is a listed monument could also bring about obstacles to its use. As a result, there appears to be an inherent risk of the experts increasing the gulf between the building and daily life. In the most extreme cases, listed church buildings are just things to wonder at (Noppen 2011), mere objects, appraised by experts by means of a vague attribution of (universal) values.

By making use of the existing 'universal' approach, the experts involved ignore what church buildings mean on a more concrete level; in particular, the experts ignore what church buildings do and what they bring about. The main effect of the current modus operandi is that church buildings are being reduced to a few generic values. The heritage approach is not equal to commodification as such, although buildings are seen as objects, but it does not rule out commodification either, not even with the discovering of the appealing aura of monuments by some strictly commercial actors, shop and hotel owners for example. Moreover, for the Flemish administration, it is perfectly possible to turn a monument into a shop or a hotel, as long as the 'intrinsic heritage values' are being respected, that is, as long as the material aspects of the building are being safeguarded. The immaterial social effects of, for example a church building, seem to be of less importance. That is why it might be interesting to examine the social aspects by way of another method, one that truly values the social.

One of the most prolific contemporary writers on the interface between architecture and the social sciences is Jeremy Till. Till's main critique is that 'architectural culture' has a tendency to forget about process, occupation, nature and society (Awan et al. 2011, p. 28). Against an architecture that many architectural theorists in the second half of the twentieth century regarded as a strictly autonomous and artistic affair, Till and his colleagues introduce the notion of spatial agency. Agency, according to the authors, is 'change through the empowerment of others, allowing them to engage in their spatial environments in ways previously unknown or unavailable to them, opening up new freedoms and potentials as a result of reconfigured social space'(Awan et al. 2011, p. 32). The participation movement that started in the 1960s with advocacy and community architecture (Jenkins and Pereira 2010, p. 40) plays an important role in the book *Spatial Agency: Other Ways of Doing Architecture* (Awan et al. 2011), as well as some visionary architects of the twentieth century. The practices included in *Spatial Agency* are underpinned theoretically by Till (2009) in *Architecture Depends*, his book on architectural connectedness and contingency. By citing authors as diverse as Henri Lefebvre, Zygmunt Bauman and

9 Making Church Happen

Bruno Latour, Till confronts the present 'architectural culture' with (among other insights) Latour's 'proliferation of the hybrids'. Till (2009) quite literally copies the most important of Latour's (1993) arguments into architectural discourse. By doing so, he implies that most architects today are 'moderns' since their discourses and their practices are about purification. A 'non-modern' architect would know how to appreciate the hybrid character of the complex issues that architectural problems actually are.

According to Till, architectural culture resents contingency and because of this 'pure' discourse it fails to connect with daily life. Many architects reason in terms of freeze-frames: The conceived building only 'exists' for them when it is being finished and when the photographer is there to take pictures of it in its mint condition (Till 2009, pp. 77–92). Thus, time is being erased from the architectural process, as are time-related concepts such as decay and occupation. Time inevitably means change, whether decay through the elements for example, or unexpected patterns of use through occupation. Most architects, Till argues, cannot deal with such contingencies and tend towards a 'pure' and autonomous architecture that is unavoidably disconnected from daily life and its many uncertainties. Autonomous architecture is not conceived of as 'lived' or 'inhabited', let alone being taken care of by non-architects.

Consequently, trying to (re-)connect architecture and the social is a somewhat contrarian act. However, the notion of performance, as understood by the advocates of spatial agency, does exactly that. Originally, the term was used in design theory to describe how a building performs technically: how efficient it works in terms of energy, fire-protection, structural strength and so on. Most of the time performance thus refers to calculable matters, whereas Till (2009, p. 162) adopts a broader, more social, definition that attempts to describe the effects of the building on the (social) environment, mostly due to the occupation of the building. He talks about 'people whose political and phenomenal lives will be affected by the construction of a building and its subsequent occupation' (Till 2009, p. 173). Isabelle Doucet and Kenny Cupers (2009), influenced by Latour as well, also talk about a general move towards performance in architecture, as do some important contemporary American architectural theorists (Somol and Whiting 2007).

A more social understanding of architecture need not clash with a more artistic understanding. Even the most passionate advocates of spatial agency do not reject architecture's dimension of (artistic) authorship; however, process and performance become more important than the finished product. There are architectural interventions which succeed in blending precisely the right amount of architecture with the right performance for the job. For example, the German firm Raumlabor's *Eichbaumoper* project in one of the Ruhr area's derelict metro stations turned the near-ruin into a vivid and locally supported cultural node which now works as a generator for civic engagement. The architect(s) need not always design completely new structures—after all, a lot of areas in the Western world, Flanders to name but one—are already built up. Contemporary spatial agency even makes us believe that the more connected the architect is to local (social) demands, the less he or she actually builds, though what the architect builds has an important social performance.

By opening up the act of architecture towards society, spatial agency overtly declares itself in favour of an architecture that is intrinsically social, committed and relying on volunteers. At the same time, spatial agency does not deny that buildings have autonomous components as well. The new focus on architectural performativity might have important implications for the discourse on church buildings. Up until now, parish churches and architectural performativity were two separate worlds, but church buildings also do something. Indeed, one might even say, especially church buildings, because traditionally they make people believe. They are not static objects; they influence their (social) environments and their (social) environments influence them.

By referring to the case study, the next-to-last section will investigate how some spatial agency-inspired actions work in Schulen, how they are able to ignite processes with volunteers and others and also whether these processes are able to be long-lasting or not. But first, let us take a closer look at (some of) the key literature that inspired Jeremy Till to support the field of spatial agency.

A Parish Church as a Network

Key to the new approach to Flemish parish churches would be to find a new, broader definition of what a parish church really is. Such a definition could be similar to Clifford Geertz's (1973) 'thick description'. The point is to discover a line of reasoning that does not ignore contingency, the local feelings towards the building and the many ways in which the building itself performs. Therefore, this section attempts to find a way to look at 'the social' regarding parish churches. The acts of mapping, as proposed in this section, will help to trace a possible social basis to redefine and reassess the parish church.

Contemporary thinkers such as Bruno Latour and Michel Callon dismiss abstract notions of 'the social'. Instead, they talk about the collective (Latour 2005b, p. 116), a more concrete but at the same time somewhat contingent and unstable assembly of people and other things. They say things because their ontology is a symmetrical one: For them there is no a priori difference between humans and nonhumans. What is more, Callon and Latour question every possible theoretical (for example historical or hermeneutic) presumption. As leading theorists in Actor-Network Theory (ANT), they understand knowledge and agency as distributed through networks. Success, power and truth (Latour 1988) depend on the strength of these networks; they are effects of networks. Nothing is foundational (Latour 2008) in ANT, rather, everything is relational, as is the case for American pragmatism, William James's and John Dewey's philosophical method.

ANT has already been transposed successfully to the realm of architecture and urban design: Over the past 10 years, several academic publications were dedicated to actor-network descriptions of buildings in their complex contexts and to an ANT-inspired scrutinizing of architectural firms in their daily practice (Yaneva 2009; Houdart and Chihiro 2009). Latour himself wrote about architecture and design as well (see for example Latour 2008; Latour and Yaneva 2008). The major strength of ANT is that it does not flee from complex *imbroglios* (Latour 1993, p. 3) or matters of concern (Latour 2005b, p. 175), mixtures of social, cultural, scientific and technical affairs for example. Above all, ANT is particularly interested in controversy. It is no coincidence that today's debates on trans-disciplinarity (Doucet and Janssens 2011) to tackle complex societal problems build heavily on ANT. When it comes to architecture, ANT informs architects to adopt a broad definition of what design is, since the networks as described by ANT do not suddenly stop beyond the architectural firm's threshold, or beyond the plot one intends to build on.

Is it possible, then, to transpose this theory of relations, which at first sounds like something more suited to complex urban contexts, to a more pastoral and rural setting such as Schulen? It is, because ANT is only a way to look at things, to describe them and by doing so to gain new perspectives. Yaneva's (Yaneva 2009) and Houdart's (Houdart and Chihiro 2009) ethnographies of design turned tons of previous architectural theories and design theories inside out. As Yaneva and Houdart pointed out: Some very impressive buildings came into being very pragmatically; they were not plain products of mythical authorship, nor were they produced using strictly logical and rational methods. Our own case study research in Schulen reveals new perspectives as well. Saint John's networks, however peaceful the surroundings might look, are as complex as any.

One can, of course, trace many networks starting from 'church' in Schulen. 'Church' today is brought into being as the effect of complex relationships and gentle controversies between actors as diverse as the church building, the parishioners, the church choir, the fabric committee, funding from the municipality, other incomes, the sexton, the dean and the deanery of Herk-de-Stad, the central church board, the diocese of Hasselt and the Flemish government's decree on cults and more actors which there is no space to mention here. Because of many common interests, Schulen's 'church network' looks rather strong; lots of actors want 'church' to happen in Schulen, and it does happen. However, cracks in the network are starting to show in terms of a lack of priests, the decreasing numbers of parishioners and the questioning of the funding.

An ANT account of a church, in its spatial and social environment, has important advantages. Tracing local networks and local knowledge reveals a certain basis, not only for a more pragmatic way to look at church buildings, but also for a new way to actually and pragmatically deal with the building, as a new layer on top of the ANT account.

Restricting the approach to involving actors, however, is no guarantee to keep future processes of church reuse from becoming just economic. There is a double inherent danger hiding in the current general situation in Flanders regarding parish churches which cannot easily be dealt with. In a recent note from the civil authorities on the future of Flemish parish churches (Bourgeois 2011), it is written that local associations should be involved in the discussions between the fabric committees, the central church boards and the municipality. However, no explicit guidelines or protocols for the discussions with local associations are expanded on, which presents a first problem. When these discussions take place across the region of Flanders, will the associations be truly consulted or just informed? Or, in more architectural terms, will there be participation or pseudo-participation (Till 2005, p. 23; Jenkins and Pereira 2010, p. 51)? The simple involvement of 'stakeholders' is not enough to ensure a rich future for the parish churches. Flanders is in need of a policy, but currently a general aversion to all things reeking of social engineering appears to stop politicians from acting firmly. For some authors (BAVO 2008; Vanstiphout 2008), this dislike of social engineering is actually a guarantee for a very restrictive and neo-liberal line of reasoning and politics. Secondly, the scale on which these discussions will take place, the scale of the central church board that is (which at the same time is the scale of the municipality), might erase a lot of local knowledge. In the worst-case scenario, which is not at all impossible, the individual church building will be treated as a commodity, as a simple object which performs a simple function today and another function tomorrow, and that can easily be bought or sold. Although local actors may get involved, a sheer top–down approach of, say, developers who only inform the locals cannot be excluded unless more regulation is put in place.

An ANT account of a concrete, church-related situation is able to at least resolve part of this double problem. Whenever a thorough account of a church building is being drawn up, it will most probably show that the church is not an object but rather a mediator (Latour 2005b, pp. 37–42) with an unpredictable and complex performance. It will show that many volunteers and others are implicitly and explicitly taking care of the building, that they make 'church happen', and that each church building has its own particular network. When the future of the church building becomes an issue, however, an ANT account will not suffice to explore future possibilities. That is why the next section will focus on a theoretical basis for a protocol for concrete action, while still relying on the performativity of the church building.

A Parish Church as a Forum

A search for guidance, for a democratization even, of the future discussions and actions regarding parish churches in a way compatible with ANT's focus on performativity, brings us to the text *Acting in an Uncertain World* by Callon et al. (2009). The central notion developed by Callon and his co-writers is that of the hybrid forum.

What is the hybrid forum? Simply put, the hybrid forum is a public space that makes the layperson the expert. The discourse on the hybrid forum stems from the Science and Technology Studies (STS) and ANT traditions, in which the social is understood as being assembled time after time (Latour 2005b) between humans and non-humans. Callon and his coauthors (2009) describe meetings where laypersons and experts get together and in which they practice science (the accumulation of knowledge) and (micro-)politics (deliberative processes which affect people's lives) at the same time, hence the use of the term hybrid. Although Callon et al.'s

9 Making Church Happen 181

(2009) cases are mostly about health and always about a quest for new science, the authors state that the hybrid forum might well be translated into other fields, for example religious or ethical ones (Callon et al. 2009, p. 253).

The hybrid forum is dialogical, rather than delegative (Callon et al. 2009, p. 10). This means that it is open. Consequently, everyone is invited to contribute. According to Callon et al. (2009), during the hybrid forum, which is always a succession of several 'rendezvous' (Callon et al. 2009, p. 222), new identities, and especially new group identities, can form. Together, experts and laypersons design possible worlds they can share, they gradually investigate possible scenarios. As Latour quotes William James in a text about what he calls 'collective experiments': 'action is never the realization, nor the implementation of a plan, but the exploration of the unintended consequences of a provisional and revisable version of a project' (James in Latour 2001). Hybrid forums encourage others to join and, equally importantly, they encourage controversies to come to the fore and these are best dealt with sooner, before positions have 'hardened' (Callon 2009, p. 252), rather than later. Uncertainty is the hybrid forum's driving force. Thus, complexity, contingency and uncertainty are tackled without effacing them.

In order to explore common worlds, Callon et al. (2009, p. 189) suggest that each rendezvous leads to small and reversible measures, rather than to big and final decisions. As regards church buildings and their future, this understanding can correspond to experimenting with new (temporary) uses that can coexist with liturgy and which do not need major refurbishment. Because almost all Flemish church buildings, however empty, are still used as, precisely, church buildings, the networks surrounding and involving these buildings are still there. Therefore, it might be better to already start rethinking them while still in use because of the networks present. This in turn is in line with what the Flemish Minister wrote in his recent note on local actors and local needs. Callon et al.'s guidelines can help to keep future discussions between the fabric committees, the central church boards, the municipalities and local associations truly dialogical.

The hybrid forum, however, is no easy solution. Its lack of interest in a general consensus and its apparent coming into existence spontaneously do not correspond with what one might expect from a protocol regarding the future use of churches. Callon et al. would go as far as to state that the concept of consensus undermines the dialogical democratic nature of the forum (2009, p. 4) and one can, of course, understand the hybrid forum's lack of consensus as some sort of 'permanently postponed consensus' and as a plea for non-stop experimenting, yet this is still quite a relativist position. Because money is involved and, according to many, central to the problem, most actors, even the locals are in favour of a rather rigorous scenario for the future and Schulen is no exception as we discovered. Participation (or a quest for a common world) is fine, but it must lead to something. The second problem, the hybrid forum 'coming into existence spontaneously', is equally hard to tackle. Hybrid forums appear, for example, when parents of children with very rare diseases organize themselves to demand new research on the subject. Very fast, these parents then become specialists themselves and a new group identity is born. The hybrid forums Callon et al. talk about concern life-threatening issues. Churches which might cease to be churches do not bring about life-threatening situations, so no hybrid forums are formed 'spontaneously'. Hybrid forums, according to Callon, need whistle-blowers (2009, p. 200). When it comes to church buildings, and even when whistle-blowers are there to address the issue—the Schulen fabric committee's 'youngster' once appeared in a newspaper, claiming that the church was too expensive to maintain (no author 2006)—no hybrid forum will form overnight, let alone spontaneously, however vital it may be to bring together specialists and the local community.

Many of the hybrid forum's aspects, however, are highly challenging, and probably most useful with respect to future protocols. Callon et al.'s 2009 text acts as an important update for older texts on participation. Maybe *Acting in an Uncertain World* is too relativistic, but older texts on participation were too mellow on the surface and often pedantic, dictatory and ideological underneath, as Berit Moltu's (2008, p. 164) critique of participatory action research and Jeremy Till's (2005, pp. 21–23) critique of Carole Pateman's *Participation and Democratic Theory* show. To solve the problems of the hybrid forum, while not dismissing Callon's important guidelines, a certain grip or support is needed as well as a spark to ignite the discussions and to make the issue of the near-empty church buildings clearly visible in the public sphere. In Schulen, there is some solid ground (the elder men and women who take care of the parish church network) for initiating a process, but that seems to be it. The media can help to make the issue (more) visible (Callon et al. 2009, p. 181), but even that is not enough. More awareness, a sense of urgency even, is needed. But how can this come about? And how can this be streamlined into a process? To answer these questions, the Schulen case study resorted to architecture.

The Schulen Scale Model Trials

In Schulen, the performativity of the parish church and the view of the inhabitants on the future of the church were tested through several research actions. As already mentioned, the Schulen case is used to discuss and exemplify theory. The sequence of research actions came into being slowly and via consultation of the Church's hierarchy and the local fabric committee. Grants were found via the Belgian King Baudouin Foundation to make this process happen, a large part of it being a joint effort between the researchers and a small group of local volunteers. 'Volunteers' here means both church and other volunteers. The most active volunteers, when it came to supporting the researchers, were the fabric committee's treasurer and the president of the local branch of the pluralistic 'Family Union'. Both volunteers are loyal parishioners, although they have only weak ties with the higher Church hierarchy, not unlike most other volunteers in Schulen. Apart from two questionnaires (one with Schulen's volunteers only and one with about one sixteenth of the total population) and a 'village meeting', the authors organized two separate 'scale model trials'. The Schulen scale model trials took place in the parish church itself,

Fig. 9.3 A conversation with participants during the first scale model trial; behind the model are the white cubes of model foam that represent dwelling space. (Photograph by Jeroen Gielen)

more precisely in a 'forum setting' as inspired by both the hybrid forum and the contemporary field of spatial agency. Central to the methodology were two large scale (1/50) wooden models of Schulen's Saint John's.

The first scale model trial (April 30–May 1, 2011) was set up to examine the current performance of the parish church. It was not the first research action in Schulen, as it took place after the first questionnaire and the village meeting. The three objectives of this experiment were to explore: (1) the inhabitants' view on the strengths and weaknesses of their church building, (2) their ideas as to future use and (3) the way they decided about these issues. At the same time, this research action was a way of testing the scale model methodology. About 40 people participated, most of them in their fifties, sixties or seventies, both male and female. Several core volunteers, also being loyal parishioners, took part in both the organization of the particular action (which was combined with a photo exhibition on the old and 'new' Saint John's) and the experiment itself. Everyone was free to participate; people were informed of the research action via Schulen's diverse associations and an advertisement for the photo exhibition circulated in a door-to-door brochure.

Two identical models of the church were used during the first trial. The first one questioned the participants' preferences vis-à-vis future use. This was tested by means of icons representing (groups of) proposed uses which the participants could pick up and allocate a place within the model. The second model examined the possibility of dwelling in the church building. After configuring one or more icons in the first model, the participants were free to position cubes of model foam (representing dwelling space) in the second model. (Fig. 9.3).

Apart from (1) the fact that cultural use, Catholic rite use and more general spiritual use were the most popular options for the church, (2) the fact that most participants made their own scenarios for the future of the church by combining different uses and (3) the fact that dwelling in the church was not to be ruled out for most of the participants, the most interesting information was gathered from the motivation of their choices, which they openly shared with the researchers. These motivations showed that a pragmatic viewpoint regarding the church building was not taboo (anymore). After a first series of local actions organized by the authors and some key local actors, Schulen's community went past the stage of habituation. For many inhabitants, the need for rethinking the church building has become obvious. The empirical research points out that some people, however, do reason in terms of a priori's. For them, the chancel is not to be touched in any way at all since it is the most holy part of the building. Others, conversely, see it as a dark and unattractive space, which was better to transform into dwelling space, into an office or into a meeting room for local associations. A third group of participants designed well-thought-out scenarios in which several uses would strengthen both the original church use and each other. This third group was typically the volunteers, the ones who realized they felt attached to the church building and knew how it worked and as a result had strong opinions on how it could work.

The empirical research disclosed some local controversies and passions. Two features play a special role here: the organ and the glass-stained windows, especially those of the transept. Whenever progress was made during the in-situ research in Schulen, 'expert values', such as those typically constructed by heritage specialists, were put into perspective. Most locals preferred to preserve for liturgical matters not the chancel but the transept (the transverse section), precisely because of its beautiful windows and because it is the best lit space in the building. What does matter here is the performance of the building, how the building acts in relation to its users and its (social and spatial) environment, in other words, what it does and what it gives, or, according to James J. Gibson (see Maiera et al. 2009), what it affords. In order to describe the building and its significance, the notion of performance acts as an alternative to a top–down approach imposed by heritage values. Performance, as already mentioned, is as much the effect of design measures as it is of contingency and situational factors, or in ANT terms: Performance can be understood as the effect of complex networks. Schulen's inhabitants indeed perceived the church building not as an autonomous and isolated object, as many an expert assessment did, but rather as an actor with a specific performance that is related to other actors.

The use of scale models as in the case study of Schulen has proven to be an appropriate way to both trace the church buildings' performance and trigger locals to get involved. The models, to use Callon's (2005) words, act as 'socio-cognitive prostheses': They help laypersons to express opinions on an issue they are not necessarily familiar with. Latour (2005a, p. 24), in the volume *Making Things Public*, even states: 'Who could dream of a better example of hybrid forums than the scale models used by architects all over the world to assemble those able to build them at scale 1?' Using models of a building as research instruments inside that very building has a special effect; people respond very well to the models, as their gazes constantly oscillate between the models and the real building. The participants thus trace the building's performance. The models enable the researchers and the locals to speak an easily understood common language, that of the performance of the building. What is more, the models function as catalysts, spurring on to further research and action. After a while, however, boredom sets in in the ever-peaceful village of Schulen, as everyone who felt like doing so had ventilated his or her opinion in the course of the in-situ research. To keep a triggering effect going proved to be hard and laborious. When applied rightly, however, architectural action (via the models) is able to spark the local citizen's creativity. The actions as undertaken in Schulen gathered local knowledge and got (new) local agency circulating. They brought dormant controversies to the fore and made them public.

The reuse of churches is a complex issue with important social and architectural aspects and this causes difficulties as well as interesting effects, as the case of Schulen demonstrates. The citizens involved in the actions, the architecture of the existing church and the new proposals for the building have their influence on every next research action. People have their own opinions, since they are advocates of the building as found, or of certain parts of it, or they keep a close eye on specific financial issues, but they are also keen to hear what the architect (the researcher) has to say. (Fig. 9.4).

The first model trial informed a second one, involving two possible scenarios for the church building which were inserted by means of cardboard inside the wooden models; the uses and corresponding places within the building, which the participants preferred during the first trial, were translated into two concrete but very different future architectural schemes for Saint John's. Since the models now demonstrated actual possibilities for Schulen's church building, they kept the process going. As was the case for the first model trial, the second one, which was another joint effort between the researchers and the local core volunteers, was not solely an act of research; it was linked up with a church quest, tours of the building, organ music and a dance performance. Putting on these 'events on the side' would never have succeeded without volunteers and their social and creative capital.

The second scale model trial (November 13 and 20, 2011) was set up to examine (1) how the participants would judge the proposed scenarios and (2) whether new temporary uses were a possibility for the future. This experiment doubled as a way of additional testing of the scale model methodology. About 50 people participated; this time the population was mixed, both age-wise and according to residency. People were informed of this research action via a flyer that was delivered to all of Schulen's private mailboxes.

Apart from the more quantitative results, the second scale model trial uncovered a certain wish for a rigorous rather than an open-ended scheme. However, Schulen's inhabitants, when compared to the other participants (such as the members of the dance group that performed that day), were a bit more in favour of the open-ended plan. They still preferred a durable solution for their church over a (design) process extended into eternity. Therefore, an architectural scheme based on research and on

Fig. 9.4 The second scale model trial's two architectural scenarios: *above* the rather rigorous 'community centre' scheme with among other things, a space for cultural uses in the nave and a new church room in the transverse section; *below* the rather indeterminate 'agora' scheme, with much open space, curtains to create separate areas and a residential unit in the tower. The models rest on the podium, constructed for the elementary school's musical that took place that same month. (Photographs by Sylvain De Bleeckere)

local knowledge, agency and creativity might be an answer. Apart from that, the architectural schemes generated new conversations, and again the common language was the parish church's performance rather than expert values. By means of the models, the degree of realism was gradually being enhanced. Schulen's inhabitants increasingly talked about the concrete technical and financial aspects; in a way, they were becoming experts themselves. A similar result is that the outcomes of a questionnaire (November 25, 26 and 27, 2011), which was conducted during the local elementary school's musical, which itself took place in the parish church, show that Schulen's inhabitants feel attached to the church building and that they are less indifferent to Saint John's future than those not living in Schulen. More than 500 people, about 180 of them from Schulen, were questioned for the duration of the musical. The research advantage of the musical was that a good cross-section of Schulen's population was present, which was not the case for the model trials, because the latter only attracted those who were at least interested in or curious about the researchers' approach (and who were not necessarily faithful parishioners or active volunteers).

The results of the second model trial also indicate that architectural expertise (from outside the community) could feed local agency and keep a process going.

Expertise, when applied based on research, dialogically and proceeding step by step, does not necessarily force the locals into a discourse of universal values.

Both the actions and the events on the side are themselves examples of (gentle) temporary use of the church building; they invite others to use the church as well, the best example of this being the local elementary school's musical (November 25, 26 and 27, 2011), which 'sold out' the church building three evenings in a row. The mere organization of the musical, which was an immense endeavour, proves that there still is a basis for putting on public manifestations, albeit in untraditional forms. In addition, it proves that the church building is well suited to such uses.

Conclusion

By making local interests and local agency explicit and public, in terms of, among other things, volunteering, the continued public relevance of a typical, even ordinary, Flemish church building was detected. Through the sustainable involvement of the local civil society and 'ordinary' citizens, the Flemish parish churches might have a future which is not as bleak as the general public opinion suggests. What is more, the Flemish churches and their futures can be dealt with in a democratic way.

The notion of 'performance' was examined as a possible tool to accompany the communication between the locals and their church building. On a theoretical level, this notion was underpinned via both the discourse of spatial agency and ANT. The concept of performance puts into perspective the rather directive deployment of expert opinion and paves the way for a richer, more 'thick' description of the parish church in which local agency and local interests are included.

As a methodology to put these findings to the test, and as a possible guideline for future protocols of (re-)use, the hybrid forum was examined, theoretically as well as via concrete (research) actions in Schulen's parish church. To a certain extent, and as Callon et al. (2009) alleged, laymen did become experts in Schulen. Through the Schulen scale model trials, creative and social capital and local skills slowly became visible and public. The key actors surprised themselves in a positive way, especially when organizing the temporary uses of Saint John's, and awareness on the church issue matured. The church building became a matter of concern in Schulen, visible in the public sphere, for those who stopped visiting it on a weekly basis (or never did in the first place) as well. The people of Schulen do now see it more explicitly as their building and they also see that they themselves are able to claim the church building for purposes they consider suitable.

Moreover, the approach outlined in this chapter might act as a counterbalance to the Flemish policy's jump in scale from the level of the individual fabric committee to the level of the entirety of the municipality, a scaling up that was recently institutionalized in a new Flemish decree on cults. As a result of this Flemish decision, the inherent danger of overlooking local agency and local knowledge of the church building arises. When the problem of the emptying churches will only be looked at from the top down, it is more likely that parish churches will be seen as commodities or marketable objects only. A thick description of the church building which, as explained above, incorporates social capital, creative capital and local agency, makes clear that a church building is much more than a commodity; it is more than the result of a typical conservation expert's assessment as well, as Schulen's Saint John's, which always was below the radar of heritage experts, proves. Although well known for some time in other parts of the world (see for example Davie 2001), these and similar findings have not yet found their way into Belgian or Flemish discourse and policy on the future of the parish churches. For regions that are already acquainted with Davie's 'vicarious religion' and new types of civic commitment, which are effects of secularization, the results of this chapter provide new support. In Schulen, a village with very low attendance figures, new commitment emerged from just discussing the parish church's future, while traditional commitment, for example, that of the fabric committee's treasurer and the Family Union's president, is being strengthened.

By means of sociological methods that provide opportunities for talking about architecture and religion in terms of (messy) performance, researchers are able to let go of definitions which describe both architecture and religion as 'pure' and substantial. Thus, they are able to provide richer descriptions too as well as an approach to parish churches and their present and future potential. As a matter of fact, the field of architecture (or architectural theory), whenever it is seen as having a social dimension, as Jeremy Till does, for instance, can help to understand complex processes of secularization.

As regards the exploration of new uses, the hybrid forum approach, as a second layer on top of the tracing of the church's network, promises to be a fruitful strategy. However, there is a need to deal with the hybrid forum's propensity towards relativism. The fact that a hybrid forum requires a 'spark' to get started, and the fact that it is, unlike the actors involved in processes of church reappraisal, not interested in a general consensus, were dealt with via the emphasis on architectural creativity and authorship. In the case of Schulen, scale models were used to (fully) initialize the process, to keep it going and to give it a certain direction. However, the long-term effects, whether volunteer action resulting from the reappropriation of parish churches is sustainable or not, were not examined; they need more thorough research.

Instead of seeing church buildings as architectural envelopes only (empty or not) to be preserved for the future, which runs the risk of letting the church-related social capital dry up, it would be wise to make this existing social capital and local agency central to the processes of reuse. Radical reuse might not be the solution, as the (traditional) local capital is not just eroding but also transforming itself into newer shapes (e.g. the musical). Therefore, the church building as a major public amenity might be better off as part of these transformations. New uses are best implemented gradually and dialogically, precisely in order to be able to detect the local capital in time and make the most of it. That way, small step after small step, the resulting 'new' church building (which would still be able to accommodate religious use, or not) might well be able to have positive effects of its own.

9 Making Church Happen

References

Achterberg, P., Houtman, D., Aupers, S., de Koster, W., Mascini, P., & van der Waal, J. (2009). Dialectiek van secularisering. Hoe de afname van christelijke religiositeit samengaat met een sterkere nadruk op haar publieke belang in achttien westerse landen. *Sociologie, 5*(3), 324–342.

Awan, N., Schneider, T., & Till, J. (2011). *Spatial agency. Other ways of doing architecture.* Londen: Routledge.

BAVO (2008). De nieuwe mythe van de relatieve maakbaarheid. *Open, 15,* 175–182.

Bevers, H., Gelders, D., Martens, M., & Raymaekers, P. (2011). Verkennend onderzoek naar de sociale samenhang en de betekenis van sociaal-culturele verenigingen in vijf plattelandsdorpen. In H. Bevers, D. Gelders, M. Martens, & P. Raymaekers (Eds.), *Sociaal-culturele verenigingen: Het sociaal kapitaal van de samenleving?* (pp. 13–117). Tielt: Lannoo Campus.

Billiet, J. (1998). Sociaal kapitaal, levensbeschouwelijke betrokkenheid en maatschappelijke integratie in België. *Tijdschrift voor sociologie, 19*(1), 33–54.

Bourgeois, G. (2011). *Conceptnota "Een toekomst voor de Vlaamse parochiekerk".* Brussel: Vlaamse Regering.

Callon, M. (2005). Disabled persons of all countries, unite! In B. Latour & P. Weibel (Eds.), *Making things public: Atmospheres of democracy* (pp. 308–313). Cambridge: MIT Press.

Callon, M., Lascoumes, P., & Barthe, Y. ([2001] 2009). *Acting in an uncertain world. An essay on technical democracy.* Cambridge: MIT Press.

Davie, G. (2001). The persistence of institutional religion in modern Europe. In L. Woodhead, P. Heelas, & D. Martin (Eds.), *Peter Berger and the study of religion* (pp. 101–111). London: Routledge.

De Pooter, P. (2003). *De rechtspositie van de erkende erediensten en levensbeschouwingen in staat en maatschappij.* Brussel: Larcier.

Delbeke, G. (2007). Herbestemming en/of herwaardering van kerken. *Collationes, 37*(1), 23–45.

Doucet, I., & Cupers, K. (2009). Agency in architecture: Rethinking criticality in theory and practice. *Footprint, 4,* 1–6.

Doucet, I., & Janssens, N. (2011). Editorial: Transdisciplinarity, the hybridisation of knowledge production and space-related research. In I. Doucet & N. Janssens (Eds.), *Transdisciplinary knowledge production in architecture and urbanism. Towards hybrid modes of inquiry* (pp. 1–14). Dordrecht: Springer.

Draulans, V., & Witte, H. (1999). Initiatie in de vrijwilligerskerk. Verkenningen in vergelijkend perspectief. In L. Boeve (Ed.), *De Kerk in Vlaanderen: Avond of dageraad?* (pp. 167–188). Leuven: Davidsfonds.

Elchardus, M., Huyse, L., & Hooghe, M. (2001). Samenvatting en besluit. In M. Elchardus, L. Huyse, & M. Hooghe (Eds.), *Het maatschappelijk middenveld in Vlaanderen: Een onderzoek naar de sociale constructie van democratisch burgerschap* (pp. 211–238). Brussels: VUB-Press.

Geertz, C. (1973). Thick description: Toward an interpretive theory of culture. In C. Geertz (Ed.), *The interpretation of cultures.* (selected essays by Clifford Geertz) (pp. 3–30). New York: Basic Books.

Havermans, N., & Hooghe, M. (2011). *Kerkpraktijk in België: Resultaten van de zondagstelling in oktober 2009.* (Rapport ten behoeve van de Belgische Bisschoppenconferentie). Leuven: KU Leuven Centrum voor Politicologie.

Hooghe, M. (2000). Inleiding: Verenigingen, democratie en sociaal kapitaal. In M. Hooghe (Ed.), *Sociaal kapitaal en democratie: verenigingsleven, sociaal kapitaal en politieke cultuur* (pp. 9–22). Leuven: Acco.

Hooghe, M., Quintelier, E., & Reeskens, T. (2006). Kerkpraktijk in Vlaanderen: Trends en extrapolatie: 1967–2004. *Ethische Perspectieven, 16*(2), 113–123.

Houdart, S., & Chihiro, M. (2009). *Kuma Kengo. An unconventional monograph* (trans: L. Lyall Grant). Paris: éditions donner lieu.

Jenkins, P., & Pereira, M. (2010). International Experience. In P. Jenkins & L. Forsyth (Eds.), *Architecture, participation and society* (pp. 39–59). Londen: Routledge.

Latour, B. (1988). *Wetenschap in actie. Wetenschappers en technici in de maatschappij* [trans: de Lange, B.]. Amsterdam: Uitgeverij Bert Bakker. English Edition: Latour, B. (1987). *Science in action: How to follow scientists and engineers through society*. Cambridge: Harvard University Press.

Latour, B. ([1991] 1993). *We have never been modern* (trans: C. Porter). Cambridge: Harvard University Press.

Latour, B. (2001). Which protocol for the new collective experiments?, *Boletin CF+S*. http://habitat.aq.upm.es/boletin/n32/ablat.en.html. Accessed 21 June 2011.

Latour, B. (2005a). From realpolitik to dingpolitik or how to make things public. In B. Latour & P. Weibel (Eds.), *Making things public: Atmospheres of democracy* (pp. 14–41). Cambridge: MIT Press.

Latour, B. (2005b). *Reassembling the social: An introduction to actor-network theory*. Oxford: Oxford University Press.

Latour, B. (2008). A cautious Prometheus? A few steps toward a philosophy of design (with special attention to Peter Sloterdijk). In F. Hackney, J. Glynne, & V. Minton (Eds.), *Networks of design: Proceedings of the 2008 annual international conference of the Design History Society* [University College Falmouth, September 3–6] (pp. 2–10). Boca Raton: Universal Publishers.

Latour, B., & Yaneva, A. (2008). "Give me a gun and I will make all buildings move": An ant's view of architecture. In R. Geiser (Ed.), *Explorations in architecture: Teaching, design, research* (pp. 80–89). Basel: Birkhäuser.

Maiera, J. R. A., Fadela, G. M., & Battistob, D. G. (2009). An affordance-based approach to architectural theory, design, and practice. *Design Studies, 30*(4), 393–414.

Moltu, B. (2008). Satirical and romantic stories about organisational change. Actor network theory and action research. *International Journal of Action Research, 4*(1+2), 155–179.

Noppen, L. (2011). Quebec's churches: Converting from the faith. *L'Architecture d'Aujourd'hui, 386*, 41.

Sellam, K. (2009, September 9). Dorpskerken hebben dringend Vlaamse steun nodig. *De Standaard*. http://www.standaard.be/artikel/detail.aspx?artikelid=772ES457. Accessed 3 Oct 2012.

Smith, L. (2006). *Uses of heritage*. Londen: Routledge.

Somol, R., & Whiting, S. ([2002] 2007). Notes around the Doppler effect and other moods of modernism. In W. S. Saunders (Ed.), *The new architectural pragmatism* (pp. 22–33). Minneapolis: University of Minnesota Press.

Till, J. (2005). The negotiation of hope. In P. Blundell Jones, D. Petrescu, & J. Till (Eds.), *Architecture and participation* (pp. 19–40). Londen: Spon Press.

Till, J. (2009). *Architecture depends*. Cambridge: MIT Press.

Van Lierde, E. (2012, April 4). Dossier: Kerk in ombouw. Parochies zoeken toekomst. *Tertio*, 7–9.

Vanstiphout, W. (2008). Maakbaarheid van stad en stedenbouw. Ideologie als achilleshiel. *Open, 15*, 60–85.

Yaneva, A. (2009). *The making of a building: A pragmatist approach to architecture*. New York: Peter Lang AG.

Zijn dure kerkrestauraties nog wel verantwoord? (2006, August 16). *Het Belang Van Limburg*. http://www.hbvl.be/archief/guid/zijn-dure-kerkrestauraties-nog-wel-verantwoord. aspx?artikel=fcd61889-b26e-4a6c-83d6-4f2a36b17f32. Accessed 4 Oct 2012.

Chapter 10
Restorative Justice and Volunteering in a Secular Age

Erik Claes and Emilie Van Daele

Introduction

In the past two decades, many western democracies have seen the rise of restorative justice practices in the margins, and even within the very heart of their criminal justice systems. Restorative justice is a broad umbrella term referring to what has been called an alternative approach and response to crime. Participation of the conflicting parties, restoration of the harm caused by crime as well as healing and peacemaking are considered to be the core elements of these approaches and practices in Canada, New Zealand and Europe.[1] Restorative programmes such as victim–offender mediation, family group conferences, peacemaking circles, all aim to put aside, or at least to temper, the punitive twist of our current penal practices. They ambitiously aim to trigger change in, and reform of, our dominant ways of penal thinking.

Where does this restorative approach come from? It belongs to the canon of the restorative justice literature to point to underlying democratic ideals such as empowerment and civic participation, but also to refer to religious and spiritual antecedents which range from early Christianity to the world views and practices of first nations people in Canada or the Maori in New Zealand. Restorative justice practices such as mediation, conferencing or peacemaking circles should thus also be seen as a rediscovery of these spiritual worldviews. What are the concrete implications of such a rediscovery? Some advocates of restorative justice plead for giving communities more space to develop a healing response to crime, its consequences and causes. Authors such as Howard Zehr link restorative justice with

---

[1] For an overview of restorative justice practices in Europe, see Aertsen, et al. (2006).

E. Claes (✉)
HUB, Pragodi, School of Social Work, Warmoesberg 26, 1000, Brussel, Belgium
e-mail: erik.claes@hubrussel.be

E. Van Daele
Socius, Steunpunt Sociaal-Cultureel Volwassenenwerk, Brussel, Belgium
e-mail: emilie.vandaele@socius.be

L. Hustinx et al. (eds.), *Religion and Volunteering,* Nonprofit and Civil Society Studies, 191
DOI 10.1007/978-3-319-04585-6_10, © Springer International Publishing Switzerland 2015

'biblical justice', a justice that is fundamentally respectful as the only way to break the cycle of violence and revenge (Zehr 1994). Other advocates of restorative justice stress the importance of ceremonies and rituals aiming at restoring a deep sense of interconnectedness (Pranis et al. 2003). Some even go a step further. In their critique of the retributive response to crime, they also claim that our current and still dominant criminal justice system should be regarded as a powerful, but brief, secular episode in human history, which aimed to sever criminal justice from its deeper sacred and spiritual dimension. In such a view the restorative justice movement strives to put an end to this episode, by reconnecting the practice of answering to crime with its ancient spiritual resources of forgiving, healing and peacemaking (Weitekamp 2002).

If a rediscovery of spirituality and religious roots belong to many restorative justice practices, and if this spiritual turn shows itself to be important to the aspirations of the philosophy of restorative justice, how could one adjust these aspirations to the actual modern world with its secular institutions? How can one combine these aspirations with the ambition to trigger change within the existing criminal justice system with its heritage of the rule of law? Should we, advocates of restorative justice, temper our spiritual aspirations in order to improve our chances for penal reform? Or, is there a framework available in which we can together think about a spiritual view of justice with ideas of criminal justice that are rooted in liberal values such as neutrality, right to liberty, democratic participation and the rule of law?

In order to address these difficult questions, it is important to acknowledge the fact that restorative justice practices in many parts of the world stem from grass roots initiatives. Volunteering citizens, together with social work professionals often supported by social scientists and criminologists, and driven by their passions and beliefs in an alternative response to crime, were the first to start off restorative practices and programmes. Even now, in countries such as Norway, Finland and New Zealand, the continuation of these practices depend to a large extent on the commitment of voluntary mediators. The idea of engaging voluntary citizens to work at the heart of restorative justice practices should not come as a surprise, since the philosophy of restorative justice is deeply influenced by the belief that citizens are capable of resolving their conflicts themselves. Empowering volunteering citizens to organize and offer restorative justice practices is just another instance of this basic belief that the response to crime should be handed back to society, to a society of participating citizens. Some of these citizens are members of religious communities, but others do not have any strong religious affiliations, they are just committed citizens willing to take responsibility in the aftermath of crime.

If active and participative citizenship seems to constitute one of the central aims of voluntary work in restorative justice, what are we to think of the spiritual roots of restorative justice and their impact on voluntary commitment? Should we build our volunteering projects on these spiritual roots and on ideas of healing justice? And should we, advocates of restorative justice, make it important that the civic engagement of volunteers is inspired by a spiritual world view's conception of justice?

10 Restorative Justice and Volunteering in a Secular Age 193

Should we then promote voluntary work and even select voluntary candidates on these spiritual grounds?

In this chapter, we will reflect upon the connection between: (1) the rediscovery of spirituality in restorative justice practice and theory, (2) the ambitions of its proponents to expand their ideas in a modern world, and (3) the prospects for voluntary commitment. The aims of this chapter are broad and ambitious.

We are, firstly, seeking for coherent ways to bring together the spiritual dimensions of restorative justice practices and their ambitions to develop in relation to the criminal justice system as it is currently organized in modern, secular democracies.

Secondly, we are ambitiously searching for a coherent framework that grounds voluntary work in active, participative citizenship, while at the same time responding to the spiritual aspirations of restorative justice.

These ambitious aims indeed raise many difficulties and challenges that cannot be dealt with extensively within the scope of this chapter. Only some of them will demand our attention.

Naturally, given the immense variety of existing restorative justice practices located in different countries and embedded in different histories and cultures, the design of a coherent conceptual framework is quite difficult. In the face of this variety, it is not sure whether this rediscovery of spirituality has and should have equal importance for restorative justice practices in order to flourish and develop. Do we really have to draw on spiritual worldviews in order to ground and develop our ideals of restorative justice in each country?

Furthermore, it is also unclear what this spiritual dimension of restorative justice precisely consists of. Is there a common spiritual philosophy that can be derived from various religious resources? Are all types of spirituality of a restorative nature? What are the claims flowing from such a philosophy with regard to penal reform in a liberal democracy?

Lastly, efforts to bring coherently together spiritual aspirations in restorative justice with ambitions of penal reform in the modern world—or with ambitions of grounding voluntary work in active citizenship—inevitably raise questions as to the secular nature of our modern society. How do we (re-)think our modern societies, our secular institutions and our secular public life in order to once again make space for spiritual ways of dealing with crime? What is the precise nature of our secular condition and how does it bear upon restorative justice practices and their spiritual aspirations? Is it really necessary to step out of a secular framework in order to develop restorative justice practices?

In the following sections, we will develop five arguments that modestly contribute to the general aims mapped above.

- *Argument 1.* In line with the first aim (combining discovery of spirituality with development of restorative justice practices in the modern world), we will, first, argue that advocates of restorative justice who favour a strong connection between spirituality and ideals of restorative justice lack a strong conceptual framework to think their claims of spiritual justice together with a state-based criminal justice system (Sect. 2). This prevents them from really understanding how restorative justice practices can accomplish penal change in close cooperation with judicial state actors.

- *Argument 2.* Given the variety of restorative justice practices, it seems wise to recognize that not all restorative justice practices and theories need to draw upon spiritual worldviews. While certain restorative justice practices undeniably do, others do not. A close examination of a concrete Belgian practice of restorative justice, its aspirations and relation to the criminal justice system shows that both the practice and theory of restorative justice can be fully expressive of the basic tenets of a secular age yet also ground voluntary work (Sects. 3–4). Belgian practitioners have developed a moderate version of restorative justice which is deeply secular in its nature, because its approach and response to crime express at least two important modern social imaginaries (the state as a political artefact originating in a contract between individuals, and the idea of a civil society as a sphere outside the state). This moderate version of restorative justice also testifies to a secular spirit because it strongly embodies a secular moral ideal (the ethics of authenticity). The point of our second argument is that these Belgian restorative justice practices are not just embedded in secular, legal institutions, but are also supported by a conceptual framework which is secular in its essence. Because of its secular mind-set, a moderate version of restorative justice seems to better channel penal change that is in line with the values of our actual criminal justice system based on the rule of law.
- *Argument 3.* This, of course, does not dispense us from searching for a conceptual framework in which it is possible to valorise the spiritual dimension of restorative justice and at the same time to favour cooperation with judicial state actors as well as grounding voluntary work in the values of a democratic constitutional state. In Sect. 5, we will develop a third argument based upon a moderate view of restorative justice. This view, with its ideal of participative and communicative justice, offers an interesting perspective allowing us to dig channels of dialogue between the logic both of restorative spirituality and of state-based justice.
- *Argument 4.* Our next argument also derives from the Belgian case and clearly tempers the ambition of our second aim (coherently connecting spirituality with grounding restorative volunteering in active citizenship) (Sect. 6). Starting from the Belgian case, it is perfectly possible to ground voluntary work in a secular version of restorative justice without having to bother with the spiritual sources of restorative justice. Within the framework of a moderate view of restorative justice, spiritual categories such as healing and forgiveness do not shape the main objectives of engaging volunteers in restorative justice programmes. Articulating the value of voluntary commitment from within a moderate view of restorative justice leads us deeper into secular waters instead of reaching the shores of religion and spirituality.
- *Argument 5.* Finally, we will focus on possibilities for creating a space for spirituality in restorative volunteering within a secular framework of restorative justice (Sect. 7). Our argument, derived from Charles Taylor's complex account of secularity and the process of secularization, is that in a secular age the conditions for religious belief have changed profoundly, opening a variety of spiritual

10 Restorative Justice and Volunteering in a Secular Age

paths. Restorative pratices are responsive to these varieties, and, consequently, to a variety of spiritual aspirations that drive volunteers into the realm of restorative justice.

The Spiritual Roots of Restorative Justice

In 'The Ethics of Traditional Communities and the Spirit of Healing Justice', J. Sawatsky reports on his visit to the hollow water community in Canada (Sawatsky 2009). The story of this community became very influential in restorative justice literature because it is a successful introduction to healing practices based on the traditional wisdom of Canadian first nations people. A community once broken, with massive alcohol and sexual abuse problems, transformed into a community with a recidivism rate 'more than six times lower than the national average rate for sexual abusing' (Sawatsky 2009, p. 99). Sawatsky's visit teaches us how the community, by setting up a partnership with the western system of justice as well as a local social service, struggled to bring back their Anishinabe way of living. Their restorative aspirations consist of finding ways of rediscovering a holistic community in which both the traditional criminal justice system and the social service systems tend to become superfluous.

Sawatsky discovered that a spiritual approach to justice is more than just responding to crime differently. Here, healing justice comes down to bringing about a shift in ways of living and living together. Respect for a transcendent force (the Creator) and the sacredness of life, structuring daily life with ceremonies and rituals, making people aware of their interconnectedness with the land and with their communities, all these aspects of spirituality help nurturing respect for oneself, for others, for the community and for the earth.

Instead of incarcerating sex abusers, the hollow water community launched a partnership with official judicial actors and social workers (the Community Holistic Circle Healing). Together they set up a 13-step healing process involving different stages. There is the stage of disclosing of sexual abuse. This process of truth finding is steered by an intervention team consisting of representatives of the justice system, child protection service and community members trying to discover what really happened. There is the stage of establishing safety for the victim through the support of a social worker. In a next step, the healing process proceeds in confronting the victimizer with the offence. In this stage, it is important to assure that the offender feels safe enough to acknowledge the facts and take responsibility. After having admitted the charges and agreed to embarking on the healing journey, the victimizer will appear before court. He will be released back into the custody of the Community Holistic Circle Healing. In the further stages, circles are organized with the victimizer and his family and between victim and victimizer, everything culminating in a sentencing circle which includes the criminal judge, the victim and his family, as well as the victimizer with his family. All the stake holding parties are carefully prepared for the sentencing circle. This circle, as well as its preparatory practices, are highly ritualized (preparing of a sweat lodge by the victimizer for his family three nights before the sentencing circle, circle dialogues going clockwise by means of an eagle feather, closure of the sentencing circle by a feast in which everyone, including the judge, is taking part). In all these rituals, a sense of wholeness and sacredness, an interconnectedness between victims, victimizers and families, is evoked through contact with nature.

Of course, the spiritual sources of restorative justice are not confined to a return to aboriginal healing practices in Canada (or in New Zealand or Australia). In 'The Spiritual Roots of Restorative Justice' (Hadley 2001), a collection of essays on the restorative dimension of various religious traditions, Pierre Allard and Wayne Northley, throw an intriguing light on the complex relation between Christianity, restorative justice and the current penal state apparatus (Allard and Northley 2001). They argue that our current criminal justice system, which is still primarily focused on retribution by a punishing state, still retains the alliance between Roman Church and state going back to Emperor Constantine. Since then, integration of the Christian faith into the political institutions of the Romans has led to a marginalization of the essence of Christianity in its response to crime, to what they call a burying of 'the richness of biblical Restorative Justice' (Allard and Northley 2001, p. 124). This richness stems from the essence of Christianity: God's all-embracing love for each of us, even for the rejected, and his rejection of violence, as embodied in the life and death of Jesus. According to the authors, this biblical message points to another model of justice in which forgiving, healing and reconciliation are the central values. The emergence of restorative justice practices in many western countries can be interpreted as a rediscovery of this early Christian view of criminal justice. The position of Allard and Northley clearly testifies to what many proponents of restorative justice endorse, namely that restorative justice practices are continuous with a spiritual view of justice and with a variety of religious traditions that favour a peacemaking response to crime for all the stakeholders involved. Not retribution, but love, compassion and mercy are the true spiritual aspirations of justice with regard to crime, and this because these aspirations draw their force from a sacred, divine power beyond earthly life.

Other authors in the volume of 'The Spiritual Roots of Restorative Justice' are tracing a similar dividing line between restorative justice and its spiritual aspirations on the one hand, and state justice, on the other. In his 'Healing Justice: A Buddhist Perspective', David Loy argues that our penal state system derives from a world view that sees crime as an attack on the 'sacred' authority of the nation state, embodying the sovereign will of the people. Loy's plea for restorative justice from a Buddhist perspective contains a double attack on the current, criminal justice system: (1) To him, the modern state monopoly on violence should not be seen as a secular answer to crime but as the result of the sanctification of the state and of a 'discredited Christianity'. (2) Legal protection by the state through law-enforcement should be seen as a response to our fears with regard to others. According to Loy, human fears as the grounding for the state monopoly of violence, as well as the impersonality of a state bureaucracy enforcing the law through punishment, are the main obstacles to Buddhist justice. According to this spiritual tradition love and compassion (instead of fear), the voices of the stake-holding parties (instead of the state) and the mobilization of interpersonal trust within communities (instead of state bureaucracies) are seen to be the driving forces of a criminal justice system. It is the merit of restorative justice practice to reconnect with these forces and to explicitly oppose itself to the current penal state system.

Advocates of restorative justice not only make an effort to retrieve spiritual roots and to introduce them in restorative practices; despite the differences of their religious traditions, they also come up with converging claims with regard to the foundations and central aims of restorative justice. Practitioners and researchers who favour a strong connection between restorative justice and spirituality join in a similar restorative justice philosophy.

Firstly, they bring the essence of restorative justice down to its religious and spiritual roots, referring thereby to the importance for victims, offenders and communities of living a fuller life in contact with a sacred order and transcendent powers beyond earthly life. Sawatsky is very clear in this regard when he argues that healing justice practices such as those of the hollow water community could help to deepen the scope of restorative justice, making it less incident-focused and more holistic (Sawatsky 2009, p. 269).

Secondly, proponents of a strong link between spirituality and restorative justice identify love, compassion and respect as some of the central keys of the spiritual roots. Restorative justice is essentially spiritual because it revolves around the search for non-violent ways to heal victims, offenders and communities.

Thirdly, they see a strong dividing line between restorative justice and its spiritual essence on the one hand, and state based justice, grounded in fear and retribution, on the other hand. For them, the assumptions of our modern, retributive criminal justice system (individualism, infliction of punishment as a necessary evil, focus on rule breaking, on the monopoly of the state in imposing coercive measures, neutrality of the state and judicial actors) sit ill with the spiritual essence of restorative justice.

Lastly, these advocates understand state-based justice in terms of a false sanctification of state authority. Our strongly institutionalized criminal justice system with its monopoly on violence is rooted in a 'wrong' spirituality based upon a narrow reading of Biblical writings.

So much for these four claims. How do we respond to these claims and how convincing are they, given the variety in the actual practices of restorative justice? Does the rediscovery of the spiritual roots of restorative justice necessarily imply a need for pulling down a modern state-based criminal justice system? Should we reconnect with spiritual worldviews such as those of early Christianity and Buddhism in order to fully develop a restorative justice response to crime? In order to prevent us from hastily addressing these questions affirmatively, we will deploy two critical strategies.

The first is analytical and calls for clarification of concepts such as spirituality, religion and healing justice. Advocates of restorative justice tend to use them as if they are interchangeable concepts, when they argue that restorative justice is and should be spiritual in its essence, but are they? A close reading of Sawatsky's book on traditional communities and the spirit of healing justice offers us interesting perspectives in this regard. In line with recent theological writings (Waaijman 2011), Sawatsky sees spirituality as a way of experiencing oneself, others and nature on a deeper and fuller level in relation to a transcendent power surpassing and guiding the earthly life of humans. A spiritual life does not require strong identification with the authority of religious confessions, but it demands curiosity about, and reflective exploration of, religious texts, religious traditions and rituals in order to maintain contact with this fuller life open to a transcendent power (God, the Creator). Religious traditions are the concrete forms in which spirituality takes shape, unfolds and develops, and, inversely, a spiritual reflection on religious practices and texts has the potential to change religious traditions (Sawatsky 2009, p. 220). Sawatsky's book also has the merit of being analytically clear about the logic of healing justice. He distinguishes six features of this logic: (1) 'Healing Justice does not begin with states and institutions, but begins and ends with the spirit and the land' (Sawatsky 2009, p. 239). It is a kind of justice that is fully aware of the gift and vulnerability of life. The land, our ecological environment, manifests itself as 'a teacher of justice'. (2) The procedures of healing justice aim at transforming structures and patterns that cause and condition harm. (3) Healing justice seeks to cultivate conditions of loving kindness and deep respect as a way of remembering for those who have forgotten how to act according to these attitudes. (4) Healing justice follows a logic of finding true identity, it helps victims, offenders, citizens and professional workers to remember and rediscover what constitutes their deepest humanity. (5) Healing justice draws on a logic of interdependent relationships and stresses the interdependence of responsibilities with respect to addressing the harm. (6) The logic of healing justice sees conflicts, wrongs and harms as an opportunity to work at healing for all, it contains the belief that all can heal, can rediscover the gift of life and can live a fuller life in deep respect for oneself and others. Sawatsky reminds us that spirituality and religion do not automatically bring us to healing justice. Religious traditions, like Christianity, can nurture forms of spirituality that obscure healing justice instead of fostering it. To him the logic of healing justice is also a framework that helps us to critically reflect upon our religious practices.

So far, our analytical strategy has led to a clearer view of what the spiritual nature of restorative justice refers to. When some advocates of restorative justice claim that spirituality makes up the essence of restorative justice, they seem to refer to a specific logic of healing justice that draws our attention to a variety of specific forms of spirituality in which this logic surfaces. These forms of spirituality are nurtured by a critical and reflexive reading of religious texts and by accomplishing and reinventing certain religious practices within the framework of restorative justice programmes.

But can we say that all restorative justice practices, in order to flourish, should give expression to a logic of healing justice? This question begs for a more practical strategy. We should attentively examine how restorative justice practices are concretely embedded in contemporary legal institutions and how they are developing their philosophy of restorative justice as a reflection upon the development of their practices. In order to assess whether, if at all, restorative justice should be spiritual in its essence, one ought first to examine, carefully, how restorative justice approaches are shaped by concrete practices which are embedded in the real modern world.

A similar practical approach can be inspiring with regard to a puzzling issue that relates to the third claim, the claim that restorative justice, because of its spiritual nature, does not fit with a state-based criminal justice system with its procedures and rule of law values. What puzzles us here, and what requires a more practical strategy, is the following ambiguity. On the one hand, this third claim presupposes a kind of hostility vis-à-vis the logic of a state-based criminal justice system and its assumptions. If one wants to give a chance to healing justice, state-based penal responses to crime should be pushed to the margins of our social and public life. On the other hand, concrete restorative justice practices with strong spiritual roots, such as seen in the hollow water community, seem to be far less radical in their claims. They have organized close cooperation with key judicial actors, such as magistrates and public prosecutors, in a spirit of mutual respect.

These observations bring us to our first argument, announced in the introduction of this chapter. Advocates of restorative justice who favour a strong link between restorative justice and spirituality are not equipped with a conceptual framework that promotes spirituality and, at the same time, gives space to cooperation between restorative justice programmes and the interventions of the state. It is as if their story of spirituality prevents them from seeing cooperation with the classical criminal justice system in a constructive way. Once again a plunge into concrete restorative justice practices might be fruitful. Instead of focusing on the ideal theory of restorative justice, we should carefully analyse practice theories of restorative justice that are built from the ground up and see whether these practices contain conceptual frameworks that could help in thinking together the spiritual dimension of restorative justice on the one hand, and the importance of dialogue and communication with a state logic of criminal justice on the other.

In what follows, we will focus on just such a practice theory that emerged from the Belgian practices of victim–offender mediation. We will call this practice-based view of restorative justice a moderate conception of restorative justice because it explicitly rejects an abolitionist project according to which the existing criminal punishment system should be abolished and replaced by socially constructive restoration (Walgrave 2008) or by non-violent, healing ideals.

A Moderate Plea for a Multidimensional Approach to Criminality

The genesis of Belgian restorative justice practices is a complex story with too many turns and twists to be recounted within the space of this chapter. Three currents have determined the outlook of the restorative justice landscape in Belgium. The first began with a local experiment in a public prosecution service, in which the public prosecutor proposed using victim–offender mediation in some selected cases. If its outcome of the mediation process proved to be successful, the prosecution was to be dropped. This experiment was legalized in 1994 and led to the practice of penal mediation in the early stage of the criminal process. The second current began with experiments in mediation and family group sessions first organized by academic researchers in the field of youth protection, and which was in its turn legalized in a reform of the Youth Protection Act in 2006. Since then, public prosecutors and juvenile courts have been backed by a legal basis, allowing them to propose these restorative justice practices to juvenile offenders. The third current was initiated by academic researchers (Victimology Research Unit) and practitioners (victim aid organization), again in cooperation with a local public prosecution service. This innovative project focused on victim–offender mediation in serious offences committed by adult offenders. In these programmes, the public prosecutor, after having summoned the defendant to the criminal court, offered the conflicting parties the possibility to engage in a process of mediation organized by an independent mediation service. This project developed into a mature practice, steered by two Belgian non-governmental organizations (NGOs) and supported by a federal criminal justice policy. Through the efforts of these independent organizations, victim–offender mediation for adult offenders was gradually implemented in each Belgian judicial district and this led to a legislative initiative in 2005 that provides a legal framework for this third restorative justice current.

It is, to a large extent, in this third current that an interesting practice theory surfaced. The driving force of practitioners and academics and, later, of the NGOs, led to what we have called a moderate view of restorative justice. This view starts from victim–offender mediation in serious cases with adult offenders who are summoned to court and admit responsibility for the alleged wrongs. The content of this view draws heavily on this starting point, but also on a continuing history of cooperation between independent organizations that are officially recognized as mediation services and policy makers and the criminal justice system. Proponents of a moderate view of restorative justice can refine their ideas at the very heart of this cooperation and through constant reflection on their premises.

What is the outlook of this moderate view of restorative justice today? In line with restorative justice philosophy, advocates of this view endorse an alternative approach to crime but, precisely because of their commitment to cooperation with judicial authorities, their view diverges from the canon of restorative justice.

First of all, they have an eye for what Pelikan and Pali call the life–world element of a crime—one of the key elements of any restorative justice approach (Pali and Pelikan 2010). Through this life–world lens, crime is seen as a disruption or disturbance of human relations. Attention is drawn to the immediate emotional experience of the persons involved and the concrete needs originating from this experience—the experience of hurting or harming somebody and the experience of being harmed or being hurt (Suggnomè 2005). All these lived experiences bring proponents of this moderate view of restorative justice to see criminality as a disruption of interpersonal relationships. Crime manifests itself as a clash between personal lifeworlds, as a complex tale of wounded identities.

10 Restorative Justice and Volunteering in a Secular Age

But within a moderate conception of restorative justice, criminal wrongdoing is also seen through a second lens. Besides an interpersonal dimension crime also has a civic dimension. Through this public lens victim and offender are involved in the aftermath of a crime as citizens. Moreover, crime also appears as a violation of values and norms that affect other fellow citizens who are not necessarily directly involved. Their reaction indicates a loss of public trust and social indignation, as well as a commitment to public debate and a search for a shared opinion.

Finally, advocates of a moderate conception of restorative justice take into consideration a third perspective on crime: the formal legal dimension. According to this approach, a criminal offence is a violation of a law established by the state that makes some conduct punishable. A criminal offence is a violation of the authority of the legal norm. Here, a moderate conception of restorative justice proves to be a fully fledged practice theory emerging from a mediation practice involving cooperation between an independent mediation service and public prosecutor services. The latter would already have qualified the alleged facts in terms of the legal definition of a criminal offence and thus already decided to summon the defendant to court. Victim–offender mediation is organized as a voluntary offer given to both parties after referral by the public prosecutor.

In line with this practice, advocates of a moderate conception do not reject the classical legal approach of crime as endorsed by public officials. Unlike leading authors such as Howard Zehr, they do not discard the formal legal lens but keep it close at hand (Van Garsse 2004; Aertsen and Peters 1997). Instead of seeing this legal approach as an obstacle for realizing the normative aspirations of restorative justice, they fully acknowledge the normative stakes underlying a legal, reductionist approach, and integrate them in their practice theory of restorative justice.

A society that reduces criminal wrongdoing to a legally constructed criminal offence makes an important normative choice: it accurately delineates what is and what is not punishable. One of the cornerstones of the criminal law system is the principle of legality: There is no criminal offence without a clear, ascertainable and non-retrospective definition in the law. This principle of legality is taken to be one of the cornerstones of a state governed by the rule of law: It creates clarity for citizens and their rights and restricts the monopoly on violence of the state (Claes 2001).

To sum up, given its practice-based grounds, advocates of a moderate conception of restorative justice see criminality as a multidimensional phenomenon: Crime is highlighted in its interpersonal dimension, its civic dimension and its formal legal dimension. The core of a moderate view of restorative justice comes down to the message that all these dimensions of criminal wrongdoing need to be heard and involved when organizing an appropriate response to crime. How does such a moderate view of restorative justice relate to a spiritually rooted conception of restorative justice? In the following paragraphs, we will argue that advocates of this moderate view strongly diverge from those hardliners who defend a strong link between restorative justice and spirituality. Their moderate view helps us to develop the second, central, argument of our chapter.

We will argue that a moderate view of restorative justice use a completely secular framework, embodying modern social imaginaries and secular values. From this it follows that it is perfectly possible to develop restorative justice practices without drawing on a logic of spirituality or healing. Embedding a moderate approach in a secular age inevitably leads to a contesting of the claims that restorative justice is spiritual in its essence, that its message of love and compassion is necessarily spiritual, that it is essentially hostile to state justice and that state-based justice inevitably comes down to a sanctification of state authority. It seems wise, then, to recognize that not all restorative justice practices and theories need to draw upon spiritual worldviews *(Argument 2)*.

Restorative Justice in a Secular Age

To what extent can we say that a moderate view of restorative justice is continuous with a secular understanding of the world? In order to address this question, one should first ask: What does it mean to live in a secular world? According to Charles Taylor, secularity is a multilayered notion. It refers, first, to a typical modern western process of a growing number of people 'falling off of religious belief and practice' (Taylor 2007). Secularity has, secondly, also a practical and institutional dimension. It relates to the separation between the state and religious institutions, and, more fundamentally, to a withdrawal of religion from public life. Secularization refers to the basic idea that our public life is not grounded anymore in any reference to God, nor in any other transcendent power or order. Secularization removed us from 'a story of action-transcendent grounding of society in higher time' (Taylor 2004, p. 186). Human interactions, between citizens or between governments and citizens, no longer derive their worth and legitimacy from sacred powers or from a sacred time; their worth stems from values and ideals embodied in our human earthly life. This retreat of religion and religious beliefs from public life became possible because of the emergence of a complex set of modern social imaginaries. But this institutional change (separation between public life and religion) betrays a complex interplay of the manifold ways that we moderns understand our social life and our stance. Taylor unfolds this complex conceptual story and argues how it brings us to a third layer of understanding: We are living in a secular age because the social and intellectual horizons against which people's belief in transcendental powers (God, spiritual forces) changed profoundly. 'The change is one', we quote Taylor, 'which takes us from a society in which it was virtually impossible not to believe in God, to one in which faith, even for the most staunchest believer, is one human possibility among others' (Taylor 2007, p. 3).

Saying that contemporary restorative justice practices are secular can therefore mean different things. Either we mean by this contention that restorative justice practices develop in societies in which state practices have been emptied from any allegiance to religious beliefs, or reference to God, and in which the public legitimacy of restorative justice does not depend upon any particular religious belief (secularity in an institutional sense). In such a case, there is no doubt that the bulk of contemporary restorative justice practices is embedded in a secular context, including the moderate view we have reconstructed above. Or we could say that restorative justice practices and theories are secular in their conceptual structure. In that case we defend the position that the underlying conceptual framework that underpins restorative justice is tributary to a complex interplay of modern, social imaginaries. This is a much stronger thesis that is empirically questionable, given the variety of restorative justice practices. We will, therefore, confine this stronger thesis to the moderate view of restorative justice as developed in Belgium since the mid-1990s of the twentieth century. In order to give substance to our point, it is important to further consider Taylor's notion of modern social imaginaries. This notion refers to the way we, moderns, imagine our social interactions and our living together, but also to concrete social practices in which these representations of the social order are embedded (Taylor 2004, p. 30). Modern social imaginaries are dynamic and, due to a complex interaction of historical events, changing economic conditions and new ideas, they have been subject to several mutations. To Taylor, the beginning of our modern understanding of our societies begins somewhere in the seventeenth century, with the idea of a new moral order. In this view, human interactions are no longer ordered according to a sacred, divine plan. Instead, social order is built on a logic of mutual interest between individuals. Their natural rights as individuals to liberty, and their mutual interest to preserve these rights, are the basis of a social contract which gives the state legitimate power to enforce laws in the service of these mutual interests. Two dimensions of our contemporary society grew out of this idea of a new moral order: Firstly, there is 'the picture of society' in which individuals 'come together to form a political entity against a certain pre-existing moral background and with certain ends in view' (Taylor 2004, p. 3). This political entity finds its expression in the state with its public officials and bureaucracies, regulating human interactions by means of a complex set rules, principles and institutions. But, secondly, society is also pictured as the pre-political sphere in which citizens, as private individuals, exercise their rights, and keep critical watch whether the state is legitimately defending their rights. As we will see, throughout modern history this pre-political sphere has been structured by different modes of interlocking, social imaginaries.

According to Taylor, this idea of a new moral order is truly secular in that it grounds the legitimacy of ruling authorities in the mutual interest of individuals, and not in a higher, divine order. The legitimacy of state intervention depends upon respect for these interests and the rights of individual citizens.

Given its dependence on concrete practices of victim–offender mediation, on referral by the public prosecutor, and given the cooperation between mediation services and judicial state authorities, one should not be surprised that a moderate view of restorative justice and its multidimensional approach to criminality is partly in line with this secular understanding of society in terms of 'a new moral order'. By stressing the importance of the formal-legal dimension of criminality (violation of legal norms enacted by the state), proponents of the moderate view still continue to imagine criminal wrongdoing against the backdrop of a state whose legitimate use of coercive power depends upon respect for the rights of all the stake-holding citizens. Only a strict legal basis, and not a disruption of a sacred order, or the authority of sacred power, allows the state to intervene and to limit the liberties of the offender after a fair trial guided by an independent judge.

From this connection between a moderate view of restorative justice and a new moral order, we can easily dismantle at least two claims upheld by proponents of a spiritual view of restorative justice. A moderate view clearly contests the idea that state-based justice and its foundations are irreconcilable with restorative justice. It also contests the sanctification of state authority, because grounding the state in a new moral order testifies to its real fragility. The legitimacy of the state can be always contested by its contracted citizens when they critically defy the exercise of state power.

There is more, however. A moderate view of restorative justice can also be traced back to modern secular roots because it has both an interpersonal and a civic approach to criminal wrongdoing. In order to flesh out this argument, Taylor's reconstruction of civil society and the public sphere as a mutation of our modern social imaginary (Taylor 2004), as well as of the growing importance of the modern ideal of authenticity, shows itself to be quite helpful (Taylor 1991).

Let us first focus on the idea of a civil society. According to Taylor, this notion is closely linked to the idea of a public sphere and should be understood against the background of a process of mutation with respect to the idea of a new moral order. Gradually the pre-political sphere outside the state began to take on a different shape: the free market, on the one hand, and the public sphere on the other hand. Again, the idea of a public sphere should be seen as an emerging social imaginary, embodied in practices of public opinion making, as well as of practices of citizens organizing themselves (Taylor 2004). Three features can be listed in order to characterize the idea of a public sphere.

First, through notions such as the public sphere or civil society, we imagine our social interactions as common, public spaces in which citizens come together to deliberate and act together to realize a public interest or common good. Or, we imagine our society through the idea of public opinion. An essential ingredient of living together consists, then, of informing oneself through various forms of public media, to formulate one's own public opinions and to submit one's views to a public debate. One of the preconditions of this capacity of citizens to enter a common space of mutual encounter is the existence of basic, social trust: the trust that people are treated on an equal basis, and are respected in their fundamental rights and liberties.

Secondly, the public sphere has to be distinguished from the political system of the state, for it is a sphere the essence of which is constituted by the power of citizens to position themselves constructively and critically in relation to the power of state officials. According to Taylor, the public sphere 'is a space of discussion that is self-consciously seen as being outside power. It is supposed to be listened to by power, but it is not in itself an exercise of power' (Taylor 2004, p. 89).[2]

---

[2] Different views exist, however, as to the question whether this space outside power is of a political nature. In his illuminating essay 'Invoking Civil Society', Taylor distinguishes two different

10 Restorative Justice and Volunteering in a Secular Age

Thirdly, the emergence of a public sphere is closely connected with the formation of a collective agency through the process of acting and deliberating together. This process is secular in nature, for the public sphere is 'an association that is constituted by nothing outside the common action we carry out in it: coming to a common mind, where possible, through the exchange of ideas' (Taylor 2004, p. 94).

By stressing the civic dimension of criminal wrongdoing, proponents of a moderate view on restorative justice, explicitly draw upon the social imaginaries of the public sphere and civil society. It follows from this that criminal wrongdoing is not considered to be an attack on a sacred order but a violation of basic social trust allowing people to come and act together in a common space. Theft, violence and other offences inevitably breach the basic trust between citizens. Citizens are violated in their trust that respect for their fundamental rights is guaranteed. When such a violation occurs, many people will find it difficult to trust their fellow citizens when acting together or interacting in public places (neighbourhoods, streets, schools, etc.). Of course, in a constitutional state, citizens expect that the state is first of all charged with the responsibility of restoring basic trust among citizens when it has been violated. It is first and foremost the task of the state to bring the accused before an independent judge. There, the defendant is called upon to answer publicly for his actions. If he has been found guilty, it is up to the state to enforce respect for the rights that were infringed. But this does not always suffice to restore basic, social trust between citizens. It is part of the originality of restorative justice practices that they support initiatives of citizens to engage in these, often difficult, healing processes of trust as a complementary response to criminal wrongdoing. Again, a moderate conception of restorative justice clearly contests one of the central claims of a spiritual view of restorative justice. Spirituality is not the core of this moderate conception because this latter is far removed from the reaffirmation of a sacred, transcendent order. Instead, a moderate view of restorative justice affirms the restoration of citizens' capability to participate in social life against a background of mutual social trust.

What about the interpersonal dimension of criminality? Could this approach not be linked to deeper spiritual sources of healing, forgiveness and reconciliation? Departing from concrete victim–offender mediation practices, the development of a moderate view of restorative justice borrows its inspiration from the values of self-expression, dialogue and self-restoration. Through an indirect, or direct encounter, through an exchange of views and lived experience, victims as well as offenders are given the opportunity to express their needs, feelings, expectations and to reposition themselves as human beings with regard to their roles as victim and offender. For both parties, entering into dialogue could be part of a process of restoring broken identities, a process in which both voices could be heard. These intimate encounters also embody the hope that both can take up their lives again freed from the suffocating burden of crime. Again, these values of self-expression and dialogue are to be

---

conceptions: the Lockean version which claims the non-political nature of civil society, and a version which can be traced back to Montesquieu (the M-stream), which gives civil society a counterbalancing political role (Taylor 1997, p. 214).

traced back to our modern, secular age. In his 'sources of the self', Taylor (1989) lucidly explained how the romantic period discovered the idea that each person was unique, and that his individual flourishing depended on his capacity for expressing his uniqueness in the intimacy of love, in friendship, in public spaces and, not least, through work and production. This ethics of authenticity (Taylor 1991) is strongly linked with a belief in the equal worth of each individual life. It is also closely linked to an affirmation of our ordinary, mortal lives, and with the aspiration to relieve people as much as possible from human suffering. Restorative justice ideals undoubtedly take up this secular ethic of authenticity in the process of victim–offender mediation, to the extent that it acknowledges the unique ways in which crime affects victims as well as offenders, but also in the ways it supports the restoration of individual flourishing through the empowerment of both victims and offenders. What is asking to be restored is not a higher, sacred order, but broken self-trust and, often, immense human suffering. Advocates of a moderate view on restorative justice seek the re-affirmation of authenticity and the relief from suffering in the daily lives of people.

This concern for human flourishing, for compassion and for the mitigation of human suffering, obviously echoes Christian ideas of benevolence and universal love and care for humans. The point of secularization, however, has been that these concerns have gradually lost their reference to a transcendent power going beyond our human lives. Therefore, to claim that universal love and compassion define the spiritual essence of restorative justice fails to acknowledge the crucial, secular transformations these concerns underwent in the last two centuries.

So far we have argued that a moderate view of restorative justice is not a spiritual conception of justice that stands in opposition to a formal, legal one. It is instead a complex web of ideas constructed around concrete practices, containing a multidimensional approach to criminality which is at the same time expressive of a set of secular, modern imaginaries. Of course, one could reply that a moderate view of restorative justice is just one practice theory, confined to the Belgian context. Given the worldwide scale of restorative justice practice, many other practice theories exist in different countries and different settings. In these contexts, restorative volunteering might be grounded in other values that could more easily chime with the religious roots of restorative justice. Whether true or not, the Belgian, moderate view of restorative justice clearly shows in any case that there are good reasons to loosen the ties between spirituality and restorative justice ideals that are strongly anchored in concrete practices and relate to more formal settings of criminal justice.

This brings us to another, second argument in favour of tempering a strong link between spirituality and restorative justice. A moderate view of restorative justice, which is firmly anchored in a secular framework, has the advantage that it provides within a framework of understanding that stresses positively, instead of obscuring, the importance of cooperation between judicial actors with the state-based system of restorative justice. As already explained above, a moderate view of restorative justice understands criminality as a multidimensional phenomenon, in which the legal-formal dimension deserves as much attention as the interpersonal and civic approach. It is by fully embracing this multidimensionality that advocates of a moderate view can underline the importance of cooperation with official actors of the criminal justice system, but also affirm the legitimacy of the rule of law (such as legality, proportionality, presumption of innocence, etc.).

Channelling Interaction Between Restorative Spirituality and the Secular State

Up till now our strategy consisted of tempering the connection between spirituality and restorative justice, departing from a moderate view of restorative justice which is firmly anchored in a secular framework. However, this strategy does not dispense us from developing what we announced as the third, central argument of our chapter. What we need to track here is a route that conceptually brings together restorative justice practices with strong spiritual roots on the one hand, and the secular assumptions of state-based justice on the other. One could draw here on what has recently been called post-secular thinking (Habermas 2006), which comes down to rehabilitating the public expression of religious worldviews and practices in the public sphere in a manner that is compatible with the grounding logic of public life, such as equal rights to self-expression and to religious freedom, equal rights of participation and deliberation for the sake of the common interest. Another route, which we will follow within the framework of this chapter, can be traced on the basis of what we have called a moderate view of restorative justice.

In order to build this path, further clarification is needed with respect to the content of this moderate view. Advocates of such an approach not only favour a multidimensional understanding, but also a multidimensional response to criminal wrongdoing, which is often captured under the umbrella of 'participative and communicative justice'. How should we understand this notion?

The idea of participatory and communicative justice, *firstly*, refers to the importance of enabling a participative and communicative process between the stake-holding parties. According to the proponents of a moderate view of restorative justice, victim–offender mediation allows people to exchange views and to take part actively in the process of searching together for a just response to crime. This communicative and participatory process enables the conflicting parties to regain the ownership of their conflict (Christie 1977).

Secondly, those who embrace this participatory and communicative account take their view of restorative justice even further. The ideal of communicative and participative justice implies more than just giving a voice to the personal stories of victims and offenders. It also asks that room is made for a response from civil society. Furthermore, an armed robbery necessitates state intervention within the clear limits of a previously defined criminal offence. In a moderate account of restorative justice, it is important that all the stake-holding parties (conflicting parties, civil society, the state) take part in developing a social response with regard to the criminal facts committed each from their own distinct view on criminality.

But the idea of communicative and participatory justice harbours yet another, a third, layer. For a moderate view of restorative justice, the ideal of participatory and communicative justice also requires that judicial actors, conflicting parties as well as fellow citizens, exchange their views in their response to crime. The distinctness of a moderate view lies in its ambition to enable communication between an interpersonal, a civic and a formal-legal response on criminal wrongdoing, without giving up the distinctness of their perspectives. This implies that these three perspectives relate and interact with each other (Aertsen 2006, pp. 83–84).

Thus, advocates of a moderate conception of restorative justice want more than organizing victim–offender mediations, independent and apart from the classical criminal procedures, and completely isolated from public debate in civil society.

Part of the restorative dialogue, firstly, aims at encouraging victim and offender to reposition themselves in relation to the civic dimension of the wrongdoing, or, more concretely, a moderate conception of restorative justice also invites conflicting parties to reflect on what it means for fellow citizens to be diminished in the assurance that their fundamental rights will be respected.

Secondly, according to the advocates of a moderate view of restorative justice, a just answer to crime also invites the conflicting parties to reflect upon the outcome of their dialogue seen from the perspective of the judge. Such a view not only promotes a horizontal dialogue but also a 'vertical communication' between, on the one hand, the parties involved and, on the other, the judiciary (Aertsen and Peters 1997, p. 379; Aertsen 2006, p. 83). Parties would then engage in a learning process as active citizens, for they would convey their common efforts, wishes and agreements to the judge and thus expose their views to a classical, legal perspective on the criminal offence. According to Van Garsse, Aertsen and Peters, this vertical communication reveals an essential part of participatory justice (Van Garsse 2001; Aertsen and Peters 1997).

Given the ideal of communication between interpersonal, civic and formal-legal responses to crime, it should not surprise us that a moderate view of restorative justice is deeply secular in its nature. Its mediation practices activate the voice of the state as well as the voice of civil society. Such a view explicitly articulates the importance of making the legitimacy of judicial interventions by the state dependent upon the participative process of victims and offenders (and not upon some sacred power). It also invites conflicting parties to position themselves within a society seen as a common, deliberative space in which citizens can come to a shared conclusion.

It is precisely this secular interaction between the mediation process, on the one hand, and the criminal intervention of judicial actors on the other hand that offers a promising conceptual framework for dialogue between the spiritual, healing dimension of restorative justice and the rule of law of the classical criminal justice system. In the following paragraphs, we will develop three ideas to make our point:

1. The ideal of participative and communicative justice, as articulated in a moderate view of restorative justice, fully affirms the existence of different and distinct rationales for responding to criminality, without denying the vulnerabilities and

limits implied in each logic. Both practices of state-based justice and restorative justice practices such as mediation have their own 'geographies', to use a nice metaphor of Sawatsky (2009, p. 262), with their own particularities and borders. A moderate view of restorative justice, one that embraces the ideal of participative and communicative justice, reminds us to recognize these distinct particularities and limitations. Applied to restorative justice practices with a strong healing dimension, such as the hollow water community, this conceptual framework of participative and communicative justice invites practitioners and public officials to spell out the distinctness of their positions, as well as the vulnerabilities and limitations of their perspectives. One of the vulnerabilities of the healing ceremonies could be, for example, the absence of a legitimate, coercive framework that would invite the victimizer to take the healing path seriously as a fully fledged alternative to incarceration. A characteristic vulnerability of a state-based criminal justice system is that its process of making people accountable for crime is based upon the premise of individual responsibility and does not create space for interconnected responsibilities. The ideal of participative and communicative justice offers itself as an attractive way of bringing restorative spirituality and state-based justice together, to the extent that it invites both geographies to accept the limits and limitations of their territories.

2. The ideal of participative and communicative justice strives to create communicative channels in which these distinct rationales, the different 'geographies' of justice, can be complementary to each other and can respond to each other's vulnerabilities. Applied to the relation between restorative spirituality and state-based criminal justice, the ideal of participative and communicative justice invites us to search for these complementarities. The concrete cooperative partnership between the members of the hollow water community and the criminal judge seems to us the fruit of such a search for synergies. The sentencing circles that take place in the presence of the criminal judge seem to complement the limitations of sentencing as a practice of holding the individual offender publicly responsible for criminal wrongdoing and are based on a logic of interdependence of relationships and responsibilities.

3. Finally, characteristic for the ideal of participative and communicative justice is that each logic of responding to crime is invited to reflect on and reshape its own premises in dialogue with other types of responses. Because of the reality of a civic dimension of criminality affecting communities, neighbourhoods and citizens, victims and offenders in their exchange of views and lived experiences, in their need for the restoration of their broken selves, are invited to break out of the purely interpersonal response to crime and to reflect upon the broader causes and effects of the type of crime committed and the circumstances in which they are committed. Applied to the relation between 'the geography' of restorative spirituality and 'the geography' of state-based justice, the ideal of participative and communicative justice might serve as a promising conceptual framework to coherently think both geographies together. By deploying this framework of self-understanding, restorative justice practitio-

ners would be stimulated to enter into a reflective learning process and reinterpret the religious sources of their healing practices in the light of the values of human rights and the rule of law, such as the right to cultural identity, participatory rights, the right to individual self-determination, the right to privacy, the presumption of innocence and the right to a fair trial. To be sure, this is a difficult process of translation, but we think it is an indispensable one if restorative justice practices with a strong spiritual dimension are to have any chance to broaden their horizons and expand their territories to the real world of modern, western democracies.

Volunteers and the Secular Grounds of a Moderate View of Restorative Justice

So far we have focused only on the first aim of our chapter: How to adjust the spiritual dimension of restorative justice to the development of its practices in the modern world which is dominated by a state-based criminal justice system governed by the values of the rule of law. It is now time to shift our attention to the second aim: How to think restorative spirituality and the importance of civic volunteering in restorative justice practices together. In this section, we will pursue our practical approach. We will focus on the Belgian context and ask how to understand the values and aims of voluntary work in this secular picture of restorative justice. Is there any place for spirituality given the secular nature of a moderate view of restorative justice? This question is not so easy to answer, taking into account the fact that the role of voluntary work in the Belgian practices of restorative justice is still very marginal. Besides a local experiment in a mediation service in Flanders, and in contrast with other countries, there is no tradition of actively engaging volunteers in restorative justice practices in Belgium. Several reasons can be given for these findings but this would lead us beyond the focus of our chapter. More interesting in this respect is to explore the prospects of voluntary work within the framework of a moderate view of restorative justice, and then, in a subsequent step, to explore how such an ideal scenario of voluntary work might be congruent with broader spiritual roots. As already announced in the introduction, our central thesis can be divided in two parts. The critical part (*Argument 4*) holds that understanding the prospects of voluntary work in a moderate view of restorative justice reaffirms secular ideas and social imaginaries which are constitutive of a broader secular framework. The constructive part of the thesis (*Argument 5*) comes down to the idea that we have to understand the importance of a restorative spirituality in voluntary work quite differently from how it is often understood in restorative justice literature. Again, Taylor's view on spirituality and secularism shows itself to be an illuminating perspective.

Let us focus on the critical part by further examining the moderate view of restorative justice, with its multidimensional approach and response to criminality.

10 Restorative Justice and Volunteering in a Secular Age

What are the implications of such a view for the grounding and development of voluntary work within restorative justice practices?

Firstly, given the importance of reactivating the public sphere as a restorative response to crime, one could see voluntary work and the recruiting of volunteers as a contribution of civil society to the rebuilding of social trust. By giving signals of trust to victim and offender alike, citizens might empower them to regain confidence in an inclusive and respectful society. Their civic commitment could express exactly this hope and trust. Moreover, their commitment could be seen as one of the dynamics that mobilizes trust within civil society.

This message of trust can be of special significance to the offender. Someone is interested in him and is willing to believe in his capabilities. This experience of trust can motivate the offender to restore the broken trust inflicted upon the victim (but also his family, his friends, his neighbourhood, etc.). This message of trust might also be meaningful for the victim. The latter might receive the signal that there are trustworthy people in society who recognize and take interest in his suffering as a victim of crime.

One could develop an even stronger version of the preceding argument in favour of volunteering. If a moderate conception of restorative justice wants to give a voice to the civic dimension of criminal wrongdoing, then such a view not only has to give space to, but also requires the presence of volunteers who take up the role of trust builders. Following this line of thought, one could even argue that, because of their strong social commitment, voluntary citizens are better placed than professionals to fulfil this trust-building role (embodying and representing a trust-building society). Volunteers have no professional interests. They volunteer in their free time. They can make time for social commitment because they are more free from professional pressures (status, income, power play of an employer) (Arendt 1990).

Secondly, the civic dimension of restorative justice, at least in its moderate version, implies reactivation of deliberative citizenship. Completely in line with the social, secular imaginary of a public sphere, the ideal of communicative and participatory justice also invites conflicting parties to see interpersonal conflicts as chances for deliberating together on broader social issues and on more structural responses to these issues. This implies that mediators and social care workers who facilitate and support the mediation process should themselves be responsive to this broader, civic perspective. It is up to them to empower the conflicting parties to discover this civic dimension of criminal wrongdoing. Here, engaging voluntary citizens could be an added value, and this for three reasons that reactivate the secular nature of restorative justice rather than affirming its religious and spiritual roots:

1. Engaging volunteers in the mediation process could have an important expressive meaning. By assigning volunteers the role of active fellow citizens who help the conflicting parties in disclosing the civic dimension of their conflict, one could give a strong signal to the parties that an active, committed and cooperative society is at work. In contrast with a spiritual conception of restorative

justice, the role of volunteers is not to bring in values of unconditional love or forgiveness (even if it can be part of their personal motivation), but to let their commitment help reinforce the idea that citizens are able to deliberate on their conflicts and to come to a shared opinion. Imagine, for example, that in the aftermath of a tragic traffic accident, a volunteering citizen facilitated a face-to-face meeting as a mediator. Imagine this citizen sensitively helping the parties unravel the broader social issues underpinning the legal offence. Imagine this citizen respectfully coaching them in this common deliberative process. Would it be vain to say that such a voluntary commitment conveys a strong message to both victim and offender that they are supported by an active, responsive society of citizens which empowers them in turn to discover their chances of active citizenship?

2. Engaging voluntary citizens might also lower the threshold for victims and offenders to break out of their cocoon of grief and guilt and to focus on the more general, public issues related to the particular criminal offence committed. Volunteering citizens are not messengers of God, or of a religious community, they are fellow citizens who might be better placed than professionals to ease broader issues (like driving under the influence) into the dialogue of restorative justice.

3. Finally, the voluntary commitment of citizens might introduce a lot of life experience and civic competence into mediation services, which in Belgium are steered only by professional mediators. These civic competences relate to a sense of equality, to an openness to diversity and difference, but also to an ability to take part in cooperative practices. They are secular, in the sense that these competences do not exclusively depend on religious beliefs, on a belief in transcendental powers, outside the realm of human action. The inspiring role of volunteering citizens, which might bring professional mediators out of their comfort zone and challenge them to refine their sense for the civic dimension of crime, does not primarily and exclusively derive from their capability to connect with the spiritual and religious roots of restorative justice but from their sense of responsible citizenship.

In the previous lines, we argued that within the framework of a moderate view of restorative justice, the grounding values of restorative volunteering (trust-building, expressing the solidarity of a cooperative civil society, facilitating deliberative citizenship in mediation practices) are quite far removed from a religious, spiritual vision of restorative justice. Of course, one could reply that a moderate view of restorative justice is just one practice theory, confined to the Belgian context. Given the worldwide scale of restorative justice practices, there are many other practice theories in different countries and different settings. In these contexts, restorative volunteering might be grounded in other values that could more easily chime with the religious roots of restorative justice. Though this might well be true, and deserves further research, our Belgian case with its moderate view of restorative justice clearly shows that there are good reasons to temper the connection between the spiritual roots of restorative justice and the aims and values of 'restorative volunteering'.

Spirituality, Meaningfulness and Restorative Volunteering

We now come to the more constructive part of our thesis, which boils down to exploring and imagining how spiritual belief and religion can still play a role in restorative volunteering as rooted in a secular background. To make our point more intelligible, we will once again draw on some intriguing insights of Taylor in his secular age. As already explained, Taylor's account of secularity acknowledges different layers. The third one refers to the idea that the general background to our religious believing has fundamentally changed. Christians, Muslims or Buddhists, who believe in a transcendent goodness beyond this human life, all experience their faith differently because their religious belief manifests itself as just one option among many other profound but non-religious aspirations. Therefore, these religious beliefs inevitably have to position themselves in relation to other, non-religious paths through which individuals and groups make sense of their human existence. These routes borrow their inspiration from the emergence of modern moral sources, as well as from the birth of modern social imaginaries. From this it follows that, in a secular age, the notion of 'spirituality' should be interpreted in a wider sense, also embracing non-religious responses to deep existential issues. Applied to restorative volunteering, one could argue that the profounder motivations of volunteers for engaging in restorative justice practices should be qualified as 'spiritual' in this broad sense. Some of these spiritual aspirations will be religious, referring to transcendent powers beyond earthly life; others will refer to moral sources available in this worldly life.

What, roughly sketched, are the various routes to spirituality in our secular age? In his 'Dilemmas and Connections', Taylor (2011) distinguishes three spiritual paths.

The first, he calls the path of secular humanism, which starts off from the ideal of human flourishing for each through the affirmation of our ordinary lives, our lives of work, family and friends. This spiritual aspiration situates meaningfulness and goodness in secular spaces and times, and the ideal of human flourishing depends on the ambition of people to relieve suffering and reduce it as much as possible in the world. In this view suffering and death are seen as the negation of life.

The second, Taylor calls neo-Nietzschean. This way of positioning oneself in human existence begins by affirming the ambivalence of life, with order and disorder, harmony and violence as its essential ingredients. Such a route can bifurcate in different directions: It might result in a fascination for the will to power, or it might bring us to develop strategies to accept human suffering and human finitude, and to limit and temper the powers of destruction.

The third one goes back to the great religious traditions. In these traditions, the point of life is not exhausted by the fullness and goodness of life. Entering the forest of religious spirituality is seeing a point beyond life. Such a view enables believers to see 'in suffering and death not merely negation, the undoing of the fullness of life, on which life itself originally draws', but also an entrance to a deeper, sacred sense beyond life (Taylor 2011, p. 16). This path requires 'an opening yourself to a change of identity: a radical decentring of the self in relation with God' (Taylor 2011, p. 17).

How do we deal with this multiplicity of spiritual paths? How do they bear on the motivations and the experiences of meaningfulness of the citizens volunteering in restorative justice practices? Two remarks should suffice to make the final point of our chapter.

Firstly, it is important to stress, at least within a moderate view of restorative justice, that these three spiritual paths serve as a roadmap to understand the deep, individual and intimate choices of individual volunteers. It belongs to the predicaments of our secular age to respect and accept the differences between these variants of spirituality and to restrain ourselves from our inclination to give prescriptive force to one of these paths. Moreover, it belongs to the challenge of our times, in restorative justice practice as elsewhere, 'to discover in humility and puzzlement, how we on different paths are also fellow travelers' (Taylor 2011, p. 16).

Secondly, the existential stakes related to crime (loss of trust, suffering, fears, loss of meaning and identity, on the side of the victims; shame and guilt on the side of the offender) are often very high in restorative justice programmes. Therefore, accompanying both parties as a volunteer can inevitably raise deep existential questions for a volunteering mediator: a sense of powerlessness with respect to the immensity of suffering and grief, an acknowledgment of the tragic quality of human existence, etc. In such victim–offender cases, volunteering citizens are inevitably provoked in their spiritual worldviews, because these views provide us with a framework of meaning that enables volunteers to personally and intimately respond to these cases. It follows from this, and this corresponds with our first remark, that volunteers are to be given a free hand in choosing for themselves which of the three stances (humanist, Nietzschean or religious) fits the best with their own personal integrity. Take, for example, exclusively humanists whose commitment as restorative volunteers provides them with a framework of aspirations to relieve the suffering of both victims and offenders, convinced that life's ultimate end refers to the flourishing of each human being (victim and offender). As sworn humanists, it is part of their personal integrity as volunteers to incorporate these aspirations into their voluntary work. But the same goes for neo-Nietzscheans, their sensibility as active citizens will be coloured by a strong awareness of human ambiguity, of the possibility of destructive power games, even in restorative encounters. Their spiritual framework can help in detecting these potentials for restorative violence and in finding ways to cool these forces down. Again, there surely is space too for volunteers upholding Christian beliefs. Within this framework of meaning, it is perfectly legitimate to mediate between victim and offender as a responsible citizen and to support them in their encounters. Inspired by the idea that both victims and offenders are children of God and deserve unconditional love and forgiveness, volunteers can support a mediation process, even if the concrete circumstances clearly show that such an unconditional stance is not possible in this earthly life and is not to be expected from the conflicting parties. Forgiveness and reconciliation are then experienced, not as a central goal to be achieved, but as an emerging force, reflecting an ultimate good beyond life. All these three spiritual paths have their strengths and pitfalls, but our final point here is that, because of their deep existential nature, none of these three stances can be excluded from the field of restorative volunteering. It should depend on the intimate, personal choice of each volunteer to respond to the existential challenges of restorative justice practices according to the particular spiritual stance he (or she) endorses.

References

Aertsen, I. (2006). The intermediate position of restorative justice: The case of Belgium. In I. Aertsen, T. Daems, & L. Roberts (Eds.), *Institutionalizing restorative justice*. Cullompton: Willan Publishing.

Aertsen, I., & Peters, T. (1997). Herstelbemiddeling in slachtofferperspectief. *Victimologie*, 372–383.

Aertsen, I., Daems, T., & Robert, L. (2006). *Institutionalising restorative justice*. Cullompton: Willan Publishing.

Allard, P., & Northley, W. (2001). Christianity: The rediscovery of restorative justice. In L. Hadley (Ed.), *The spiritual roots of restorative justice* (pp. 119–141). New York: State University of New York Press.

Arendt, H. (1990). *On revolution*. London: Penguin Books.

Christie, N. (1977). Conflicts as property. *British Journal of Criminology, 17*(1), 1–15.

Claes, E. (2001). *Legaliteit en rechtsvinding in het strafrecht. Een grondslagentheoretische discussie*. Leuven: Universitaire Pers Leuven.

Habermas, J. (2006). Religion in the public sphere. *European Journal of Philosophy, 14*, 1–25.

Hadley, M. L. (2001). *The spiritual roots of restorative justice*. New York: State University of New York Press.

McCold, P. (2000). Toward a holistic vision of restorative juvenile justice: A reply to the maximalist model. *Contemporary Justice Review, 3*(4), 357–441.

Pali, B., & Pelikan, C. (2010). *Building social support for restorative justice. Media, civil society and citizens*. Leuven: European Forum for Restorative Justice.

Pranis, K., Stuart, B., & Wedge, M. (2003). *Peacemaking circles: From crime to community*. St Paul MO: Living Justice Press.

Sawatsky, J. (2009). *The ethic of traditional communities and the spirit of healing justice*. London: Jessica Kingsley Publishers.

Suggnomè, V. (2005). *Waarom? Slachtoffer-dader bemiddeling in Vlaanderen*. Antwerpen: Garant.

Taylor, C. (1989). *Sources of the self*. Cambridge: Harvard University Press.

Taylor, C. (1991). *The ethics of authenticity*. Cambridge: Harvard University Press.

Taylor, C. (1997). *Philosophical arguments*. Cambridge: Harvard University Press.

Taylor, C. (2004). *Modern social imaginaries*. London: Duke University Press.

Taylor, C. (2007). *A secular age*. Cambridge: The Belknap Press of Harvard University Press.

Taylor, C. (2011). *Dilemmas and connections*. Cambridge: The Belknap Press of Harvard University Press.

Van Garsse, L. (2001). Op zoek naar herstelrecht: Overwegingen na jaren bemiddelingswerk. *Panopticon, 5*, 438.

Van Garsse, L. (2004). Bemiddeling in de strafrechtelijke context. Suggesties voor de regelgeving op basis van jaren bemiddelingspraktijk. *Panopticon, 5*, 47–63.

Waaijman, K. (2011). Spirituality as theology. *Studies in Spirituality, 21*, 1–43.

Walgrave, L. (2008). *Restorative justice, self-interest and responsible citizenship*. Cullompton: Willan Publishing.

Weitekamp, E. (2002). *Restorative justice. Theoretical foundations*. Devon: Willan Publishing.

Zehr, H. (1994). Justice that heals: The practice. *Stimulus, 2*(3), 69–74.

Chapter 11
Short-Term Mission Voluntarism and the Postsecular Imaginary

Mary Hancock

Introduction

Short-term mission (STM) has become an annual pursuit for more than 1.5 million American Christians, both mainline and evangelical, with the highest participation rates among evangelical Christians (Priest 2006, 2008; Wuthnow 2009, p. 171).[1] STM projects amalgamate leisure tourism, evangelism, and voluntary development work; the projects are sponsored and coordinated by denominational bodies and specialized para-church agencies with participants paying fees that vary with destination and covering their costs of travel, meals, and lodging (Bramadat 2000; Dearborn 2003; Hoke and Taylor 2009; Priest 2006, 2008; Stiles and Stiles 2000). Most projects are conducted in Christian communities, with only a minority carried out

---

[1] "Evangelical" is usually used to describe Protestant communities whose core tenets include conversionism, activism, Biblicism, and crucicentrism (Bebbington 1989). While such traditions are longstanding in the USA, following the second world war, evangelical Christians, in an effort to distinguish their concerns and orientations from Fundamentalist Protestants, established a network of nondenominational seminaries, parachurch organizations, and media outlets to develop a more activist, mission-oriented identity. This resulted in the expansion of nondenominational churches and other sorts of agencies. This growth, which was centered in the "Sunbelt" (western and southwestern US), was entwined with the development of suburban settlements and small-government conservatism and produced alliances between white evangelical Protestants and conservative political interests—a phenomenon that resulted in their identification in the 2000s as a crucial political base for the Republican Party and related formations such as the Tea Party and Libertarian movements (Luhr 2009; McGirr 2001). While whites are indeed overrepresented within evangelical communities, there are also self-identified liberal evangelicals, as well as evangelical bodies dominated by African-Americans, Asian-Americans and Latin-Americans (e.g., Walton 2009; Wolfe 2000, 2006). Following the US Religious Landscape Survey (2008, pp. 16–17), I use "evangelical" in this chapter to refer to communities who espouse the tenets of evangelicalism; these communities in the USA encompass nondenominational bodies as well as Baptist Pentecostal, Restorationist, Holiness, and Adventist denominational families. "Mainline" is used to refer to Methodist, Lutheran, Presbyterian, Anglican/Episcopal, and Congregational families.

M. Hancock (✉)
Departments of Anthropology and History, University of California, Santa Barbara, California
e-mail: hancock@anth.ucsb.edu

L. Hustinx et al. (eds.), *Religion and Volunteering,* Nonprofit and Civil Society Studies,
DOI 10.1007/978-3-319-04585-6_11, © Springer International Publishing Switzerland 2015

among non-Christians, often dubbed "unreached" or "least reached," among whom Muslims attract the greatest interest (see also Gallaher 2010).

Volunteers of all ages are recruited, though over the past two decades, STM has become a staple within evangelical youth ministry where it is valued for its ability to contribute to the development of Christian personhood, to world Christianization and to improving material conditions among the world's poor and disenfranchised masses. Its instrumental goals are framed colloquially as matters of personal transformation and personal relations with the divinity—of deepening faith by encountering god experientially, be it "seeing God" in the faces of orphaned children, "experiencing God's love" in fellowship with others, or "surrendering to God's will" through the personal sacrifices demanded in mission service (e.g., Hoke and Taylor 2009).

Its proponents value STM as a mission practice that, along with other new styles such as "reverse" mission, is adapted to an increasingly globalized world in which transportation and communication technologies enable denser and more frequent connections between geographically dispersed communities. Advocates contrast STM with colonial-era missions noting the latter's sharp, usually racialized, distinctions between the "home" church and the "foreign" mission field and the dependencies it fostered between home and mission. They regard STM's emphasis on the parallels, as well as organic connections, between work at "home" and that carried out abroad as signs of progressive change. More fundamentally, they present STM as the product of a theological paradigm—the "missional church"—that views the mission field as lying as much in one's immediate surroundings as in the distant worlds of non-Christian Others (Barth 1962; Bosch 1991; Guder and Barrett 1998; Newbigin 1989). While eschewing the colonial associations of "mission," they assert that STM, like other forms of contemporary mission, comprises practices at the center of Christian life, pointing to the centrality of notions such as "witness" (assertions of Christian principles through action), "fellowship" (relations of mutuality and support), and "servanthood" (emulation of Christ through self-sacrifice and service) in STM practices (see also, Fickert and Corbett 2009; Howell 2009; Koll 2010; Priest 2006, 2008; Priest et al. 2006). Assertions of the missional core of Christianity are hardly new but their expression through STM practices and institutions raises questions about how, why, and to what ends mission practices are transposed from "mission field" to "home." For STM volunteers and agencies, the answers to these questions lie in the extended and ever more durable networks, both national and transnational, that link communities and instantiate a "global Christendom".

As this brief sketch suggests, STM can be compared to other kinds of voluntarism, including that associated with secular institutions, inasmuch as it contributes to the thickening of social ties that sociologists describe as social capital (e.g., Putnam 1994). My interviews with STM leaders and volunteers, as well as my review of web site content, guidebooks, and theological works, revealed that some STM projects are indeed represented by their architects and participants as generators of social capital, with the enhancement of social capital glossed as the means by which missions contribute to a "holistic" form of development that addresses both spiritual

11 Short-Term Mission Voluntarism and the Postsecular Imaginary   219

and material needs. I found that the projects that invoked social capital, or equivalent terms, in presenting their goals, were usually sponsored by mainline denominational bodies, such as those with Presbyterian, Lutheran, or Congregational orientations. The explicit valuation of social capital expressed by these groups, who also tended to downplay conversion in favor of more ecumenical approaches to mission outreach, contrasted with the more muted attention to social capital expressed by nondenominational evangelical groups, especially those who understood mission as having conversion as its ultimate goal. Regardless of specific religious orientation, however, respondents from all groups employed similar framing idioms to gloss the pro-social practices of STM and to ground them theologically. Idioms such as "relational ministry" (in which friendships are encouraged as vehicles of Christian action and communication) enabled them to present their work in ways that diminished distinctions between their activities and those of secular, voluntarist actors. At the same time, while some borrowed the analytic category of social capital to frame their operations, especially for secular audiences, all qualified the value of broader and/or denser social networks and relations, distinguishing those that promoted Christian values from others that did not (i.e., volunteer tourism or secular development work). For example, I encountered frequent expressions of skepticism about the effectiveness of sociopolitical institutions in effecting beneficial change with many respondents disavowing affiliations with the types of secular social and political institutions, such as the civic and sociopolitical associations that scholars associated with the generation of social capital. Continuing this theme, missionaries, especially those with nondenominational evangelical affiliations, placed secular societies of the US and western Europe alongside the "unreached" communities whom they targeted for Christianization. And, most strikingly, volunteers expressed admiration for the very public presence of religious discourse and practice in societies that were religiously Other, notably in Muslim-majority countries.

I argue that STM and the communicative practices it comprises, while generating social capital, are predicated on a radically different social imaginary than that which sustains the neo-Tocquevillean models of sociality and associational life implied by social capital (e.g., Lichterman 2005, pp. 23–30). In shifting focus from the relational outcomes of STM to the social imaginary that informs it, I adopt Charles Taylor's understanding of a social imaginary as a schema that is both conceptual and ethical in orientation and is

> much broader and deeper than the intellectual schemes people may entertain when they think about social reality in a disengaged mode…[it is] rather…the ways people imagine their social existence, how they fit together with others, how things go one between them and their fellows, the expectations that are normally met and the deeper normative notions and images that underlie these expectations (Taylor 2004. p. 23).

If a neo-Tocquevillean social imaginary, as held by both everyday actors and social scientists, frames sociality, and societal institutions as humanly authored and historically contingent—characterizations that themselves rest on a normative and historically specific conception of the secular (Asad 2003)—that which is invoked by STM treats the temporal world as a space in which divinity is immanent, if unrecognized, and expressed affectively and relationally, through experiences of spirituality. For audiences of fellow Christians (e.g., when recruiting STM volunteers), STM's generation of social capital is framed within a social imaginary that is deeply theological, that understands human action and societal institutions as products of god's will and as the media through which it is expressed. The betterment of worldly conditions is understood to be contingent on divine agency and disclosed biblically and prophetically, rather than on the machinations of social and political institutions. STM practice, especially that targeting non-Christians, might be considered as a laboratory or improvisational stage for experimenting with this social imaginary. This experimentation is carried out through the communicative work of creating both bonds and boundaries among volunteers and between volunteers and local communities—it is the sort of *"communication about social ties* that... matters...for *creating social ties"* (Lichterman 2005, p. 16, italics original). This communicative work may involve learning and deploying techniques of outright conversion and/or relational ministry to create a body of believers; it can involve the discourses on spiritual experience that volunteers develop as they reflect on mission experience; it might also entail encounters with other critical discourses on secularity, such as are found in Islamic societies. The latter, while targets of conversionist practice, may also be recognized as exemplars of a postsecular way of life that mirrors that which evangelical Christians also desire.

My characterization of this social imaginary as postsecular is meant to signal the ways in which, for Christians committed to missional practice, it works both to critique the secular and to promise an alternative that will succeed it. It is such critiques that have occasioned recent scholarly debates on secularism (see, for example, Asad 2003; Connelly 1999; Gorski et al. 2012; Taylor 2007). Within scholarly discourse, "postsecular," while ambiguous, is valuable in signaling the presence of a variety of critiques of secularism, the thrusts of which are both normative and descriptive, as well as the social arrangements and imaginaries in which these critiques are lived out. It suggests the limits of the secularization thesis and indexes the complexities of a world in which the constitutional underpinnings of secularity (i.e., formal separation of church and state in the USA) exist alongside the growing presence and significance of plural religiosities and faith commitments in social action and institutions (Beaumont 2010, p. 6; see also Casanova 1994; Connelly 1999; Habermas 2008; Milbank 2006; Taylor 2007). STM, and the socio-moral imaginaries that it sustains, can help us think through the formation and significance of postsecularity in these domains. The postsecular world that evangelical Christians imagine is one in which the political apparatus of the secular state is modified or eliminated and replaced by institutions and rule-making practices based on theological norms. For some US evangelicals, this world can only be made if gay marriages are prohibited and reproductive choice narrowed. For others, this world rests on immigrant rights and environmental stewardship. Rather than treating those who advocate these positions as residues of "premodern" or traditional lifeways, these positions can be framed in relation to the historical and cultural contingency of secular institutions. Moreover, the secularity that may incite resistance or invite adherence is not an abstract matter of constitutional provisions, legislation, or policy regulations, but is lived and felt, as the "sensed context" in which beliefs are developed (Taylor 2007,

p. 13; see also Bender and McRoberts 2012). This includes bodily comportment, body modification and embellishment, dress and accoutrements, and speech norms and idioms; through all of these, it is expressed in everyday social practices. It is in these same domains, therefore, that postsecular social imaginaries may take shape.

In the pages that follow, I discuss how STM volunteers with three para-church agencies framed and negotiated both boundaries and bonds among themselves and between themselves and non-Christian, predominantly Muslim, Others. Projects in Muslim-majority regions, while constituting a minority within STM overall, are the settings in which volunteers are themselves prompted to evaluate the secular norms of the USA through a process of comparison and contrast, and to re-imagine the boundaries of the secular. The further comparison of agencies reveals a gradient of theologically inflected differences in the ways that they both expressed their goals and related them to notions of "social capital." Of the three agencies, one (International Mission Project and Cross-Cultural Training, IMPACT) is affiliated with the Presbyterian Church (USA), while two (InterVarsity Christian Fellowship, IVCF and Campus Crusade for Christ International, Cru) have ties to nondenominational, evangelical bodies. IMPACT's goals and methods are closer to the ecumenical style of mainline denominations; Cru and IVCF, by contrast, are more overtly conversionist in aim and tend to draw participants who are more theologically conservative. This qualitative analysis of the ways that volunteers from each agency framed and engaged with Muslims allows me to compare their different understandings and usages of the notion of social capital, while also showing how, in both mainline and evangelical projects, a postsecular imaginary arises from the activities and discourses of STM.

Data and Methods

Research was conducted in southern California between 2009 and 2012. It included participant observation at events sponsored by evangelical churches and para-church organizations (STM recruitment and planning meetings, prayer and bible study sessions, and worship services). Besides the interviews and informal conversations with local church members, I conducted semi-structured interviews with 21 STM trip leaders, 29 volunteers, and 9 prospective volunteers. These 59 respondents, representing both nondenominational and mainline communities, participated in mission projects sponsored by 27 sending agencies and all respondents quoted are referred to with pseudonyms. Among the respondents was a subset of 18 individuals (5 trip leaders and 13 participants) who had participated in mission projects with non-Christian—predominantly Muslim—communities in Europe, the Middle East, and Asia, sponsored by three agencies. Four interviewees were recruited from IMPACT, a mainline agency affiliated with the Presbyterian Church (USA); 14 others were recruited from agencies with nondenominational evangelical affiliations, 6 from the IVCF and 8 from the Cru.

The three agencies discussed here, like most other STM sending organizations, designed short-term projects meant to support the efforts of career missionaries, the in-country staff of organizations, and/or local Christians. Their respective organizational structures differed, however. Cru and IVCF recruit participants through chapters based on college and university campuses, sponsoring hundreds of volunteers annually on projects that mix evangelization with service. While both have core agendas that are centrally controlled, flexibility in operations is built-in by allowing decentralized specialized ministries to implement agency goals. IMPACT recruits five to seven teams of volunteers annually through a regionally based board; its agenda is not set by the church's national governing body but by trip leaders, local ministers, and volunteers.

A Brief Overview and History of Short-Term Mission in the USA

The operations of STM exemplify what Robert Wuthnow (2009) calls "boundless faith." Along with church partnerships and pastoral exchanges, they are enabled by, and participate in, contemporary processes of economic globalization, such as travel and migration, transnational flows of capital and commodities, and the global circulation of information and images. The globalization of national political economies during the past few decades has enabled mission growth while also contributing to the patterns of deprivation that mission may seek to ameliorate (Han 2010; Velho 2009; Wuthnow 2009). Equally important are the cultural exchanges, interactions, and debates that accompany and often mediate the economic changes of globalization. Mission transmits forms of life, objects, and ideas across geopolitical boundaries, while also embodying and reproducing globalization's dialectical tension "of engagement and alienation" (Mazzarella 2004, p. 361) in its efforts to engage with Christian and non-Christian Others while necessarily distinguishing itself from those Others. STM demonstrates this in its complex relations with the burgeoning and ever-diversifying tourism industry. Although STM's proponents contrast their own aims with those of leisure tourism, tourism's expansion has yielded various niche styles, marketed by a raft of agencies that include NGOs, and includes critical and reflective practices (e.g., alternative, poverty and volunteer vacations) that overlap with STM. Also, some STM sponsors deliberately incorporate elements of leisure tourism, such as recreational sports and day trips to tourist sites and entertainment venues.

Although its growth has paralleled and been entwined with tourism, STM originated in the reconfiguration of evangelical institutions that followed World War II (Balmer 1989). It emerged in the 1960s, with the founding of the nondenominational agency, Youth with a Mission (YWAM). Soon after, Cru added STM to its ministries, as did IVCF. STM's place in the new postwar wave of evangelical institution building reflects the changing value of mission for evangelicals. While interests in mission waned among many mainline denominational bodies in the

1950s, new para-church ministries (e.g., IVCF, Young Life International) and seminaries (e.g., Fuller Theological Seminary) made mission a cornerstone of evangelical praxis. Underwritten, in some cases, by millennialist theological principles and by conservative interpretations of missionary Christianity, new evangelical bodies stressed the urgency of the conversion of non-Christians. The short-term model, buoyed by the renewed embrace of mission among evangelicals and sustained by the new styles of missiological training and theory provided in evangelical institutions, steadily gained popularity in the decades following its founding, thereby increasing its participation rates and spawning scores of sending agencies (Priest et al. 2010; Wuthnow 2009).

This growth has been further fueled with the incorporation of STM projects within the US government-sponsored development projects that Christian faith based organizations (FBOs) have pursued since the early 2000s (Bornstein 2003; Clarke 2006, 2007; Hancock 2013; Hearn 2002; Thomas 2005). These shifts in development and foreign policy frameworks began with the private sector ventures that burgeoned in the 1980s and grew following the 2002 adoption of policies supporting faith-based initiatives in domestic social services and international development. Although the US Agency for International Development prohibits use of public monies and goods for religious proselytization, by framing their activities as "holistic development" with no sectarian restrictions on beneficiaries, Christian para-church bodies have successfully expanded mission practice within the context of economic development (Shah and Grigsby 2011; see also Bornstein 2003. p. 65).

With the wider adoption of STM, its theological emphases have diversified. STM operations now rest on principles that range from the overt conversionist goals embraced by its original adopters to more ecumenical forms of engagement, with a broad middle ground amalgamating elements of both. Although Cru is mostly allied with conversionist goals and the direct forms of evangelism that accompany them, some of its programs, like those of IVCF, also advocate "relational" forms of ministry, by training volunteers to seek friendships through informal interactions and, within the context of those friendships, to introduce non-Christians to Christian principles. Both agencies also sponsored service projects in which efforts to convert were downplayed in favor of Christian witnessing and fellowship. Even less emphasis on conversion exists among those, like IMPACT, with mainline denominational affiliations, which emphasize humanitarian service, yoked to Christian witness, during the mission period and work in partnership with local Christian churches.

Engaging Others in Short-Term Mission

The now-standardized format for STM begins with volunteers assembling prior to travel for preparatory activities that may include trust exercises, training in communications, and personality assessments. Participants are also coached on fundraising strategies—usually the solicitation of donations from family, friends, and fellow church members—and brief tutorials on destinations that include basic socio-demographic information and cultural etiquette are offered. Volunteers travel, live, and work together during the period of mission service, carrying out assigned duties (e.g., construction projects, Vacation Bible School) on behalf of host communities and participating in local liturgy. They also gather regularly for prayer and reflection, and prepare web journals or maintain Facebook pages to share their experiences with family, friends, and home churches. Service in the field is followed by one or more days of debriefing, during which they are guided in reflecting on how god has revealed himself in the course of their work. They are expected to continue this reflection in the weeks and months that follow by sharing their stories with home audiences and by maintaining contacts with fellow participants and communities in mission locales, through social media, web logs, and email.

"Getting Out of the Comfort Zone": Preparing for Short-Term Mission

The training sessions that precede STM projects may start as early as several months prior to travel. The training contexts are, on the one hand, spaces of bonding, constituting volunteers as "teams" through various exercises and spiritual practices. This anticipates the field experience and is meant to create relational ties that can persist after its conclusion. On the other hand, training is intended to impress upon volunteers the distance, cultural, and geographic, between mission fields and home. Prospective volunteers learn that STM will take them "out of their comfort zone," a phrase that recurs in respondents' narratives, as well as in guidebooks and marketing materials and signals the perceived privation the mission field brings (regardless of actual socioeconomic characteristics) and its "foreignness," in the form of linguistic and cultural barriers (e.g., Howell 2009, 2012). Agencies gleaned much of the socio-demographic and geographic information that they presented about mission destinations from encyclopedic works, especially the Joshua Project (http://www.joshuaproject.net, January 30, 2013) and *Operation World* (Mandryk 2010), both of which are published by evangelical Christian organizations having millennialist theological orientations.[2] These sources compile data retrieved from a variety of sources, including CIA Factbooks and Human Relations Area Files as well as mission agency databases (e.g., Barrett et al. 2007) and use that information to categorize ethno-linguistic, sectarian, and regional populations according to their

---

[2] Both organizations draw on the theology of the "10/40 Window" and the "AD 2000" (later renamed "AD 2000 and Beyond") movements founded in late 1980s, and their cartographic media, databases, and image archives are used by mission agencies (Han 2010). Collectively, these groups are rooted in premillennial dispensationalist theology, with its expectation that Old Testament covenants will be fulfilled in the near future with the Christianization of the world's population understood as a condition that precedes the fulfillment of these covenants. Populations targeted for mission are located between the tenth and fortieth northern latitudes and defined as "least reached" by Christianity and most in the grip of poverty, illiteracy, disease, and other societal problems.

exposure to and acceptance of Christianity. Muslims are consistently identified as most resistant to and thus least "reached" by evangelization; indeed, Muslims are depicted not only as "unreached" but as hostile toward Christianity. While vividly depicting the worlds that lay beyond volunteers' "comfort zones," these materials also suggest that the de-familiarization of STM is virtuous, that the feeling of dislocation and disorientation in the face of difference is also a space of connection with divinity, and that the sacrificial demands of mission will create and deepen volunteers' experience of being (in their words) "in a relationship with God."[3]

All agencies treated Joshua Project databases and *Operation World* as objective representations of religious diversity but they differed in the degrees to which they incorporated the date of those sources in STM training. Cru relied most extensively on data from the Joshua Project and *Operation World* in representing boundaries between Christian Selves and non-Christian Others, and its visual and textual representations of Islam depict it in terms of the threats it poses to Christianity. IVCF and IMPACT, by contrast, did not emphasize sectarian or cultural boundaries as consistently as Cru in representations of STM projects. Their web sites foreground bonding with images of mission fields emphasizing affective relationships. Missionaries are shown working and worshiping with local community members, caring for children, providing medical assistance, playing soccer, or sightseeing. These visual vocabularies were consistent with the textual glosses for "relational mission" on the sites, as exemplified in the IVCF's focus on the "lingua-cultural work" of language acquisition and training and the creation of friendships through "sharing world views" (http://gp.intervarsity.org/projects/china-silk-road, 21 January 2012).

The different treatments of geographic and cultural boundaries by agencies are also found in the ways that their training programs seek to move volunteers beyond their "comfort zones." Cru's training for summer mission trips began with meetings scheduled several months ahead, during which volunteers chose destinations and formed mission teams, each of which was expected to train (incorporating prayer and bible study) and to carry out fundraising together. In seminars, volunteers were introduced to Cru's ranking of destination countries according to their "openness" to Christianity. Japan, Kuwait, Pakistan, and China, for example, were less open than Thailand, Mongolia, or Australia. Rudimentary information about regional history and society were offered, but with a focus on developing strategies for engaging non-Christians in interactions that would open the door to effective forms of evangelization. Some volunteers chose to participate in the Jesus Film Project, a ministry organized around screening and distribution of "Jesus," a 1978 film based on the gospel narrative of Luke and since translated into thousands of languages (http://www.jesusfilm.org, 30 January 2013). All were expected to distribute and discuss a pamphlet, *Four Spiritual Laws*, published by the Campus Crusade for Christ and long used in its proselytization (http://www.campuscrusade.com/fourlawseng.htm, 30 January 2013). Volunteers were also introduced to their roles in helping generate data for Cru's own databases: They were taught to administer various Cru-produced surveys on religious composition, as well as to record the numbers of persons with

---

[3] See Hancock (Forthcoming) for a more extended discussion of these materials.

whom they "shared" their faith and, of those, how many "accepted Jesus." A more intensive team orientation took place just before the scheduled trip, comprising trust- and team-building exercises along with spiritual preparation. The practices and routines in which they were trained were all explained as vehicles for god's agency, as a veteran Cru volunteer put it: "God is what makes things happen on a trip." Volunteers, in other words, learned to see themselves as the means of divine intervention in temporal worlds.

IVCF- and IMPACT-sponsored trips were preceded by training sessions that began months prior to travel and concluded with several days of intensive training immediately preceding departure. In the early sessions, volunteers formed teams and usually initiated some kind of regular interaction, such as Bible study. They also were introduced to information about regional society and history. Closer to travel, logistical preparations and team-building exercises were pursued. Idioms of relationality, such as "friendship," "relational ministry," "servanthood," were stressed, as was attention to vulnerability and self-disclosure, all of which were presented as the means by which volunteers' own relations with divinity would grow.

IVCF training for volunteers on its Bosnia and Herzegovina trips emphasized the region's religious composition and its history of ethno-religious conflict. Strategies for "relational ministry" appropriate to this setting were introduced. These strategies essentially involved volunteers' seizing opportunities to "share" their faith in the context of the English-language classes that they led and the informal conversations that they pursued. Furthermore, the approaches rested on the vulnerable personas that volunteers were enjoined to assume: They were allowed only limited amounts of clothing, personal goods, and money and were counseled to be ready for an "extreme cross-cultural friendship" (http://gp.intervarsity.org/, 30 January 2013).

IMPACT's volunteers were trained to be "learners, storytellers, and servants" (http://www.impact-sbp.org, 30 January 2013). Some groups began preparations months beforehand by studying the Bible or other theological works and devising devotional exercises. More intensive preparation came with "cross-training," a 5-day camping trip scheduled shortly before departure. "Cross-training" was meant to cultivate bonds between team members, to orient them to the kind of work they would do, as "servants," and to prepare them for the adaptability that would be required as "learners." They also learned to create a "story," a short narrative about themselves and their faith appropriate for cross-cultural interaction. Those traveling to Turkey acquired some basic information about Islam, though participants' sense of Muslim Otherness was a by-product of the agency's main goal of extending support to a small Christian community, based in Antalya. James, an Anglo-American trip leader in his fifties explained that because Islam had displaced Christianity in the region he felt "this grief for Anatolia…it was the most significant Christian community in the first four hundred years. That was the strongest, most imbedded part of the Roman Empire, where Christianity flourished and [now] it's just all relics." James related this historical decline to the current minority status of Christians, including their difficulties in competing for jobs and in school: "just your presence there as believers from another country is encouraging…to them because they are an extreme minority in this Islamic country." At the same time, he hoped that volunteers' presence might open Muslims' "hearts" to Christianity and hoped that their presence, as Christians—even without direct evangelization—could bridge those gaps.

In recruitment and training, therefore, volunteers with all agencies were introduced to various kinds of boundaries between Christian Selves and non-Christian Others and urged to move "out of their comfort zones" in engaging with those Others. What STM promised, through this experience of defamiliarization, moreover, was the volunteers' own closer relationship with god. The types of boundaries emphasized, and the corresponding strategies for mission outreach, differed among the agencies, however. Cru emphasized the antagonisms between Christians and the world's "unreached," Muslims, in particular. Volunteers were challenged to step out of their "comfort zones" by entering worlds whose inhabitants were hostile toward Christianity and conversionary strategies were developed to deflect or overcome this perceived hostility. IVCF, while also aiming for Christian conversion, emphasized the possibilities for connection across sectarian difference with idioms of relationality and openness. It trained volunteers to achieve this goal through "relational ministry"—engagements with non-Christian Others through "friendship"—rather than direct evangelization. IMPACT, while abandoning the goal of conversion, also urged volunteers to step "out of their comfort zones" through training that emphasized the cultivation of vulnerability through engaging with difference—in this case, by adopting the tripartite persona of "learner, storyteller, servant" rather than "missionary." For all volunteers, regardless of the instrumental goals or methods of mission, being "out of the comfort zone" was a prelude to the "relationship with God" that mission practice promised.

"It's cool to see God in another place...": Mission Practice

Mission practice often centered on service and yielded practical benefits such as repaired buildings, sewage trenches, and vaccinations. Service was predicated, however, on affective ties both with the Others (Christian and non-Christian) of the mission field and among the volunteers themselves (see also Bramadat 2000; Howell 2012). These connections were glossed with terms like "heart," "love," and "sharing" which is understood as conduits of divine agency. That is, affective orientations were framed as expressions of what STM discourse calls "God's global heart" and portended new, unexpected encounters with god. For example, after telling me that ordinary tourist travel had given her "a heart for the world," 24-year-old Denise, an Anglo-American volunteer with Cru, explained that STM involved "learning about what the people are about and where their hearts are" and further, "sharing with them why you're there and what your heart is about." Again, mission and the sacrifices it demanded were meant to deepen volunteers' relations with god. Kim, a 21-year-old Asian-American volunteer with Cru, put it this way: "I was able to see people's lives changed, not through me, really, but because I sacrificed myself to do that."

When in the field, STM volunteers usually lived together in houses or apartments provided by agencies and local affiliates. Their days usually began with group prayer and Bible reading, and each day included time to "share" what god had "told" them in the course of their activities and interactions. They carried out service and educational projects as teams. Meals were taken together and, because participants were rarely competent in local languages, they communicated in English and relied on translators. Their stays included visits to tourist sites, but they avoided poorer areas and other sites deemed dangerous. Most STM trips, therefore, were experiences of enclavement for volunteers; while generating within-group dependencies, these arrangements also contributed to their sense of the mission field as a space of difference, risk, and vulnerability.

Efforts to bridge the differences between Christian Selves and the non-Christian Others took varying forms. While IVCF and IMPACT volunteers emphasized that they were honest about their desires to share their faith, Cru volunteers, like 20-year-old Peter, characterized their work as "mission on the down low," meaning that it was covertly carried out. Teams in Muslim-majority areas usually participated in educational or cultural exchange programs, for example, by enrolling in university-sponsored classes. These strategies enabled them to interact with a variety of local residents with whom they might engage in conversionary discourse. Twenty-three-year-old Adriana (Anglo-American) explained that Cru's volunteers were expected to "meet as many new friends as possible, get their [telephone] numbers" and follow up with them. She outlined several typical encounters in which conversational gambits, such as requests for directions, could be used to initiate more extended interactions. Volunteers also relied on Cru's established technique of using written surveys as ice-breakers (see Ingram 1989). Pearl, a 21-year-old Asian-American volunteer, described the survey that she used in a Muslim-majority area as including questions about respondents' sectarian affiliations which would then, as she put it "slide into Christianity," by asking them what they knew about it, and finally offering to teach them more about it. The survey and other techniques, however, were only means to create opportunities for more targeted conversations using Cru's pamphlet, *Four Spiritual Laws,* as the guide. In the evenings, the students re-assembled to talk about their day's activities—what they accomplished and failed to accomplish, what they learned; on some nights, they held worship sessions to which local Christians might be invited.

Although Cru's web site materials suggested antagonism between Christianity and Islam, volunteers' actual experiences were more nuanced. Some suggested that Muslims' past and present experiences with European imperialism generated antagonisms toward Christianity, but felt that the relationships that they had established, even if not leading to conversion, might eventually overcome that hostility. Denise, quoted above, recognized the presence of resistance but insisted that the field situation could be framed by "love": "I would love our team to become unified with one another, to just grow and lean on each other and love on each other. I would love for our team to honestly and earnestly love on the people there." (Her colloquial usage of the preposition "on" after the verb, "love," is common among American youth.) Volunteers saw the willingness of Muslim youth to engage in conversations

11 Short-Term Mission Voluntarism and the Postsecular Imaginary

on spiritual matters as another sign of how hostilities might be overcome. As Peter, quoted above, offered:

> They definitely are more hospitable than we are and that is like hands down…one of my favorite parts. I think they, they know how to treat people well. They know how to welcome people well. …as far as spiritual life, goes, I think they are a more spiritual people, at least they identify more with Islam than Americans would with Christianity or Judaism or Islam over here…

The spirituality that volunteers attributed to Muslims contrasted with Americans' reticence when approached in a similar manner. Americans, they felt, adhered to behavioral norms of secular society, such as the avoidance of professing one's own religious identity or seeking the identifications of others in casual conversations. This, which some coined as "apatheticism," was sometimes described as a more significant hurdle to Christianization than Islam. Cru volunteers, whose STM practice began with the recognition of boundaries between Christian Selves and non-Christian Others and who sought to overcome boundaries through conversion, found themselves in the unexpected position of recognizing, in that non-Christian Other, a shared critique of secular society as well as a model for inter-religious dialogue.

The possibility that conversionist encounters could work, both as polemical exchanges and as a discovery of shared critiques of secular society, was recognized among volunteers with other agencies. IVCF's volunteers were coached to interact in ways similar to Cru, though without the props of pamphlets, scripts, or videos. IVCF volunteers traveled to Muslim-majority areas in China and in Bosnia and Herzegovina, and I interviewed individuals who had participated in the latter. At 4 weeks, those trips were longer than the typical STM project. Their goals were described by Liz, an Anglo-American trip leader in her mid-twenties, as follows: "So we teach conversational English. We're very up front about [saying] 'We're Christians, we want to serve you. We want to teach you English, and we would love to talk to you more about God if you want to'…. We're not, like, doing any shady business, but we develop relationships because that's how you share." This brief quote reiterates the idioms of social connectivity that recur in volunteers' discourse while investing these connections with theological significance.

The daily schedule of volunteers included 2–3 h of English conversation classes, coupled with much lengthier, and less structured, interactions usually over coffee. Like their Cru counterparts, IVCF volunteers were also excited by Muslim youths' willingness to engage them on spiritual matters. Liz's description of her experience with a young Muslim man captures this dynamic:

> I had a really, really powerful conversation with one of our friends. He was involved in kind of an equivalent to InterVarsity, but a Muslim student organization…. I think he wanted to improve his English too. He basically told us like, "I'm trying to convert you." And we were like, "Great! We are trying to convert you!"… And we would joke about it and that's what I love about over there is, like, it's not taboo. In the United States people are, like, "Don't push your religion on me." But there, I mean, he felt strong enough in his faith that he could talk about it, you know? I'm like "Great." And we just had this deep trust and relationship with him that it was, like, "Let's get into it."

These conversations often reached an impasse, though volunteers still found the opportunity to engage encouraging. Liz explained that one of their conversations had turned to the subject of justice and that her friend had stressed that "God is just, therefore he has to keep track of all the good I do and all the bad I do because, since he's just he can't let these bad things go unnoticed, and God is constantly recording it. And then when I die I'll find out if the good outweighed the bad." Liz admitted to him that his account of god's punitive (and unpredictable) authority was "scary," and went on to explain her own notion of god's justice, telling him: "I think God is just also…and let me tell you why, because of Jesus. Jesus was justice; he did pay the price, so now God doesn't have to keep track because that is justice." She described his reaction: "And he's, like, 'Uhhhh.' And he didn't like what he heard… He didn't have a rebuttal." For Liz, this exchange was one of "sharing" and the impasse with which the conversation ended confirmed to her that she had conveyed something important and potentially transformative to her friend. And, although it appeared to involve an exchange of doctrinal principles, it also confirmed her own notion of Christianity's more encompassing "truth" and her own sense of mission's ability to solidify her own "relationship" with god.

Contrasting with Cru and IVCF, IMPACT projects did not involve evangelization, although engagement, formal and informal, with Muslims was anticipated. The agency's program in Turkey developed out of a two-decade-long partnership between the presbytery and a small Christian church in Antalya, and it operated out of a cultural center. Consistent with the relational and familial themes of its web site, IMPACT's projects in Turkey centered on parenting classes. Trip leader James explained that such projects were devised with the goal of enhancing "social capital," the only reference to social capital that any of my interviews yielded. The classes were not represented as "Christian," nor were they restricted to Christians. Instead, they incorporated Christian principles in ways that IMPACT's leadership considered generally applicable to family life, regardless of sectarian affiliation and attendees included both Muslims and Christians. James elaborated:

> [In the classes] I'm not preaching the Gospel directly, but I'm teaching parenting principles that reflect the parenting nature and character of how God, in a sense, parents us. But I'm not saying that. And by doing that, I'm helping families raise their children in a healthier way, so they're gonna be more receptive and able to understand that there is a God who loves them, and I'm creating harmony in homes, or helping to facilitate harmony in homes, and I'm giving the church a tool to connect with the community in a way that doesn't feel religiously threatening. Because everybody wants to be a good parent, and [the community] says, "Wow, they're doing this. That's a good thing." So it gives the church a good rapport in the community and I believe that's missional—meeting a real need, you know, of people.

Some of the volunteers understood this sort of outreach as being consistent with American political values of free enterprise and of freedom of speech and religion, as this excerpt from an interview with 67-year-old Anglo-American, Alicia, indicates:

> I believe so strongly that the church will grow because of God working through us…we're not doing good deeds to get into heaven; we're just doing it because we believe so firmly that people should have the freedom of choice in everything they do. …Freedom of worshiping God as they would like. Freedom of being able to have maybe some alternative ideas of how they can support and sustain themselves and their kids and their church.

11 Short-Term Mission Voluntarism and the Postsecular Imaginary

While ideas about the virtues of social capital and other American values underwrote the formal programs, many interactions were casual and serendipitous, arising from everyday commercial and recreational activities. Alicia asserted:

> You don't want to convert them or anything, but just discuss things.... In different careers that I've had...I can work with everybody. So, believe it or not, they would sit me down, they would have a discussion on religion. They said, "Are you a missionary?" I said, "No, no, no, no. I'm here as an assistant teacher for parenting over at [the cultural center]".... So we got into religion every day with different men.

As was the case with Cru and IVCF, then, IMPACT projects created opportunities for dialogue that surprised and gratified volunteers like Alicia. Indeed, the idea that god was present in culturally unfamiliar surroundings was a mainstay in all STM discourse. The possibility of god "showing up" in another, very different circumstance—a different country, a different style of worship—is a draw of mission and it is predicated on the notion of divine immanence, that god is already present, incarnate, in these multifarious places and activities. STM works though this possibility, even as it recognizes boundaries, that there are "unreached" who form the targets of conversionist outreach. The placement and permeability of these boundaries are indicative of the theological distinctions played out in mission practice. At the same time, the possibility of god's presence in the quotidian and strategies for recognizing that presence arise from a postsecular imaginary, shared across these theologically distinct projects, that engages and interrogates everyday norms of secularity and assumptions about the boundaries between secular and religious institutions. How volunteers try to bring mission home speaks to this imaginary.

Bringing Mission Home

Mainline projects, such as IMPACT's, often accommodate the norms and practices of social capital. They explicitly sought to work across linguistic, cultural, and sectarian boundaries to impart skills (e.g., parenting) that would strengthen communities. In a similar vein, some respondents ventured that mission trips offered lessons for living in multicultural society and enlarged their capacity for tolerance. Although these volunteers would insist that their actions arose from motivations associated with Christian faith, they did not necessarily seek to spread that faith. This approach accorded with the principles of secularism (privatization of religion, the separation of church and state, and freedom of religious expression) that are nominally endorsed in the USA. The perceived relation between these values and "free enterprise" as expressed by Alicia further underscored this as an accommodation to such principles and the socioeconomic and political landscapes that they shaped.

Nevertheless, even projects that included enhancements of social capital among their aims, rested on theological (rather than sociological) grounds, as James' analysis of IMPACT's role in Turkey confirms:

> In Antalya, there were people sent from a church in the UK, from Russia, from Switzerland, from the Netherlands. And I'm realizing, Oh my gosh, the Holy Spirit is at work in the hearts and minds of people everywhere, like this giant chessboard, moving pieces, where there is a need and where God calls us. And there's this moving back and forth.... God is this international traffic cop, you know, saying, "Ok, go here. Wait a minute...." And just directing the traffic of his followers that are open and are responding to his leading.

It was the perception of divine agency and intent, such as voiced by James, that constituted a common thread among STM projects. If some conceded that social capital might be enhanced, with corresponding benefits for community welfare, all understood the capacity to undertake mission and the experience of vulnerability and sacrifice as disclosures of divine agency. By embracing the spiritual and bodily risks of travel to a different place, one might gain an experiential connection with god's power. "People have been blessed when we go. I've seen it with my own eyes, people getting healed, people having churches built up for them, people's lives being changed...in front of my eyes because we were there," declared Cru volunteer Cindy. Liz learned that "God could answer prayers" when she traveled to Bosnia with an IVCF team; Adriana, working with Cru in the Middle East, described her experience as a "test" imposed by God, and "nothing of myself." Some described the process of choosing a mission travel site as one of experiencing god's agency: Cru volunteer, Pearl, described how her original intention to travel to Australia was overturned by god, who engineered a series of coincidences that resulted in her traveling to a region classified as "less open" to Christianity. These perspectives were accompanied by the devaluation of political institutions and affiliations. The majority of respondents, and all who self-identified as "evangelical" or "nondenominational." participated minimally in formal or informal political institutions and often described themselves as "apolitical" or simply "undecided." Even Jerry, a 30-year-old IMPACT volunteer who distanced himself from the conversionist goals of organizations like Cru, maintained, "I am not an American Christian, I am a Christian who lives in America, an ambassador."

These experiences set the stage for developing "boldness" in faith, by which they meant a willingness to witness and proselytize at home. STM provided a space in which to practice various techniques for communicating with and about their faith. It also offered models of a social world in which such speech styles were acceptable. In particular, they encountered in their relations with Muslim Others, a model for engagement, whether pluralist, dialogical, or polemical, that departed from the secular norms that consigned spirituality to private realms of the home and religious institutions.

The same agencies that sponsored trips also played crucial roles in channeling these impulses and ways of imagining the social into concrete practices. IMPACT, working through the presbytery, provided opportunities for volunteers to participate in other church-based networks, domestic and international, and thereby deepen and sustain the ties between local churches and their partners (secular and faith-based). Through their campus-based chapters, Cru- and IVCF-sponsored Bible study, worship, and prayer groups; they also helped members establish co-housing arrangements, such as shared apartment or house rentals. Veteran volunteers with all agencies coached others in methods of "sharing faith" closer to home (e.g., with fellow students and co-workers), while also retaining within their everyday speech the idioms and speech styles that characterized mission discourse, such as references to being "in a relationship with god," "seeing god show up" in unexpected places, and "having a heart" for various causes and communities. Moreover, those who adopted conversionist approaches often re-framed the secular spaces of home as "unreached" and devised mission projects for engaging that world. In the course of my research, I learned that at least one southern California nondenominational church, the Seaview Church (pseudonym), traces its origins to STM. Its co-founder, Gwen (now married to its pastor, Les) described the church as a divinely directed outcome of a STM experience in Zimbabwe that had been sponsored by an organization with ties to IVCF. She explained its origin using the same idioms that other STM volunteers employed to characterize the kinds of sociality that mission prompted: "During our debriefing…the Lord spoke to me and told me that…my ministry would be at [the university that borders Sea View]." She continued: "It was not enough to have only one or two believers focus on the lost. We needed a radical community of believers loving one another supernaturally and loving the city with that same love. Only then could a whole city be saved." While further discussion of Seaview Church is beyond the scope of this chapter, it serves as a telling example of how missional idioms may re-circulate at home and, in that context, serve to anchor a postsecular imaginary through embodied practices of prayer and the "love" engendered and expressed through those practices.

Conclusion

This chapter has offered a comparative analysis of how three Christian STM agencies engaged with non-Christians in the context of international projects that mixed service, evangelism, and tourism. I examined how volunteers with each agency employed theological idioms to frame both boundaries and bonds among themselves and between themselves and non-Christian Others. STM's contribution to thicker, more durable relational networks suggests that STM might be understood in terms of social capital and some agencies, especially those affiliated with mainline denominational bodies, borrowed this analytic category to describe their aims and operations. I discovered, however, that although the paradigm of social capital may suggest ways to explain the functions and social effects of STM, it does not capture the social imaginary from which STM arises nor the critique of secular norms, practices, and institutions that it promulgates.

My approach in this chapter, therefore, has not begun with assumptions about the normative status of social capital as an outcome of STM but with the aims and aspirations voiced by its proponents, analyzing whether and how STM achieves those ends and on those bases considering what it tells us about postsecular moral imaginaries. Although STM can easily be placed among the forms of voluntary action that sociologists have categorized as "plug-in" because of their coordination by service agencies and recruitment of participants for specific tasks, it is not my aim to explicate its contributions to voluntarism in functionalist terms. Nor are my concerns aligned with those of STM practitioners, who aim to identify the benefits, spiritual and quotidian, of STM in order to pursue those goals more effectively. Instead, I am interested in how STM's postsecular imaginary, the world of global Christendom that it both assumes and anticipates, is felt and understood in counterpoint to the everyday secular institutions and practices

Both the experience in "mission field" and the way that that experience is framed and extended at home show how STM may work as a node for cultivating a postsecular imaginary—a mode of understanding and experiencing the temporal world as the space of immanent divinity. By placing STM within the context of the postsecular, I am proposing that it be interpreted among other contemporary phenomena that indicate the limits of the secularization thesis and that attend to the existence of plural spiritualities and faith commitments in social action and institutions. Geographer Justin Beaumont (2010) explains:

> I use the term to indicate that within secularized social structures of modern late capitalism, religions, referring both to religious actors and organizations are very much present and will not disappear irrespective of widespread aversion to the idea among certain liberal and secularist commentators. In other words, postsecular refers to the limits of the secularization thesis and the ever-growing realization of radically plural societies in terms of religion, faith and belief within and between diverse urban societies. (Beaumont 2010, p. 6)

This critique and re-framing of secularity has attracted scholars' attention in recent years. It can unfold in the consequences, intended and unintended, of the projects of urban development, gentrification, or beautification and of their own relations to property by religious actors (e.g., McRoberts 2003; Elisha 2011). It may arise in debates about the presence and influence of religious norms, bodies and practices in institutions, and spaces that make up the public realm (e.g., Habermas 2008). It can also emerge in the insertion of signifiers (material, embodied, pragmatic) in ways that conform to codes and conventions of secular spaces, such as the guarantees of free speech that allow crosses or menorahs to be displayed, and thereby blur the boundaries of publicity and privacy. This, in overly simplified terms, is the phenomenon that Matthew Engelke (2012) described as "ambient" religion, a locution deliberately meant to parallel the phenomenon of ambience in advertising and thus to place religious action and expression within the landscape of consumer society.

I want to draw on the example of STM and its effects to posit a third option for the critique of secularity, one that is less concerned about the categorical boundary between "religion" and the "secular," but instead focuses on the affective and experiential qualities of spirituality as media that put "inner worlds" in conversation with material and political realities, rather than "cordoning off…inner spiritual states from external publics." (Bender and McRoberts 2012, p. 20) STM, especially projects carried out in Muslim-majority areas, offered volunteers new models for thinking about the boundaries of the secular. Although many STM projects, regardless of destination, were pitched as training grounds for volunteers growing in "boldness" in professing and sharing their faith, volunteers working in Muslim-majority sites discovered in these social spaces new, non-Christian styles for the expression of this "boldness." These styles, manifest in public spaces, were

11 Short-Term Mission Voluntarism and the Postsecular Imaginary

expressed acoustically in calls to prayer and amplified sermons, in dress and in murals and posters. They also existed in interactional norms, notably Muslims' willingness to engage in conversations and debates on spiritual topics and in the perceptions, voiced by some, that Muslims were more "spiritual" than Americans. Ironically, it was in the worlds of non-Christian Others that they found models for critiquing everyday norms of secularity in the USA that favor discretion and treat religion and spirituality as private concerns to be shared with family and like-minded others rather than co-workers or casual acquaintances (see Connelly 1999). It suggests how STM may work as an anchor for a postsecular imaginary in which social spaces of everyday life are treated as spaces of moral experimentation, and in which diverse faith commitments may confront one another, both as polemical opponents and as converging imaginaries.

Acknowledgments Research was supported by grants from the Institute for Social, Behavioral and Economic Research and the Academic Senate of the University of California, Santa Barbara (USA) and assistance provided by Audra Kosh, Steve Hu, Kerry San Chirico, Kristy Slominski, and Lindsay Vogt. Versions of this chapter were presented to audiences at UCSIA, the University of California Santa Barbara, the Society for Anthropology of Religion, the American Anthropological Association, and the UCHRI Working Group on Religion and Urban Place-Making.

References

Asad, T. (2003). *Formations of the secular: Christianity, Islam, modernity.* Palo Alto, California: Stanford University Press.

Balmer, R. (1989). *Mine eyes have seen the glory: A journey into evangelical subculture in America.* New York: Oxford University Press.

Barrett, D., Johnson, T., & Crossing, P. (2007). Missiometrics 2007: Creating your own analysis of global data. *International Bulletin of Missionary Research, 31*(1), 25–32.

Barth, K. (1962). *Church dogmatics IV.3b.* Edinburgh: T. & T. Publishers.

Beaumont, J. (2010). Transcending the particular in postsecular cities. In A. Molendijk, J. Beaumont, & C. Jedan (Eds.), *Exploring the postsecular: The religious, the political and the urban* (pp. 3–17). Leiden: Brill.

Bebbington, D. (1989). *Evangelicalism in modern Britain: A history from the 1730s to the 1980s.* London: Unwin and Hyman.

Bender, C., & McRoberts, O. (2012). Mapping a field: Why and how to study spirituality. Paper of the Working Group on Spirituality, Political Engagement and Public Life. Social Science Research Council. http://blogs.ssrc.org/tif/wp-content/uploads/2010/05/Why-and-How-to-Study-Spirtuality.pdf. Accessed 15 May 2013.

Bornstein, E. (2003). *The spirit of development: Protestant NGOs, morality and economics in Zimbabwe.* New York: Routledge.

Bosch, D. (1991). *Transforming mission: Paradigm shifts in the theology of mission.* Maryknoll: Orbis.

Bramadat, P. (2000). *The church on the world's turf.* New York: Oxford University Press.

Casanova, J. (1994). *Public religions in the modern world.* Chicago: University of Chicago Press.

Clarke, G. (2006). Faith matters: Faith-based organizations, civil society and international development. *Journal of International Development, 18,* 835–848.

Clarke, G. (2007). Agents of transformation? Donors, faith-based organizations and international development. *Third World Quarterly, 28*(1), 77–96.

Connelly, W. (1999). *Why I am not a secularist*. Baltimore: Johns Hopkins University Press.

Dearborn, T. (2003). *Short-term missions workbook: From mission tourists to global citizens*. Downers Grove: InterVarsity Press.

Elisha, O. (2011). *Moral ambition: Mobilization and social outreach in evangelical megachurches*. Berkeley: University of California Press.

Engelke, M. (2012). Angels in Swindon: Public religion and ambient faith in England. *American Ethnologist, 39*(1), 155–170.

Fickert, B., & Corbett, S. (2009). *When helping hurts*. Chicago: Moody Publishing.

Gallaher, C. (2010). Between Armageddon and hope: Dispensational premillennialism and evangelical missions in the Middle East. In J. Dittmer & T. Sturm (Eds.), *Mapping the end times: American evangelical geopolitics and apocalyptic visions* (pp. 209–232). London: Ashgate.

Gorski, P., Kim, D., Torpey, J., & Van Antwerpen, J. (Eds.). (2012). *The postsecular in question: Religion in contemporary society*. New York: New York University Press.

Guder, D., & Barrett, L. (1998). *Missional church: A vision for the sending of the church in North America*. Grand Rapids: Eerdmans.

Habermas, J. (2008). Notes on post-secular society. *New Perspectives Quarterly, 25*(4), 17–29.

Han, J. H. J. (2010). Reaching the unreached in the 10/40 window: The missionary geoscience of race, difference and distance. In J. Dittmer & T. Sturm (Eds.), *Mapping the end times: American evangelical geopolitics and apocalyptic visions* (pp. 183–207). London: Ashgate.

Hancock, M. (2013). New mission paradigms and the encounter with Islam: Fusing voluntarism, tourism and evangelism in short-term missions in the USA. *Culture and Religion: An Interdisciplinary Journal.* doi:1:10,1080/1475560.2012.758160.

Hancock, M. (in press). Short-term youth mission practice and the visualization of global Christianity. *Material Religion.*

Hearn, J. (2002). The 'invisible NGO': US evangelical mission in Kenya. *Journal of Religion in Africa, 32*(1), 32–61.

Hoke, S., & Taylor, B. (2009). *Global mission handbook: A guide for crosscultural service* (Revised edition). Downers Grove: IVP.

Howell, B. (2009). Mission to nowhere: Putting short term missions into context. *International Bulletin of Missionary Research, 33*(4), 206–111.

Howell, B. (2012). *Short-term mission: An ethnography of Christian travel narrative and experience*. Downers Grove: IVP Academic.

Ingram, L. (1989). Evangelism as frame intrusion: Observations on witnessing in public places. *Journal for the Scientific Study of Religion, 28*(1), 17–26.

Koll, K. (2010). Taking wolves among lambs: Some thoughts on training for short-term mission facilitation. *International Bulletin of Missionary Research, 34*(2), 93–96.

Lichterman, P. (2005). *Elusive togetherness: Church groups trying to bridge America's divisions*. Princeton: Princeton University Press.

Luhr, E. (2009). *Witnessing suburbia: Conservatives and Christian youth culture*. Berkeley: University of California Press.

Mandryk, J. (2010). *Operation world* (7th revised edition). Colorado Springs: Biblica Publishing.

Mazzarella, W. (2004). Culture, globalization, mediation. *Annual Review of Anthropology, 33*, 345–367.

McGirr, L. (2001). *Suburban warriors: The origins of the new American right*. Princeton: Princeton University Press.

McRoberts, O. (2003). *Streets of glory: Church and community in a black urban neighborhood*. Chicago: University of Chicago Press.

Milbank, J. (2006). *Theology and social theory: Beyond secular reason*. New York: Wiley Blackwell.

Newbigin, L. (1989). *The gospel in a pluralist society*. London: SPCK.

Pew Forum on Religion and Public Life. (2008). *U.S. religious landscape survey*. Washington, DC: Pew Forum on Religion and Public Life.

Priest, R. (Ed.). (2006). Short-term missions. *Missiology (Special Theme Issue), 34*(4).

Priest, R. (Ed.). (2008). *Effective engagement in short-term mission: Doing it right!*. Pasadena: William Carey Library.

Priest, R., Dischinger, T., Rasmussen, S., & Brown, C. (2006). Researching the short-term mission movement. *Missiology (Special Theme Issue), 34*(4), 431–450.

Priest, R., Wilson, D., & Johnson, A. (2010). U.S. megachurches and new patterns of global mission. *International Bulletin of Missionary Research, 34*(2), 97–103.

Putnam, R. (1994). *Bowling alone: The collapse and revival of American community*. New York: Simon and Schuster.

Shah, R., & Grigsby, C. (2011). *2011 VolAg: Report of voluntary agencies*. Washington, DC: U.S. Agency for International Development. PDF File downloaded from http://www.pvo.net/usaid/. Accessed 30 Oct 2011.

Stiles, J. M., & Stiles, L. (2000). *Mack and Leeann's guide to short-term missions*. Downers Grove: InterVarsity Press.

Taylor, C. (2004). *Modern social imaginaries*. Durham: Duke University Press.

Taylor, C. (2007). *A secular age*. Cambridge: Harvard University Press.

Thomas, S. (2005). *The global resurgence of religion and the transformation of international relations*. Hampshire: Palgrave MacMillan.

Velho, O. (2009). Missionization in the postcolonial world: A view from Brazil and elsewhere. (trans: D. Rodgers). In T. Csordas (Ed.), *Transnational transcendence: Essays on religion and globalization* (pp. 31–54). Berkeley: University of California Press.

Wuthnow, R. (2009). *Boundless faith: The global outreach of American churches*. Berkeley: University of California Press.

Websites Consulted

InterVarsity Christian Fellowship (http://www.intervarsity.org/).
Cru (formerly the Campus Crusade for Christ International) (http://www.cru.org/).
The Joshua Project (http://www.joshuaproject.net).
The Jesus Film Project (http://www.jesusfilm.org).
IMPACT Missions Organization of the Santa Barbara Presbytery (http://www.impact-sbp.org).
Access dates for above sites were from 1 December, 2011 to 30 January, 2013.

Part IV
Politics of Religion and Volunteering

Chapter 12
Religion and Social Solidarity

A Pragmatist Approach

Paul Lichterman

Religion and Solidarity: The Neo-Tocquevillian Synthesis

Classical sociology gave religion a strong role as social integrator. Sociology's first and foremost challenge, the problem of social order in a modern society, arose from the assumption that religious commitment was inevitably in decline. What force would strengthen social togetherness in a post-religious world? Powerful criticisms of the secularization thesis (Casanova 1994), not to mention daily news headlines, ushered in the observation, which has since become routine, that religious identity and practice still do play roles in public life around the globe. They promote a variety of collective, civic acts, from charitable volunteering (Wuthnow 1991; Baggett 2000) to broad-scale social welfare assistance (Davis and Robinson 2012), to risky anti-war protest (Nepstad 2004). How should we think of religion as a basis for social solidarity today?

Different approaches answer the question with different understandings of "religion" and "social solidarity." One common approach selectively adopts Alexis de Tocqueville's oft-repeated arguments about American democracy (*Democracy in America*, 1969 [1835]). De Tocqueville argued that voluntary associations, rather than fragmenting the citizenry, cultivated in American citizens a willingness to take political life as well as other citizens seriously and to work together across different interests. In this way, de Tocqueville supposed that over time associations strengthened not only American democracy but cohesiveness or social solidarity, by giving citizens practice in interacting with other citizens and by broadening their sense of engagement in a larger, common project as a public "we." Associations might play weaker or different roles in other democracies; in the USA they were a crucial counterbalance to the habit of Americans of withdrawing from that larger "we" into their small circles of friends and family. Many US scholars have tended to read de Tocqueville's complex arguments selectively, simplifying them in ways that

---

P. Lichterman (✉)
University of Southern California, Los Angeles, CA, USA
e-mail: lichterm@usc.edu

L. Hustinx et al. (eds.), *Religion and Volunteering*, Nonprofit and Civil Society Studies, DOI 10.1007/978-3-319-04585-6_12, © Springer International Publishing Switzerland 2015

complement the needs of empirical researchers (Putnam 2000; Verba et al. 1995; see Berman 1997).

The approach that I will call the "neo-Tocquevillian synthesis" treats social solidarity as an aggregate of individual and collective, "pro-social" acts. In practice, this often means counting voluntary, face-to-face associations, voluntary group memberships, or discrete acts of charitable volunteering or, sometimes, political participation. The thinking is that if associations, memberships or acts of participation in public life are increasing, then solidarity is increasing—if we assume that these groups and acts have some pro-social purpose; a decrease in the count implies the opposite. In the past two decades the neo-Tocquevillian version of the social capital concept (Putnam 1993, 1995, 2000; but see Edwards and Foley 1997) has become a prominent tool for researching voluntary associations and ties. Treating solidarity in terms of voluntary acts of participation that can be counted, it complements research on cross-national data sets that can tell us whether or not religiously sponsored associations contribute a lot or only a little to social solidarity, understood in this neo-Tocquevillian vein.

The neo-Tocquevillian synthesis assimilates currently common understandings about religion. In the past two decades, sociologists (Warner 1993) have come to see religion as a flexible, multi-vocal resource for diverse group solidarities and collective identities, rather than as an overarching "sacred canopy" of meaning, or a guarantor of societal integration, as older views had it (Berger 1967). From this more recent point of view, we expect to find religion's contribution to social solidarity working at the level of small groups or organizations and not society as a whole. We can tally up "religious social capital" (Smidt 2003) as the sum total of religious group memberships or acts of participation in groups that call themselves religious. Like the older sociological view of religion as a sacred canopy, this newer understanding depends on what I will call the "unitary actor model" of religion. According to this model, individuals and groups either are or are not religious, all the time.

Studying religion and social solidarity by means of the neo-Tocquevillian synthesis is a relatively clean, yet risky, research strategy. I would argue that this strategy has become an increasingly inadequate way to understand religion's relation to social togetherness in complex, diverse, socially unequal societies. The neo-Tocquevillian synthesis can produce rough overviews of religious associational life and that is useful for some purposes. As a perspective on religion and social solidarity it also has limits. After reviewing those limits—particularly the problematic assumptions about religious actors in the neo-Tocquevillian synthesis—I propose an alternative, "pragmatist" approach to religion that works better for understanding religion's relation to social solidarity. A case of voluntary, civic action by a church-sponsored organization that advocates for homeless people's needs in a large US city will illustrate the benefits of the pragmatist approach. The case will clarify why we need a conceptual alternative that shows how, if at all, religion plays a part in local acts of solidarity.

12 Religion and Social Solidarity

Troubles with the Neo-Tocquevillian Synthesis

The Unitary Actor Model of Religion

Designating individuals or groups as religious or not religious, as neo-Tocquevillians have usually done, depends on a unitary actor model of religion.[1] Its guiding assumption is that when religious identity or sensibility is manifest at all, it is not substantially affected by the setting. Religious people, or groups, are always being religious. The unitary actor model is easy to take for granted partly because many people, especially Christians, tend to understand religion as an identity-pervading belief (Neitz 2004), deeply lodged in the self. Typical research practice designates actors as either religious or not religious on the basis of affiliations they name in response to survey questions, or affiliations they carry in contexts other than the one under study. Such research goes on to correlate the presumed religious beliefs or motives of the actors with actions of interest. Invoking the unitary actor model, research ends up assuming that the actors we researchers have designated as "religious" are acting on religious beliefs continuously. Yet everyday life offers many examples of people—clergy as well as laity—who express religious sentiments in different ways in different social circles, and who express it in some settings but not others. Sociological research has tended to neglect this variation until very recently.

A brief example from the case developed below helps illustrate the problem. In a large US city, 60 community advocates, clergy people, and volunteers met over breakfast to trade ideas on what to do about homelessness in their urban neighborhood. The breakfast was hosted by an association called the Caring Embrace of the Homeless and Poor (CE) which was sponsored by a Protestant church. Its participants included Christian clergy, church volunteers, and religious and secular social activists. The breakfast meeting opened with a welcome to "religious and non-religious" people, followed by a short prayer to an unnamed divinity. Some speakers embraced religious commitments, others criticized religious ideas or people. Some participants were ordained clergy, but it would have been hard to tell purely on the basis of what they said. Were they necessarily religious actors anyway? Should we categorize this as a religiously inspired gathering?

We can find the unitary actor model continually reappearing in the sociology of religion. The privatization thesis that became the current consensus about religion (Lichterman and Potts 2009) at least implicitly if not explicitly depended on a unitary religious self as a lynchpin of moral order. In one version (Parsons 1967, especially pp. 418–421), stable and private religious selves promoted pro-social values; in the more pessimistic view (Berger 1967), modern society's "sacred canopy" of religion was fraying in the glare of modern scientific thinking, voluntarism, and role segmentation. Neither view would sensitize observers to the existence of variety in an individual's or organization's religious identity in different situations. A more

---

[1] For a fuller development of this argument, with additional empirical material beyond the case in this essay, see Lichterman (2012b).

recent paradigm of American religion research (Warner 1993) dropped the notion of religion as society's canopy of ultimate meanings and argued that different religious traditions facilitate group empowerment in a pluralistic, fragmented world (Roof 1998; see Luckmann 1967). Change in religious identity from setting to setting still flew under an intellectual radar more attuned to religion as a force for group if not societal integration.

Very recent moves to highlight everyday practices of religion have taken more interest in the ways an individual's or group's religious expression may vary by context or be ambiguous, as in the case of the convocation on homelessness pictured above (Ammerman 2003, 2007; Bender 2003). When contrasted with earlier research on similar topics, these new studies clarify the dangers that result when we consider religious identity as "a singular guiding 'core' that shapes how others respond to us and how we guide our own behavior" (Ammerman 2003, p. 209). Older studies of conservative social movements of women, for instance, imply that a continuous sense of religious self is present across different settings, from national conferences to local church settings, to private interviews (Klatch 1987, pp. 20–31; Press and Cole 1999). In contrast, very recent research on pro-life activists shows that the setting of an abortion protest action can carry religious and/or non-religious meanings for participants who identify religiously in other settings; the action does not rest on a single sense of religious self (Munson 2007).

Unitary actor assumptions in studies of religious groups also at the very least encourage a soft form of "groupism," a tendency to attribute to members of a religiously identified organization the same shared religious sensibilities and identities. As Brubaker conceives it, groupism is the tendency to take "internally homogenous, externally bounded groups as basic constituents of social life" and the main actors in social conflicts (2002, p. 164). For one example of this tendency, a prominent study of American local activists generalized that "religious commitments to community caring, family well-being, and social justice inspire and sustain political participation" in citizen's organizations that fight for better schools and more job opportunities (Warren 2001b, p. 4). The study claimed that those religious commitments were shared by clergy and lay members of congregations that supported these citizens' initiatives (191–210). One could infer that these citizen's organizations were pervaded by a shared theology and uniform religiosity. Yet, Warren's study also shows along the way how religiously based, local citizen advocacy must juggle overlapping social identities, especially ethnic identities, that inhibit solidarity based on religious commonalities.

In contrast, other research on citizen organizations shows how local meetings with municipal leaders become powerful forums for "identity work." Instead of "compartmentalizing themselves into a 'secular self' enacted in other settings", participants integrate secular and religious identities (Wood 2002, p. 167). This remarkable observation on the power of settings comes with the quiet assumption that the prayer at these meetings "roots political work in the shared faith commitments of participants." This assumption of group homogeneity may be difficult to leave aside entirely in social research, but again, we can ask more about how religion promotes solidarity if we stop assuming that unchanging religious motives are shared by everyone under study.

Multiple Acts of Solidarity: A Closer Look at the Meanings of Volunteering

The neo-Tocquevillian synthesis highlights activity in voluntary associations as a society's means to maintaining or strengthening solidarity. It is important to keep in mind, though, that voluntary activity can be structured in widely different ways, with different meanings and potentially different contributions to social togetherness. Let us take the USA as one locus of examples.

Many Americans say they benefit society by "volunteering." A half-century ago, Americans thought of "volunteering" as membership in a local association whose members routinely carried out charitable activities that ordinary citizens could plan, such as raising money for a hospital or a school or visiting the sick (Wuthnow 1998). Some of these associations belonged to the kind of self-organizing, national federations that might lead some local members to develop a broader view of national society (Skocpol and Fiorina 1999).

While this "club"-style volunteering certainly still exists (Eckstein 2001), when Americans speak of "volunteering" today, they often have in mind "hands-on," task-oriented and unpaid acts that serve some charitable purpose and involve short-term, scheduled commitments. They imagine serving homeless people dinner once a week for two hours, or acting as a summer camp counsellor for several hours a week in a program for low-income children (Lichterman 2005, 2006). They fill volunteer slots, carrying out tasks under the management of social service professionals. This "plug-in" volunteering (Lichterman 2006; Eliasoph 2011) is currently one of the most popular forms of voluntary participation in the USA, and one of very few forms of participation found to be growing, not declining, at the turn of the century (Putnam 2000). Americans currently tend to think of it as the act of social solidarity *par excellence* because they consider it apolitical and hence non-divisive, and because they think this kind of volunteering expresses sincere caring "from the heart." Americans tend to disregard the organized planning and administrative oversight that makes plug-in volunteering possible (Wuthnow 1991, 1998; Eliasoph 1998; Lichterman 2005). American religious congregations sponsor a lot of plug-in volunteering and some argue that religious congregations are particularly well suited to host it (Chaves 2004).

Individual choice-driven, temporary voluntary action is not unique to the USA. It also is an important form of participation for young people in Belgium and the Netherlands (Hustinx et al. 2012).[2] In the USA too, individual-driven, choice-enhancing participation continues to compete with other, more group-centered forms of voluntary action, inside as well as outside the arena of groups we might call "po-

---

[2] Different studies (for instance, Hustinx et al. 2012; Lichterman 2006; Eliasoph 2011) have identified individual choice-driven volunteering with somewhat different examples. They are not all exactly the "plug-in volunteering" illustrated in US examples by volunteers who sign up for short shifts of voluntary work once a week under the direction of a volunteer recruiter. They are similar enough to warrant being considered together for this discussion's purposes, especially when compared to club-style or "collectivistic" (Eckstein 2001) volunteering.

litical" (Lichterman 2005). Highly personalized forms of participation in political and religious groups have become widespread since the 1960s in a variety of other societies (Lichterman 1996; Juris and Pleyers 2009; Melucci 1989; Mische 2008). Though different in various ways, they share with plug-in volunteering a focus on individual choice.

Compared with clubs in national federations, plug-in volunteering results in fewer projects of ordinary citizens collectively organizing themselves since it relies on expert management. Whether or not the club-style of volunteering represents a stronger act of social solidarity than the task-oriented one is at least partly a matter of moral or political viewpoints.[3] Empirically, it is safe to say that plug-in volunteering is a very distinct form of contributing to social solidarity, and is not universally widespread. While common in the Low Countries among the college students that Hustinx and colleagues studied, it might still confound expectations among members of the same demographic in Germany, who are used to volunteering financed and regulated by government through the *freiwillige Soziale Jahr* program (Kaiser 2007). Treating any single form of voluntary action as a prime indicator of social solidarity may short-circuit our understanding of cross-national differences in religion's contribution to social solidarity, if by solidarity we mean a mutual regard among socially unequal or culturally diverse groups that results from intentional acts.

Despite its limitations, the Tocquevillian synthesis can produce worthwhile research. If our goal is mainly to correlate types of religion or religious institutions and types or rates of voluntary action, then the neo-Tocquevillian synthesis does the job. It may suggest hypotheses regarding religious influence on associational life or on solidarity that deserve further research. We simply cannot use it to say a lot about how religion relates to acts of social solidarity or what religion means for people who share those acts, whichever way we discern the presence of religion. These questions benefit from an alternative framework that detaches religion from unitary actors and uses a larger theoretical category of civic action to encompass historically and culturally varying acts of solidarity such as volunteering.

---

[3] In the USA, widely read social critics argued in the 1980s that a growing focus on individual expression and choice was diminishing social solidarity, perhaps weakening collective efforts for social change too (Bellah et al. 1985); from this viewpoint, the growth of plug-in volunteering might signal declining solidarity. From a different point of view, another critic (McKnight 1996) argued, analogous to Habermas, that administrative planning disempowered the collective will of American citizens. Given that plug-in volunteering depends on planners and recruiters who direct volunteers and often are state-employed (Wuthnow 1998), we might infer, again, that participating in this kind of volunteering is a weaker act of solidarity than the older kind, in which citizens decided on and carried out charitable or pro-social deeds together. On the other hand, plug-in volunteering accommodates a highly mobile society (Wuthnow 1998) and other kinds of individualized participation welcome socially diverse people who do not all share the same expectations and cultural experiences (see Lichterman 1996).

Religion and Solidarity in a Post-Tocquevillian Scenario

Solidarity Amidst Porous Boundaries

Classical social theorists such as Durkheim and Marx imagined society as a unitary if perhaps deeply fractured or strained social formation. The neo-Toquevillian vision of social solidarity imagines diverse voluntary associations pursuing pro-social ends from inside the sphere of civil society, counterbalancing the market and state. Robert Putnam's much-cited research on declining associations and memberships in the USA has been read as a paean to an age of social solidarity and civic virtue that is now past (Cohen 1999). Other work, however, takes into account changing American cultural and institutional conditions.

Robert Wuthnow suggests that we conceive of a highly modernized society as a loosely connected society of "porous institutions" (Wuthnow 1998). He uses metaphors of network and loose connections to imagine solidarity in the contemporary social order. Social cohesion in a loosely connected society is much more a matter of detachable, portable, and multiple social ties than enduring loyalties to groups that all embody the central symbols of a single societal community (for instance, Hustinx and Lammertyn 2003). That does not mean solidarity is necessarily diminished in some absolute sense; rather, it has a different form from that of solidarity in a society with bonds that are tight (but therefore exclusive) and institutions that are less porous (but therefore inflexible). Shared tasks, temporary projects, and individual choice, more than compulsory communal values and certainly more than shared religion, sustain such a loosely bound society (see Merelman 1984). In this vision, it makes less sense to expect that actors will sound and act either religiously or non-religiously, at all times and in all settings whether institutional or informal. Some settings may invite implicit or explicit religious expression while others do not, and the difference does not always depend on an organization's identity as secular or religious (Ammerman 2007). Individual actors may cross the porous boundaries between religion-friendly and secular institutional spaces with relative ease (Lichterman 2012b). In this post-Tocquevillian scenario, it is better to ask how religious expression relates to civic or voluntary action differently in different kinds of settings. From this view, the unitary actor model of religion reifies religious actors and over-simplifies the contexts that enable and constrain religious expression.

The post-Tocquevillian scenario views social solidarity in a somewhat different light too. It starts with the valuable Tocquevillian idea that social cohesiveness in a democracy grows from participation in the civic realm of voluntary, face-to-face associations that act for some public good (Warren 2001a). In the contemporary USA, however, it makes sense to include within the realm of "civic" or voluntary action the informal networks and individual choice-driven projects of a "loosely connected" society, projects that use plug-in volunteers as well as complex, "non-profit" organizations or NGOs and local, face-to-face volunteer and advocacy groups (Lichterman and Eliasoph 2013). The civil sphere of social solidarity (Alexander 2006), then, includes a variety of relationships intended "on behalf of society" in some sense.[4] Researching relations between religious expression and any of the sites of civic action reveals important and varying aspects of the relation of religion to social solidarity.

A Pragmatist Focus on Religious Expression

Once we recognize a society of porous institutional boundaries and diverse civic settings, the unitary actor model of religion seems increasingly inappropriate. Contemporary writing on culture and institutional relations bolsters the argument for an alternative to simple ideas about individuals as unitary actors. As Ann Swidler argued (2001), people are rarely consistent in their use of the cultural repertoires they have available to them; they use different repertoires of action to address different kinds of problems in different contexts. From this point of view, it makes more sense to trace actions to the different kinds of institutional relationships within which actors find themselves instead of treating actors as first-movers (Jepperson 1991).

Building on these kinds of insights, my alternative to the neo-Tocquevillian synthesis is a "pragmatist" approach in a very restricted sense of the term. It focuses on situated action and situated identities in settings (Mead 1934), in this case, the settings of civic action. Rather than follow the performance of religious or other texts (for instance, Burke 1945), this approach starts with everyday action, similar to Goffman's studies of interaction (1961, 1959). The pragmatic approach, similar to many studies using the unitary actor model, treats religion as culture, one that is not fundamentally different from other kinds of culture. In this perspective, religious culture is not a set of silent beliefs, as popular common sense still has it, but patterned communication (Riesebrodt 2008; Ammerman 2003; Lichterman 2008). The pragmatic approach goes on to say that those patterns of communication—whether we call them vocabularies, discourses, or narratives, for instance—are always inflected by specific social settings (Eliasoph and Lichterman 2003; Lichterman 2005, 2007). The following discussion offers elements of a method we can use to study how settings enable and constrain what people can say and do religiously.[5]

Settings are structured by group styles. Group style is a concept from recent cultural sociology that improves the Goffmanian approach to settings. Group style is a pattern of interaction that arises from a group's shared assumptions about what constitutes good or adequate participation in the group setting. While Goffman treated culture mostly as a static backdrop, more recent work finds there are loose patterns of creating "group-ness" which have their own histories and make up part of a society's cultural repertoire. Sets of understandings about what constitutes appropriate participation in a setting, or group styles, are sometimes shared by many groups across a society. Group style is what gives settings their power to shape interaction

---

[4] For a much fuller development of these claims in theoretical and methodological terms, see Lichterman and Eliasoph (2013). A partial, preliminary sketch of some of these ideas is available in Lichterman (2012a).

[5] For a full presentation and conceptual justification, see (Lichterman 2012b).

and identity, in ways potentially different from how they would unfold outside the setting (Eliasoph and Lichterman 2003). By setting I mean the social and material coordinates of an interaction scene (see Lichterman 2012b). The same setting, however, may host more than one group style, if the participants' implicit idea of adequate participation were to change. In my research, a church sanctuary may become the scene of private devotion, then a citizen's meeting, and then a service of worship, all in the same evening. Each of these is coordinated by a different group style. Neither does the same group style always characterize the same "group" of people. Rather than saying that a group exists and has a style, it makes more sense from this viewpoint to say that the same people may coordinate themselves and define the meaning of membership in different styles, creating different kinds of group each time. Different group styles elicit different abilities, perspectives, and even religious beliefs, which individuals may not exercise or express outside the group.

For the scholar of religion it is important to recognize that a group's style has a reality of its own. It is not simply a derivative or logical consequence of the religious beliefs of members or sacred texts. A new body of research is showing that group styles shape not only how people work together but how people interpret their beliefs differently in different settings and how the same people welcome or eschew religious or political claims in different settings.[6] When we study different settings for public religion, we are studying how group style, the meaning of membership in a setting, itself shapes opportunities for religious expression. To discover group style, a researcher can focus on several aspects of action in common; for present purposes, two are the most important. Firstly, organizations draw boundaries around themselves on a wider social map; those boundaries bring "the organization" itself into being, defining what is "inside" or "outside" it, who it is like, and who it avoids. Secondly, organizations sustain bonds that define a set of obligations good members have towards each other.

To assess boundaries and bonds in relation to religious or potentially religious culture, the observer may pursue two related questions. What implicit understandings guide the actors' ways of relating to the (potentially) religious identities of others in the setting? And how do individual actors relate to their own potentially religious identities in the setting? The task, then, is not to figure out "what religion the participants have" or "how strongly they hold their religion," but how they construct religious identities and how they relate their religious commitments to those of others in a setting. Why should we bother focusing on settings rather than groups and individual actors?

This pragmatist approach to religion may sound counterintuitive. Its focus on religious communication rather than "religion" *per se* is a strong departure from the common understanding, especially among ordinary Christians, that religion is

---

[6] For the main expositions of this viewpoint and methodological guidelines for using it, see Eliasoph and Lichterman (2003), Lichterman (2005, 2012b), and Eliasoph (2011). For other applications of the group style concept to cases in the USA, South America, and western Europe, see Lichterman (1995, 1996, 2007, 2008), Mische (2008), Faucher-King (2005), Yon (2009), Luhtakalio (2009), Citroni (2010).

a deeply internalized core of the self that drives action. Drawing as it does on the interactionism of Erving Goffman along with contemporary cultural sociology, this approach does not claim to access the deep internal self that psychologists—and many religious people—may assume is central to religious experience. Neither does this approach deny that many people would say they are consistently deeply motivated by religious teachings. The pragmatist focus on religious communication is a matter of methodological and theoretical principle (see Wuthnow 2011; Lichterman 2012b). From this pragmatist viewpoint, we would not phrase research questions in terms of "the social effects of religion," as if religion already exists as a psychological force and then has social effects. Instead, we investigate how religious communication, conveyed in the context of different group styles, can facilitate or hinder different kinds of relationships. The same religious teaching on paper can facilitate or hinder different kinds of action depending on the group style through which it is conveyed. Certainly, theological and other approaches to religion define "religion" and its consequences differently; scholars and citizens too gain from a pluralist appreciation of different approaches to such a fraught topic.

Some scholars inquire into the social effects of religion because they want to know which religious groups summon people's charitable impulses most effectively, especially if they suppose that religious traditions are repositories of humanitarian concern. Correlating religious groups or traditions with different rates of voluntary participation can be informative from an instrumental point of view, if our main concern is to know what religions "do for society." The neo-Tocquevillian synthesis complements that point of view. Scholars concerned with religion and solidarity should also want to ask the pragmatist questions: How do religious teachings and language work in everyday acts of solidarity? How do they become part of action? Otherwise we risk just inferring very simple accounts of motivation from correlational models that leave out meaning.

A Case of a Religiously Sponsored Voluntary Association

The case example, Caring Embrace of the Homeless and Poor (CE), was a loose-knit group of congregational leaders, housing, and homelessness advocates. A shifting core of members met monthly at an urban Protestant church with a decades-long history of engagement in progressive causes, located near a university in neighborhood of working-class residents and students. Monthly meetings gathered between five and twelve people who expressed different religious identities or no religious identity during meetings. The group's facilitator, Theresa, was the lead staff person for the hosting church's network of social advocacy projects and identified as a liberal Presbyterian. Other core participants included the hosting church's pastor, a long-time Lutheran pastor of a nearby congregation, a graduate student intern who professed no particular religious identity, a Korean evangelical real estate agent, two members of a theater troupe made up of homeless and formerly homeless people who did not identify themselves in religious terms, the congregational liaison person for a charitable organization who identified simply as Christian, and, early

12 Religion and Social Solidarity 251

on in the study, two activists from a citywide housing advocacy organization who expressed no religious identification at the meetings.

CE's main activity was a campaign to educate religious congregations about myths regarding homelessness and to advocate that the real solution to homelessness is affordable housing. The Nails Project, as it was named, asked local religious congregations to collect nails, which CE would then donate to Habitat for Humanity®, the large non-profit organization that builds houses for low-income families. CE set the goal of collecting 74,000 nails so that the number of people homeless on an average night in the sprawling city could be symbolized dramatically. During this study the group collected roughly 55, 000 nails, at a pace that the group's facilitator considered slow. The group also kept members informed of meetings and protest events related to housing and homelessness, and became a stop-off point for a variety of homeless and community advocates looking to involve religious groups in their own projects.

CE does not sound like "volunteering" in the currently common sense of a "hands-on," task-oriented activity, and it was not. It is, however, an appropriate example of civic action, that is, a conceptual and less culture-biased category of action we can use in cross-national research on social solidarity regardless of whether the citizens tapped in the study were all familiar with plug-in volunteering. As a voluntary association of citizens committed to educating non-homeless citizens and promoting problem solving about homelessness, we can reasonably state that CE's activities were acts of social solidarity, ones that both Alexis de Tocqueville and pragmatists such as John Dewey (1927) would have recognized as such.

Data for the case came from participant observation, the method of choice for studying how people enact religious identities in everyday settings in real time (Bender 2003; Lichterman 2008). I studied CE for 24 months; in addition to observing, I volunteered for outreach and other tasks, and tried to get two congregations interested in hosting a speaker from CE on homelessness.

Personalized Inspiration in a Community Education Project

Orchestrated Ambiguity and Inclusiveness

The unitary actor model bids us see individuals or groups as carrying religious culture in monovalent ways. The ethnographic scenarios that follow would frustrate that attempt. We can now return to the breakfast meeting sponsored by Caring Embrace of the Homeless and Poor. The director planned this meeting in order to share ideas on how to deal with the growing presence of homeless people in the neighborhood surrounding the church. It included pastors or representatives from a variety of Protestant churches, both mainline and African American, a Catholic homeless shelter employee, several homeless or formerly homeless people from the city center, a rabbi from a Jewish college student organization, an affordable housing developer and two affordable housing advocates from a city-wide housing coalition, an imam from a local mosque, and several African American Muslims. Though many of the participants were clergy or religious leaders, their varied ways of professing, alluding to or ignoring religious identity make it very difficult to apply the unitary actor model. I quote from field notes at some length to illustrate the great variety of ways people related to religion at this meeting:

Theresa, the meeting director, asked the pastor of this church to make some opening comments. Pastor Frank W. said that "more and more [homeless] people are coming to our doorstep...How can we make a compassionate response to homelessness? How can we make a compassionate response to poverty in this area? ...How can we make a response with dignity...How can we work together as religious people, as non-religious?" He added that "we all have resources to bring" to the issue—and he listed several qualities including "compassion" and "courage." Then he asked us to pray: "Thanks for the children" he said, first of all...and "thanks for the food we have today." There followed a mild petition to bless our work together, "and we ask in your name, amen." The prayer contained no specific names for the divine.

Theresa then asked us to do a go-around of introductory statements so that everyone could say a little bit about "what group we are from and why we are here." This go-around session took the great majority of the meeting time. Following are a sample of responses.

Rabbi Kenneth from Campus Hillel: "...Instead of thinking of the campus as a fabulously wealthy university—let's think of homelessness (in this area) as an opportunity to learn about social consciousness."

Thomas: He said that homelessness has grown so that now it included "people who used to be middle-class who are getting pushed down—on the verge of being on the street." He also described homeless people as "people trying to deal with issues alone, rather than getting together and working collectively."

Wes, pastor of a nearby mainline Protestant church: "I came here to learn, and to pray."

Two pastoral interns from St Mark's introduced themselves. The second one described her church as "open all the time for people in need."

Two actresses from a theatrical troupe made up of homeless people said they were from "the other LAPD"—the Los Angeles Poverty Department. (This is a local, bitter joke in reference to the Los Angeles Police Department). Each said she was homeless, lived downtown, and that "I'm a child of God, a social activist, a prayer warrior."

Francis, staff person with a housing advocacy organization:

"Our response, traditionally, in many religious communities has been immediate service. But we need to broaden our imagination to think about what we can do to end homelessness."

A man from the "homeless artists local foundation" talked about them himself, saying that he "had been homeless, but ten years ago spiritual principles were applied" and now he no longer was homeless. Later he said "we need to do more networking with other churches. A lot of us don't realize that when we detach ourselves, our families still want us—they may be looking for us...it's an emotional issue...I didn't realize how much people wanted me back."

The leader of a nearby mosque said there "was more need" than there used to be, and that homeless people were not all on drugs but that rather it was "people down on their luck." He told us also that his mosque started a charter school.

Henrietta: She told us how when she was homeless, she and her family lived in their car. They parked it outside a church in Hollywood. She recounted to us how she told her children, "if these are good Christian people, they'll say something to us". Then she told us bitterly, "No one said anything. Children laughed and pointed at us!"

It is extremely difficult to generalize about the religious or non-religious character of the setting as a whole, and hard to infer confidently the presence or absence of religious identities or motives in individuals as they are speaking. Speakers ranged from two "prayer warriors" and a man who "came to pray" to those who made no clearly religious comment at all. Some of the people were ordained, but one would not be able to guess that solely on the basis of what they said. For instance, Thomas, the man who said some homeless people were once middle-class but had been pushed down the social ladder, was associate pastor of a large, mainline Presbyterian congregation. His comments and his appeal to collective action made him sound more like the (non-religious) housing advocate Francis than his fellow mainline Protestant pastor, Wes. We cannot know if Thomas was more motivated by social justice activism than religious piety or if Brown was more motivated by the power of prayer than the image of collective political action; staking these claims would require inferring basic, continuous motives, religious or irreligious, and then using those to explain speech—making the kind of epistemological move associated with the unitary actor model.

The pragmatic perspective would ask, instead, how participants collaborated in creating a kind of setting for both religious and non-religious expression. The style that coordinated this setting featured fluid boundaries and an affirmation of individual voice. Pastor Frank set the stage to begin with. "How can we work together as religious people, as non-religious?" he asked. *The stage allowed us at the meeting to decide whether or not we wanted to sound religious or not, and to decide whether or not someone else meant to be religious or not.*

In terms of group style, the pastor's comment bid us make the boundaries between religious and secular fluid. This was not a "religious group" bringing religious compassion to a secular world; it was a group of caring people who may or may not claim religious identities. At the end of the session, Theresa validated all of the comments, from appeals to treating homeless people with dignity to calls for collective political action, saying that each had a place in an overall response to homelessness. The group's "map" welcomed a wide variety of caring responses into the circle of "we" who address homelessness.

Some individuals, like the homeless women from the theatrical troupe, interpreted the meeting as an opportunity to testify to their religious conviction; others, including pastors, did not. Others spoke in language easy for many Americans familiar with congregational life to associate with religion, such as "people in need." The pragmatic approach does not ask what their deep religious or secular motives were. Rather, it helps us study how people co-created a setting that could accommodate religious, non-religious, and even anti-religious identification. It tells us to listen to what people say about themselves in relation to religion—how they sustain boundaries between different kinds of religious or irreligious expression.

This stage invited participants to relate to their religiosity in a very personalized way. In terms of group style, the bonds holding together the participants in this setting were very personalized. They obligated each to hear the other respectfully as individuals with personal inspiration, not necessarily as representatives of a creed or community, whether religious, irreligious, or anti-religious. Pastor Frank set the tone when he said we all have resources to bring to the problem of homelessness, and then named some which non-religious or religious people might just as easily contribute, such as "courage." Whether or not people expressed strong opinions—

as Henrietta did, above—no one tried to convince anyone else to adopt hers or his. Everyone got a hearing.

Ritual go-arounds of individual sharing will not sound remarkable to anyone familiar with the personalized style of bonding common in contemporary American group life (for instance, Wuthnow 1994; Lichterman 1996), but this way of coordinating a group does not have any natural affinity with religious people. Some individuals on this stage perform as religious people in different ways in other settings and those performances are not nearly as individualized. Pastor Thomas, for instance, participates in faith-based community organizing efforts groups whose members all promote a shared, obligatory collective identity as "people of faith" who identify with Judeo–Christian traditions, not individuals who may or may not be "of faith" as in the case of CE's homelessness effort.

One might ask if the pragmatic approach works mainly when the people we study are "performing" in the conventional sense—trying to be polite in interfaith settings. Examining the group's monthly meetings suggests that a focus on the setting is useful even when the stage is much smaller and has a less diverse cast.

Personalized Inspiration at Monthly Meetings

Personalized inspiration was the norm for monthly meetings, and new participants learned it even if they expressed religious identity or reasoning differently in other settings. Lines between religious and secular inspiration continued to be ambiguous. An awkward moment for the facilitator at the start of one meeting helps illustrate:

> At the start, Theresa was talking about a friend of hers with a terminal illness, muscle degeneration, who was at the point that she could no longer move anything but her eyes and her mouth enough to talk. Theresa said this woman's daughter, also a family friend, carried pent–up anger at her mother and said her mother's illness seemed not to upset the daughter, but Theresa knew better. Theresa took off her glasses and wiped her eyes.
>
> Theresa: "So whatever you do—pray, mediate, send energy—do it for them."
> Raquel, the representative from Habitat for Humanity® asked, "What's her name?"
> Theresa: "Marta, and Rita."
> Raquel wrote down the names. I thought of the evangelical Protestant practice of taking names and praying for people.
> Theresa took her glasses off and wiped her eyes again.
> Chuck, the student from School of Social Work: "Will their names be able to get into the program (at Theresa's church, which hosted our meeting in the Peace Center library) for Sunday worship?"
> Theresa said they already had.
>
> We still were waiting for the printed agendas for our meeting, which were not ready yet.
> Theresa: "In some circles, it would be bad to come in unprepared—but I don't think that. I think it's part of our shared humanity."
> Raquel gave her an understanding look.

Theresa signalled here that the stage was one for people with religious commitments, or spiritual commitments, or maybe humanistic and non-theistic ones. She invited us to see "our shared humanity." The appeal would have sounded out of place at a corporate business meeting or school board meeting, and probably at many meetings where friends might gather (Bakhtin 1988). Theresa's appeal might suggest that this was a stage for subtle religious expression. The professed Christian woman Raquel might have written down the names of Theresa's unfortunate family friends because she intended to pray for them. It is safer to observe, however, that the participants on the stage here were maintaining a forum with fluid boundaries. It was a forum in which people could guess wrongly each other's motives, yet keep going, as long as all sincere, individual expressions of inspiration were safe. Identifying with religious faith was welcome though not mandatory, as long as any kind of inspiration, including faith in "our shared humanity" was welcome too.

On this inclusive stage, participants could affirm a religious teaching directly as long as they did not use them to promote some faiths to the exclusion of others. One of very few direct endorsements of religious conviction during two years of field research was an inclusive-sounding interfaith affirmation as well:

Raquel, a Christian, told us about a comment she heard a rabbi make about homelessness:

If we are all made in the image of God, then the image of God sleeping on the street should be unconscionable." Raquel said her own pastor had said almost exactly the same thing. Raquel: "When people from two completely different directions say almost the same thing—Wow, that is a truth!

Throughout my time with CE, facilitator Theresa worked to keep the group's identification with religion inclusive. Often she used the phrase "churches and synagogues and mosques" to describe both CE's audience and its own potential constituency. Since no one engaged with a mosque ever came to any of the monthly meetings I attended during 24 months, and only two, short-term participants identified with Judaism, I inferred that the phrase symbolized the intent to project a diversely inspired, inclusive effort.

Non-clergy as well as clergy members participated in more tightly bound religious groups and promoted more specific religious identities in settings outside CE meetings. Conversations with Theresa after meetings made clear to me that she identified with liberal Presbyterianism, and not only inclusive spirituality in general. Yet she never suggested or implied CE members should care about Presbyterianism. At a volunteer session for CE members at a Habitat for Humanity® builders' warehouse, Raquel read from the Bible and applied the reading to her non-profit organization's work. At CE meetings, in contrast, Raquel presented herself as a churchgoer but never used Biblical language to articulate either her own or CE's stance on housing and homelessness.

Since religious identity was not mandatory but welcome as long as it made no claims on others, "personalized inspiration" also took interactional work for participants who distanced themselves from religious faith in other contexts. I never heard housing advocate Francis identify himself openly in religious terms during this study. Yet he spoke in the first person plural when he urged religious people at the breakfast meeting pictured earlier to address homelessness in more political ways than by sheltering homeless individuals. Non-religious community advocates quietly stood by when CE participants identified themselves in religious terms.

While observing the office of the housing advocacy organization that employed Francis as a participant, I heard his co-worker Zina express disappointment that a core CE member was religious. But neither Zina nor Francis or any other participant questioned the value of basing homeless advocacy on religious identity during my observations at CE meetings.

Religious Expression, Settings, and Social Capital

Neo-Tocquevillian scholars laud religious congregations as rich stores of "social capital"—the networks and mutual trust that make collaboration between citizens possible (Putnam 2000; Smidt 2003). Social capital is a much used, much debated concept that has strongly influenced the way social scientists think about voluntary associations, governance, and economic development, to name just three areas.[7] When we focus on group styles in settings rather than on religious actors and look beyond congregations, we learn more about conditions that may disable as well as enable religious people's networking for civic ends. We learn that social capital is situational and not something actors carry continuously with a continuous value for social ties.

The example of the Nails Project in CE shows that it is not religion, or religious expression itself, but one's preferred style of relating to religion in specific settings that determines whether or not people can use religion to recruit others for acts of solidarity. The director of Caring Embrace, for instance, knew many local leaders in her city's social activist and religious circles. Theresa attended a large variety of meetings and events related to homelessness, affordable housing, gentrification, and urban redevelopment by different organizations. Through her, CE should have had access to a lot of religious social capital since she was known widely as an activist who led her church's social justice center and had access to its phone lists, administrative staff, and money. Two mainline Protestant pastors who attended CE meetings said at different times in the same words that getting congregations to collect nails for an awareness-building project on homelessness "should be a no-brainer."

Yet the inclusive, personalized style of setting that Theresa preferred prevented her from attracting a wide range of religious people, even from liberal Protestant churches, to work together on the project. The Nails Project realized relatively little benefit from the director's potential social capital. The simple quest to collect 74,000 nails was still in progress after two years, many months behind its projected schedule. Theresa hesitated to make her inspiration the guiding inspiration of CE; she wanted hers to be one of a variety of voices. The director may have had lot of

---

[7] The discussion here refers to Robert Putnam's distinctive version of the social capital concept, the most widespread one. For extensive reviews and critiques, see Somers (2005), Lichterman (2006).

social capital in an abstract sense, but the group style that she preferred in settings of religious people made it difficult to prevail upon other people even for a good cause.

Social capital does not empower voluntary, pro-social action by itself. Rather, social ties empower collective action depending on how people create settings for mobilizing those ties. Studying religious people teaches us about how different forms of group cohesion can lead to powerful campaigns that sway governmental leaders, or to well-intentioned group efforts that frustrate even the own goals of their members.

Discussion: Public Religious Style in Different National Contexts

A neo-Tocquevillian focus on unitary, individual, or collective actors would leave some public expressions of religion beyond our grasp and distort the meaning of others. The pragmatic approach bids us ask how people create a social space for expressing religious sensibilities and linking them to acts of social solidarity in a diverse, unequal society.

I propose that this approach is also useful for studying public religion across national contexts, not only in the USA. It can illuminate the variety of public religious expression in different religious "regimes" (Lichterman and Potts 2009), or the institutional configurations that give citizens routine expectations for the public presence of religion. As widely institutionalized relationships, often taken-for-granted (DiMaggio and Powell 1991), religious regimes do not change easily, but local actors enact different group styles that may roughly re-instantiate the regime over time without simply reproducing mass uniformity. In societies that play out something like the post-Tocquevillian scenario briefly sketched here, such as the USA, boundaries between potentially religious and non-religious settings are ambiguous and sometimes people may even work to maintain the ambiguity. The US religious regime calls for governmental religious non-favoritism alongside an expectation that citizens may affirm religion in general—or "faith" in brief, non-exclusive terms—in public outside governmental settings. Generic religious appeal is in fact a basis for solidarity across social differences in the USA as long as it aligns with vaguely Judeo–Christian understandings of religion.[8] Some openness to ambiguity is, in effect, built into this regime. In everyday life, Americans might occasionally puzzle over which style of religious expression is appropriate in which setting. Ambiguity can lead to mutual tolerance or respect, or simply uncertainty, as in the case of the local civic association observed here, much as overt avowals of specific, exclusively religious precepts by high political officials in the USA is polarizing.

---

[8] Alexis de Tocqueville (1969 [1835]) made the argument elegantly 170 years ago; modern observer Robert Bellah (1967) re-articulated and updated the argument in a classic essay on American "civil religion". Research suggests that Americans hold atheists in lower repute and trust them less than many other widely identifiable groups, such as African Americans or Muslims (Edgell et al. 2006).

Table 12.1 Two ideal typical models of religion and social solidarity. (This is adapted from a fuller table in Lichterman 2012b)

	Neo-Tocquevillian synthesis	Pragmatic model
Main unit of analysis	Actors, individual, or collective and their shared religious beliefs	Religious communication in settings
How actors carry religion	Individual and collective actors "are religious"—they carry religion continuously, monovalently	Religious communication is setting-specific for individuals and collectivities
How religion shapes public action	Religion suffuses identity and action for the actor under study	Actors cue each other in to a shared group style that shapes religious communication. Religious communication embedded in a style, in turn, enables or constrains public action
Examples of research themes: 1. Religion's effects on public action. 2. Religion and social solidarity	Questions representing a neo-Tocquevillian approach to the theme: 1. Which religious groups pursue which kinds of voluntary action? 2. Which religious traditions create more or less social capital?	Questions representing a pragmatic approach to the theme: 1. Which settings and group styles enable people to link religious identity to collective action? 2. Which settings and group styles allow participants to use religious identity to mobilize others for acts of solidarity?

In the context of a different religious regime, tolerance for ambiguity is narrower and public religious identification more easily invites, not flexibility, but harsh disagreement, at any level of public life. Recent controversies over Muslim women's headscarves in France offer a quick, compelling example. The current religious regime in France is constituted culturally and legally by a version of republicanism that proscribes most performances of religious identity in public spaces. French republicanism makes the headscarf into a contentious display, much as republicanism says nothing about whether or not French citizens may hold Muslim beliefs privately. French citizens with Muslim beliefs nimbly craft different performances of religious visibility, some self-consciously resistant to the regime of *laïcité* or secularity, and others far more circumspect and selective (Amiraux and Jonker 2006).

This is but one more reason to study public religion from the pragmatic perspective rather than start from the common sense assumption that the religious beliefs of actors tell us everything we may want to know about what they do with religion and where. The neo-Tocquevillian and pragmatic models build on different assumptions about religion's influence in public and lead to different kinds of research questions (see Table 12.1). If we want to know how religion acts as a resource or a facilitator of voluntary action in public, then the pragmatic model offers a more precise view.

References

Alexander, J. (2006). *The civic sphere*. New York: Oxford University Press.

Amiraux, V., & Jonker, G. (2006). Introduction: Talking about visibility-actors, politics, forms of engagement. In G. Jonker & V. Amiraux (Eds.), *Politics of visibility: Young muslims in European public spaces* (pp. 21–52). New Brunswick: Transaction Publishers.

Ammerman, N. (2003). Religious identities and religious institutions. In M. Dillon (Ed.), *Handbook for the sociology of religion* (pp. 207–224). Cambridge: Cambridge University Press.

Ammerman, N. (Ed.). (2007). *Everyday religion: Observing modern religious lives*. New York: Oxford University Press.

Baggett, J. (2000). *Habitat for humanity: Building private homes, building public religion*. Philadelphia: Temple University of Press.

Bakhtin, M. (1988). *Speech genres and other late essays*. (trans: C. Emerson and M. Holquist). Austin: University of Texas Press.

Bellah, R. (1967). Civil religion in America. *Daedalus, 96*(1), 1–21.

Bellah, R., Madsen, R., Sullivan, W., Swidler, A., & Tipton, S. (1985). *Habits of the heart: Individualism and commitment in American life. Berkeley*: University of California Press.

Bender, C. (2003). *Heaven's kitchen: Living religion at God's love we deliver*. Chicago: University of Chicago Press.

Berger, P. (1967). *The sacred canopy: Elements of a sociological theory of religion*. Garden City: Doubleday.

Berman, S. (1997). Civil society and the collapse of the Weimar Republic. *World Politics, 49*(3), 401–429.

Brubaker, R. (2002). Ethnicity without groups. *Archives Européennes de Sociologie, XLIII*(2), 163–189.

Burke, K. (1969 [1945]). *A grammar of motives*. Berkeley: University of California Press.

Casanova, J. (1994). *Public religions in the modern world*. Chicago: University of Chicago Press.

Chaves, M. (2004). *Congregations in America*. Cambridge: Harvard University Press.

Cohen, J. (1999). American civil society talk. In R. Fullinwider (Ed.), Civil society, democracy and civic renewal (pp. 55–85). Lanham: Rowman and Littlefield.

Davis, N., & Robinson, R. (2012). *Claiming society for God: Religious movements and social welfare*. Bloomington: Indiana University Press.

Dewey, J. (1927). *The public and its problems*. Denver: Alan Swallow.

DiMaggio, P., & Powell, W. (Eds.). (1991). *The new institutionalism in organizational analysis*. Chicago: University of Chicago Press.

Eckstein, S. (2001). Community as gift-giving: Collectivistic roots of volunteerism. *American Sociological Review, 66*, 829–851.

Edgell, P., Gerteis, J., & Hartmann, D. (2006). Atheists as 'other': moral boundaries and cultural membership in American society. *American Sociological Review, 71*(April), 211–234.

Eliasoph, N. (1998). *Avoiding politics*. New York: Cambridge University Press.

Eliasoph, N. (2011). *Making volunteers*. Princeton: Princeton University Press.

Eliasoph, N., & Lichterman, P. (2003). Culture in interaction. *American Journal of Sociology, 108*, 735–794.

Foley, M., & Edwards, B. (1997). Escape from politics? Social theory and the social capital debate. *American Behavioral Scientist, 40*(5), 550–561.

Goffman, E. (1959). *The presentation of self in everyday life*. Garden City: Doubleday.

Goffman, E. (1961). *Encounters: Two studies in the sociology of interaction*. Indianapolis: Bobbs-Merrill.

Hustinx, L., & Lammertyn, F. (2003). Collective and reflexive styles of volunteering: A sociological modernization perspective. *VOLUNTAS: International Journal of Voluntary and Nonprofit Organizations, 14*(2), 167–187.

Hustinx, L., Meijs, L., Handy, F., & Cnaan, R. (2012). Monitorial citizens or civic omnivores? Repertoires of civic participation among university students. *Youth and Society, 44*(1), 95–117.

Jepperson, R. (1991). Institutions, institutional effects and institutionalism. In W. Powell & P. DiMaggio (Eds.), *The new institutionalism in organizational analysis* (pp. 143–163). Chicago: University of Chicago Press.

Juris, J., & Pleyers, G. (2009). Alter-activism: Emerging cultures of participation among young global justice activists. *Journal of Youth Studies, 12,* 57–73.

Kaiser, M. (2007). Volunteering as a topic of intercultural learning. Experiences from German-American exchange programs. In A. Liedhegener & W. Kremp (Eds.), *Civil society, civic engagement and Catholicism in the U.S.* (pp. 203–212). Trier: Wissenschaftlicher Verlag Trier.

Klatch, R. (1987). *Women of the new right.* Philadelphia: Temple University Press.

Lichterman, P. (1995). Piecing together multicultural community: Cultural differences in community building among grass-roots environmentalists. *Social Problems, 42*(4), 513–534.

Lichterman, P. (1996). *The search for political community.* Cambridge: Cambridge University Press.

Lichterman, P. (2005). *Elusive togetherness: Church groups trying to bridge America's divisions.* Princeton: Princeton University Press.

Lichterman, P. (2006). Social capital or group style? Rescuing Tocqueville's insights on civic engagement. *Theory and Society, 35*(5/6), 529–563.

Lichterman, P. (2007). Invitation to a practical cultural sociology. In I. Reed & J. Alexander (Eds.), *Culture, society and democracy: The interpretive approach* (pp. 19–54). Boulder: Paradigm Publishers.

Lichterman, P. (2008). Religion and the construction of civic identity. *American Sociological Review, 73*(February), 83–104.

Lichterman, P. (2012a). Reinventing the concept of civic culture. In J. Alexander, R. Jacobs, & P. Smith (Eds.), *Oxford handbook of cultural sociology* (pp. 207–231). New York: Oxford University Press.

Lichterman, P. (2012b). Religion in public action: From actors to settings. *Sociological Theory, 30*(1), 15–37.

Lichterman, P., & Eliasoph, N. (2013). *Toward a new sociology of civic action.* Paper presented at the American Sociological Association: Annual meeting, New York (August).

Lichterman, P., & Potts, C. B. (Eds.). (2009). *The civic life of American religion.* Stanford: Stanford University Press.

Luckmann, T. (1967). *The invisible religion: The problem of religion in modern society.* New York: Macmillan.

Luhtakallio, E. (2009). *Group styles in local civic practices and the place of politics in France and Finland.* Paper presented at the Social Sciences History Association, Annual Meeting, Long Beach, CA (November).

Mead, G. H. (1934). *Mind, self, and society.* Chicago: University of Chicago Press.

Melucci, A. (1989). *Nomads of the present.* Philadelphia: Temple University Press.

Merelman, R. (1984). *Making something of ourselves: On culture and politics in the United States.* Berkeley: University of California Press.

Mische, A. (2008). *Partisan publics.* Princeton: Princeton University Press.

Munson, Z. (2007). When a funeral isn't just a funeral: The layered meaning of everyday action. In N. T. Ammerman (Ed.), *Everyday religion: Observing modern religious lives* (pp. 121–135). New York: Oxford University Press.

Neitz, M. J. (2004). Gender and culture: Challenges to the sociology of religion. *Sociology of Religion, 65*(4), 391–403.

Nepstad, S. (2004). *Convictions of the soul: Religion, culture and agency in the Central America solidarity movement.* New York: Oxford University Press.

Parsons, T. (1967). *Christianity and modern industrial society. In Sociological theory and modern society* (pp. 385–421). New York: The Free Press.

Press, A., & Cole, E. (1999). *Speaking of abortion.* Chicago: University of Chicago Press.

Putnam, R. (1993). *Making democracy work.* Princeton: Princeton University Press.

12 Religion and Social Solidarity

Putnam, R. (1995). Bowling alone: America's declining social capital. *Journal of Democracy, 6,* 65–78.

Putnam, R. (2000). *Bowling alone.* New York: Simon & Schuster.

Riesebrodt, M. (2008). Theses on a theory of religion. *International Political Anthropology, 1*(1), 25–41.

Roof, W. C. (1998). *Spiritual marketplace.* Princeton: Princeton University Press.

Skocpol, T., & Fiorina, M. (1999). *Civic engagement in American democracy.* Washington, D.C.: Brookings Institution Press.

Smidt, C. (Ed.). (2003). *Religion as social capital.* Waco: Baylor University Press.

Swidler, A. (2001). *Talk of love.* Chicago: University of Chicago Press.

Verba, S., Schlozman, K., & Brady, H. (1995). *Voice and equality: Civic voluntarism in American politics.* Cambridge: Harvard University Press.

Warner, R. S. (1993). Work in progress toward a new paradigm for the sociological study of religion in the United States. *American Journal of Sociology, 98,* 1044–1093.

Warren, M. E. (2001a). *Democracy and association.* Princeton: Princeton University Press.

Warren, M. R. (2001b). *Dry bones rattling: Community building to revitalize American democracy.* Princeton: Princeton University Press.

Wood, R. (2002). *Faith in action.* Chicago: University of Chicago Press.

Wuthnow, R. (1991). *Acts of compassion.* Princeton: Princeton University Press.

Wuthnow, R. (1998). *Loose connections.* Cambridge: Harvard University Press.

Wuthnow, R. (1994). *Sharing the journey.* New York: Free Press.

Wuthnow, R. (2011). Taking talk seriously: Religious discourse as social practice. *Journal for the Scientific Study of Religion, 50,* 1–21.

Yon, K. (2009). Quand le syndicalisme s'éprouve hors du lieu de travail: La production du sens confédéral à Force ouvrière. *Politix, 22,* 57–79.

Chapter 13
'Your Prayer Moves God'

On the Relation Between Voluntarism, the Emergent Charismatic Movement in Beirut and Social Capital

Oleg Dik

Introduction and Theoretical Framework

Since the end of the civil war in 1990, Beirut has seen the emergence of new Charismatic/Pentecostal (C/P) groups and churches. The C/P movement can be found across varying denominations such as the traditional churches (Maronite, Roman Catholic, various Orthodox churches, Protestant), independent Lebanese C/P churches, migrant worker C/P churches from Asia and Africa and ecumenical independent groups with no institutional ties (including Armenian groups and Muslim converts to the C/P groups).

Established religious communities mostly mobilize their volunteers through religious welfare organizations (RWO). The effect of RWOs on social solidarity has been discussed extensively (Khalaf 2002; Jawad 2009). On the one hand, religious communities care for the material and social wellbeing of their own members. On the other hand, this control widens social divisions by reinforcing communitarian divides. Khalaf poignantly summarises this double effect: 'The ties that bind, in other words, also unbind' (Khalaf 2002, p. 259). While confessional loyalties 'continue to serve as viable sources of communal solidarity' they also 'undermine civic consciousness and commitment to Lebanon as a nation-state' (Khalaf 2002, p. 259). The dilemma lies in this double effect of the confessional identity, which secures 'vital needs and benefits' (Khalaf 2002, p. 260) on the one hand and, on the other hand, creates animosity towards 'the other' thus undermining the social solidarity of a nation-state.

According to Khalaf, the role of the confessional community grows proportionally in relation to the absence of secular forms of group affiliation. Khalaf proposes a solution to this dilemma, which I have heard voiced almost unanimously by Lebanese intellectuals during my 4-year stay in Lebanon. He states: 'Under the spur of visionary and enlightened leadership, groups can, through a revitalized voluntary

---

O. Dik (✉)
Department of Religious Studies and Intercultural Theology, Humboldt University,
Berlin, Germany
e-mail: olegdik@hotmail.com

L. Hustinx et al. (eds.), *Religion and Volunteering*, Nonprofit and Civil Society Studies, 263
DOI 10.1007/978-3-319-04585-6_13, © Springer International Publishing Switzerland 2015

sector, at least be re-socialized to perceive differences as manifestations of cultural diversity and enrichment; not as dreaded symptoms of distrust, fear and exclusion' (Khalaf 2002, p. 262). In particular Khalaf envisions gifted professional multiculturalists who acquired new insights abroad and are therefore in a better position to transcend Lebanese communal divisions. The voluntary sector must be comprised of people with no particular communal loyalties but rather with a vision for a common good. Khalaf thinks in particular of 'urban designers, architects, intellectuals, humanists of all shades and persuasions'. Khalaf then quotes Walzer in a desire for all Lebanese to unite 'for the sake of sociability itself' (Khalaf 2002, p. 267).

This structural sociopolitical analysis captures the institutional reality well. However, due to the structural approach and quantitative methodology, it overlooks heterogeneity and the fluid nature of social reality which emerges through various modes of interaction. In particular, emergent social movements such as C/P must also be studied through qualitative methodology. While the overall sociopolitical structure influences the volunteering possibilities of specific religious groups, the religious volunteers are not exclusively determined by it (On further discussion of structure-agency see: Outhwaite 1998; Manicas 1998). A qualitative approach in Social Anthropology focuses on the agency of social actors or specific social settings and styles of communication (Lichterman 2012), which shape the nature of volunteering and its contribution to wider society. While quantitative analysis of the larger sociopolitical structure aims to describe static conditions, the qualitative approach underlines the dynamic, indeterminate and contextual nature of social groups. Traditionally, ethnographic methods sought to provide a view from within, emphasising the local actors. Recently, some researchers have advocated a shift in study from actors and groups to settings and communication styles (Lichterman 2012). The larger sociopolitical structure influences the culture of C/P volunteering. However, C/P believers relate to the larger sociopolitical context through various modes, including both resistance and subversion. Thus, the communication processes and ritual performances within the religious culture on the one hand, and the social setting and interaction between religiously motivated volunteers within the public sphere on the other hand, influence the final outcome of how religious volunteering shapes social solidarity.

Methodological Procedure

This chapter is based on my field research conducted in Beirut from November 2009 to April 2011 during which I focused on C/P rituals and everyday practices. I attended 15 C/P groups and then narrowed my study down to three particular groups due to the diverse institutional associations. During the field research, I noticed a high degree of volunteering. This observation led me to research the relation between the C/P culture and volunteering.

'Abundant Life' is a growing Pentecostal Church in the poor, mainly Armenian, neighborhood of Borj Hammoud and is loosely associated with the Evangelical

Church. 'Chemin Neuf' is a Catholic/Maronite Charismatic group and meets in a Church in Jounieh, on the outskirts of Beirut. 'Chemin Neuf' is under the umbrella of the Roman Catholic Church. Finally, I attended 'Meeting with God', a Charismatic group which has no institutional ties. Attending these Churches, I attempted to capture all possible institutional affiliations in order to gain perspective on the religious and political arrangements which account for differences between C/P groups, while still highlighting the correspondences between them that distinguish them as C/P expressions of Christianity. The C/P movement emphasizes the Holy Spirit, the third person of the trinity. Since the Holy Spirit is seen as actively at work in the world, these groups view themselves as co-agents of the Holy Spirit which often leads to a high degree of religiously motivated activism in all spheres of society. The C/P transgression of the line between religious space and activism in the public sphere accounts for the intriguing relations between C/P performance and other social spheres.

As I immersed myself in the Lebanese context, I attended a seminar entitled 'Cultural and Religious Dynamics in the Middle East' at Saint Joseph University in Beirut. An American researcher presented a paper on the question of religious identities that he had conducted on various campuses. A Lebanese scholar challenged him about the usefulness of formal interviews within an institutional setting. In particular, he pointed out that most students would probably be guarded in expressing their view on politics and religion in the public sphere as they would not want to compromise their social status. When I spoke to students on the campus of the American University of Beirut (AUB), they shared with me that they answered the questions posed by western scholars according to the expectations of the AUB professor through whose permission the western scholar got his field entry. It seems that the expectations of the western scholar implied in the set questionnaire already predetermines the answers.

There are several reasons as to why quantitative methods and interviews conducted in isolation fail within the Lebanese context. In Lebanese society, the concept of honour and shame regulates the social status of the clan, the family and the individual. The insiders usually provide an outsider with information which will enhance their communal honour.

Mary,[1] the founder of one of the Charismatic groups, when asked about researching social solidarity in Lebanon, gave me the following answer:

> Sometimes, western Christians come and want to find out how Christians live with Muslims and Druze. Muslims and Druze tell them: 'Oh, we love Jesus!' We have three Bibles at home. We love Jesus and Christians. And the Westerners go home and tell that Lebanon is an open-minded country with peaceful coexistence. However, in reality, they are hiding the truth. They do not say what they mean. We have a saying here: 'I show you a lot but not what is in my stomach.'

---

[1] I have changed the names in order to protect the identity of people. Though there is a relative degree of freedom in terms of practising one's religion, and even though a change of religion is permitted by the state, such an act could bring about severe retribution from the religious community.

In the course of my entire field research, I conducted 13 semi-structured interviews after getting to know the interview partners and establishing trust, thus hoping to diminish the representational dynamics mentioned by Mary. Most of the data was gathered through participant observation and informal conversations rather than the staged setting of the interview process in order to come as close as possible to the everyday context of C/P believers. I base my interpretation on my field research notes. However, I do not distinguish clearly between empirical findings and analytical interpretation. Instead, I follow interpretative anthropology (e.g. Geertz 2000), which advocates a close link between social reality and interpretation.

Sociopolitical and Religious Context of the Emergent Post 1990 C/P Movement

The end of the civil war in 1990 was followed by busy rebuilding efforts and hopes among the public for a new beginning. However, these hopes were soon dashed with the political stalemate and what seemed for many the déjà vu of the previous history. As some Lebanese remarked to me, they feel as though their history is circular as opposed to linear. I noticed some dilapidated bus stops within the city that are no longer used. They were built right after the civil war ended as a symbol of a new order. However, these bus stops were in use only for a short time and then the old order took over again. Now the bus stops again at random places for every person and not at the prescribed locations.[2]

Of the Lebanese communities, it is the Christians who have sustained the largest demographic, sociopolitical and economic losses. With the end of the civil war, the Christian community found itself in a disadvantageous demographic position. It had shrunk from 51 % of the population to only 35 % due to both lower fertility rates and immigration (Harris 2006, pp. 59–93). The Maronite community, which held the greatest political power before the war, lost much of its former influence through the Ta'if Accord (Salam 2003, pp. 39–53). I encountered a prevailing victim mentality among many of the Lebanese Christians. Within this victim mentality, the belief persists that the diffusion of their political power also led to limited opportunities within Lebanese society. As pre-war mixed communities shrunk, Christians lost a lot of their former territory in the process of displacement, which affected the Christian community more than others (Khalaf 2002, p. 215). The feeling of threat that prevails in homogeneous communities creates a climate of paranoia and fear of the other leading to further tribalism and exclusion. Most C/P members I talked to voiced a negative view of the role of established Christian churches during the war. I heard numerous stories of clerics supporting and blessing warring Christian militias. The role of religion in mobilising sectarian and political identities is well documented (Hanf 1990; Khalaf 2007). The disappointment with traditional insti-

---

[2] Charles Malik, writing before the civil war, denounced the lack of rule of law and confirmed the popular saying: 'nothing works in this state' (see Malik 2004, p. 19).

tutional religion led some Christians to seek other forms of Christian expression. The C/P movement offered the Christians an avenue to express their disappointment while acquiring a new identity within the old confessional community.

I use the term 'Charismatic/Pentecostal' in order to classify a local movement. However, this definition of a communal identity is to some extent problematic. At the local level, the three particular groups I have observed would not necessary classify themselves as C/P for fear of the possible connotations that may come with this title. The Evangelical Pentecostals are wary of the term 'Pentecostal' because of its political association with Christian Zionism which could lead to charges of state treason as Lebanon is formally at war with Israel. The Roman Catholic, Maronite and various Orthodox Charismatic groups are wary of the Charismatic practices which could compromise their position within the official Churches. One of the founders of the Roman Catholic Maronite C/P group shared with me a story about a Greek Orthodox priest who became more open towards the Catholic Charismatic movement. He then travelled to the USA and visited some C/P mega churches only to return and shut off any further interaction with the local Lebanese Charismatic movement. The Charismatic leader interpreted that this behaviour meant the Greek Orthodox bishop must have 'met some emotionally unstable people and took it for the Charismatic church'. Some C/P believers expressed their worry that the local C/P movement could quickly be branded as an agent of the West trying to gain political power through religious means, much in the same way as Hizb'allah embodies both political and religious powers and is therefore viewed as a proxy of Iran. Locally, the groups I have attended use names which express the essence of their identity within a particular context. By giving themselves a local name the groups were able to disassociate from the worldwide C/P culture and the baggage which it carries for them and thereby underscore their particularity. However, all C/P group leaders revealed to me, as an outsider, their connections to the worldwide C/P movement. Due to the similarity of practice between the Lebanese C/P movement and the worldwide C/P movement, I retained the term 'C/P movement'. All C/P groups I observed exhibit a more lively and expressive worship style than traditional Churches. For example, it is not uncommon for believers to break out in spontaneous exclamations and dance. Moreover, 'speaking in tongues', which refers to speaking in a language unknown prior to the C/P ritual and which is believed to be given miraculously by the Holy Spirit, is emphasized as well. Finally, another common trait consists of the strict ethical expectations which follow from the conviction that the Holy Spirit resides within the believer's body rather than being restricted to a church building.

Within the Lebanese context, there are no clear demarcation lines between the Charismatic and the Pentecostal movements. Often, these two terms are used interchangeably. The Pentecostal missionaries arrived in Beirut during the 1960s and worked mainly within the narrow denominational confines of the Evangelical churches. The earliest Charismatic movement in Beirut began in the late 1960s within the Roman Catholic Church. While the Pentecostals contributed to change within the mainline Evangelical Church, the Charismatic movement has been interdenominational from its beginning, having the strongest impact among the Roman

Catholics and Maronites. Consequently, while the Evangelicals lean towards the term 'Pentecostal' and other, non-Evangelical groups prefer the term 'Charismatic', their similar practices justify their joint classification as the C/P movement.

Religious belonging drives the delicate equilibrium of power within the confessional democracy of Lebanon. Therefore, any inter and intra religious conversion, even if in small numbers, touches the core of the political balance within such a small country as Lebanon. For this reason, even a small, but growing, movement such as C/P, which emphasizes conversion and proselytises across religious boundaries, might have a strong political impact over time. My estimation of the number of C/P members is based on my tentative projections and the information I received from C/P believers. The question as to who can be classified as a C/P believer depends on the organizational structure of the C/P groups. I have discerned an organizational parallel within diverse groups which I call the 'three concentric circles structure' (tccs). The outer circle is the public opening towards the general C/P culture. Within this outer circle, the groups address the wider Lebanese culture through their weekly public events. As in the case of 'Sword of the Spirit', a public meeting is held in a large church where 800–1,000 people gather weekly. Also, certain practical seminars are designed, for example marriage seminars in the case of 'Chemin Neuf', in order to address the outsiders. My neighbour in Furn el Chebbak, who attends the Greek Orthodox Church several times a week, knew about the C/P movement through their marriage seminars.

Certain rites of passage, such as testimonies about the working of the Holy Spirit, stand at the threshold of the crossing into the middle circle. Belonging to one of the circles is not a static given, but has to be re-enacted and depends on continuous volunteering. Thus, membership in C/P communities is not static due to birth, as in the official Churches, but has to be continuously earned through participation in C/P activities and the volunteering of specific skills.

The inner circle consists of more committed believers. Meetings are held during the week in houses in smaller gatherings that address specific needs of the community and exhibit particular C/P practices such as speaking in tongues. The central circle consists of believers who form the normative circle of authority. Their commitment does not only involve time but also money and material goods. The innermost circle of believers consists of those who embody visibly what it means to be and to act as a C/P believer. Based on my participation within 15 C/P groups, I would project the total number of committed Lebanese C/P believers as being between 5,000 and 8,000. This figure does not take into account the C/P domestic worker churches. The middle circle encompasses another 6,000–8,000 and the number of those who came into some contact and are aware of C/P movement might amount to 80,000, which would comprise almost one-tenth of the Lebanese Christian population. Since the C/P brand of Christianity is relatively new to Lebanon and the Asian and African impact is only just beginning, I believe that the growth of this movement has not yet peaked. As the level of participation determines belonging to these groups, the C/P members outweigh by far the commitment of believers within traditional Churches.

The emergent C/P groups position themselves in relation to the wider culture. The closest reference points are the already existing Churches since C/P practices are framed in terms of religious activity. Further reference points are other religious communities and political/social negotiations. I noted four possible institutional reference points which are contingent on the self-positioning of C/P groups inside or outside the state-recognized Christian denominations.

The differences between various C/P groups largely depend upon their negotiating process towards traditional Churches. The Evangelical C/P Churches (EC) are in the process of being fully recognized by the state as another Evangelical expression. At this point, Evangelical C/P groups, although recognized by the wider Evangelical constituency, do not receive recognition from the state and therefore do not possess the full rights of ordinary Evangelical members, such as dealing with civil law issues for example. Moreover, many migrant C/P groups prefer Evangelical association as it is the most flexible in allowing the migrant C/P groups to practice their expression of C/P Christianity while at the same time acquiring a recognized institutional framework. Since the Evangelical Church in Lebanon is comprised of various Protestant denominations, it offers new C/P groups more flexibility than Roman Catholic, Maronite and various Orthodox Churches with a longer historical tradition and less plurality within their ecclesiological structure. The Charismatic Movement within Traditional Churches (CMTC) seeks to integrate various C/P practices within hierarchical clerical structures where a strong continuity of tradition is upheld through rituals and institutions. Although some C/P Migrant groups/ Churches (MC) are under the Evangelical umbrella, many still meet independently from any institutional framework in private homes. Like the Independent Lebanese C/P Churches, their status outside TC allows them a high degree of flexibility within their practice and self-governance. This self-positioning of the emergent C/P movement within or outside the already existing religious institutions influences the possibilities and aims of volunteering.

Interpretation of Field Research Findings

C/P Bonding Capital

Most C/P members referred throughout their conversion narratives to various benefits found within C/P groups which attracted them to joining and volunteering in C/P communities. I define 'bonding capital' as benefits resulting from human relationships within a particular group. The perception of benefits is rooted in particular historic and cultural factors.

Spiritual Family

Samir Khalaf described the Lebanese family bonds as 'intense and all-embracing' (Khalaf 2002, p. 226), influencing every aspect of a person's everyday life. According to post-1990 sociological surveys, the primordial ties of family and com-

270 O. Dik

munity have grown stronger (Hanf 2003, pp. 197–228; Khalaf 2003, pp. 107–143; Beydoun 2003, pp. 75–87) after the war. Various explanations have been given for this post-war reversal in the process of secularization with its accompanying effects of fragmentation and individualization. Khalaf attributes the main reason for this development to the diminishing of trust in the state and secular institutions due to their collapse and complete absence during the war. Moreover, as the war continued, each community witnessed internal power struggles. Many of the Lebanese Christians I interviewed recounted losing their belief in the 'Christian cause' during the fierce Christian infighting during the final stage of the war (1989–1990). As one interview partner put it:

> As long as we fought Muslims, we believed in a common cause. However, when Christians started to kill Christians, one neighbor against the other, that's when I lost hope for the Christians in Lebanon.

The disillusionment with the state and the sectarian community caused many to seek shelter in the private haven of family. While perception of the ideal of a close-knit family increased, the actual family dynamics are often caught in socioeconomic cross pressures.

The Lebanese youth often long for emotional bonding within their families and seek to know their family history in order to find their own social orientation.[3] The war affected virtually everyone in this tiny country, leaving many with emotional and psychosomatic post-war disorders (Khalaf 2002, p. 219; Karam 1999, pp. 272–282). At the same time, psychological help carries with it a taboo, as anyone who seeks such help will be labelled crazy (*majnun*). Psychology, even as an academic discipline, is widely stigmatized in society. Young adults do not have a clear picture of the involvement of their family in the war as their parents in many cases do not talk about their experience to their children. The children are therefore left with fragmented knowledge, mostly from conversations they overheard within their immediate family circle. The inability to articulate their war experiences[4] seems in many cases to lead to emotional withdrawal.

The lack of emotional empathy, paired with the lack of time to invest in their families, places an increasing strain upon individuals. I lived in Furn el Chebbak, a Christian suburb of Beirut. Many of my neighbours recalled with nostalgia 'the good old war times' when families had a lot of time on their hands to socialize and visit neighbours. After the war ended, many Lebanese felt they had lost economic opportunities and expressed frustration at their socioeconomic standing (Labaki 2003, pp. 181–197). Young educated Lebanese either emigrate or compete for scarce employment opportunities. The death toll of war combined with a steady stream of emigration after the war served to diminish the traditional Lebanese extended family as the main support structure for the individual.

---

[3] As the state failed to implement a common historic account, the family and community took on the main role in the transmission of historic knowledge (Bashshur 2003, pp. 163–168).

[4] While many talk about the war in general terms, there is reluctance, particularly on the part of those who were actively engaged in the war, to reflect upon their personal experiences and involvement (see Dyck 2010).

The projected family ideals stand in tension with the ordinary, hard-pressed Lebanese family, thus leading to the increasing frustration of their individual members. A family must struggle to balance the high individual expectations of emotional closeness and traditional roles on the one hand, and the effects of the war, increasing post war modernization, mobility and the fragmentation of extended families on the other hand. Additionally, the educated segment of the post-war generation seeks a higher participation in society and is wary of traditional authority which they identify with the mistakes of the past. In particular, many young Lebanese are appalled that the old warring militia leaders now occupy the seats of Parliament.

C/P members refer to their communities as 'spiritual families'. While 'spiritual families' differ in some aspects from kinship relations, many resemblances do evoke a sense of being a family. Besides the larger gatherings in public spaces, the C/P groups also gather in private homes. During these meetings, family traditions are enacted. The members eat together, socialize and celebrate rites of passage. These informal times together create bonding opportunities and a climate of emotional warmth. In fact, I have observed that many younger members of C/P groups spend more time in the homes of their C/P leaders then with their own families. As one C/P member put it:

> The priest preaches from the pulpit on Sunday morning and I do not know him. My group leader talks with me about Jesus and the Holy Spirit over a coffee at Starbucks. He shares with me his life.

The emotional closeness to the C/P leaders stands in contrast to the distance from the traditional authorities, whether from the home, church or the state. Moreover, while traditional religious education creates a ritual and spatial distance between the clergy and the laity, the average C/P leader is a young urban professional who seeks to engage his/her followers on a horizontal level, thereby diminishing the difference in power.

Traditional family roles and expectations are determined by social norms and expectations which are beyond the control of the individual. In contrast, the involvement of the believer and the benefits he receives from his 'spiritual family' depend on his continuous participation. Most groups seem to install control mechanisms in order to exclude free riders from their most intimate circles. At the beginning, people are initiated into the outer circle, which usually consists of weekly public meetings. With increasing commitment, the newcomers are allowed to move into the more private and intimate circle. The investment of time and resources secures for the members the reciprocal care of their chosen community. Compared to the traditional family, which is a given, the involvement within the spiritual family appears costly due to this continuous volunteering. So why do C/P members continue to 'pay' with their resources and their time? Voluntary group associations make the C/P community appear highly unstable, as membership depends on the choices of the individuals and is not reinforced by wider historic or cultural expectations. At the same time, this structural instability is balanced by stability of values. In a postwar society which is perceived as chaotic, a community of predictable norms lends the individual a sense of security and trust.

Trust

The overall trust of people in their political, social and religious leaders has decreased during the war. The credibility of the traditional churches was tarnished as many churches took sides during the sociopolitical conflict and this blurred any demarcation lines between victims and perpetrators. Some C/P members suspect the church leaders of having been complicit in the violence during the war. Some were also angered by the high prices demanded for the services of the church, thus leading the individual to equate the church with the corrupt Lebanese clientelist system from which the believers wanted to break free. Within the neighbourhood of Furn el Chebbak, I encountered some young men who professed to have a strong Maronite identity despite never having visited a Maronite church. They shared stories with me about Maronite priests who travelled to Europe during the civil war to collect funds for the suffering Maronite population and then ended up spending this money on their houses and cars. In contrast to these negative images, the C/P leaders are perceived as caring family members who open up their homes and share their time and resources.

Through C/P voluntary membership, the Lebanese understanding of how the individual interacts within the sacred communal sphere gets reinterpreted. A believer must constantly renew his/her own commitment to God through a personal confession which is validated by actions. At the same time, the C/P groups hold strong expectations as to the lifestyle of the believer. In contrast, within the traditional Christian churches, belonging to the church is not through individual choice but rather through birth. Individuality and independence are promulgated through lifestyle. The predictability of behaviour within C/P communities requires a high degree of authenticity, which is continuously reproduced through C/P rituals.

Robbins points out a clear link between linguistic and ritual ideologies. Where a general scepticism about language prevails, a ritual becomes crucial in establishing the social order. Although a ritual has no inherent meaning in itself, its strength lies in its function of bringing 'into being the worlds they [rituals] are about' (Robbins 2001, p. 595) by rendering the inner states of the individual socially irrelevant. In contrast, if deeper individual interpretation is valued, rituals become suspicious due to their role in establishing only a shallow social coherence, which is then perceived as lacking the inner truthful consent of the participants. Robbins explains the strong commitment of Pentecostals and Charismatics to rituals with the demise of the Protestant 'sincerity culture'. Globalization and new technology have undermined the trust of people in the veracity of language leading once again to 'ritual as a way of being together and communicating shared commitments to one another' (Robbins 2001, p. 599).

Although I agree with this basic thesis, the relation between linguistic and ritual ideologies as it relates to C/P believers is more ambivalent than Robbins' projection allows for. Charismatic believers in Beirut are caught between suspicion of traditional church rituals[5] and language. They seek sincerity and the capacity to commu-

---

[5] Without going further into the definition of ritual, I have chosen the definition that I consider most useful for my field research. I view a ritual as a repetitive act of communication and perfor-

nicate their experience of being filled with the Holy Spirit. Throughout this search, they are caught in a constant tension between ritual and language. On the one hand, they distrust public religious rituals, viewing them as merely promoting a religious-political identity devoid of deeper spiritual commitment. On the other hand, certain shared forms are necessary for a communal ritual to function. However, repetitive religious acts are seen as potentially harmful to the spiritual life of a believer as the repetition may cause the believer to cease searching for personal interpretation and the expression of the work of the Holy Spirit in his own life. Often, the leader of worship or preacher would remind the believers:

> If you come here just to sing some songs, meet people, listen to a sermon and have a good time, do not come. It is not about what we do together. It is about meeting the Lord. This should be first and everything else comes after it. We should not get complacent. God wants to meet us anew.

Charismatics are suspicious not only of rituals but of language as well, as they perceive language in Lebanese culture to be a tool for masking true intentions. At the same time, the believers seek for an unmediated and sincere encounter with God. However, in order to meet God, certain rituals are required, presenting the Charismatic believer with a dilemma. It is exactly this tension to 'fill' and to authenticate the rituals in place that generates a constant creative revision of the ritual form. The degree of ritualistic and linguistic commitment distinguishes a member from a non-member. Members who attend the group more often are seen as more committed to the core group. Committed members are also expected to be creative in their ongoing interpretations of the Charismatic meta-narrative. This requires them to engage in reflexive practices in order to express their beliefs and practices.

Freedom

In addition to the benefit of acquiring a new alternative family and the production of trust, most C/P believers, and young adults in particular, are drawn to a feeling of freedom and empowerment which is reproduced in C/P rituals and lifestyle. Many Lebanese describe the post-war situation as 'cold war' and 'being stuck'. Lebanon has one of the highest unemployment rates in the world for young adults. This leads to feelings of resignation and powerlessness. C/P members of a lower social class have no *wasta*[6] within Lebanese society. Charismatic rituals offer them a platform to be heard. Within Lebanese society, the right of expression depends on the social, political and economic status of the person. For example, Armenians are a minority within Lebanese society and often the object of jokes. At first, Armenian members at the 'Meeting with God' felt insecure worshipping with the Lebanese Arabs in Arabic. Within the wider Lebanese context, age also lends authority for a person to speak. An older brother of one leader and his father became believers and joined the

---

mance (see Wulf 2007, p. 181, and Bloch 2005, p. 124).

[6] Wasta can be described as a sociopolitical aspect of a Patron–Client relationship. 'Patron-client ties involve the reciprocal exchange of extrinsic benefits and therefore both patron and client have a vested interest in maintaining this reciprocity' (Khalaf 2003, p. 100).

group. I asked him how it felt to be in a role of spiritual authority over his father and his older brother. He replied that it felt strange at times. However, in C/P circles, spiritual maturity cannot be equated with biological maturity. At the moment of ritual expression, the person is filled with the Holy Spirit, who, being the creator of the universe, has greater authority than human authority. In this way, the person is freed from the restrictions imposed upon him by cultural norms. 'Speaking is the act by which the speaker overcomes the closure of the universe' (Ricoeur 1974, p. 82). C/P believers experience the opening up of their possibilities for action as liberating.

Once the newly introduced members experience these C/P benefits in their personal lives, they choose to give their time and resources to volunteer on behalf of the needs of the community. Thus, in order to keep claiming these benefits, volunteering must be ongoing. The in-group volunteering includes various tasks depending on the ability of the person. Leaders are concerned with finding volunteering tasks for everyone so that new members can invest in the communal benefits. I have observed many volunteering groups organising spiritual retreats, working in the kitchen, designing a website for the Church, organising a camp for the children, cooking, singing, distributing food and providing education in the neighbourhood and in Muslim communities, taking evangelistic trips to Lebanese rural areas and other countries in the Middle East. The in-group volunteering takes place mostly within a particular C/P location such as a church building, church basement, shopping mall or a private house, where C/P services and activities take place. The physically closed spaces restrain the volunteering activities of C/P members within a particular setting. These volunteering actions within an enclosed space and a particular religious community seem to reproduce a pre-institutionalised, sectarian welfare regime. However, before drawing conclusions on the relation between in-group volunteering and social solidarity, the religious culture motivating volunteering must be examined further.

Religious Motivation for Volunteering Within a Third Cultural Space

In contrast to the traditional churches, the C/P groups offer their members a greater number of opportunities for participation. A C/P leader constantly imagines new areas of involvement. From preparing a rock-like, worship concert, a theatre sketch, a Bible study or even cleaning the toilets, C/P leaders imbue the tasks with sacral meaning. The participants feel that with their actions, they 'advance the kingdom of God', which is God's reality on earth. Not only do the young adults consider themselves co-agents with God, but they also see themselves as capable of introducing divine intervention into the spatio-temporal realm. In one of his sermons, the pastor of the 'Abundant Life' Church called out: 'Your prayer moves God'! The C/P belief, in which words have intrinsic power to bring about possible worlds and influence material culture, is an immense motivation for people, whose words otherwise do not matter.

While the space and rituals of the traditional churches embody a stable universe, the dynamic C/P worship with rock-style music, dances and spontaneous exclamations embody a dynamic world order. The emphasis on the Holy Spirit evokes change as something desirable. Change and mobility, which are a hallmark of postwar capitalist values, are appropriated through spiritual means. C/P communities mediate between tradition and global modernization processes. Samir Khalaf rightly argues against dichotomies between tradition and modernity. Instead, he proposes a theoretical model of 'adaptive modernisation' (Khalaf 2002, p. 62). The C/P groups can be described as adaptive modernization agents. Khalaf states that 'a large measure of modernisation can and does take place by mobilising traditional networks and loyalities (Khalaf 2002, p. 62)'. The C/P movement mobilizes communal, religious and family networks.

The C/P movement uses the latest technology in their rituals and communications. Moreover, the C/P networks extend globally as they free their preachers for travel. Many believers shared with me that their pastors and preachers have travelled extensively. One of the C/P leaders told me how initially his parents were against him becoming a preacher at a Pentecostal church after he completed his degree in business, but after he travelled to many countries his parents began to realize that 'serving the Lord' can also lead to a successful lifestyle. Mobility defines Lebanese culture with more than four times as many Lebanese now living abroad as in Lebanon itself. Mobility suggests power and extended networks, both of which are crucial in such a tiny country with limited resources. With this shift in ontology, C/P believers begin to perceive the world, not as a static, changeless order, but as dynamic and offering endless possibilities as the Holy Spirit permeates all of reality. In C/P rituals, believers move their bodies to the rhythmic music, no longer mere observers of divine events which are performed by a priest on a platform. Instead, each believer becomes a divine agent co-acting with God and acting upon material culture. As one C/P member put it:

I used just to sit at home and watch TV. After the Holy Spirit filled me, I became alive, I got many friends, I entered university, I started to believe that God has a plan for me.

This powerful position of having a divine co-agent stands in stark contrast to the impoverished, immobile and ghettoized physical reality of many C/P believers. I am not arguing here for a form of deprivation theory. Broad sociological arguments of deprivation and disorganisation as a cause for new religious movements, if applied in isolation, are tautological and could be used to explain any phenomena.[7] Instead, I propose that while the C/P groups appeal to specific social needs, their role as adaptive agents of modernization is crucial in understanding their emergence. Volunteering is one of the visible forms for members of expressing their being filled with the Holy Spirit, who acts, changes and creates. Thus, volunteering becomes a confirmation of the inner sacred reality which is otherwise not directly observable.

---

[7] Throughout my field research, I also met members of the Charismatic movement within the Maronite Church who were from the upper middle class but chose to join the group with lower middle class people. Deprivation theory is too limited in its explanatory scope. Robbins and Hunt give a satisfactory summary of the critiques concerning deprivation theory (see Robbins 2004, p. 124, and Hunt 2002, pp. 23–26).

The post-war capitalist consumer culture, while evoking dreams of material wealth, allows only a few who have established networks to benefit. The lower middle class masses are left disenchanted. While the majority of Lebanese want to break free from the past, which they associate with backwardness and violence, they also lack a vision for the future. The C/P culture is seen as a third space. On the one hand, traditional Lebanese institutions such as family, marriage and certain cultural values are reaffirmed. On the other hand, the same institutions and values are transformed and imbued with modern values such as the emphasis on the individual's autonomy. The individual is not a passive part of a universal global order, but an active agent, experiencing the Holy Spirit and in turn initiating change. Through C/P and its performative narratives in preaching and rituals, the believers embody a culture, which seems to engage the past and the present, yet at the same time offers an alternative vision of the future distinct from what they perceive as western materialism and hedonism. While C/P believers perceive C/P culture as fullness, they brand both traditionalism and western values which contradict their vision as empty. The believers view the Holy Spirit as 'filling them' and 'empowering them' to break free from the oppressiveness of the capitalist market. However, on closer inspection, the consumption of C/P culture enables its members to afford the material advantages that come through modernization, as they are disciplined to be active social agents. Thus, over a longer period, C/P believers come to benefit from the material advantages of capitalism as well. I have observed some Pentecostal churches preaching a 'health and wealth gospel'. The C/P members are called on to invest their money in the kingdom and expect an abundant return from God. The result of disciplined, self-responsible consumers is an improved financial situation.

The pull towards participation and action hinges on the process of C/P identity negotiation as an alternative cultural space beyond traditionalism and 'western' consumerism. What is perceived as 'bonding capital' is conditioned culturally and historically. As I have described above, the distinct C/P benefits must be understood within the post-war urban context. The dynamic appeal of C/P identity depends on the delicate balance between a meaningful engagement with the traditional and 'western' cultures and the transformation of these spheres.

Every C/P group attempts precariously to balance its identity and create a third cultural space. This fragile C/P identity mirrors the unstable sociopolitical and economic situation of many Lebanese. While this tension of a third cultural space appears as fragile due to voluntary associations, it is, paradoxically, also the instability which creates a pull and attraction as members must continuously recreate this fluid space through participation and volunteering.

C/P Volunteering Between a Vision for Social Solidarity and the Pull of a Sectarian Sociopolitical Context

The high degree of volunteering within the clearly marked C/P space is motivated by the specific benefits C/P believers receive from membership in the emerging communities. Membership and benefits hinge on continuous participation of the individual. Thus, the C/P culture motivates volunteering and the volunteering further shapes the C/P culture. Furthermore, the C/P culture of volunteering also impacts the larger sociopolitical context.

C/P members negotiate between their former sectarian identity and the newfound desire to see the Holy Spirit at work on the national level. The prevalent siege mentality among Christians is being challenged through stories of God's universal presence and the special role C/P members claim in affecting the wellbeing of the whole nation. The sharp distinction between 'us' and 'them' is further deconstructed by the emphasis on the active working of the Holy Spirit in other communities as well. It becomes more difficult to view 'the other' as an enemy if he/she is a potential member of the C/P community. A free competition among religions based on voluntary association prevents religious communities from being inward looking and demonising 'the other', since each community must understand 'the other' in order to successfully communicate their religious offer.

C/P volunteering practices further contribute to Lebanese social solidarity by undermining sectarian identity. C/P emphasis on continuous decision-making regarding belonging opens up a free market in religion, thus weakening its the role in reinforcing tribal and territorial ties. Belonging, in this case, must be established through continuous involvement rather than remaining a given birth right. Once the 'blood and earth' ties are disentangled from the sacred ties, the mythical structure of kinship and territorial sectarian identity is weakened. A religion based on individual interpretation and choice is not as easily mobilized in cohorts who have political, tribal and ethnic agendas. Some C/P believers I interviewed, although feeling closer to the traditional Christian groups, question and transcend these boundaries at the same time, as in their view a Muslim could be closer to becoming a C/P believer than a traditional Christian. While traditional Christians volunteer within their respective community in order to benefit their sociopolitical community, some C/P believers volunteer in Muslim communities as well in order to emphasise through their actions the presence of the Holy Spirit in these communities. Identity politics are primarily maintained through anchoring of sociopolitical identities in the sacred. The Maronites emphasize the Maronite origin of Lebanon through various saints who built monasteries in the valley of Qadisha.[8] This sacred tradition excludes other religious communities and reaffirms communal boundaries. These boundaries are transcended by C/P groups through their emphasis upon the Holy Spirit, which acts universally and is embodied by every believer. As a result of this perceived immediate divine indwelling, many C/P believers distrust traditional authority. The rejection of authority strengthens individual interpretations which in turn lead to an array of religious groups each competing with each other and thus creating a highly pluralistic society, which in itself is a hallmark of modernity (Taylor 2007).

I observed that the more committed C/P believers were, the less likely they were to align themselves with a particular political party. However, this does not mean that they became less political. As one person put it, 'I used to follow Aoun because my family did. I did not care about what he stood for. But now I care more about

---

[8] On the role of the saints for anchoring the Maronite identity, see, for example Heyberger (2002).

values than about politicians'. Within C/P communities, unreflective communal practices and traditional ties are critiqued. In the same way that C/P members have learned to critique traditional religious structures through the empowering of the Holy Spirit, critique is also levelled against political parties and their subsequent actions. Once religious, self-reflective practices and volunteering are set in motion, other social spheres are necessarily affected as well. Thus, individualization of religion leads to reflective political thinking as well. As tribal political affiliation decreases and more people are challenged to seek the common good, sharp sectarian boundaries are blurred. Social solidarity does not necessarily require weak communal boundaries, only actors who are able to cross these boundaries for the sake of the common good. The C/P culture of volunteering weakens traditional sectarian boundaries and motivates its members to cross them.

The overall C/P culture tends to contribute to social solidarity, as described above. However, the particular institutional alignment of emerging C/P groups has the potential of restricting their volunteering vision and activities. I observed the Roman-Catholic/Maronite C/P groups focusing their volunteering activities primarily on their own constituency. C/P Christians often think that Christians need to encounter the work of the Holy Spirit before the Christian can have any impact upon the Muslim community or Muslims themselves. Despite this hope for a trickle down effect towards improving social solidarity, the result confirms the double effect described by Khalaf.

Evangelical and C/P groups without formal ties to the existing traditional churches have more flexibility of engagement. Some volunteer as individuals with non-Lebanese international organisations such as, for example, World-Vision. Some leaders explained to me that this choice stemmed from their desire to avoid clear sectarian affiliation in order to 'express the love of Jesus' practically to Muslims as well. Thus, their self-positioning outside the traditional church structures informs their volunteering commitment to organisations which attempt to avoid sectarian positioning.

I have also observed these groups organising educational and practical help for the socially disadvantaged Muslim neighbourhoods. For example, C/P members visited families of lower socioeconomic standing at home and discussed their needs together before offering help. During the war in 2006, it was mostly the Shi'a quarters of the city that were bombed by the Israeli army. As the Shi'a refugees sought shelter in Christian quarters, Christian RWO's and various C/P groups volunteered to provide food and shelter. Often, C/P groups decide spontaneously, as unpredictability is the mark of the Holy Spirit, whom and when to help. These volunteering activities, which cross boundaries, subvert the sectarian RWO system.

Some C/P believers acknowledged that doing good for Muslims initially went against their negative feelings towards Muslims, rooted in the experience of the civil war. However, their C/P culture motivated them to share their benefits with those outside their community. Thus, they volunteered by providing material help to the Muslim population while hoping that some would join their community and be transformed from being 'other' to a C/P member. As an emerging movement, the C/P community seeks to extend its benefits to other communities while the expectations of an individual's reciprocal participation in the community limit the extent of this outward movement.

However, C/P motivation can become irrelevant as social solidarity is also shaped by a concrete setting and mode of interaction, which is independent from the concrete intentions of religious actors. For example, I have observed a group of volunteers travelling to Muslim rural areas and offering help. Before their travels, they imagined that their practical help would allow them to pray for and share their beliefs with Muslims thus prompting some Muslims to become C/P believers. I was not at the specific site of this interaction. However, upon their return, the C/P believers shared stories of unexpected encounters and observations that were not limited to religious motives. They talked about the dress, the smells, the different dialect and unknown practices. The initial religious intention shifted to a thick cultural exchange between very different socioeconomic and rural-urban groups.

Shared understanding thus arises from a concrete setting and mode of interaction. The particular C/P vision of expressing the unconditional love of Jesus through volunteering in other communities does not necessary lead to conversion of the other. Thus, if Muslims remain in his community, a continuous interaction also requires negotiation of any common understanding. The way that one communicates one's religious identity shifts in relation to the setting. For example, some C/P members preferred not to mention their Christian identity to Muslims as they feared it could lead to a false identification of C/P intentions with a particular political agenda. Both communities then must negotiate their understanding of each other and the public good. Such reflection changes both the C/P believer and the recipient of C/P volunteering.

Conclusion

Religious welfare organisations in Lebanon fill the state vacuum in providing various services to their constituencies. Thus, volunteers within these established RWOs contribute to the 'double effect'. In contrast, C/P groups without institutional ties are less restricted and therefore subvert the established religious and political landscape by volunteering outside of the established RWO's, creating new, trans-sectarian possibilities for volunteering. Positioning themselves outside the established religio-political institutions allows these C/P groups to cross the boundaries into Muslim communities more easily than the C/P groups that depend upon the structure of traditional churches. The concrete settings and communications between such diverse groups as urban C/P believers and the Sunni rural population weaken sectarian divides thereby providing the possibility of more inclusive identities over time, which would then contribute to social solidarity. Therefore, the style of volunteering impacts on the religious culture, since the encounter with the religious other challenges a religiously motivated volunteer to reflect on his/her own practices.

The C/P vision for social solidarity and volunteering for the common good stands in stark contrast to the actual Lebanese sociocultural and political reality. The C/P vision of God's unconditional love conflicts with both the conditional working of C/P identity negotiation and the sectarian welfare regime. The dynamics of C/P culture hinges on excluding free riders, who would seek to take the benefits without volunteering themselves. C/P groups subvert the sectarian culture through their C/P culture of individual choice and continuous volunteering. The emphasis on the Holy Spirit serves to diminish ethnic, cultural and political divisions, as the Holy Spirit cannot be confined to concrete sociopolitical categories.

Thus, the effect of volunteering in Lebanon depends on three interrelated factors. First of all, the positioning of volunteering either within or outside the sectarian welfare regime. Second, the role of the particular religious culture is central as it anchors and feeds volunteering practices across or within sectarian divides. Third, the setting and communication style that prevails between C/P volunteering believers and receivers affect the concrete outcome of the social discourse. Social solidarity, as an outcome of mutual understanding and appreciation between members of differing religious communities, is one of the possible positive outcomes in such a fragmented country as Lebanon.

Although Khalaf recognizes the primary role of family and religious community for the identity formation of individuals, he seems to ignore the thick embedding of volunteering actions in these communal settings. Accordingly, both social solidarity and social strife, stem from particular, religiously motivated practices. Through concrete encounters, members from diverse group associations are given the possibility of developing a common identity. Social solidarity grows out of particular negotiations and is established at the grassroots levels. Therefore, Khalaf's vision of a top down, secular, unbiased volunteering to achieve social solidarity is naïve and mistaken. At worst, the top–down approach to social solidarity could provoke communal resistance towards foreign ideas and create an unnecessary rift between projected 'religious tradition' and 'western modernity'. In Lebanon, national identity remains primarily a discourse of the elites, while the families and religious communities on the ground shape the primary identity and actions of the individual. If, however, values such as individual reflectivity, national unity, critique and freedom are rooted in the communal religious practices, the volunteering actions will have a more profound effect than volunteering motivated by abstract, seemingly universal ethical imperatives imposed by state institutions and academic elites. The understanding of ethics and the common good is informed by communal identities (MacIntyre 1997). Therefore, any imposition of a non-historic and non-cultural ideal upon such a complex society as Lebanon will inevitably fail. Contrary to Khalaf, my field research shows that religiously motivated volunteering is not *per se* negative when viewed in relation to social solidarity. Instead, each case must be analysed within its particular context, considering the larger sociopolitical context, the religious culture and the particular setting and interactions of volunteering, as outlined in my study.

A closer ethnographic and comparative look at other religious cultures such as, for example Hizb'allah, would provide a fuller picture of the Lebanese relation between religious volunteering and social solidarity. So far, the sociopolitical accounts provide insights into the relation between the emergence of Hizb'allah in achieving

13 'Your Prayer Moves God' 281

a strong link between bonding capital and volunteering (Harb 2010). These accounts, do not, however, hold further conclusions for social solidarity. The peaceful future of religiously pluralistic countries depends on the ability of each community to mobilize their members for the common good. With Pentecostalism and Islam being the fastest growing religious movements globally (Robbins 2004), the issue of religious volunteering and social solidarity will remain central to increasingly global cities across the world.

Acknowledgments I would like to thank my advisor Prof. Dr. Andreas Feldtkeller at the Department for Intercultural Theology and Religious Studies, Humboldt University, Berlin, who commented on my developing ideas and stimulated further reflection. Moreover, I am thankful for the very helpful criticism of Johan von Essen, who patiently guided me through the process of writing this chapter.

Bibliography

Bashshur, M. (2003). The deepening cleavage in the educational system. In T. Hanf & N. Salam (Eds.), *Lebanon in limbo: Postwar society and state in an uncertain regional environment* (pp. 159–181). Baden-Baden: Nomos Verlagsgesellschaft.

Beydoun, A. (2003). A note on confessionalism. In T. Hanf & N. Salam (Eds.), *Lebanon in limbo: Postwar society and state in an uncertain regional environment* (pp. 75–86). Baden-Baden: Nomos Verlagsgesellschaft.

Bloch, M. (2005). *Essays on cultural transmission.* New York: Berg.

Dyck, L. F. (2010). *Entanglement of past and present: Civil war postmemory in Lebanon.* Unpublished MA paper in Islamic-Christian Relations, Saint Joseph University, Beirut.

Geertz, C. (2000). *The interpretation of cultures: Selected essays.* New York: Basic Books.

Hanf, T. (1990). *Koexistenz im Krieg. Staatszerfall und Entstehen einer Nation im Libanon.* Baden-Baden: Nomos Verlagsgesellschaft.

Hanf, T. (2003). The sceptical nation: Opinions and attitudes twelve years after the end of the war. In T. Hanf & N. Salam (Eds.), *Lebanon in limbo: Postwar society and state in an uncertain regional environment* (pp. 197–228). Baden-Baden: Nomos Verlagsgesellschaft.

Harb, M. (2010). *Le Hezbollah à Beyrouth (1985–2005). De la banlieue à la ville.* Paris: Karthala.

Harris, W. (2006). *The new face of Lebanon—History's revenge.* Princeton: Markus Wiener Publishers.

Heyberger, B. (2002). Saint Charbel Makhlouf, ou la consécration de l'identité maronite. In C. Mayeur-Jaouen (Ed.), *Saints et héros du Moyen-Orient contemporain* (pp. 139–161). Paris: Maisonneuve et Larose.

Hunt, S. J. (2002). Deprivation and western pentecostalism revisited: Neo-pentecostalism. *Pentecostudies, 1*(2), 1–29.

Jawad, R. (2009). *Social welfare and religion in the Middle East: A Lebanese perspective.* Bristol: The Policy Press.

Karam, E. G. (1999). Women and the Lebanon wars: Depression and post-traumatic stress disorder. In L. R. Shehadeh (Ed.), *Women and war in Lebanon* (pp. 272–282). Florida: University Press.

Khalaf, S. (2002). *Cultural resistance: Global and local encounters in the Middle East.* London: Saqi Books.

Khalaf, S. (2003). On roots and routes: The reassertion of primordial loyalties. In T. Hanf & N. Salam (Eds.), *Lebanon in limbo: Postwar society and state in an uncertain regional environment* (pp. 107–143). Baden-Baden: Nomos Verlagsgesellschaft.

Khalaf, S. (2007). Resurgent communal identities and protracted collective violence in Lebanon: A dialectical reading. In P. Molt & H. Dickow (Eds.), *Kulturen und Konflikte im Vergleich* (pp. 237–253). Baden-Baden: Nomos Verlagsgesellschaft.

Labaki, B. (2003). The postwar economy: A miracle that didn't happen. In T. Hanf & N. Salam (Eds.), *Lebanon in limbo: Postwar society and state in an uncertain regional environment* (pp. 181–197). Baden-Baden: Nomos Verlagsgesellschaft.

Lichterman, P. (2012). Religion in public action: From actors to settings. *Sociological Theory, 30*(1), 15–36.

MacIntyre, A. (1997). The virtues, the unity of a human life, and the concept of a tradition. In L. P. Hinchman & S. K. Hinchman (Eds.), *The idea of narrative in the human sciences* (pp. 241–264). New York: State University Press.

Malik, C. (2004). *Lebanon in itself.* Beirut: NDU Press.

Manicas, P. (1998). A realist social science. In M. Archer et al. (Eds.), *Critical realism: Essential readings* (pp. 313–339). London: Routledge.

Outhwaite, W. (1998). *A realist social science.* In M. Archer et al. (Eds.), *Critical realism: Essential readings* (pp. 282–297). London: Routledge.

Ricoeur, P. (1974). *The conflict of interpretations: Essays in hermeneutics.* Evanston: Northwestern University Press.

Robbins, J. (2001). Ritual communication and linguistic ideology: A reading and partial reformulation of Rappaport's theory of ritual. *Current Anthropology, 42*(5), 591–614.

Robbins, J. (2004). The globalization of pentecostal and charismatic Christianity. *Annual Review of Anthropology, 33,* 117–143.

Salam, N. (2003). Taif revisited. In T. Hanf & N. Salam (Eds.), *Lebanon in limbo: Postwar society and state in an uncertain regional environment* (pp. 39–53). Baden-Baden: Nomos Verlagsgesellschaft.

Taylor, C. (2007). *A secular age.* Cambridge: Harvard University Press.

Wulf, C. (2007). Die Erzeugung des Sozialen in Ritualen. In A. Michaels (Ed.), *Die neue Kraft der Rituale.* Heidelberg: Universitätsverlag Winter.

Chapter 14
Faith-Based Organizations and Civic Engagement in Egypt

Can FBOs Be Agents for Change?

Moustafa Khalil

Introduction

Islamic faith-based organizations (FBOs) have dominated civil society in Egypt for many years, controlling most of its financial resources as well as voluntary human resources (Clarke 2008). They have been the main destination for the limited numbers of young people who chose to volunteer before the 2011 revolution (Barsoum et al. 2010). Despite this, Islamists have never been able to bring about any change of the ruling regime in the Middle East's most populated country. The revolution that broke out on the streets of Egypt in January 2011 toppling the regime of former President Hosny Mubarak was a movement driven by mostly secular and young middle class activists (Teti and Gervasio 2012). Although for many of those young people it was their first encounter with civic commitment, the magnitude of the revolution brought many to expect that those who sparked it would be able to step forward to play a major role in shaping its aftermath. Instead, however, the voting fixtures that took place in the months following the revolution showed that popular support was mostly leaning towards other forces, particularly the Islamist movement (Lynch 2012).

The causes of the electoral success of Islamists have been a matter of extensive discussion in the literature pertaining to the 2011 Egyptian revolution. In some reports, the role of voluntary Islamic FBOs was overlooked in favor of focusing on the identity question so closely related to the Islamists.[1] In other accounts, however, the role of Islamic FBOs, which are mostly powered by volunteers, was probably overestimated, with claims accusing them of buying the loyalty of the population with their social service activities. This chapter will put the role of voluntary Islamic

---

[1] I mean here the ongoing debate on the identity of Egypt between those who argue that Egypt is Arab, those who argue that it is Islamic and those who argue for an independent Egyptian national identity. Islamists have usually used this debate within an emotional discourse to mobilize the masses against those who are allegedly trying to "strip Egypt of its Islamic identity."

M. Khalil (✉)
Institute of Development Policy and Management, University of Manchester, Manchester, U. K.
e-mail: mykhalil@hotmail.com

L. Hustinx et al. (eds.), *Religion and Volunteering,* Nonprofit and Civil Society Studies,
DOI 10.1007/978-3-319-04585-6_14, © Springer International Publishing Switzerland 2015

283

FBOs in shaping the political scene during the transition to postrevolutionary Egypt into perspective. The present chapter will use qualitative data from three volunteer-based FBOs in Egypt to understand how some Islamic FBOs have used their religious background not only for mobilizing volunteers and resources on behalf of their community service work but also for contributing to the ongoing political transformation in a volatile and turbulent postrevolution Egypt. This chapter will try to find what role these FBOs and the volunteers working through them have played in the rise of the Islamist movement to power in Egypt.

This chapter will start by explaining what it means by FBOs and will discuss two of the theoretical frameworks for their role in political transformation. It will then move to present the three case study organizations as they stood before the revolution together with the research background and methodology. The main part of the chapter will focus on the behavior of the three case study organizations after the revolution and will conclude with a critical analysis of the empirical findings.

FBOs and Political Transformation

The research objects in this chapter are FBOs, seen here as a distinct category of civil society organizations (CSOs). The definition of FBOs has been a controversial issue for a long time due to the, often ambiguous, link between faith and CSOs. For example, there are many organizations, such as the Edhi Foundation (the biggest humanitarian welfare organization in Pakistan), whose leaders and staff state that their main motive is their faith; but they would not consider their organizations to be FBOs (Bano and Nair 2007). Also, the use of the word "based" in the definition of FBOs is by no means a settled issue. For instance, Smith and Sosin (2001) used the term faith-related instead of faith-based because the latter excludes many organizations that have their resources and activities related somehow to elements of faith without being totally based on or affiliated to it. These disagreements about the terminology may lead to either an exclusive definition or a widely inclusive one that includes each and every organization where faith plays any role in its purpose, structure, or practice. A decent attempt to solve this problem is the detailed description of FBOs listing seven characteristics provided by Ebough et al. (2003), all of which apply to the case study organizations that will be presented below. Ebough et al. outlined detailed criteria to distinguish FBOs from other CSOs. The most important elements in these criteria identify CSOs as organizations that are: "1. Self-identified as religious organizations […]. 2. Participants […] tend to be religiously committed individuals, 3. Material resources [are] primarily provided by religious people or organizations. 4. Organizational goals, products, and services provided […] are usually of a religious nature, and are performed on the basis of religious values. 5. Organizations rely on religious values, beliefs, activities, or experiences in information processing and decision making" Ebough et al. (2003, p. 413).

Religious organizations have played paradoxical roles when it comes to political transformation. They have used their advocacy and community service activities to legitimize various existing political and social conditions. On the other hand, there

14 Faith-Based Organizations and Civic Engagement in Egypt

were cases when they challenged these conditions and managed to change them. These contradictory functions, as Hart and Dekker (2005) point out, are a reflection of the equally contradictory functions often played by religion itself since it can be used both to "comfort" and to "challenge" its followers, as seen in Max Weber's reference to the roles of priest and prophet in religion. De Tocqueville (in Warren 2001) and Putman (1993) have provided two of the leading theories regarding the role of civil society in democratization, which I shall refer to here as replacing democracy with political transformation.[2] De Tocqueville highlighted the impact of "social mores, political culture and habits of collective action" on democratization. According to him, CSOs, of which FBOs are a subcategory, provide venues for representation, for developing political culture and collective action. This role has been as important as the role of estates in establishing democracy in Europe. He theorized that associations, starting with individuals who join them at the level of narrow, primary associations (family clans or neighborhoods), develop as they acquire their civic culture into entities that can meet their interests collectively. They come to realize that they need to be dependent on others as being part of bigger groups that work for their collective interests.

Putman (1993) followed this by stating that he was concerned about the social context in which institutions operate (Howel and Pearce 2001). He specified how dependency within associations resulting from social and economic inequalities makes it hard to achieve the establishment of democratic civic culture. He noted that democratization (political transformation here) could not be founded within vertical ties. He explained that the failure of CSOs in Southern Italy to achieve political transformation was due to the chains of dependency and vertical relations that resulted from the prevailing social structures. This was in contrast to Northern Italy, where ties within CSOs tended to be horizontal rather than vertical allowing the association members greater freedom of movement and therefore greater ability to be transformed.

Bearing this in mind, we shall now move to providing the contextual background of the research by describing the state of civil society and volunteerism within it as it stood before the revolution.

Civil Society in Egypt on the Eve of the Revolution

Prior to 25 January 2011 (the date of the beginning of the protests), Egypt was a country ruled for more than 30 years by a nominally democratic military dictatorship regime headed by President Mubarak. The Egyptian Ministry of the Inte-

---

[2] I am using the term political transformation rather than democracy or democratization, which tend to dominate in the literature on the political role of civil society. Huntington (1993) believes that civil society is key to understanding the transformation to democracy. I argue that it can also be key to understand political transformation in general whether it to democracy or to other forms of political organization. The relation between civil society and democracy can be either positive or negative. It is not, therefore, necessary that civil society leads to democracy.

rior with its secret police arm called the State Security Department (SSD) and a 1.25 million man-strong paramilitary force had worked hard to crack down on any form of political activism they saw as a threat or a potential threat to the regime (Lynch 2012). The only exception to that seemed to be the Muslim Brotherhood (MB). This movement, which was established in 1928 with the aim of reviving the lost glory of the Islamic nation, had been legally banned after a turbulent history in relation to all the regimes that ruled Egypt since the mid-1940s. However, the legal ban was hardly implemented and the group was allowed to exist through its service-provision activities, especially in the fields of health care and education (Pargeter 2010). The group was also allowed to participate in some elections by fielding its members as independent candidates. Despite claims of widespread vote rigging, the MB succeeded, or perhaps was allowed, to win some seats in parliament as well as in trade unions and syndicates. This was described as an attempt by the regime to use the MB's conservative agenda as a scarecrow to gain popular approval for themselves as being the only possible alternative (Selvik and Stenslie 2011).

In this environment, civil society was left to exist as long as it mostly stayed clear of political activism. It was in effect contained by the authorities, in order to prevent it from growing strong enough to become a threat to the regime. Those who had studied civil society in Egypt before the revolution seemed to agree on describing it as a rather weak, fragmented, and contained element. It suffered various problems that included, but were not restricted to, lack of skills and capabilities, weak management, elitism, red tape and bureaucracy (UNDP 2010) as well as lack of funding and strong financial dependency on the government (Becker 1997). The relationship with the government was governed by the emergency law, which has been in effect throughout the entire era of President Mubarak's rule, from 1981 to 2011. It was also influenced by the strong presence and involvement of the SSD within the Ministry of Social Solidarity (MoSS), which was the government's arm dealing with CSOs (Zahid 2010). Being sidelined by the State, civil society was left to offer only service provision and economic development functions without any serious involvement in policymaking. The ousted regime's persistent policy of promoting nonreligious development organizations and containing advocacy and political NGOs had severely restricted the capability of civil society to achieve any significant political change on the national level and resulted in a situation which Langohr (2005) described as "too much civil society and too little politics."

FBOs comprised the largest portion of CSOs in Egypt. It is difficult to know the exact size of its share because official registers do not record the degree to which organizations are affiliated with religion. Yet, looking at the names of organizations as they appear in the register of NGOs in Egypt (issued by MoSS) and some of the activities that are typically associated with FBOs (such as funeral services and organizing pilgrimage trips to the Holy mosques in Saudi Arabia) shows that they existed in abundance.

Most staff members of Egyptian FBOs are volunteers and most of them are older, middle class educated people (UNDP 2008). However, detailed statistics about volunteering in Egypt could only be found for youth as a detailed study on a sample of Egyptian youth was published by the Egyptian Population Council only a month be-

14 Faith-Based Organizations and Civic Engagement in Egypt

fore the revolution in December 2010 (Barsoum et al. 2010).[3] The study described the picture of volunteering and participation in civil society among young Egyptians by highlighting a number of observations.

Firstly, young Egyptians seemed to have had little interest in volunteering in civil society. Less than 4% of the sample reported membership in a community group of any sort; and in most of the cases, these memberships were in sports clubs and youth centers. Around 1% of the sample reported belonging to any CSO or political party. Second, young Egyptians were very attached to religion. Eighty-eight percent of the sample covered by the survey reported that they were "religious." About 83% said they prayed at least once a day (Islam requires five prayers per day) and more than 97% of the surveyed females wore the Islamic headscarf with more than 90% of them considering that not wearing it would bring them disrespect from society. The adherence of young people to religion was reflected in attitudes towards volunteering. About 66% of the minority who reported actively looking for volunteering opportunities had gone to mosques to find what they were looking for. Only 19% went to search for a volunteering opportunity at an orphanage (something that might still be managed by an FBO) and only 14% went to nonreligious organizations.[4]

The Case Study Organizations

The previous paragraphs summarized the context within which the case study organizations have been located before the revolution. The data used for this chapter was gathered during the research fieldwork conducted for the author's PhD project. This research fieldwork included case studies of three volunteer-based FBOs operating in the field of poverty reduction in Cairo. The pilot fieldwork that included examining the records of the local Social Solidarity Department had concluded that most FBOs in the research area (which is the lower middle class urban neighborhood of *El-Wayly* in Cairo) are actually mosque-based CSOs that can be divided into three main categories:

1. Community-based mosques without affiliation to any political groups or religious orders.
2. Mosques that are part of one of the two main ultraconservative Islamic *Salafi*-mosque networks, which are *El-Gameya El-Shareya* (GS) and *Ansar El-Sunna*.
3. Mosques that are officially independent but affiliated with the MB (officially banned before the revolution).

---

[3] Although the study was issued by a government agency, the list of its authors show a number of prominent academics whose involvement would grant the document an acceptable level of integrity and reliability.

[4] Visiting orphanages on Fridays and religious feasts is a common practice for youth community service groups and enthusiasts in Egypt. Perhaps that is why orphanages featured in this statistic as a category on their own attracting almost one fifth of all volunteer efforts.

Based upon this examination of the records, the following criterion was established in order to select three comparable and typical CSOs, so that each would represent one of the three major categories above:

4. The FBOs must be affiliated to mosques.
5. The mosques had to be of medium size where Friday prayers are held but not located in a main street or considered to be the main mosque of the neighborhood. This condition was set to capture the community aspect of the organizations yet to limit them to a size that it is possible to study within the specified time for each case.
6. They had to be fully dependent on volunteers for providing their human resources.
7. They had to have regular year-around activities aimed at community service (poverty reduction in particular).
8. The activities had to be dependent on the mosque for their location, funding, management, and other logistics.

The first of the selected case study organizations is *Gameyet Magales El-Tayebeen* (GMT), which is affiliated to a community-based mosque that does not represent any particular ideological or political beliefs. The second FBO is affiliated to a mosque that is part of a nationwide Salafi network called *El-Gameya El-Shareya* (GS). The Salafi movement is an ultraconservative Islamist order, which believes that true Muslims are the ones who strictly imitate the lifestyle and actions of the early Muslims who lived with Prophet Mohammed and the two generations that followed them (all commonly known as the *Salaf*). They do not apply the Islamic legislation rule of *Ijtehad,* which allows Muslims to reinterpret sacred religious texts to coincide with the needs of life in each particular stage of history or social surroundings (Meijer 2009). The third case studied looked at the *Mohammed Farag Association* (MFA), which is affiliated to a mosque largely under the dominance of the MB, the biggest and most organized Islamist political group in the country, considered by many as being relatively moderate (Sulivan and Abed-Kotob 1999).

Before the revolution, the GMT was a typical charity applying a redistributive, basic needs approach to poverty reduction. The organization worked to raise donations from the better off members of society in order to redistribute them through regular monthly cash installments to poorer members of the community. In doing that, there was no pressure applied on the beneficiaries to give their allegiance to any particular political organization or ideology. No conditions whatsoever were imposed on the beneficiaries. The organization tried to address poverty by providing poor people willing to work with capital to start their own microprojects. The plans failed several times because most of the targeted beneficiaries failed to keep their projects afloat. They were in the habit of selling their assets to finance their consumption once they faced any difficulty. The organization is run by an all-volunteer team with most of the work being done by one person, the treasurer of the organization, and with the mosque's imam providing major assistance. According to their statements in the interviews, the motives of the board members for working in the organization varied from a feeling of social responsibility towards their local community to the charitable obligation, which satisfied their religious consciousness.

The Salafi GS, which represents a more fundamentalist element of Islam, was very different. While it also applies a mostly basic-needs approach to charity without the element of empowerment or capacity-building, there was a significant difference in the form of the assistance it provided. In addition to regular cash payments, it provides beneficiary households with food assistance, free medical prescriptions, free school textbooks, exceptional payments for a daughter's marriage or death, and more. However, the biggest difference is the organization's strong commitment to maintain a link between the mosque as a religious institution and the poverty reduction activities conducted through the mosque. Beneficiaries would be required to attend religious lessons in order to receive the assistance. They would also be required to come in person to the mosque to receive their payments. The FBO team kept an eye on their attendance levels to pray in the mosque. All of this made perfect sense when I asked the General GS board member[5] Moustafa Ismail in an interview about the main motive behind GS's poverty reduction activities. He said it was about "reforming society through maintaining strong ties between people and their mosque because the closer these ties are, the more religious people become and consequently become better members of society."

The third case (the MFA) was originally a community-based mosque similar in location and structure to that of GMT. However, the difference is that the mosque was infiltrated by the MB as represented by the mosque imam, a devoted MB member. He was appointed to this mosque by the Ministry of Endowments and Islamic Affairs (MoE) in 2006. After a few years in office, he persuaded the mosque's board members to establish an NGO linked to the mosque. It is important to note that none of the board members is an MB member. In fact, at least one of them had very strong opinions against it. The imam was authorized by the board to utilize his personal knowledge and experience to go through the lengthy procedure of establishing the organization, as well as designing and implementing its poverty reduction activities. As his role became more central and dominant at the mosque and the organization, he used the connections and socialization opportunities his positions granted him to promote the agenda and ideology of the MB. With the tight grip of the SSD on CSOs before the revolution, doing that was not possible in public, through Friday sermons for example. Instead, the imam had to lobby and try to get his message to mosque regulars when he was off the microphone by establishing friendships and social ties with them, which allowed him to get his message through to them. His image as an initiator of good works done by the mosque's MFA helped him in doing that.

In a similar pattern to GMT, both the Salafi and the MB-affiliated organizations were mainly powered by volunteer board members who were mostly middle class pensioners motivated by similar motives to those of the GMT board members. In both organizations most of the work was handled by one person. MFA was the only exception to that, as the imam was a young man in his mid-30s and he used to get

---

[5] There is a General GS that is like the mother to a network of smaller local and independent CSOs carrying the same name. They relate to the General GS in a way that is similar to retail franchises where the branches take the name and apply the methods of the General GS, but enjoy independent finances and decision-making in areas that do not contradict the religious principles or the main features of activities design of the GS.

Table 14.1 Case study organizations before the revolution

Case study FBO area	Community-based GMT	Salafi GS	MB-affiliated MFA
Human resources	All volunteers	All volunteers	All volunteers
Motive to volunteer	Religious/personal	Religious agenda	Political agenda
Poverty reduction activities	Simple top–down charitable	Sophisticated top–down charitable	Simple top–down charitable
Requirements for recipients	None	Attend religious lessons and attend mosque regularly	None
Political advocacy practiced	None	None	Pro-MB but not in public

FBO faith-based organization, *GMT* Gameyet Magales El-Tayebeen, *GS* El-Gameya El-Shareya, *MB* Muslim Brotherhood, *MFA* Mohammed Farag Association

some assistance from members of the MB youth groups who were all volunteers. The following matrix explains the main characteristics of the three case study organizations as they stood before the revolution. (Table 14.1).

The Research Methodology

Before returning to explore the case studies in detail, we pause to look at the data-gathering methods of this study. The gathering of data was done mainly by using the two methods of participant observation and interviews. Participant observation was used to collect data from the daily activities of case study CSOs. These activities include the daily interaction (in formal meetings or in everyday dealings) between leaders of case study organizations and their field staff on the one hand and the donors, recipients and other community actors on the other. Participant observation is a research method where the researcher is involved in social interaction with the "informants" within the "milieu" of the latter (Taylor and Bogdan 1998). The method is based on the first-hand experience that researchers could get from living themselves within the context of their research objects. This increases the reliability of the research findings because it becomes difficult to deceive the researcher in contrast to what might be done with a total outsider (Burns 2000). Participant observation does not necessarily require the researcher to participate in the activities they are observing. Instead, researchers are allowed to choose their level of participation anywhere between a "complete participant" and a "complete observer" (Burgess 1984). In this research, the choice was for the latter.

In addition to observing meetings and activities, semi-structured and informal interviews were used to gather data from the organizations' staff, donors and recipients as well as other key informants. Interviews were used to get feedback about their understanding and interpretation of the activities that are observed in the field as well as to examine their attitudes towards studied concepts such as political trans-

14 Faith-Based Organizations and Civic Engagement in Egypt

Table 14.2 Number of interviews per case study

Case study category	GMT	GS	MFA
Board members	6	5	4
Donors	10	8	6
Recipients	12	16	10
Mosque imams	1	0	1
CSO staff	1	2	0
Other key informants	5	6	2
Total	35	37	23

GMT Gameyet Magales El-Tayebeen, *GS* El-Gameya El-Shareya, *MFA* Mohammed Farag Association, *CSO* civil society organization

formation and civic commitment. Interviews were utilized as an effective tool to gather data that might explain valuable observations recorded from the field by trying to understand the motives and justifications of these observations. Interviews that supplement a participant observation method ideally use open-ended questions and do not extend over long sessions (Stake 1995). This was convenient to the characteristic of the research area where most of the respondents were not available on a full-time basis. Table 14.2 summarizes the main categories of informant interviewed and the number of interviews conducted in all case studies:

Some of these informants were interviewed twice: before and after the revolution, when their corresponding case was revisited. In such cases, the questions were not repeated to compare changes in attitude. Instead, there were mostly new questions on what changes had happened and what new realities had emerged. The reason for revisiting the case studies after the revolution was to understand the process of transformation that they had been going through rather than to establish a comparison between what was before and what was after the revolution. Therefore, those who were interviewed twice had their second interviews transcript merged into the first one and they were both considered as one interview in Table 14.2.

It is worth noting that the third case study (the MB-affiliated mosque) was rather under-researched when compared to the other two because it was added to the author's initial PhD research only after the revolution. However, that should not cause any major methodological problem for this study because the MB, unlike other wings of the Islamic movements, has been covered extensively in the literature and there have been ample sources about the conduct of the MB before the revolution.[6] Finally, rapid comparative assessment, which is a technique developed from Robert Chambers' (1983) Rapid Rural Appraisal, was used to validate the applicability of the gathered data to the wider communities of the areas examined. This was only applied for the Greater *Wayly* area, which has a total of 83 mosques including the

---

[6] The author's PhD study does include a case study on a fourth secular organization. However, this will be ignored in this chapter due to methodological complications emerging from the fact that the revolution had erupted during the conduct of that case study and it would be difficult to include it within the limited space of this text.

three case study International Bathymetric Chart of the Southern Oceans (IBCSOs). The exercise was conducted with the help of the local MoE officer.

FBOs' Reaction to the Revolution

With the bleak picture of civil society and volunteering in Egypt before the revolution shown above, there were few expectations for the emergence of a nonviolent participatory movement demanding political and economic change in the country. However, all these assessments were dashed in the course of a few days with the outbreak of the 18-day uprising on 25 January 2011, when millions of people took to the streets to demand an end to the 30-year rule of President Mubarak (Lynch 2012). The events of the days that followed have shown an unprecedented boom in volunteering and civic commitment.[7] The author's own personal experience as a participant in the revolution was of how people who had never volunteered before were engaged in all sorts of voluntary activities to serve the public, including people they had never known before. This included helping the wounded protesters with medication, guarding the entry points of the main protest area in Tahrir square, supplying blankets, cleaning the square and removing the garbage. Medical and paramedical professionals staged an all-volunteer clinic that later developed into a field hospital, which kept growing in size and equipment as the revolution progressed in order to provide the casualties with basic treatment. Outside of the protest areas, volunteers quickly replaced the withdrawn police forces and organized their own neighborhood patrols and checkpoints to protect lives and properties. They replaced traffic police forces and took responsibility for organizing the traffic. They even cleaned streets and painted the pavement sides. After more than a week without effective government in many parts of Cairo, volunteers kept the city up and running in a manner that was surprising when taking into account that Egypt has lived most of its history as an extremely centralized state (Marfleet 2009). After the revolution, the trend continued as manifested by the formation of Revolutionary Youth Coalitions (through which young volunteers practiced civic commitment), the establishment of 35 new political parties and the founding of many NGOs and community initiatives and activist movements.

For CSOs, there was also a significant change. On the fourth day of the revolution, Mubarak's notorious police force was defeated by the huge waves of protestors and the army was called in to maintain security. When Mubarak departed a few weeks later, the State Security Department's grip on civil society was broken. On 5 March 2011, protesters stormed the SSD headquarters in Cairo to confirm the end of an era of restraint for Egyptian civil society. In the following paragraphs, I will tell the story of the reaction of each of the three case study organizations to the revolu-

---

[7] There is little distinction between the two concepts of volunteering and civic commitment in the Arabic literature, which leads to both of them usually being treated equally. Civic commitment is not always related to acting for change. Instead, it is described as active participation in civil society.

14 Faith-Based Organizations and Civic Engagement in Egypt

tion and how they dealt with the opportunities made available by it to use a wider pool of participants in their activities within an environment that was now cleared of most of the old SSD restraints on civil society. I will then conclude the chapter by analyzing the implications of these stories for our understanding of the role of FBOs in political transformation in volatile environments.

At the community-based GMT, things mostly remained the same. The charitable, distributive activities conducted through the mosque continued in the same pattern. There was no significant element of mobilization or any attempt to utilize the rising will to volunteer and act in the public domain. The focus of the organization on poverty reduction and its approach to issues related to development, political changes or transformation continued to be as neutral as they used to be. The imam of the mosque in which the FBO was based had certainly become more vocal in expressing his political views, but he chose not go any further without any attempts to organize local collective actions. Even his politicized sermons during Friday prayers did not call for any action in favor of any particular political agenda. Instead, they focused on aspects such as the threat of corruption to society, the importance of participation and voicing opinion and the ideal characters of the just leader. The mosque, however, extended its community service activities introducing a burial service for the dead and managing to install air conditioning in the mosque. "People are willing to act and play a positive role in their community. Not only had they volunteered to pay the costs of buying the funeral car and renovating the mosque, but some of them that we have never seen before have volunteered to recruit donors and help us with the logistics," the GMT mosque imam said.

Interviews with members of the community who received poverty assistance from GMT, held after the first postrevolution parliamentary elections in December 2011, showed higher rates of political participation by voting in elections. This was a very remarkable change as compared with the prerevolutionary scene when only 1 out of 20 interviewed recipients said that they had ever voted before. Most of the GMT mosque affiliates who declared their voting allegiances after the revolution said they had voted for the MB that won the majority of votes of the community's constituency. The reasons for their voting for the MB varied from "to give them a chance" to "see if they would be any better" or simply because "one can't find better options." While the community-based mosque organization managed to attract more participation in community-service-related fields centered around the mosque, it was neither interested in, nor able to play any role in the political success of the Islamic movement in elections despite the relative sympathy with the Islamists within the FBO. The motive for volunteering to work with the FBOs for its board members and staff remained the same; to earn the religious reward resulting from the service they provided to their community and the assistance they gave to the poor. Inflecting some sort of a political change, or contributing to that through the mosque, was hardly thought of at GMT despite the opportunities that would have made such thinking possible.

At the Salafi GS, the situation was different. However, we first need to look at the reaction of the Salafi movement at large to the revolution. The first sign of the Salafi's shift from their prerevolution, neutral position was a rally organized in the streets of Giza shortly after Mubarak's departure to demand the implementation of Islamic Sharia Law in Egypt. That event shocked many of those who were hoping for a better time under the secular and youthful spell of the revolution. This was soon followed by a series of arson attacks in which Salafi youth groups torched and vandalized the shrines of Sufi *Awleyaa* (saints), who, according to the Salafis, are pagan idols that contradict the pure practice of Islam (Newswires 22 March 2011, 2 April 2011, and 6 April 2011). These events, carried out by what was then an ambiguous, aggressive and violent group resulted in mounting fears and brought back memories of the violence committed by radical Islamist groups in the 1980s and 1990s. The scholars of the central council of *El-Daawa el Salafeya* (the main body of religious leaders behind the organized Salafi movement) seemed to have picked up the signals and decided to satisfy the demand for participation in politics of their followers by forming the El-Nour Party in June 2011 to integrate the unleashed Salafi elements into a legitimate process. Initially, opinion polls were not very favorable to the newly formed party (Al-Ahram 26/9/2011). This was soon proven wrong when the party managed to secure about 22.5 % of the seats in the general elections of 2011 and finished runners-up to the MB's political arm, the "Freedom and Justice Party" (FJP) that topped the polls. The result came as a shock since a party that was mainly composed of inexperienced and mostly unknown politicians managed to control about 35 % of the Islamist representation in parliament (Topol 2012).

Back at the GS, the FBO's activities had seen a significant rise. According to board members, "donations have significantly increased following the revolution." In addition, the General GS began to implement new activities that were not permitted during the times of Mubarak through its branches of mosques present all over the country. For instance, the GS began a project to help poor families in rural areas by providing them with livestock and farming equipment. In addition, the organization expanded on infrastructure projects; the most important of them was a project to install water pumps in villages that lacked access to fresh water. More than 600 of these were installed over a few-weeks span according to statistics obtained from the GS. However, from the detailed description of activities, it was possible to understand that this expansion mainly took place in rural areas. GS branches in urban areas, such as the GS case study organization in this research, continued working at their prerevolution capacities. This included the breadth and depth of volunteering with the organization.

Moreover, research has not detected any direct link between the studied GS branch and the El-Nour Party during the elections. The mosque advocacy activities such as Friday sermons and religious lessons did not involve any political content and continued to focus on the ultraconservative teachings of Salafi Islam as was the case before the revolution. Interviews with the GS beneficiaries showed that many of them have not understood the meaning of the term Salafi nor do they know much about the principles of Salafi doctrine or have ever declared belonging to it. Yet, they showed considerable levels of trust in the mosque and valued its central role in the community. For many of them, the mosque was the place to approach whenever they require help or faced hardships.

The El-Nour Party capitalized on these high levels of confidence in the Salafi's religious image. The party designed its campaign to revolve around religious rather than political discourse (unlike that of the MB). The Salafi campaign was centered on the party's plans to apply the "rule of God" without a clear outline of what that actually means. It depended on the endorsements of popular Salafi TV-preachers, such as Mohammed Hassan, Yaser Borhamy, and Abu Ias'haq El-Huwainy. The use of the images of bearded fathers taking their daughters to schools and refraining from putting the images of women candidates in their publicity posters all reflected the uncompromisingly conservative agenda of the campaign, which, unlike the MB's, did not try to appeal to the nonreligious crowd at all. Apparently, the Salafi's focus on their religious message was enough to achieve what they needed from politics.

The MB, with a richer political experience, did not follow suit. Instead of using the space becoming available after the revolution to establish a line of religious advocacy activities that could compete with the Salafis, the Brotherhood depended on infiltrating mosques and mosque-affiliated FBOs for later use as networking and mobilization bases, in the same ways that they successfully used with other organizations before the revolution, such as labor unions, syndicates, and student organizations (Tadros 2008). The MFA was one of those FBOs infiltrated by the MB before the revolution as explained above. After a few years of working in the mosque and its CSO, the imam gained the trust of the board members that allowed him to run the daily affairs of the mosque and the organization by himself. A dependency relationship with board members was created. They needed him to run the organization and manage its complicated paperwork. In return, he obtained a mandate to use the mosque as a platform to preach the political discourse of the MB. During three Friday sermons held over the period of the two rounds of general elections (18 November 2012, 25 November 2012, and 2 December 2012), the imam rather aggressively attacked the political opponents of the FJP, deconstructing their arguments and warning against voting for them.

In the last sermon, delivered just before the election, he began his speech by explaining that the mosque should not be used to campaign for any particular political group. Instead, he said it was the mosque's duty to enlighten people on "how to choose" the most useful candidate for themselves and their community. He then offered to perform that task himself and began eliminating one group after the other. He first denounced anybody with obvious ties to the former regime, dismissing them as "corrupt and proven incompetent." After that, he said that each person should be voting for those who represent their own "principles and ideals." He then gave a carefully chosen question: "Do you think that we should be a secular state and throw our marvellous religion away and get it out of our lives?" He answered promptly: "If the answer is yes, then vote for those who advocate that, but if you think that we are good Muslims and we should stick to this religion and to its rule, then you ought to vote for those who represent what you believe in." However, that was not all. There was still one group that needed to be eliminated, namely the Salafis. He accomplished this by saying that voters must also be careful when they choose who represented their religion by not voting for those "who are taking Islam too far" in a clear reference to the more conservative Salafi. Finally, he emphasized to the prayers that the best candidate would always be the "Muslim who is capable of serving Islam and is knowledgeable as well as experienced in doing that. Those are the ones who have stood firm in opposition for many years unlike the young and inexperienced ones who might have good intentions but are not up to various serious challenges we are facing in such a critical time."

Later on, after the prayer, the imam offered to take the data (names, ID numbers, and phone numbers) of the would-be voters. The ostensible purpose of the exercise was to text them the addresses of their assigned polling stations where they were supposed to vote. This process of data collection, that continued in the mosque for 3 days and was advertised after every prayer, was carried out by a number of young assistants who all belonged to the MB youth groups. According to some local informants, some of them had never been seen before in the mosque, which showed that they had been dispatched by the MB from somewhere else to help the imam. The practice of moving Brotherhood members to assist others in campaigning elsewhere seemed to be a common practice because the imam of MFA mosque himself was later asked to move to help at another mosque in the poor northern Cairo suburb of Bahtim where elections took place on a different day. The elections took place in three stages because there were not enough judges to cover the whole country on 1 day after new rules enforced a system of one judge per polling station. In this case study, the FBO's role was simply to act as a platform where many people could be gathered and where they were forced to sit still to listen to the sermon for 1 h and could not walk away or grab the remote control to change the channel. Needless to add that this same scene was repeated in many similar institutions in other places. According to a local MoE officer interviewed in October 2011, the MB managed to control the boards of at least three big mosques and their affiliated organizations during the 8 months that immediately followed the revolution and they were "on course to add more."

On the side of the recipients, there was no evidence to show that they were particularly targeted by MB campaigning. Patterns observed at GMT and the GS continued with the MFA recipients interviewed who had shown a diverse set of political opinions. Some voted for the Salafis and others for the Brotherhood with only one voting for one of the former members of the NDP (The National Democratic Party, Mubarak's former ruling party). Reasons for their voting decisions varied, but most of them (all were women) mentioned receiving advice from their sons or brothers. They all denied having been contacted by the association or any of its members, or even by any of the individual MB campaigners at their homes, in order to vote for the Brotherhood.

Throughout the election campaign, general observations outside the MFA mosque reflected similar conclusions. Organized, politically oriented mobilization and not social service provision was evident in the field throughout the election campaign. During the polling days, I encountered the phenomena of buses provided by the MB used to transfer the members of certain syndicates or neighborhoods to polling stations in several places in Cairo. MB youth also worked on providing help for voters who were looking to find their registration information or to know their polling station data by installing stalls equipped with laptops that carried electronic copies of the electoral registers. This information provision service was particularly useful in elections where most people were voting for the first time ever and did not know much, neither about the voting process nor about the candidates. In the media, and unlike the Salafis who focused their message on those who would sympathize with their religious message, the Brotherhood extended its appeal to voters of all types, including non-Muslims, and tried, through putting forward many of its moderate members such as Mohammed El-Beltagy and Rafiq Habib, to reflect a moderate image. The MB simply dominated the political scene in ways that were not matched by any other group giving the feeling that they were almost the only major contender competing in them.

In the above three stories, we have seen three models of FBOs reacting to the events that suddenly allowed civil society activity to become more open than ever to participation and volunteering. In the first example, a community-based FBO had used its social capital and credibility within the local community, which was based on its religious nature as well as on the reputation of its respected leaders, to enhance participation for providing better community service. In the second example, the Salafi movement invested its association with very conservative religious values meant to appeal to a wide audience in mobilizing support for its political agenda. The community service and poverty reduction efforts effected by the Salafi FBO have expanded horizontally to enhance the centrality of the Salafi mosques and consequently the Salafi religious values to many followers. Finally, the experienced political group MB managed to use its affiliated FBOs as a recruitment base for volunteers who later used the FBOs as advocacy centers for the discourse of the MB. The following paragraphs will take these findings forward by analytically linking them to the conceptual debates on the role of FBOs in political transformation in Egypt.

FBOs: Converting Religious Capital to Political Transformation?

The behavior of the three case study organizations after the revolution showed four interesting, comparable fields that need to be analyzed in more detail. Firstly, the practice of using religion to strengthen their position within their communities; secondly, the means they had at their disposal to exploit that position to affect the process of political transformation in Egypt; thirdly, the role played by poverty reduction and community service activities in all of this; and finally, the way in which the growing will of the people to volunteer, especially the youth, was used to horizontally and vertically expand the activities of FBOs.

First, the dual functions of religion, highlighted by Weber's analogy between priest and prophet, was apparent. At all case study organizations, there was a prophet who promised a divine reward to those who volunteered to participate in their activities. This acted as a motive that was lacking in nonreligious organizations within the same community. This might explain that while there were 83 mosques in the district where the research took place, almost all of which were volunteer-powered active providers of social service, there were only a handful of struggling secular organizations that could be recognized within the same community. Those who worked in the three case study organizations did so for God; not for pity for the poor or for the public benefit of their communities. The Salafis were more focused on the religious motive with work conducted to enhance the relation between the community and the mosque. The MB had been trying to push forward the State of God through their ascent to political power; and the community-based mosque associates were simply after a personal divine reward or blessing. Despite the different ways in which it occurred, all organizations were motivated by religion. In addition to motive, religion provided these organizations with legitimacy. It made answering their appeals for help, funding and support better heard and responded to by their communities. The most significant and intensive use of religion was, not surprisingly, the one practiced at the Salafi case study organization when the recipients were forced to attend religious lessons at the mosque they received poverty assistance from. The Salafi goal was to promote a Salafi conservative way of life and religious conduct to their followers. This prepared their minds to accept the Salafi political propaganda as soon as it began to appear. The MB applied religion specifically as a packaging or "image" that did not necessarily relate to any particular way of life or personal conduct. However, it only made MB look good or decent or moral because of its religious cover or connections. It was obvious that the MB would gain the most because they managed to use religion to carry their message beyond the borders not only of the religious community but even of the communities that directly benefited from their activities.

The second area of comparison is the role these FBOs played in political transformation. Here we find that there were two fields of influence that these organizations had. The first was their influence on the direct recipients of the organizations and the second was with the general public outside the circle of the organizations. All three case study FBOs failed to exploit their recipient's potential to be agents for political transformation despite the freedoms they gained after the revolution. This failure can be explained by Putman's theory on the role of civil society in political transformation, which was outlined earlier in this text. If Putman was to analyze the data gathered from this research, he would have attributed the failure of case study FBOs to effect political transformation on the type of political culture delivered to the recipients, which resulted from the patronizing, top–down approaches used for the organizations' poverty reduction activities. This failed in breaking the strong ties that continued to connect the recipients to the primary institutions they belonged to. Case study organizations did make recipients dependent on the associations for survival, but they were not integrated into these institutions as parts of "groups" or "associations" that might have been joined by the common goal of bringing about change for the collective interest. Case study organizations did not provide a model of practice that could have shown their local communities the paths to either political or social transformation.

At the level of the general public, the Salafi and the MB-affiliated FBO succeeded in becoming instrumental for political transformation, albeit in different ways. In the case of MFA, the organization provided the arena for campaigning for change, which is a function similar to what De Tocqueville had suggested for civil society. The Salafis did something similar by providing a model for a caring and compassionate institution that could care not only for the wellbeing of the poor but also for the maintenance of the values and principles of religion as seen from a Salafi point of view. The Salafis thus enjoyed political success in elections, but it was still inferior to that of the MB because the Salafi's message was focused on a selected audience. On the other hand, the lack of a political agenda had not resulted, at least for now, in any significant influence for GMT in the political transformation arena, unless the politicized sermons provided by the mosque's imam will end up enhancing certain values among his audience. That would still need time before it can be measured as voting patterns on elections days alone would not be enough to indicate any such change in values.

The third area of comparison is the role played by the poverty reduction activities of these organizations. The key finding here is that none of the case study organizations used the assistance provided to the poor to affect their political loyalties. Interviews with recipients across the three organizations have shown how their voting patterns and their level of participation in the political activities after the revolution remained independent from the agendas of case study mosques. For example, many recipients at MFA have voted for the Salafi party in the parliamentary elections and a number of recipients of the Salafi organization have voted for secular parties. Contrary to the beliefs widely expressed in the literature on Islamic movements in Egypt, the social service activities provided by Islamic FBOs are not among the reasons for the political success of the Islamists in Egyptian politics. Instead, it seems that Islamists managed to appeal to those who voted for them by providing a discourse, an ideology, a political program and maybe just a strong and well-organized alternative that attracted enough popularity to win elections at that time.

The final area of comparison between the three case study organizations is related to their use of volunteers. Despite an apparent increase in the will to volunteer and take part in civic activity, case study FBOs mostly failed to directly utilize this in expanding their activities except in the case of MFA. At GMT and the Salafi GS, the focus was on people's will to contribute more to their economy. This included not only younger generations that took part in the revolution itself and its related activities. It also included other people, who might have not been with the youth on the streets, but were motivated to contribute by the patriotic euphoria that swept through the country as a result of the revolution. This was mainly manifested by the increase in donations and in-kind contributions to both GMT and the GS. However, the two organizations still could not convince any of those who did not volunteer with them in the past to personally take part in their activities after the revolution. On the other hand, the MB clearly had more success in recruiting more volunteers. The new faces that showed up in the MFA mosque to help the imam during the election campaign were recruited based on the motive to contribute to the political agenda and ideology of the MB. The role of politics here is crucial. During the revolution, young people increased their levels of volunteering and civic commitment. The context of this was political as the goal of the revolution was to bring about political change. When the main wave of the revolution ended, the will to continue to volunteer or take part in civic commitment continued to be political. The MB, as the only well-organized political party, managed through its sophisticated organization to find those who believed in its ideology and were willing to act for its sake and provided them with the space and guidance (the role played by the mosque imam leading the young volunteers) to volunteer. That does not mean that others who volunteered during, and right after, the revolution would not have been willing to continue volunteering through civil society organizations or other FBOs. However, so far, civil society, which has not been as well organized politically, has failed to capture this potential and to utilize it. Table 14.3 summarizes the findings across the case studies.

Summary and Conclusions

The Egyptian revolution in January 2011 resulted in the end of an era of restraint for Egyptian civil society. This report discussed the role played by some of the Egyptian FBOs in the political transformation during the postrevolution era. The data was collected via research fieldwork conducted to include case studies of three mosque-based FBOs operating in the field of poverty reduction in Cairo.

One organization was a community-based mosque without affiliation to any political groups or religious orders. The organization, which adopted a charitable top–down approach to poverty reduction and lacking any political dimensions before the revolution, exhibited no major changes in its pattern of activities after January 2011. The second organization was attached to a mosque that belongs to a large, ultraconservative Salafi network. The FBO had been using its poverty reduction activities to enhance the ties between the mosque on the one hand and the recipients and community on the other. Post revolution, the activities have seen a rise in quantity with the implementation of new development activities. The parent Salafi movement has formed a political party (El-Nour Party) that achieved remarkable success in elections. There was no direct link between the studied GS branch and El-Nour Party during the elections. However, it is believed that the poverty reduction work practiced by the FBO has helped the party in the election by earning people's confidence in the values and the effectiveness of the Salafi mosque as an institution and, consequently, in the movement it represented.

The third organization was affiliated to the relatively moderate MB organization. In the postrevolution period, the organization was utilized to recruit volunteers and support for the MB. The mosque's imam, aided by material and manpower support from the MB, participated actively in the election campaign to preach the political discourse of the MB. Apart from this, the mosque's poverty reduction ac-

14 Faith-Based Organizations and Civic Engagement in Egypt 301

Table 14.3 Case-study organizations after the revolution

Case study FBO area	Community-based GMT	Salafi GS	MB-affiliated MFA
Human resources	All volunteers	All volunteers	All volunteers
Change in participation or volunteering	More donations and participation in the mosque activities	Quantitative expansion of activities at the branch and qualitative expansion in rural areas through other GS branches	More freedom to deploy assistance from other MB members when needed
Attracting new volunteers and more participation after revolution	Revolution sympathizers encouraged to make more donations and in-kind contributions	–	Politically motivated youth believing in MB ideology volunteering to serve political ideology
Motive to volunteer	No change	–	–
The role of religion in the organization	Motivation and legitimacy	Motivation, legitimacy and agenda	Motivation, legitimacy and image
Poverty reduction activities	No change	–	–
Requirements for recipients	No change	–0	–
Political targeting of recipients	None	None	None
Political influence on the public	Advocacy for certain values such as participation and accountability	Enhance the positive image of a religious and effective institution	Direct mobilization and advocacy through Friday sermon and other political activities practiced within the mosque
Impact on political transformation	No directly recognized impact so far	Indirect help to the Salafi political campaign	Direct help to the MB campaign

FBO faith-based organization, *GMT* Gameyet Magales El-Tayebeen, *GS* El-Gameya El-Shareya, *MB* Muslim Brotherhood, *MFA* Mohammed Farag Association

tivities were quite similar in their description to that of non-MB community-based mosques.

Religion provided these organizations with motivation and legitimacy. The Salafis' goal was to promote their conservative way of life and religious conduct to their followers. The MB applied religion specifically as an "image" that does not necessarily relate to any particular way of life or personal conduct, but one that is capable of acquiring wide public approval and acceptance.

The three FBOs potentially or actually contributed to political transformation in various levels and different ways. The GS facilitated the public's sympathy for the Salafi religious agenda. MFA provided a venue for political activity for the MB and the GMT could have influenced the values of the community by emphasizing concepts such as justice, accountability and participation. The belief that Islamists win political support as a result of the poorer classes supporting them in return for social protection and poverty assistance has not been evident in this research.

Apart from the MB-affiliated CSO, case study organizations did not benefit from the rise in volunteering and civic commitment that was witnessed after the revolution. This rise was mainly related to the achievement of a political goal. Only the MB had the organizational capacity to divert that energy into active participation. Other organizations had to opt for an increase in donations and in-kind contributions by people sympathetic to the revolution.

There remains much to be learnt about the impact of voluntary FBOs on political transformation in Egypt. The situation in Egypt remains volatile and turbulent. The latest wave of major street protests in the country prompted the Egyptian military to overthrow the MB government amid significantly declining popularity for the Islamist causes. As this chapter is finalized, the country remains in turbulence and the future remains anything but clear. However, this research has proven that religion will remain a key element in the understanding of Egyptian civil society. It motivates participants, legitimizes organizations and sets the agendas for those who are willing to pursue them. And that will probably continue to be the case for a very long time to come.

References

Bano, M., & Padmaga, N. (2007). *Faith-based organizations in South Asia: Historical evolution, current status and nature of interaction with the state*. Religion and Development Research Programme, WP 12. Birmingham.

Barsoum, G., Ramadan, M., et al. (2010). *Survey of young people in Egypt*. Cairo: Population Council.

Becker, S. (1997). *Responding to poverty: The politics of cash and care*. London: Longman.

Burgess, R. (1991). *In the field: An introduction to field research*. London: Routledge.

Burns, R. (2000). *Introduction to research methods*. London: Sage.

Chambers, R. (1983). *Rural development—Putting the last first*. New York: Wiley.

Clarke, G., & Jennings, M. (2008). Faith-based organizations and international development: An overview. In G. Clarke (Ed.), *Faith-based organizations and international development* (pp. 17–45). New York: Palgrave Macmillan.

Ebaugh, H., Pipes, P., Saltzman Chafetz, J., & Daniels, M. (2003). Where's the religion? Distinguishing faith-based from secular social service agencies. *Journal for the Scientific Study of Religion, 42*(3), 411–426.

Egyptian High Commission for Elections. (2011). Website. www.elections2011.eg.

Hart, J., & Dekker, P. (2005). Churches as voluntary associations: Their contribution to democracy as a public voice and source of social and political involvement. In S. Roßteutscher (Ed.), *Democracy and the role of associations: Political, organizational and social contexts* (pp. 168–196). London: Routledge.

Howell, J., & Pearce, J. (2001). *Civil society and development: A critical exploration*. London: Lynne Rienner Publications.

Huntington, S. (1993). *The third wave: Democratization in the late twentieth century*. Oklahoma City: University of Oklahoma Press.

Langohr, V. (2005). Too much civil society, too little politics? Egypt and other liberalizing Arab regimes. In M. P. Posusney & M. P. Angrist (Eds.), *Authoritarianism in the Middle East: Regimes and resistance*. Boulder: Lynne Rienner Publishers.

Lynch, M. (2012). *The Arab uprising: The unfinished revolutions of the new Middle East*. New York: Public Affairs.

Marfleet, P. (2009). State and society. In R. El-Mahdy & P. Marfleet (Eds.), *Egypt: The moment of change*. London: Zed Books.

Meijer, R. (2009). *Global Salafism*. London: Hurst.

Pargeter, A. (2010). *The Muslim Brotherhood: The burden of tradition*. London: Saqi.

Putman, R. (1993). *Making democracy work: Civic tradition in Northern Italy*. Princeton: Princeton University Press.

Selvik, K., & Stenslie, S. (2011). *Stability and change in the Middle East*. London: I. B. Tauris.

Smith, S. R., & Sosin, M. R. (2001). The varieties of faith-related agencies. *Public Administration Review, 61*(6), 651–670.

Stake, R. (1995). *The art of case study research*. Thousand Oaks: SAGE.

Sulivan, D., & Abed-Kotob, S. (1999). *Islam in contemporary Egypt: Civil society vs. the state*. Boulder: Lynne Rienner Publishers.

Tadros, M. (2008). *The Muslim Brotherhood and Islamists politics in the Middle East*. London: Routledge.

Taylor, S., & Bogdan, R. (1998). *Introduction to qualitative research methods: A guidebook and resource*. New York: Willey.

Teti, A., & Gervasio, G. (2012). After Mubarak, before transition: The challenges for Egypt's democratic opposition. *Interface, 4*(1), 102–112.

Topol, S. (2012). Egypt's Salafi surge. *Foreign Policy, 4*(January).

UNDP. (2010). *The 2008 Egypt Human Development Report*. Cairo: UNDP.

Warren, M. (2001). *Democracy and associations*. Princeton: Princeton University Press.

Zahid, M. (2010). *Muslim Brotherhood and Egypt's succession crisis: The politics of liberalization and reform in the Middle East*. London: I. B. Tauris.

Chapter 15
'Going Back to Our Values'

Restoring Symbolic Hegemony Through Promoting 'Volunteering'

Itamar Y. Shachar

Introduction

"To give, your soul and your heart / To give, to give when you love"—when the first words of this famous Israeli song begin to play, about a dozen teenagers start to walk slowly towards the centre of the municipal square, while adding some dance movements to their steps. As the slow rhythm of the Israeli song is replaced by James Brown's cheerful song "I Feel Good", another group of teenagers leave the crowd to join in the dance. Gradually, the vast majority of the audience of some 500 teenagers moves to the centre of the square with dance steps. Some of the teenagers are dressed in everyday shirts and jackets, while the others are dressed with the blue uniforms of different youth movements: Many of the blue shirts have the white lace and logo of the Zionist-socialist movement *HaShomer HaTza'ir*,[1] and many others have buttons and white stripes along with the logo of the right-wing movement "The National Youth". Few of the blue shirts have the red lace and logo of "The Working and Studying Youth", which is affiliated with the *Histadrut*—the general federation of workers in Israel.

The music changes again, and when the Red Hot Chili Peppers start singing "give it away, give it away, give it away now", the 500 teenagers at once remove their top clothing. Blue uniforms and colourful jackets, white laces, red laces and white strips all intermingle in the air and fall to the bare brick floor of the municipal square, while the teenagers cheer and clap their hands. They continue to dance, but now all of them are wearing the same white T-shirt. On the front of the shirt blue and red lines create a heart, and underneath it there is a large English slogan in capital

---

[1] Words and phrases in Hebrew were put in italic letters.

A version of this chapter was previously published in Voluntas (Published online first in 2013), DOI 10.1007/s11266–013-9398-x

---

I. Y. Shachar (✉)
Department of Sociology, Ghent University, Ghent, Belgium
e-mail: itamar.shachar@ugent.be

L. Hustinx et al. (eds.), *Religion and Volunteering*, Nonprofit and Civil Society Studies,   305
DOI 10.1007/978-3-319-04585-6_15, © Springer International Publishing Switzerland 2015

letters: "DOING GOOD". On the back of the shirt a smaller Hebrew text is printed: "Give yourself as a gift—Good Deeds Day 2011".[2]

While dancing, the faces of the teenagers are mainly directed towards the wide stairway that leads from the square to the municipality building. On the top of the stairway, a few TV cameramen are documenting the event. Next to them stand a few dozen guests and organizers, many of them wearing the same white T-shirt as the youth underneath their formal jackets. In the middle of the stairway, about a metre above the dancing teenagers, a man with a microphone in his hand is dancing while occasionally delegating instructions to the youth. Just next to him I recognize Shari Arison, an Israeli-American billionaire and one of Israel's richest people, who inherited from her father, Ted, his powerful investment firm.[3] The main assets of the firm are privatized public companies, such as Israel's largest bank, 'the workers bank' (*Bank HaPoalim*), and a real-estate company, both formerly owned by the *Histadrut*. The Ted Arison family foundation, of which Shari and her children constitute the board, is the sole sponsor of "Good Spirit" (*Ruach Tova*)[4], the non-governmental organization (NGO) that organizes the Good Deeds Day every year.

Wearing the "DOING GOOD" shirt and black tights, Arison is smiling broadly at the teenagers while performing the dance movements together with them. At a certain point she steps down the stairs to dance among the teenagers who respond with loud cheers and applause. A bit later, the music changes to some kind of oriental melody and the teenagers and Shari are moving their bellies in tune with the rhythm and circle their open arms. After the music returns again to the faster rhythm of American pop, Shari is accompanied by the dance facilitator up the stairs and continues to dance from there. Some teenagers are also climbing up a few stairs in the course of the dance, and the facilitator responds by saying into the microphone: "Don't go up the stairs—stay down". Shari continues her dance on the stairs, above the teenagers, who keep dancing on the square until the music is over. Then Shari takes the microphone to deliver a short speech, full of compliments to the teenagers who cheer and applause with excitement in response. She ends the speech by saying: "and thank you for choosing the good!" before disappearing into the municipal building to the loud applause of the teenagers.

---

[2] Hebrew excerpts from the observations, the interviews and quotes collected from the mass media were translated by the author.

[3] On March 2011, Shari Arison was ranked 200 in the Forbes list of the world's billionaires and as the third richest person in Israel. See: http://www.forbes.com/profile/shari-arison.

[4] The Hebrew word *Ruach* can be translated as 'spirit'—a concept which can be associated with a transcendent entity as well as with the human soul. The combination of these two meanings is usually the most relevant in the contexts in which the name *Ruach Tova* is mentioned, and therefore I chose to translate it as "Good Spirit". However, *Ruach* can also be translated as 'wind': A worker in a centre for children at risk, in which a new garden was planted as part of a volunteering project organized by Good Spirit, has said that Good Spirit is indeed like a 'good wind' that blew and completely changed the place.

15 'Going Back to Our Values'

This type of ritualistic performance was presented as a 'flash mob'[5] by its organizers: the youth department of the municipality in a large city adjacent to Tel-Aviv. Participation in it was restricted to teenagers who volunteered in youth movements, community centres or NGOs. This event was one of the peaks of the fifth annual "Good Deeds Day" that was held on 5 April 2011. The Good Deeds Day was initiated in 2007, when 7,000 Israelis took part in one-day 'volunteering' activities across the country. These episodic, one-day activities included renovation, decoration and gardening at welfare institutions, community centres and houses of needy people, cleaning and recycling activities, as well as a wide range of educational activities and community gatherings. Each year, an increasing number of private firms, municipalities, military units and other institutions have participated in the project, but also a growing numbers of individual volunteers, attracted by the extensive campaign that promoted the day. In 2011, the number of volunteers reached 140,000.[6]

The expansion of the Good Deeds Day seems to reflect an ongoing growth in volunteering rates among Israelis. Surveys indicate that 13 % of the Israeli population volunteered in formal organizations (mostly NGOs) in 1997, while 19 and 25 % did so in 2006 and 2008 respectively (Shye et al. 1999; Haggai Katz et al. 2007; Haski-Leventhal et al. 2011).[7] Since the early 1990s, there has also been a tremendous growth in the number and public influence of NGOs (Gidron et al. 2002; Ben-Eliezer 2004)—the institutional framework within which 'volunteering' is mainly practiced. This phenomenon is not unique to the Israeli context but seems to be part of what a group of influential social scientists described as a "global associational revolution", that is, "a massive upsurge of organized private, voluntary activity in literally every corner of the world" (Salamon et al. 1999, p. 4). Their comparative study of 22 countries shows that no less than 28 % of the overall population in these countries volunteered in non-profit organizations in 1995 (Salamon et al. 1999).

The narrative of the growth and expansion of 'volunteering', as shared by academics and NGO workers, relies on a particular perception of 'volunteering' as an autonomous and mainly altruistic practice that commonly takes place in the institutional realm of the non-profit or 'third' sector. This perception seems to be inspired by an ideal of 'civil society' that conforms to the liberal tendency "to en-

---

[5] Molnar views 'flash mob' as "a new form of sociability" (2009), which evolved around collective artistic expressions in urban public spaces and organized through new digital media tools. She claims that only after the initial development of the 'flash mob' it was appropriated for purposes of political activism, and later on also for commercial use.

[6] The number of participants who took part in the Good Deeds Day a year later, on 20 March 2012, had risen further to approximately 250,000 volunteers, as estimated by Good Spirit. This number adds up to roughly 3.18 % of the Israeli population when the day was held.

[7] According to these surveys, roughly 15–20 % of the volunteering took place in public agencies (e.g. welfare institutions or the security forces), and all the rest volunteered in NGOs (mainly in the areas of welfare and health). The rates of informal volunteering (i.e. which is not conducted through a formal organization) demonstrate a similar, although more moderate, tendency of growth: 19 % in 1997, 26 % in 2006 and 23 % in 2008.

clave certain matters in specialized discursive arenas" (Fraser 1990, p. 73): A public realm which is separated from other social spheres, such as the economic market, the state-related political system and the family.[8] Scholarly attempts to challenge the dominant analytical and empirical distinction of 'volunteering' from its political and economic dimensions are still exceptional (Kaplan-Daniels 1988; Simonet 2005; Taylor 2005; Eliasoph 2011). The Israeli third sector of today is largely an institutional realization of the liberal, Anglo-Saxon idea of 'civil society', and serves as a main arena in which the autonomous variations of 'volunteering' can proliferate and become dominant. However, following Chambre's (1989) account of how the definition of 'volunteering' was maneuvered in American surveys according to public policy needs, we should also be careful in concluding that 'volunteering' is a broadening social practice in Israeli society based on the survey figures presented above. Nevertheless, we can indicate that 'volunteering' was constituted relatively recently as an important object of knowledge production and political attention: The above-mentioned surveys have been conducted only since 1997, by the Israeli Center for Third Sector Research established that year;[9] and the Israeli Central Bureau of Statistics began to include questions regarding 'volunteering' in its surveys only since 2002 (Abu-Ahmed 2010). This growing academic and political interest in 'volunteering' has appeared simultaneously with the increasing public visibility of this notion, created through public campaigns and enterprises such as the Good Deeds Day.

This chapter therefore proposes that the recent emergence of 'volunteering' as a publicly significant notion should become a central object of scholarly analysis. Explaining this emergence could benefit from conceptualizing 'volunteering' as a relational field of discourse and institutionalized practice (cf. Bourdieu 1983). The boundaries and content of such a field are constructed and shaped by different social actors, and especially by those who occupy prominent and authoritative positions in the field. Tracing these construction processes and the identities of the actors involved is crucial for understanding how a particular construction of the field of 'volunteering' is being both expanded and legitimized, and why this process occurs in this particular historical moment. The current chapter cannot and is not intended to fully accomplish this scholarly challenge, but endeavours to demonstrate that such an approach may yield fruitful theoretical and empirical results. Through examining the case of Good Spirit, the chapter suggests that the recent emergence of 'volunteering' in Israel signifies a successful attempt to universalize a particular construction of this notion, which corresponds to the liberal ideal of 'civil society' as an autonomous realm of voluntary participation. This notion of 'volunteering' is promoted by specific groups and grew out of concrete interests that emerged in

---

[8] This sense of 'civil society' was articulated, for example, by Anheier et al. (2001). I do not intend to claim that this definition is more accurate than alternative conceptualizations of 'civil society' (e.g. Gramsci 1971), but only that it underpins the current institutional formation of the formal third sector in many countries, among them the US and Israel.

[9] http://cmsprod.bgu.ac.il/Eng/Centers/ictr/Aboutus/. Accessed 10 February 2012.

particular socio-historical contexts, all of which should be traced and described by scholars of 'volunteering'.

Setting and Methodology

The theoretical focus on the attempts to promote and expand 'volunteering' leads us to pay close attention to the work of the actors who are mainly engaged in this promotional work. Among those actors are umbrella and intermediary NGOs, many of them facilitating the routine work of other NGOs and supporting their efforts to recruit volunteers. They thus have a substantial influence over the construction, implementation and ongoing cultivation of 'volunteering'. However, such organizations have rarely been studied by scholars of 'volunteering' as they tend to focus on the NGOs in which the voluntary activity itself takes place.[10] In Israel, there are several nationwide NGOs that dedicate themselves to promoting voluntary participation of citizens and supporting volunteer-based organizations. I decided to centre my empirical study around a nationwide intermediary organization—Good Spirit—where I conducted extensive ethnographic fieldwork.

I chose Good Spirit for several reasons: Its annual Good Deeds Day makes it highly visible to the Israeli public, its relatively large staff makes it a fertile site for ethnographic research and the ongoing financial support of the Arison Group ensures that the organization is likely to continue to play a central role in the Israeli field of 'volunteering' also in the future. As my ethnographic study was primarily focused on Good Spirit staff and board members, I will mainly describe the ways in which they have constructed and shaped 'volunteering'. These ways, however, were often developed through the interactions of the staff with employees of other NGO, volunteers, state representatives and politicians, business people, and workers in the media and advertising sector. Therefore, Good Spirit's cultivation of 'volunteering' simultaneously relies upon and shapes the wider public understanding of this notion. Furthermore, I hope that although this chapter relies on a particular case study, some of the analytical standpoints proposed here will provoke future empirical explorations and theoretical debates, which will hopefully make a "contribution to 'reconstructing' theory" (Burawoy 1998, p. 16).

Good Spirit, formally registered as an NGO in 1996, was operated solely by volunteers during its first years and was only episodically active. In 2003, the Ted Arison Family Foundation began to provide financial support to the organization, and the first employee, Oded,[11] was hired as Good Spirit executive director and held

---

[10] An exception is a pilot exploratory study on umbrella NGOs conducted in Israel, which also indicates the deficiency of the literature on this type of organizations (Katz et al. 2009).

[11] The names of Good Spirit staff members have been changed. Three prominent staff and board members have agreed to be mentioned by their real names, and although I chose to use pseudonyms, I indicated their positions in the organization. In the case of the less prominent staff members, I also changed in several instances their position, gender or other characteristics in order to avoid identification. Shari Arison is indicated by her full name as she was not one of my infor-

310   I. Y. Shachar

this position until May 2013. In 2008, Good Spirit became an official part of the "Arison Group" and its budget is increased annually by the Arison foundation, enabling the organization to recruit more employees and increase its scope of activity. Arison Group representatives dominate the Good Spirit board, which also includes Hadas, the founder of the organization, and Ilan, the current chairperson—a businessman and a former member of parliament for the Israeli labour party. The Good Spirit offices are located in the same luxurious office complex that hosts the Arison Group headquarters, in the midst of Israel's economic and cultural centre, Tel-Aviv.

At the time of my fieldwork, the Good Spirit team included 10 senior workers, six of them women, who mainly resided in the upper-middle class neighbourhoods of Tel-Aviv or in the affluent suburbs of the city. The senior staff coordinated the Good Deeds Day and other projects, and supervised a changing number of temporary workers recruited to implement these projects. One worker supervised a team of about seven youth servers,[12] who were mainly responsible for operating the Good Spirit call centre through which individuals seek volunteering placements. Each youth server is responsible for a specific geographic region, in which s/he maintains regular contacts with a wide range of volunteer-based organizations. When a potential volunteer contacts Good Spirit, s/he is directed to the youth server responsible for the geographical region where s/he resides. They then refer the volunteer to potential placements according to her/his interests and availability, and accompany her/him during the placement process. A similar, although more complex, process takes place when senior workers coordinate volunteering projects for groups such as corporations, military and police units, student groups and families. This "Volunteer Management System" enables Good Spirit to fulfil its aims: connecting "volunteers and organizations that need volunteers" and "developing volunteerism in Israel".[13]

The fieldwork was conducted between the end of July 2010 and the end of December that year. During this period, I conducted participant observation that included assisting in Good Spirit routine work of placing volunteers; being present in meetings, training sessions and the rest of the office activities; and accompanying staff members to meetings and activities outside the office. Complementary participant observation was conducted between 28 March and 7 April 2011, during the last week of intensive preparations towards the Good Deeds Day, the day itself and its immediate aftermath.[14] Taking a regular part in these professional activities also granted me various opportunities for informal interactions with the staff members

---

mants, and this article relates to her only as a public figure, based on her public appearances and on media items.

[12] In Israel, the law gives the army the authority to conscript all men and women at the age of 18. The 'national service' is a non-obligatory route available to high-school graduates, most of whom are women, who were exempted from military service due to religious, medical or personal reasons. These youth servers serve roughly 40 hours per week for 1 or 2 years in a welfare institution, state agency or NGO and receive a monthly allowance.

[13] http://www.ruachtova.org/about. Accessed 26 February 2012.

[14] Regev Nathansohn and Noa Shauer agreed to participate as volunteers in the Good Deeds Day and shared their ethnographic insights with me. I am grateful for their help as it gave me some idea of how the day was experienced by the volunteers themselves, while I observed it mainly from the perspective of Good Spirit staff.

15 'Going Back to Our Values'

that led to a deeper acquaintance. During the fieldwork period I conducted 20 in-depth interviews, which lasted on average 1.5 hours, with most of the Good Spirit staff and board members. In addition, I collected various documents, publications, media items and quantitative data from the organization's archives and database. Several complementary in-depth interviews, supported by a few observations, were conducted with volunteers who were placed by Good Spirit in other NGOs, and with a few other professionals in the Israeli field of 'volunteering'.

The Social Origins of the Israeli Field of 'volunteering'

Salamon argued that the global "increase in organized voluntary action" is a result of a multifaceted crisis in "the hold of the state": the crisis of the western welfare state, the economic crisis in developing countries that led to "an aid strategy that stressed the engagement of grassroots energies and enthusiasms", the global environmental crisis and the crisis "of socialism" (Salamon 1994, pp. 115–117). In a later publication, Salamon and his associates pointed out that this transformation in the modalities of political participation has its roots in the corrective attempts of political leaders to balance neoliberal economic policies with "broader social protections" (Salamon et al. 1999, p. 5). A similar transformation occurred in Israel during the 1990s and the 2000s, when the public legitimacy of the voluntary-based non-governmental sector grew tremendously at the expense of the traditional, state-affiliated, political structures, such as the political parties and the trade unions (Filc 2006, pp. 158–159). While this process can be explained also in its Israeli variation as a decrease in state power (Ben-Eliezer 2004), it seems useful to also consider it as an intrinsic component of the transition from a Keynesian/Fordist political-economic model to a neoliberal/post-Fordist model (Filc 2006).

Consolidating a Hegemonic Civil Order

Israel's economy has been managed according to Keynesian/Fordist principles since the establishment of the state in 1948; economic activity was mainly generated through public capital, regulated by state agencies and accompanied by strong welfare mechanisms (Shafir and Peled 2002). This political-economic model was mainly promoted by one particular segment of Jewish-Israeli society: the *Ashkenazi* Jews who immigrated to Palestine during the first decades of the twentieth century from Eastern and Central Europe.[15] In those decades, under British colonial rule,

---

[15] The term *Ashkenazim* (plural; singular and adj.: *Ashkenazi*) relates to Jews of European origin (including their Anglo-Saxon descendants). In Israel, the term is widespread in academic and non-academic discourses, and is usually opposed to the category of *Mizrahim*—Jews of Asian and African origin. The influential Israeli sociologist Baruch Kimmerling (2001) suggested terming this group *Ahusalim*, the Hebrew initials for Ashkenazi-Secular-Socialist-National, as an attempt

the Ashkenazi political elites established a national labour movement that gained immense support among the Ahskenazi migrants to Palestine. This movement was composed of a dominant labour party, a few affiliated smaller parties and a single and powerful union (the *Histadrut*); it developed ethnically-segregated trade union activity, welfare services and public economic enterprises, as a means to establish in Palestine a Jewish national entity that would be separated from the Arab-Palestinian indigenous community. Striving to realize the Zionist ideology and to transform the Jewish people from a diasporic religious community into a nation in the modern sense, the labour movement fostered a nationalistic identity that conflated religious symbols, colonial aspirations and secular-modernistic characteristics. The ideological versatility and institutional efficiency of this powerful movement enabled the political elites to successfully secure a broad popular base for the nation-building project, which later on also included the consolidation of the newly established nation-state.

In the early, formative years of the Israeli state, the nation-building project reached a hegemonic position. A central tool in consolidating this ideological hegemony was a set of symbols and rituals that generally revolved around the state as the ultimate realization of the hopes and needs of its new citizens, as well as the Jewish people in general, and was depicted by Liebman and Don-Yehiya (1983) as a form of 'civil religion'. Liebman and Don-Yehiya imported into the Israeli sociology a concept that was originally developed to describe American society, stemming from the Durkheim-inspired work of Bellah (2005 [1967]). Their approach was to "treat civil religion in functional terms – as a symbol system that provides sacred legitimation of the social order" (Liebman and Yehiya 1983, p. 5); but as this system does not include a transcendental power as one of its core components, it was termed a 'civil' religion to distinguish it from its 'traditional' counterpart. The ideological hegemony of this Israeli civil religion was reinforced through the institutional mechanisms that were created or centralized by the state after 1948, such as the education system.

However, the functionalist paradigm adopted by Liebman and Don-Yehiya neglected parallel processes that took place in the newly-established state: The welfare-state agencies and the state endorsement of the *Histadrut* enabled the political elites to consolidate a differential distribution of rights and resources that contradicted the symbolic inclusiveness of the civil religion. Ashkenazi Jews, especially their men, were granted a preferential position, while other groups—mainly *Mizrahi* Jews (of Asian and African origin), ultraorthodox Jews and especially Arab-Palestinian citizens of Israel—were absorbed into the Ashkenazi-dominated national project, while being subjected to differential mechanisms of structural exclusion (Shafir and Peled 2002; cf. Berkovitch 1999; Rosenfeld 1978; Svirsky and Bernstein 1980). As the main beneficiaries of the welfare-state mechanisms, Ashkenazi Jews became the loyal adherents of the state and its civil religion. Although

---

to create a Hebrew-Israeli equivalent to the American 'WASP'. However, the term was not widely accepted, and this dominant group is commonly referred to simply as Askenazim, or Ashkenazi Jews. I will adopt these two prevailing terms throughout this text.

the labour movement was a hybrid conflation of secular and religious elements, as the concept of 'civil religion' indicates, 'secularism' was consecrated as a signifier of the Ashkenazi group, while Mizrahi Jews were constituted as 'traditionalists'— adherents of Jewish religious traditions in a partial, non-Orthodox manner (Shenhav 2006; cf. Yadgar 2011). This dichotomy legitimized the exclusion of Mizrahi Jews, by presenting them as deviating from the modern and civil order embodied by the state, while maintaining the transparency of Ashkenazi privilege through the identification of Ashkenazi citizens with the universalist state. The 'civil religion', although presented and sometimes even analysed by sociologists as a unifying mechanism, was in fact entangled with mechanisms of differentiation and exclusion.

The Hegemony Crisis and the Rise of 'Volunteering'

The 'neoliberal regime shift' (to adopt Jessop's (2002) conceptualization) implemented in Israel since the mid-1980s included a radical transformation from a Fordist mode of production to a de-regularized economy, one dominated by knowledge-based industries and a powerful financial sector. This transformation was realized by privatizing public assets, weakening unionized labour and commodifying welfare services, resulting in growing socioeconomic gaps (Filc 2006; Shafir and Peled 2002). The neoliberal regime shift in Israel was part of the global transition to neoliberalism (cf. Harvey 2005), but was promoted locally by growing segments within the core of the (Ashkenazi-based) labour movement (Peled and Shafir 2002). During the neoliberalization processes, a few (mainly Ashkenazi) individuals and families expanded their private firms tremendously, often by purchasing privatized assets, and gained extraordinary economic and political power. Other Ashkenazi individuals achieved leading positions in the different realms of the neoliberal order and they still make up the vast majority in companies' senior management and boards, political institutions, the senior civil service, the technocracy of the business sector (law and consultancy firms) and the marketing, media and advertisement sector. However, growing segments of this former ruling group have begun to find themselves in different positions within the precarious neoliberal labour market, and experience increasing difficulties in gaining well-remunerated and secure positions.

This fragmentation within the Ashkenazi group was accompanied by an erosion of the hegemonic cultural-ideological order, including of the prominence of the 'civil religion' that had legitimized Ashkenazi privilege. One of the indicators of this decline is the parallel upsurge in the explicit self-identification of Mizrahi Jews as 'traditionalists' and in the delegation of their political support to religious parties, which were aimed at challenging Ashkenazi political dominance and revealing that the 'secular' social category is ethnically biased (Yadgar 2011; Peled 1998). As other social groups also gained more political power, the formerly hegemonic Ashkenazi group was gradually becoming just another particular sector that has to compete with other groups for cultural, ideological and political dominance

(Kimmerling 1998). As a result, the cultural-ideological character of Israel became the subject of intense political contentions, while at the same time a neoliberal/post-Fordist hegemony was not only consolidated in the realm of political economy but also maintained because of its versatile articulation in relation to the contesting cultural projects of the different groups (Filc 2006). The discrepancy between these two realms explains why even Ashkenazi Jews who have managed to retain an economic privilege nonetheless express dissatisfaction, often accompanied by a sense of disempowerment, as regards the cultural-ideological transitions that are occurring in Israel. These anxieties have been implicitly and explicitly articulated in Israeli newspapers, which are still dominated by Ashkenazi writers (Yonah et al. 2010), and were expressed by wealthy Ashkenazi business people when describing their motivation to engage in philanthropic activity (Barkay 2008; Shimoni 2008).

The ethnographic study I have conducted in Good Spirit indicates that 'volunteering' is being set up as one of the social domains through which Ashkenazi Jews come to grips with these changes in their social status; it demonstrates how this domain serves as a site to restore an updated variation of the former hegemonic order and the civil religion that accompanied it. Existing figures indicate that the Ashkenazi group heavily populates the field of 'volunteering': Ashkenazi individuals constitute a majority on the boards of voluntary-based organizations (Iecovich 2005), and they are more likely to serve as volunteers in these organizations than members of other ethnic groups (Shafransky 2007; Haski-Leventhal et al. 2011). A recent study demonstrated that Israeli-born Jews are overrepresented in the workforce of the Israeli third sector, while Jewish immigrants are roughly equally represented relative to their percentage in the overall population and Palestinian citizens of Israel are underrepresented; however, the report did not examine the ethnic divisions among the Jewish, Israeli-born employees (Hagai Katz and Yogev-Keren 2013). During my fieldwork in Good Spirit, most of the senior staff and board members were Ashkenazim, while many of the youth servers were Mizrahi Jews, supervised by a senior Ashkenazi worker. The people who contacted Good Spirit to put themselves forward as potential volunteers mainly resided in cities and towns that are largely populated by upper-middle class Ashkenazi Jews, while Mizrahi Jews who reside in peripheral towns contacted Good Spirit much less. Palestinian citizens and Orthodox Jews were strongly underrepresented among the Good Spirit constituency.[16]

My interpretation of the Ashkenazi dominance in the field of 'volunteering' is inspired by pioneering studies that imported theoretical notions from the field of 'whiteness' studies to the Israeli context and constituted the Ashkenazi group as a legitimate object of scholarship (Sasson-Levy 2008; Shadmi 2003; Chinski 2002). These works were focused on depicting the consolidation and reproduction of Ashkenazi structural privileges through the concept of 'whiteness', while the current

---

[16] The place of residence was the only detail in the form filled in by the potential volunteer that could indicate, although only indirectly, what her/his socioeconomic class and ethnic origin might be, through the information provided by the Israeli Central Bureau of Statistics on the socioeconomic characteristics of each local council. For a detailed description, see Shachar (2011).

study intends to enrich this body of literature by describing one of the paths through which white individuals tackle a decline in their status and strive to re-consolidate their privilege. The category of 'whiteness' appears as highly useful for forming a theoretical grounding that conjoins ethno-racial, political-economic and cultural-religious dimensions, in order to explain the connection between the historical moment of neoliberal uprising, the decline of civil religion and the attempts to revive it, and the emergence and intensive promotion of 'volunteering'.

Promoting 'Volunteering' in Times of White Decline

Following Frankenberg's work, I refer to 'whiteness' in this article as "a relational category, one that is constructed with a range of other racial and cultural categories, with class and with gender. [...] [It] signals the production and reproduction of dominance" (1993, p. 273). Indeed, what constitutes the 'whiteness' of Ashkenazi Jews is not their skin colour (cf. Kaplan 2002), but the privileged status of their ethno-racial identity together with their ability to maintain its transparency (Sasson-Levy 2008; Shadmi 2003).[17] In Hage's (1998) theorization of white nationalism, this ability to naturalize privilege is indicated as defining the 'national aristocracy':[18]

> It is those national aristocrats that assume that it is their very natural right to take up the position of governmentality within the nation and become the national managers they are 'destined' to be: subject whose rich possession and deployment of the dominant national capital appears as an intrinsic natural disposition rather than as something socially and historically acquired. (Hage 1998, p. 62)

The 'governmental belonging to the nation' of the national aristocrats "involves the belief in one's possession of the right to contribute [...] to its [i.e. the national space] management such that it remains 'one's home'", and in one's ability "to inhabit what is often referred to as the *national will*" (Hage 1998, p. 46). Such a 'governmental belonging to the nation' is embedded in contemporary personal narratives of many Ashkenazim, such as those collected by Sasson-Levy (2008): One of her respondents depicts the Ashkenazi group as an active historical subject that worked to establish the Israeli state, and therefore allegedly possesses the right to continue and manage the state and the nation. However, while unable to give up their aspiration to continue and manage the nation, Ashkenazi Jews experience hardships in maintaining their traditional aristocratic status: Following the social

---

[17] Yanow (1998) demonstrated how this transparency mechanism is also dominant in the domain of public policy in Israel.

[18] Hage's analysis of white nationalism in Australia has been used to gain insights into Israeli society mainly by Kalir (2010), who adopted Hage's concept of 'practical national belonging' to depict the ways in which undocumented migrants in Israel strive to improve their marginal social position within the national field. The study of the managers of volunteering illuminates the other end of the national field, which is populated by those who hold relatively dominant positions within it.

transformations indicated above, they are gradually losing their ability to 'whiten' their managerial practices and thus to deploy them.

This new situation occasionally leads Ashkenazi individuals to experience feelings of alienation, disempowerment and loss of control and even a breakdown or a crisis: "I don't like the personality this country develops and the directions it takes", one of Good Spirit senior workers told me. One aspect of this breakdown is the loss of control over the national space: When Hadas heard the name of the neighbourhood in which I was living during the fieldwork, which used to be an affluent neighbourhood populated by elitist strata affiliated with the labour movement, she told me in response that she visited a "good friend" there several times during the last years, "and the neighborhood is so different from how I remembered it [...]. It is not easy [for my friend] to live there, there are almost no Hebrew speakers, everybody are foreigners...". But these feelings of 'white decline' also lead to new forms of political organization and action: the creation of, and investment in, new social domains such as the field of 'volunteering', in which the management of the nation can be deployed and obscured simultaneously. Managing and promoting the national, all-inclusive enterprise of 'volunteering' provides Ashkenazi individuals, such as Good Spirit workers and board members, opportunities to regain a sense of control over the national space and its population, through their attempts to reposition themselves as the natural enactors of the 'national will'.

Aspiring to a 'National Unity', Renewing the Civil Religion

During our interview, I asked Hadas to reminisce about her motivation to establish Good Spirit. At that time, she was still working as the deputy of the Israeli military spokesperson.

> I think it was in 1993 [...] when suddenly all kinds of questions came to me: what is actually our role here? Each of us, as a human being, we as a nation [...] and then I started to think a bit about the history of the Jewish people, about all the separations, the detachments, the *antagonism* that there is between us [...] what mostly bothers me is the separation between us and the lack of *communicative* abilities between us, so what I aspire for is that there will be more unity here, more connections, more collaborations [...] the result of this topic of unity and connections was basically volunteering.[19]

Hadas' ideas of fostering 'national unity' through 'volunteering' echoed explicitly and implicitly in many of the observations and interviews I conducted. It even received a visual expression in the logo Hadas chose for Good Spirit (see Fig. 15.1),

---

[19] The English words in italics within the quotes were said in English by the respondent during the Hebrew interview. Most of my interlocutors used various slang expressions during the interviews, and, like many Hebrew speakers, they did not always use accurate grammatical constructions while speaking. It was particularly prevalent among the younger staff members and youth servers, but also among the more senior ones. I tried to convey this in the English translation of the quotes by intentionally including grammatical mistakes or using what may be seen as awkward language constructions.

Fig. 15.1 The Israeli flag (on the left) adjacent to the Good Deeds Day logo

which later on became the logo of the Good Deeds Day. Oded described the logo when I interviewed him: "...the different colors- it's like the difference conjoins into a heart, and into like the Israeli flag, to make it something national". "A great logo", he added.

Tackling contemporary tensions and uncertainties through an aspiration to 'national unity', accompanied by the nostalgic yearning for a harmonious past, was also prevalent in other social domains in Israel, such as the dialogue groups of secular and Orthodox Ashkenazi Jews that flourished in the late 1990s. In their study of these groups, Yanay and Lifshitz-Oron (2003) showed how 'national unity' emerged in these groups through the consolidation of an Ashkenazi identity that transcended differences in religious practice, while excluding non-Ashkenazi groups. Therefore, it is interesting to note that one of the first activities of Good Spirit in the early 1990s was a series of dialogue meetings between secular and religious Jews. While the organization quickly turned to different ways of action, the aspiration to unity—and its exclusionary character—remained.

The aspiration to 'national unity' seems to be gradually realized in the mounting numbers of participants in the Good Deeds Day each year. Good Spirit board members and workers have regularly expressed a hope that the Good Deeds Day will become "a national day", and some have even equated it with the celebration of the national Independence Day. The mass media depicted it as an event that "became an Israeli tradition" (Roichman 2011) due to its annual reoccurrence. If the Independence Day used to be a core component of the old, state-centred civil religion, the symbolic and ritual aspects of the Good Deeds Day can be seen as crucial for introducing a new symbolic order, along with the colourful heart that simulates the national flag. As demonstrated in the ritualistic 'flash mob' described earlier, the unifying notion in this new civil religion is no longer the identification with the nation-state, but the notion of 'DOING GOOD' that appears on the uniform white T-shirts.

The efforts to introduce 'volunteering' as representing a form of 'national unity' are intensified through its differentiation from 'politics'. 'Politics' was identified by the Good Spirit staff members with "the separations, the detachments, the *antagonism* that there is between us", and many of them aspired to refrain from 'politics' on a personal level and to distance Good Spirit as an organization from it. During my fieldwork, political issues or views were rarely a topic for informal conversation at lunchtime or on other occasions. During interviews, many staff members refrained from answering questions that related to political issues, or shifted the conversation back to Good Spirit activities, to 'volunteering' or 'giving' or the overall work of NGOs, presenting it as the only way to promote social change. The attitude to 'politics' that characterizes Good Spirit staff resembles prevailing tendencies in the related field of CSR in Israel (Shamir 2005; Barkay 2008) and among volunteers and community activists in the USA (Eliasoph 1998), but also corresponds to the wider dispersion of 'anti-political sentiments' in Israel since the 1990s (Arian et al. 2008; Herman 2010). Good Spirit—as an institutionalized organization, even if it was not the intention of many of its workers—became an active actor in creating a context in which discussing and actively pursuing 'politics' is devalued and delegitimized, while engaging in 'volunteering' is perceived as a positive, consensual and accessible option. Yet, when the political system becomes irrelevant and delegitimized, there is still a need to fill the vacuum with other points of collective reference. This is another factor that encourages the emergence of a new type of 'civil religion', as an expression of the desired social consensus, one that transcends 'politics' and represents the entire nation. The captivating character of this new consensus nurtures the perception of its promoters as enacting a 'national will' and obscures the political-managerial aspirations embedded in their activity.

Adopting a 'Professional' Ethos

The political dimensions of the promotion and management of 'volunteering' are being further obscured by Good Spirit staff members when they depict their activity in discursive terms borrowed from the corporate world. Ilan, Good Spirit chairperson, told me during an interview:

> We have here a compan- ehh, an NGO that deals with volunteers but is very serious – one can trust our word [...] People have in mind [regarding volunteers] that...they don't have to, they might do something and they might not do it. [In our organization] there's no such a thing. We are checking ourselves constantly to make sure that we will do what we have promised.

Other staff members have also aspired to adhere to professional and efficient working methods that will distinguish the organization from other actors in the non-profit sector, and will position it closer to the corporate world. This perception was also conveyed to the youth servers during their training sessions, and some explicitly mentioned that it was important for them to be "professional" in their work. This discourse of 'professionalism' stems from the inspiration Good Spirit draws from the corporate world: In staff meetings, and also during appointments with business persons and state officials, Oded regularly used discursive elements and examples from the corporate world to describe Good Spirit uniqueness and efficiency.

15 'Going Back to Our Values'   319

Umbrella NGOs[20] and academics (e.g. Haski-Leventhal 2007) are increasingly involved in spreading 'professional' techniques of volunteer management in the Israeli non-profit sector. This phenomenon is part of the transnational circulation of managerial knowledge and techniques in the NGO sector (Roberts et al. 2005), through which "the profit-seeking corporation is promoted as the admired model for the [...] civil society" (Connell et al. 2009, p. 334). The origin of this tendency can be traced to the historical emergence of the managerial ideology and management techniques as a remedy for turbulent labour relations. The conflation of scientific positivism and progressivism enabled the emerging class of managers to position themselves simultaneously as impartial professionals and promoters of social progress, and to serve as a buffer between the firm's owners and the workers (Shenhav 1999; Jacoby 2004). They were gradually able to demand higher material and symbolic remunerations for their work, in the form of growing wages and professional autonomy (Shenhav 1999). The rise of neoliberalism was accompanied by an escalation in the power of the managerial elites of corporations (Harvey 2005), and in the expansion of the managerial ideology to domains that were earlier considered to be subject to different logics (Connell et al. 2009). In the realm of volunteer management, the two fundamental axes of managerial ideology—the positivist and the progressive—appear as mutually connected: Progressive discourse around 'volunteering' constructs this notion as an undisputed common good; the positivist-oriented forms of managing 'volunteering' are perceived as crucial for successfully expanding this progressive activity; together, they strongly legitimize the managerial practices in the field of 'volunteering'.

Expanding 'Volunteering', Restoring a Mythical Past

In order to regain a managerial sense of control over the nation, a dissemination of the new notion of 'volunteering' throughout the national space was also needed. The efforts of Good Spirit to spread the call to 'doing good' received a powerful visual representation in an online map of Israel located in the webpages and Facebook page that promoted the Good Deeds Day (see Fig. 15.2). On the map, all of the cities and local councils in which volunteering activities were held throughout the day were indicated with the heart that appears in the day's logo. A public radio presenter interpreted this visualization as reflecting the state of the nation: "I'm looking at the map here, and there's not enough space for this country. It's all one big heart".[21]

---

[20] Two main umbrella NGOs which disseminate the notion of 'professional volunteer management' in Israel are the "Leir Institute for Volunteer Management" (See: http://www.hitnadvut.org/en/?page_id=1820) and the department for volunteering and philanthropy at the Joint Distribution Committee-Israel (See: http://www2.jdc.org.il/category/English-JDC-Israel). They issue printed and online publications, including periodic journals and a blog, organize conferences and provide consulting and training services.

[21] Michael Miro, "A Social Hour", Reshet Bet, 15 March 2010. I have located the transcription of this radio broadcast in an internal file of media items relating to the Good Deeds Day, collected by Arison Group's public relations office and stored in the group's headquarters.

Fig. 15.2 Online map of the Good Deeds Day activities (Retrieved 13 June 2011 http://www.ynet.co.il/home/0,7340,L-4398,00.html)

This geographical expansion of 'good deeds' throughout the Israeli territory was imagined by some of Good Spirit workers as a centrifugal movement from the centre to the periphery. It was strongly reflected in one of the ideas they developed for the Good Deeds Day: Exporting to the periphery an initiative that started in several cafés in Tel-Aviv, where a second-hand library is operated by people with mental disabilities. The books will be placed on a sort of bus, that will "go into neighborhoods around the country", as one worker described it, and "spread out the message"; in that way, "we [Good Spirit] help them [the NGO operating these libraries] to enter other cities [than Tel-Aviv]".

But the expansion of the 'good' also encompasses temporal aspects, as the movement of the library-bus throughout the country is also imagined as restoring a mythical past. The library project reminded my interlocutor of a popular education project promoted by the state in its formative years: "It'll also bring back a bit the... [...]

I also wasn't familiar with that, but I know that in the past there was a mobile library that used to arrive in the neighborhood […] so there is something quite nice about it". The longing for an idealized past returned in many of the interviews I held with the senior staff and the board members of Good Spirit, expressed in phrases such as "these are things that are missing today" and "going back to look at each other's eyes". Ilan said during an interview that we should be "going back to our values a bit. There are many beautiful values in the Jewish religion – of helping the other, of […] charity, of humanism". Similarly to what has been argued by Yonah et al. (2010), the longing for the past that conjoins the narratives of decline described earlier, encloses an aspiration to restore the old hegemonic order that is obscured through the mythical representation of the past. The new symbolic repertoire developed by the Good Spirit staff and board members conflates mythical motives from the 'civil' and 'traditionalist' religions, which nurture their attempts to create a broad social consensus for the new notion of 'volunteering' they aspire to promote.

Inclusion and Exclusion in the Field of 'Volunteering'

According to the interviews I conducted, the mechanisms of legitimacy deployed by the Good Spirit staff were very effective in their social surroundings, which significantly contributed to their belief that there is a wide social consensus around 'volunteering'. However, during their work the staff had to face social groups that could not be incorporated into the 'volunteering' enterprise that easily. Encounters of this type were sometimes the result of a deliberate attempt of Good Spirit staff to expand its activity to new social sectors, and sometimes imposed on the staff when individuals from non-dominant sectors approached the organization. It was only following these encounters that the homogenous ethnic composition of the staff became noticeable: A Palestinian worker was recruited only when the incorporation of the Palestinian citizens of Israel in the Good Deeds Day was defined as an organizational aim; migrants from the former Soviet Union were hired when a large number of Russian-speaking elderly people started to call the office, following a news item on an Israeli-Russian TV channel. However, the work of these new employees was perceived as a sort of instrumental mediation between 'their sector' and the senior staff. When meeting Palestinian municipal officials, Oded regarded potential obstacles to their participation in the Good Deeds Day as deriving mainly from the language differences and described the recruitment of the Palestinian worker to the organization as intending "to enable you [the officials] to communicate with us [Good Spirit] in your own language". As 'volunteering' was conceived as 'apolitical', any hesitation in cooperating with Good Spirit was usually interpreted by the staff as related to 'cultural difference', neglecting the political context that fostered the ethno-racial cleavages in Israel.

Furthermore, 'volunteering' was depicted by Good Spirit staff as a possible path to integration which minority groups were expected to follow. Indeed, some members of minority groups that I interviewed adopted this expectation, among them a Russian-speaking worker in Good Spirit who told me that:

> I think that the Russian [volunteers] in the project are [...] those who did integrate, and it is really different from most of the [Russian] population that experiences difficulties in integrating in the country [...] But you should know that we speak Hebrew with the volunteers who are Russian speakers, because they are the most Israeli one can find. [...] I'm the same; it's more comfortable for me that way [i.e. to speak Hebrew].

My migrant interlocutor internalized the perception that speaking Hebrew and becoming a 'volunteer' are important factors in being an 'Israeli', and that migrants should adapt to this hegemonic form of 'Israeliness' if they wished to 'integrate' successfully. Furthermore, these practices offer individuals a hope for making their way into a position of higher status within the field of 'volunteering', and through that, to an improved social level. However, they could only reach this aim by conforming to the apolitical character of this domain, which praises 'national unity' and delegitimizes class-based or ethnic-based grievances.

As part of the apolitical emphasis in their everyday work of promoting 'volunteering', the reflection of wider social hierarchies and conflicts amongst Good Spirit staff also remained unspeakable. During my fieldwork, the Ashkenazi-Mizrahi divide became strongly present in the office when the veteran Ashkenazi senior workers had to adjust to a new team of largely Mizrahi youth servers. However, as the tensions between the groups could not be discussed in terms of ethnic and class hierarchies, religion appeared as the terrain of explicit differentiation and contention. The youth servers used their partial religious practices and self-identification as 'traditionalists' to express and explain their difference from the Ashkenazi senior workers, who were signified as 'secular'. One of the youth servers told me:

> There is always a *distance*, also during lunch, if you have noticed, each one is separated, I mean, from the staff above us, the servers together – they [the staff] are together [...] It is also because we are religious, so it's also this difference [...] we arrive from a different place, we arrive from a religious home, and they arrive from secular homes, from Tel-Aviv – it's, it's two different ways of thinking.

In a sense, this axis of tension within the Good Spirit staff encapsulates the renewed encounter between the Ashkenazi attempt to re-constitute the civil religion, now based on the ethos of 'volunteering', and its veteran opponent—the 'traditionalist' religion. As indicated above, the widespread upsurge of 'traditionalism' was analysed by Israeli sociologists as a political challenge presented by Mizrahi Jews to the Ashkenazi hegemony, and in this sense various exhibitions by the youth servers of 'traditionalists' practices and views can be interpreted as a tactic of differentiating themselves from the Ashkenazi staff members and an implicit resentment towards their authority. Good Spirit senior workers gradually expressed greater willingness to bridge these cultural-religious gaps within the staff and to carry out various practical adaptations in the office. It seems that both sides, and particularly the senior staff, preferred to manage the tensions between them within a cultural-religious framework rather than entering the more explosive terrain of the class and ethnic hierarchies that were reflected in the intra-organizational power relations.

The tendency of Good Spirit staff to disregard structural inequalities while embracing limited cultural adaptation was equivalent to their broader construction of 'volunteering' as a highly inclusive terrain, which is capable of incorporating even 'traditionalist' motives and to embrace both 'secularists' and 'traditionalists'. This inclusive version of the outdated civil religion is better capable of circumventing potential resistance by means of religious discourse or practices, and represents a more sophisticated response within the Ashkenazi group, traditionally signified as 'secular', to the 'traditionalist' challenges to its hegemony.

Concluding Remarks

The high public visibility of Good Spirit activity, together with the organization's financial and political resources, places it in a relatively central position in the Israeli field of 'volunteering'. The position of Good Spirit enables its Ashkenazi staff members to engage in constructing the notion of 'volunteering' and shaping the field's boundaries, which in turn serves as a means through which they are able to tackle the changes in their social status that resulted from the neoliberal transition in Israel. As I have described in this chapter, Good Spirit staff members are able to reclaim for themselves a managerial position in the national field through deploying managerial practices in the field of 'volunteering' and representing their actions as an all-inclusive national project. They construct a new version of the symbolic order that underpinned the Israeli civil religion in the state's formative years; through this new symbolic and ritual apparatus, a few components of which were described throughout the chapter, Ashkenazi promoters of 'volunteering' aspire to retain their old hegemonic status. The particular and political dimensions of the actions to promote 'volunteering' are 'whitened' and universalized through the simultaneous representation of this practice as a professional and an apolitical project that enacts the 'national will'. Ethnic, class-based and symbolic-religious conflicts are transcended through constructing 'volunteering' as an apolitical, unifying and inclusive domain, in which everyone can participate and is even expected to do so.

The 'white' character of 'volunteering' seems to be tacitly recognized by the subordinate groups that this project aspires to absorb. Skeptical attitudes expressed by members of these groups might be interpreted as forms of resentment towards the attempts to disseminate the notion of 'volunteering' among them. Others, however, see in their commitment to this project a potential to improve their peripheral social position. However, analysing such forms of resentment, consent and utilization deserves additional ethnographic exploration; while the current study was focused on the prominent actors in the construction and promotion of 'volunteering', further research is needed to depict the reactions of those who are constituted as the subjects of this promotion.

Another characteristic of the universalization and whitening of 'volunteering' is its depiction as a 'civil' and 'inclusive' terrain, which is aimed at including 'religious' or 'traditionalist' tendencies alongside 'secularism'. The realm of 'volunteering' circumscribes the contra-hegemonic potential of the 'traditionalist' discourse and co-opts it into the secular logic of universalism and inclusiveness. These ethnographic findings should encourage us to reconsider a prevalent theme in the (mainly survey-based) literature on volunteering: the perception of religious beliefs and affiliation with religious congregations as antecedents of increased volunteer involvement.[22] The connection between volunteering and religion should not be understood as mainly positive and harmonious: 'volunteering' can also be engaged in and promoted by groups identified as 'secular' as a means to overcome what they see as a 'religious' upsurge. Additional research could examine whether the association of 'volunteering' with 'secularism' is unique to the case of Israel and Good Spirit, or can also be traced in other social contexts.

The broader theoretical implications of these conclusions suggest that we reconsider a predominant trend in the literature on 'volunteering' that is focused on studying the relations between an a priori defined concept of 'volunteering' with other variables. It seems useful to also examine why, how and by whom 'volunteering' is constructed and being used. The exploration of 'volunteering' as a relational field of discourse and institutionalized practice, and not just as a bounded concept, enables one to depict the construction of this field, its ongoing cultivation and extension and the power mechanisms that are entangled in these processes. In this analysis, it is crucial to notice the attempts to universalize particular constructions of 'volunteering', and the analyst's role is to de-universalize and re-contextualize these constructions. I hope that the ethnographic study of Good Spirit has contributed to this aim and will provoke further empirical research and theoretical debate in this direction.

References

Abu-Ahmed, W. (2010). *Volunteer activity in the state of Israel in 2006* (Hebrew). Jerusalem: The Minister of Industry, Commerce and Employment, The Research and Economy Department.

Anheier, H., Glasius, M., & Kaldor, M. (2001). Introducing global civil society. *Global Civil Society, 4,* 3–22.

Arian, A., Hermann, T., Atmor, N., Hadar, Y., Lebel, Y., & Zaban, H. (2008). *The 2008 Israeli democracy index: Auditing Israeli democracy—between the state and civil society* (Hebrew). Jerusalem: The Israel Democracy Institute.

Barkay, T. (2008). Neoliberalism and Zionism: Corporate social responsibility and the social struggle on Israeliness (Hebrew). *Theory and Criticism, 33,* 45–71.

Bellah, R. N. (2005) [1967]). Civil religion in America. *Daedalus, 134*(4), 40–55.

Ben-Eliezer, U. (2004). New associations or new politics? The significance of Israeli-style post-materialism. In A. Kemp (Ed.), *Israelis in conflict: Hegemonies, identities and challenges* (pp. 253–282). Brighton: Sussex Academic Press.

Berkovitch, N. (1999). Women of valor: Women and citizenship in Israel (Hebrew). *Israeli Sociology, 2*(1), 277–317.

---

[22] Due to the extensive body of literature on this theme, referencing specific studies seems too anecdotal. As part of broader reviews of the literature on volunteering, Wilson (2000, 2012; Musick and Wilson 2008) reviews a wide range of studies that examined the relations between volunteering and religion.

Bourdieu, P. (1983). The field of cultural production, or: The economic world reversed. *Poetics, 12*(4), 311–356.

Burawoy, M. (1998). The extended case method. *Sociological Theory, 16*(1), 4–33.

Chambré, S. M. (1989). Kindling points of light: Volunteering as public policy. *Nonprofit and Voluntary Sector Quarterly, 18*(3), 249–268.

Chinski, S. (2002). Eyes wide shut: The acquired albino syndrome of the Israeli art field (Hebrew). *Theory and Criticism, 20,* 57–87.

Connell, R., Fawcett, B., & Meagher, G. (2009). Neoliberalism, new public management and the human service professions: Introduction to the special issue. *Journal of Sociology, 45*(4), 331–338.

Eliasoph, N. (1998). *Avoiding politics: How Americans produce apathy in everyday life.* New York: Cambridge University Press.

Eliasoph, N. (2011). *Making volunteers: Civic life after welfare's end.* Princeton: Princeton University Press.

Filc, D. (2006). *Populism and hegemony in Israel* (Hebrew). Tel-Aviv: Resling.

Frankenberg, R. (1993). *White women, race matters: The social construction of whiteness.* Minneapolis: University of Minnesota Press.

Fraser, N. (1990). Rethinking the public sphere: A contribution to the critique of actually existing democracy. *Social text, 25*(26), 56–80.

Gidron, B., Bar, M., & Katz, H. (2002). Characteristics of Israeli organized civil society (Hebrew). *Israeli Sociology, 2*(4), 369–400.

Gramsci, A. (1971). *Selections from the prison notebooks.* New York: International Publishers.

Hage, G. (1998). *White nation: Fantasies of white supremacy in a multicultural society.* Annandale: Pluto Press.

Harvey, D. (2005). *A brief history of neoliberalism.* New York: Oxford University Press.

Haski-Leventhal, D. (2007). Volunteer management as a consolidating profession in service organizations (Hebrew). *Social Security, 74,* 121–144.

Haski-Leventhal, D., Yogev-Keren, H., & Katz, H. (2011). *Philanthropy in Israel 2008: Patterns of giving, volunteering and organ donation of the Israeli public* (Hebrew). Beer Sheva: The Israeli Center for Third Sector Research.

Hermann, T. (2010). The emergence of antipolitical sentiment in Israel. http://www.idi.org.il/sites/english/ResearchAndPrograms/PoliticsandAntiPolitics/Pages/TheEmergenceofAntipolitics.aspx. Accessed 28 May 2013.

Iecovich, E. (2005). The profile of board membership in Israeli voluntary organizations. *Voluntas: International Journal of Voluntary and Nonprofit Organizations, 16*(2), 161–180.

Jacoby, S. M. (2004). *Employing bureaucracy: Managers, unions, and the transformation of work in the 20th century.* Mahwah: Lawrence Erlbaum Associates.

Jessop, B. (2002). Liberalism, neoliberalism, and urban governance: A state-theoretical perspective. *Antipode, 34*(3), 452–472.

Kalir, B. (2010). *Latino migrants in the Jewish state: Undocumented lives in Israel.* Bloomington: Indiana University Press.

Kaplan, S. (2002). Black and white, blue and white and beyond the pale: Ethiopian Jews and the discourse of colour in Israel. *Jewish culture and history, 5*(1), 51–68.

Kaplan-Daniels, A. (1988). *Invisible careers: Women civic leaders from the volunteer world.* Chicago: University of Chicago Press.

Katz, H., & Yogev-Keren, H. (2013). *The labor market of the Israeli third sector: Data and trends 2000–2009* (Hebrew with English abstract). Beer Sheva: The Israeli Center for Third Sector Research.

Katz, H., Levinson, E., & Gidron, B. (2007). *Philanthropy in Israel 2006: Patterns of volunteering and giving of the Israeli public* (Hebrew). Beer Sheva: The Israeli Center for Third Sector Research.

Katz, H., Schwartz, R., & Zeidan, E. (2009). *Umbrella organizations in Israel's third sector: A first study towards a more comprehensive understanding.* Tel-Aviv: Tel Aviv University, The Leon Recanati Graduate School of Business Administration, The Institute for Technology and Society.

Kimmerling, B. (1998). Between hegemony and dormant kulturkampf in Israel. *Israel Affairs, 4*(3–4), 49–72.

Kimmerling, B. (2001). *The end of Ashkenazi hegemony* (Hebrew). Jerusalem: Keter.

Liebman, C. S., & Yehiya, E. D. (1983). *Civil religion in Israel: Traditional Judaism and political culture in the Jewish state*. Berkeley: University of California Press.

Molnar, V. (2009). Reframing public space through digital mobilization: Flash mobs and the futility (?) of contemporary urban youth culture. http://isites.harvard.edu/fs/docs/icb.topic497840. files/Molnar_Reframing-Public-Space.pdf. Accessed 14 April 2011.

Musick, M. A., & Wilson, J. (2008). *Volunteers : A social profile*. Bloomington: Indiana University Press.

Peled, Y. (1998). Towards a redefinition of Jewish nationalism in Israel? The enigma of Shas. *Ethnic and Racial Studies, 21*(4), 703–727.

Roberts, S. M., Jones, J. P., & Fröhling, O. (2005). NGOs and the globalization of managerialism: A research framework. *World Development, 33*(11), 1845–1864.

Roichman, G. (2011, April 5). The fifth 'Good Deeds Day': 140,000 volunteers (Hebrew). *YNET.* http://www.ynet.co.il/articles/0,7340,L-4049750,00.html. Accessed 8 April 2011

Rosenfeld, H. (1978). The class situation of the Arab national minority in Israel. *Comparative Studies in Society and History, 20*(3), 374–407.

Salamon, L. M. (1994). The rise of the nonprofit sector. *Foreign Affairs, 73,* 109.

Salamon, L. M., Anheier, H. K., List, R., Toepler, S., & Sokolowski, S. W. (1999). *Global civil society: Dimensions of the nonprofit sector*. Baltimore: The Johns Hopkins Center for Civil Society Studies.

Sasson-Levy, O. (2008). 'But I don't want to have an ethnic identity': Constructing and obscuring social boundaries in contemporary discourses of being an Ashkenazi (Hebrew). *Theory and Criticism, 33,* 101–129.

Shachar, I. Y. (2011). *Managing the nation: Privatization and nationalization in the management of 'volunteering' in Israel* (MSc Thesis). The Netherlands: University of Amsterdam.

Shadmi, E. (2003). Gendering and racializing Israeli Jewish Ashkenazi whiteness. *Women's Studies International Forum, 26*(3), 205–219.

Shafir, G., & Peled, Y. (2002). *Being Israeli: The dynamics of multiple citizenship*. New York: Cambridge University Press.

Shafransky, M. (2007). Volunteering in Israel: The findings from 'The Social Survey 2002–2004' (Hebrew with English abstract). *Working Paper Series*. Jerusalem: Central Bureau of Statistics.

Shamir, R. (2005). Mind the gap: The commodification of corporate social responsibility. *Symbolic Interaction, 28*(2), 229–253.

Shenhav, Y. A. (1999). *Manufacturing rationality: The engineering foundations of the managerial revolution*. Oxford: Oxford University Press.

Shenhav, Y. A. (2006). *The Arab Jews: A postcolonial reading of nationalism, religion, and ethnicity*. Stanford: Stanford University Press.

Shimoni, B. (2008). *Business and new philanthropy in Israel: Ethnography of mega donors*. Jerusalem: The Center for the Study of Philanthropy in Israel, The Hebrew University.

Shye, S., Lazar, A., Duchin, R., & Gidron, B. (1999). *Philanthropy in Israel: Patterns of giving and volunteering of the Israeli public* (Hebrew). Beer Sheva: The Israeli Center for Third Sector Research.

Simonet, M. (2005). *In between employment and volunteer work: Serving as a 'Volontaire' and as a 'Corpsmember' in France and the United States. Center for Social Development Research Report 05–07*. St. Louis: Global Service Institute, George Warren Brown School of Social Work, Washington University.

Svirsky, S., & Bernstein, D. (1980). Who worked where, for whom and for what: Economic development in Israel and the emergence of an ethnic division of labor (Hebrew). *Mahbarot LeMekhar Ule'Vikoret* 4, 5–66.

Taylor, R. F. (2005). Rethinking voluntary work. *The Sociological Review, 53*(2), 117–135.

Wilson, J. (2000). Volunteering. *Annual Review of Sociology, 26,* 215–240.

15 'Going Back to Our Values'

Wilson, J. (2012). Volunteerism research: A review essay. *Nonprofit and Voluntary Sector Quarterly, 41*(2), 176–212.

Yadgar, Y. (2011). Jewish secularism and ethno-national identity in Israel: The traditionist critique. *Journal of Contemporary Religion, 26*(3), 467–481.

Yanay, N., & Lifshitz-Oron, R. (2003). Mandatory reconciliation [tzav piyus]: The violent discourse of moderation (Hebrew). *Israeli Sociology, 5*(1), 161–191.

Yanow, D. (1998). From what *edah* are you? Israeli and American meanings of 'race-ethnicity' in social policy practices. *Israel Affairs, 5*(2–3), 183–199.

Yonah, Y., Ram, H., & Markovich, D. (2010). 'Family structure': Intractable Eurocentric fantasies in contemporary Israel. *Cultural Dynamics, 22*(3), 197–223.

Chapter 16
Volunteering in Religious Communities

Does it Contribute to Society? Calculating Social Yield

Welmoet Boender

Introduction[1]

In a special issue of Research on Social Work Practice 21 (4), 2011, Ram Cnaan and Thomas McLauglin launch an academic debate about ways to quantify the accomplishments of social work and social services as unique contributions to society. They argue that for too long social work has failed to claim this contribution since it was not expressed as a monetary value but only justified by recording and reporting what social work does. Cnaan and McLaughlin notice that whereas the for-profit private sector easily accounts for the value of items or services in monetary terms, the non-profit fields that rely on 'soft' technologies find it difficult to assess their value to society with the economic denominator of money as a criterion for valuation. Cnaan and McLaughlin call for a debate about valuation and cost-effectiveness in social work and social services, 'assessing the financial value of a public good or a problem' (2011, p. 386). According to them, this way is challenging, complex but needed, and will be ubiquitous in the future (2011, p. 385–387). A similar suggestion is made by Ros Scott (2011) in relation to the assessment of the value of volunteers working in hospitals: 'If volunteers are to be fully recognized as a strategic asset, we must be brave enough also to describe volunteers in business terms.'

These calls are relevant in times when European welfare states are transforming at a rapid pace and governments hand over tasks from the public sector to civil society. In relation to volunteering, Mook et al. bring up the information that monetary measures 'can be useful to funders and policy makers who want to understand the full impact of their investment in a nonprofit' (Mook et al. 2007, p. 505). Cnaan and McLaughlin argue that the non-profit social sector has to prove its value in alternative ways, also to show that they do need financial support in the form of founda-

---

[1] I am grateful to Ir. Jaap van der Sar of Oikos for his input in this article. I also thank the editors, the anonymous reviewers and Prof. Dr. Henk Tieleman for helping me structure my argument.

W. Boender (✉)
Department of Philosophy and Religious Studies, Utrecht University, Utrecht, Netherlands
e-mail: w.boender@uu.nl

L. Hustinx et al. (eds.), *Religion and Volunteering*, Nonprofit and Civil Society Studies,
DOI 10.1007/978-3-319-04585-6_16, © Springer International Publishing Switzerland 2015

tion support and/or government grants in order to survive in the new constellation. '[Their] inability to put a concrete value on the contribution of social service organizations can be detrimental. In an era of scarce resources, politicians and policy analysts search constantly to cut public allocations' (2011, p. 385).

This warning could also be applied to a special group of civil society agents: religious organizations. Everywhere in Europe and USA, the discussion about the social benefits of religious organizations is a topical one. Despite strong secularization, the decline in the number of church members, and an erosion of the willingness of European (religious and secular) populations to gather anywhere on a regular and committed basis (Davie 2007, p. 93), many studies show a positive and ongoing relationship between voluntary work in religious organizations and its impact on society (see for instance Dierckx et al. 2009; Van Tienen et al. 2011). Religious communities are known for their wide range of volunteers working in very different qualities with various tasks to fulfil. Examples are diaconal support, pastoral care, inter-religious dialogue and activities such as food aid and homework assistance for teenagers. Churches can also claim a role as the guardians of religious cultural heritage in the form of church buildings, as well as preservers of rituals related to birth, marriage and death. As we will see below, attaching a monetary value to these activities could be relevant for religious organizations as well. However, the question of how to quantify the value and impact of the work done within religious organizations is not self-evident.

This question is related to methodological, conceptual and sociopolitical questions. For some time now, social scientists have been discussing methodological ways for assessing the value of volunteer activity in monetary terms (see for instance Brown 1999; Handy and Srinivasan 2004; Mook et al. 2007). Three main estimation models are used: the replacement value (the value of tasks performed by volunteers, had they been performed by paid staff); the opportunity costs (which reflect the investment in time and energy as estimated by the volunteers) and the market value (how much value would the volunteers have generated if they had performed their tasks on a commercial rather than a volunteer basis).[2] These studies usually start with a 'disclaimer' which recognizes that it is methodologically and conceptually 'tricky' to express the value of volunteer work in monetary terms (see for instance Brown 1999. p. 4 and 7; Handy and Srinivasan 2004, p. 48; Guera 2008, p. 58.). The applicability of certain economic models is not self-evident, since the value of the work is not per se congruent with the market value and it is difficult to measure 'intangible effects' (Mook et al. 2007, p. 49). This applies in particular to volunteering, as it is inherent to volunteering that volunteers are not pursuing wages. Volunteering is motivated by other incentives, as 'some combination of self-interest and of concern for the well-being of others' (Brown 1999, p. 5).[3] In these cases, '[t]he challenge ... is to assess the monetary values of outcomes such as happiness, rehabilitation, obeying the law, neighborhood pride, and family reunifica-

---

[2] Cnaan and Kang 2011 provide an overview of possible valuation methods and explain their relevance for the non-profit sector.

[3] For an exploration of the relation between volunteering and altruism, see Haski-Leventhal 2009.

16 Volunteering in Religious Communities   331

tion without the benefit of a market-driven dollar value', as Cnaan and Kang argue (2011, p. 389).

This chapter contributes to the ongoing debate regarding the consequences of measuring 'social benefit' or 'social solidarity' in 'hard' financial terms by discussing a special case of measuring the social value of religious organizations in the Netherlands. I will present the case of the Oikos Foundation, a Dutch ecumenical non-profit organization focusing on education and research regarding sustainable development, which has developed a method for calculating the value of the work of volunteers in faith-based organizations.[4] This method expresses the benefit of volunteer work for society in monetary terms.[5] Oikos has developed this method as a way to increase the visibility of volunteer work in general and of religious organizations in particular. It is presumed to lead to increased knowledge and understanding of what religious organizations such as churches do and signify, and to increase awareness among members of the value of their work (see Guera et al. 2008, p. 49). The method starts with registering how much work is done by volunteers and paid persons within a religious organization. The counted hours are linked to the tariffs of the Dutch social service sector (*Thuiszorg*). The next step is to see which part of this work is done by a professional organization elsewhere in society (such as governmental organizations or welfare organizations). In this way, what is 'saved' by society as a whole because of the work of volunteers within religious organizations becomes visible. This is what the Oikos method calls 'social yield' (SY, in Dutch: *maatschappelijk rendement*). Quantified in economic terms, the method's primary aim is said to make the social value of the (volunteer) work of religious organizations visible.

The Netherlands presents an interesting case, being a highly secularized society yet with a strong history of social commitment on the part of the protestant and catholic churches. This historically strong position of the churches is related to the unique Dutch sociopolitical system of 'pillarization' (in Dutch: *verzuiling*). Between approximately 1880 and 1960, Protestant, Catholic, socialist and liberal lifestyles were supported through separate institutions and organized in political parties, labour unions, newspapers, broadcasting corporations, schools, hospitals and recreational facilities. These so-called 'pillars' have been eroded since the 1960s and the sociopolitical influence of the churches has greatly diminished,[6] but the remnants of the pillars are still clearly visible in politics, law and culture. Despite a separation

---

[4] In 2004, Oikos investigated the social yield ('SY') of all local Protestant church communities in the city of Utrecht, the Netherlands. In 2006, this was done for migrant churches in The Hague. In 2009, three more pieces of research were published, one about the SY of mosques, one about an Interchurch social welfare organization in Lelystad and one about Youth for Christ Netherlands. The reports (in Dutch) can be found on the website of Oikos: www.stichtingoikos.nl. The method was also used by researchers of Nijmegen University; see Guera, Glashouwer and Kregting 2008. They applied it to all 250–300 church organizations in the city of Rotterdam.

[5] The method is also applicable to volunteering in non-religious organizations; see Van der Sar and Van Rooijen 2012.

[6] See, for instance, Norris and Inglehart 2004, p. 89 for statistical figures about the steep decline in church attendees and church members.

between church and state, the social and cultural activities of religious organizations can qualify for government subsidies. In the past 20 years or so, religion in the Netherlands has undergone a 'double transformation', first through the decline of institutional religion and second in the emergence of new spiritual forms and manifestations of religious communities in the public sphere (Van der Donk et al. 2006). In this context, new questions about the relation between state and religion have appeared in the public and political debate. One question concerns the issue that the Dutch government increasingly wants to delegate public tasks previously carried out by the state to local civil society organizations. Through the Social Support Act (*Wet maatschappelijke ondersteuning*), municipalities can award local organizations 'a responsibility in fostering the life skills and social participation of citizens and to increase the social cohesiveness of Dutch society', as it is phrased by The Netherlands Institute for Social Research (SCP 2011). Partners in the Social Support Act include religious organizations like churches, mosques and faith-based organizations. These religious organizations have to adapt to this responsibility, not only by professionalizing themselves, but also by making themselves visible as capable actors. This process is hindered by at least three factors. Firstly, many of these organizations work with volunteers; secondly, religious organizations (Christian, but especially Muslim) are increasingly regarded with suspicion[7] and thirdly, churches are not yet used to their altered societal role and position. A consequence of this third factor is that churches have problems with communicating their societal message (which is not unequivocal and often subject to fierce internal and external debate) (Bernts 2004, p. 152). Against this background of the changing role of religious organizations in a secular society, the question of measuring the social benefits of religious organizations in monetary terms is highly interesting and needs careful attention.

In this chapter, I will briefly reproduce the SY method as it has been used and explained in the Oikos reports, and show how it applies the economic model of 'replacement value' to religious organizations. Then I will broach the question of the applicability of this model by discussing the main merits and limitations of its method. We will see that this method offers opportunities for religious organizations to demonstrate their societal relevance in an alternative manner, by acting as any 'normal' civil society organization, no longer leaning on their traditional 'charismatic' authority. But there is also a risk for a cultural and religious impoverishment of the value of religious institutes since a functionalistic explanation of the value of religious organizations might not show their intrinsic, substantial significance. Finally, I will discuss the question of possible societal consequences of measuring the social benefit of religious organizations in monetary terms by looking at divergent public and political responses to the various Oikos reports. We will see that in these

---

[7] Trust in the church has been low in the past 10 years, but the decline has recently been further affected by the impact of the discovery of large-scale sexual abuse of children in Catholic boarding schools in the 1960s. Grace Davie emphasizes that the trend of low institutional trust not only applies to religious institutions, but also to corresponding secular institutions (2007, p. 4). This is also visible in the SCP study (SCP 2011, p. 60–62).

studies, as well as concomitant debates, the use of certain economic terms requires a very precise way of formulating.

Calculating Social Yield

Between 2003 and 2012, the Oikos Foundation carried out several studies about the SY of various religious organizations in the Netherlands. Oikos developed the SY method in an attempt to visualize an aspect of the value of the work of religious organizations which increasingly went unrecognized or unnoticed in a secular society. This concerns religious activities like diaconal work, pastoral care and providing churchgoers with a 'sense of direction', but also the preservation of 'cultural inheritance'. The method intends to calculate the value of work done in churches, mosques and faith-based organizations by literally looking at its exchange value in monetary terms. The time and energy invested by volunteers and paid persons in their organizations is counted and captured in euros, showing the amount of money which is 'saved' by society, as it implies that a certain activity does not have to be done by professionals elsewhere in society. As such, society could consider this sum a 'return' on a 'social investment' made by fellow members of their society.

This valuation method was developed by Ir. Jaap van der Sar, a senior researcher at Oikos, in the early 2000s, at a time when academic debate about the question of how to measure the value of volunteering had just begun (see, for instance, Burger et al. 1999; Van der Sar and Schoemaker 2003). Referring to the methodology for calculating Social Return On Investment (SROI) in the context of social enterprise, developed in the USA and introduced into Europe by the Dutch consultant Peter Scholten,[8] Van der Sar considered it a challenge to work out a method which would be able to show the social benefit of volunteer work.[9] His method can be classified as a form of 'Replacement Value' calculation, assessing what it would cost to produce the same benefit or good using an alternative action, one for which the costs can be more easily deduced (Cnaan and Kang 2011, p. 390). Van der Sar's idea behind the SY method is based on two notions. The first is the aspect of ranking, the second of relativity. Using a monetary ranking system, the relative value of the work done by volunteers in the religious organization can be compared with similar work done in the public sector. Normally, the value of these two forms is determined with different ranking systems, whereas now the economic denominator of money becomes the criterion for the valuation of both. Van der Sar explains this as follows in his reports: 'Money value is determined by an economic exercise in which (at least) two parties agree on a certain "exchange value." For both, there must be an acceptable balance between costs and benefits. Another way to determine the value of a certain asset or product is "redistribution," for instance of tax money

---

[8] See http://www.peterscholten.com/english.php. Accessed 22 May 2013.

[9] For the research on Protestant Churches in Utrecht, an academic committee was formed which discussed the method and research results prior to publication (Van der Sar 2004, p. 38).

into public goods. A third form of value emerges from activities and goods that are based on the idea of the gift. However, the price of the gift is rarely accounted in monetary terms' (van der Sar et al. 2009, p. 18). This is where Van der Sar steps in. 'Sometimes', he argues, 'it can be relevant to compare exchange value and gift. Not to say that they are equal, but to relate them to each other' (van der Sar et al. 2009, p. 18). That is why Van der Sar looks at the 'social exchange value' which can be connected to a specific part of volunteer work done in churches, mosques and FBOs and then expressed in euros. This gives him the opportunity to assess their value in an alternative manner, which adds up to the outcomes of qualitative, descriptive and exploratory studies about the social benefit of religious organizations (Van der Sar et al.2009, p. 12). This relation between money as ranking system and relative value is expressed in the report titles like 'Free and Precious', 'A present to society', 'Benefit for youngsters', 'Heartily' and 'Mosques valued'.

The first step in the calculation process is to figure out what work is done under the responsibility of a selected set of religious organizations (such as all Protestant churches in one or more cities) and how many hours are invested by volunteers and paid persons across the range of activities of this organization during a year. To count these hours and activities, at least three closely involved people per organization are interviewed, mostly board members (young and old, male and female), as well as church leaders or imams. The interviews take at least 2 h. The interviewees are asked to count as exactly and completely as possible which activities took place during the previous year, how many people made these activities possible and how many hours it took for each person to make these activities possible. The interviewers use lists with both common and unusual activities to help the interviewees to think of as many activities as possible. This results in long lists that show many hours of work. The researchers always use the lowest estimate of hours and persons that make the activity possible. If someone says that he or she used 4–6 h/week for a specific activity, like organizing language lessons or a football tournament, then 4 h are registered. The question is also asked if an activity, like computer lessons or Qur'an lessons, was organized on a weekly or monthly or other basis, and whether it stopped during holidays or in the summer.

After adding up the hours, each hour spent on running an activity under the responsibility of a church or mosque is linked with a certain rates used in the social service sector.[10] The nature of the task is taken as a starting point to determine a rate; no differentiation is made between the work of volunteers and paid staff within the organization.[11] In this way, a concrete figure emerges. To calculate the SY, only

---

[10] The rates of the Dutch Thuiszorg were used adjusted for inflation. The rates of the Thuiszorg, which is a specific field within the social service sector, were used because a considerable part of the work done here bears resemblance with the work done in the volunteer organizations studied. The Thuiszorg rates provide the possibility for using different scales. Since Thuiszorg rates are relatively low, their use helps to avoid the risk of over-estimation.

[11] The Oikos studies motivate this by stating that the greatest number of the counted hours in religious organizations is realized by volunteers as well as the fact that paid staff in religious organizations are financed by the members of the congregation. Exceptions are people with a subsidized job, those who work, for instance, as janitor in a mosque.

16 Volunteering in Religious Communities

Table 16.1 Outcomes of SY-studies carried out by Oikos

Year of publication	Organization	Counted hours	Amount in 'Thuiszorg' rate (€)	SY (€)
2004	18 Protestant churches Utrecht	408,000	17,200,000	8,900,000
2006	110 Migrant churches The Hague	1,100,000	43,000,000	18,000,000
2009	16 mosques the Netherlands	270,000	10,100,000	5,200,000
2009	Youth for Christ Netherlands	285,000	10,900,000	6,200,000
2009	Interchurch Social Welfare Committee (IDO) Lelystad	50,800	2,092,000	1,613,000

those activities which have an equivalent in professional organizations elsewhere in society are counted, for instance Dutch language lessons to foreign women, a consultation hour for questions about raising children or running a 'food bank'. In this way, it becomes possible to calculate what Dutch society would need to spend in monetary terms if this work were not done by people in a church or mosque, but by paid people within the government or a different organization (profit or non-profit). Not all activities carried out within the organizations have the same social relevance. Some activities yield a social return of 100%, while others yield 75, 50, 25 or 0%. For example, if a church or mosque devotes time to running a 'food-bank', the invested hours have a social return of 100%. However, when a board gathers for a meeting about the church or mosque administration, or even about the management of the food bank, the percentage is set to 0%, as these 'overhead' activities are included in the rates of the Social Service Sector (*Thuiszorg*). Just as the 'Thuiszorg' has different salaries for different jobs, the 'volunteer rates' take into account that certain tasks, like pastoral care, require more knowledge or specialization than serving coffee in the canteen. Some religious activities are also counted as returning a certain percentage of SY.[12] In this respect, the SY method goes beyond merely registering the work of volunteers within churches and mosques. To ensure the rating is performed in a consistent manner each outcome is checked by two people. The numbers provided as SY are rounded down in thousands. Table 16.1 provides an overview of these outcomes.

In Table 16.1, the 'counted hours' column record all hours spent in the religious organization as a whole, regardless of the SY. The column of 'Thuiszorg rate' multiplies the counted hours by the applicable Thuiszorg rate for each activity. In the

---

[12] Pastoral care is set at 75% and valued in the middle range of the rates. For pastoral work, one can find an equivalent professional in general welfare organizations. Pastoral work deals with questions about faith, but it also deals with questions of how to overcome the loss of a loved one, how to deal with a divorce, etc.; all work which is also done by professionals in social work organizations. A sermon, on the contrary, has a SY of 0%. Although it can inspire listeners to do any type of work with a positive SY, in itself the SY is put at 0%.

'SY' column, the methodology explained above is applied to correct for those activities which have reduced or no SY.

Apart from these calculations in euros, the outcomes are also presented in a different format. This means that it is not only monetary figures that can provide relevant information about the social value of religious organizations. The different reports are illustrated with elaborate descriptions of activities as well as the motivations of volunteers. Although space is too limited here to provide an exhaustive list, the activities and services mentioned below provide an indication of the social activities taking place. Regarding the social role of migrant churches, the 2006 report describes how they function as 'safety nets' for a variety of people (Van der Sar and Visser 2006). Particularly youngsters, newly arrived in the Netherlands without any family or who have run away from home, are cared for and given shelter. Migrant churches offer young people relaxing and educating activities while they meet with peers and adults who care about them. Volunteers assist in finding appropriate education, housing and navigating bureaucratic systems. Volunteers and paid persons in migrant churches also invest a considerable number of hours in assisting homeless people, prostitutes, drug addicts, ex-prisoners and victims of human trafficking. From the 2009 report on mosques, it appeared that mosque board members invest much time in referring mosque visitors to professional organizations in case of social, legal, mental, housing or education problems. Similarly, welfare organizations, public health organizations, local police, the local council and housing corporations knocked on the door of the mosques, trying to reach people who are otherwise difficult to reach for these professional institutions. In most investigated cases, these mosque networks were very large. Apart from religious activities, volunteers invested time and effort in providing sociocultural activities such as language lessons, sport activities and homework assistance. The Protestant churches in Utrecht (2004) show strong SY for society through their active role in debt counselling services.[13] This is also the case for the work of the Interchurch Social Welfare Committee (IDO) in Lelystad (published in 2009), where a group of Christian volunteers supports families and/or persons with debt problems. These are highly trained volunteers who do this work at the same level of professionalism as paid professionals. The asset of the SY method is that it captures the time and energy invested by volunteers and paid persons in these activities in a single figure: the euro sum. This sum intends to show the amount of money which is 'saved' by society.

Merits and Limits of the Method: Fictitious or Real Return?

Below, I will enter into the question about the applicability of the method by discussing its main merits and limitations. Can we consider this 'replacement value' method a sound contribution to the research domain of the social valuation of vol-

---

[13] This is also the case in many other Protestant and Catholic churches, see Crutzen 2008.

unteer work done in religious organizations? An affirmative answer would emphasize two aspects. Firstly, the SY method attempts to describe a 'fictitious' return with a 'real' figure. A comparison based on a similar ranking system (money) provides insight into the relative value of this and comparable work done elsewhere in society. This enables a comparison between two different entities, which is necessarily made under clear methodological restrictions. As addressed in the introduction of this article, this holds true for all research which deals with the assessment of value to volunteering as well as social work in the non-profit sector. The Oikos study also extensively and repeatedly states its 'disclaimers'. The monetary figures only provide estimates, not precise calculations. An obvious restriction is the fact that the hours of volunteers are not or seldom managed. The interviewees might have an inaccurate or deficient memory of the invested amount of hours or insight into the range of activities. Moreover, they do not only talk about their own time investment, but also that of their fellow volunteers. On the other hand, people were often surprised to realize how many hours they spent in making the organization work. To avoid any chance of presenting 'too rosy' a picture, the method systematically chooses the lower variant whenever more than one variant is recorded. Outcomes are the 'minimal observed outcomes'. Registered hours and euros were rounded down to thousands. The rate of a certain activity within a religious organization, e.g. an hour of pastoral care to someone grieving, was rated lower than a similar activity performed by a professional, e.g. a psychologist or professional bereavement counsellor. In each organization, several people were interviewed but double counting was avoided as much as possible so that overestimation of the fictitious return could be avoided. Moreover, real replacement of such activities would be extremely costly to the public sector (see also Cnaan and Kang 2011, p. 393).[14] In their estimation of the percentage of SY, the researchers admitted that subjective choices were inevitable. Here, also, the research brings out that the aim is to avoid overestimations. Finally, the reports do not assess effectiveness or efficiency of the work done, although they assume that activities of religious organizations, including religious ones like assembling for prayer, do generate a social effect. Volunteers invest time and money assuming that it will return some benefit, although they might not see it as an investment in society but as a way to counteract loneliness or *fi sabil Allah*, for the sake of God. In this way, the method forms an alternative and an addition to other attempts to examine the social benefit of religious organizations to society, as it adds to the usual qualitative, descriptive-exploratory methods.

The second asset of the method is that it uses economic terminology to show the lasting relevance of religious organizations in a highly secularized society. Paul Schnabel, director of the SCP, foresees that this discourse will become more prominent in the near future. 'Using economic terms like investment', he says, is 'not just figurative; the metaphors also reflect a changing reality and open new perspectives on the future' (Schnabel 2006, p. 5). The benefit for society of religious organizations is brought into focus by embedding them in a secular discourse. Marginalized

---

[14] Cnaan 2009 also works with conservative estimates, meaning the lowest estimate possible.

religious organizations, which experience a decline of their traditional charismatic authority, can capture their existence in a catchy phrase to highlight their social relevance to highly secularized people. Jurgen Habermas (2006) might consider using this kind of vocabulary part of the 'complementary learning processes' that secular and religious citizens must go through.[15]

However, here we touch upon an important objection to the method: the risk of reducing the social meaning of the churches and other religious organizations to a calculable, identifiable number. Their full social meaning might not become completely visible, nor understandable, when it is couched (only) in 'hard' economic terms. The method may challenge religious organizations to show, or even prove, their functional rationality. Religious organizations do have a functional rationality and their functional solidarity with society may become visible through the research technique. However, religious organizations do not have to be considered as primary welfare producers. Their rationality is, pre-eminently, not purely functional but also substantial. 'The reality in which [these organizations] operate is also a cultural reality, a reality of values, norms and meanings which direct and structure people's lives' (Zijderveld 1987, p. 104, translation WB). Can this attachment to or solidarity with society also be made concrete in monetary terms? Labour, particularly when it concerns voluntary labour is often a combination of what Max Weber called *Zweck- und Wertrationalität*, of functional and substantial rationality. The sociologist Kees Schuyt catches this with the term convivial labour. He describes convivial labour as 'work done in the service of living together, geared towards preserving this coexistence and making it qualitatively as good as possible. This labour does not exclusively focus on economic benefit; it is also focuses on a self-imposed responsibility, kinship, the will to live together, in order to expand joy in living' (Schuyt 1995, p. 90, translation WB). Precisely since 'convivial labour' is not exclusively in the service of economic benefit, the SY method carries within itself the risk of reducing the meaning of this kind of work to a functional economic one. Working in the service of society should not be brought under the same financial-economic yoke as economic labour, Schuyt argues. According to him, 'it would be a gross cultural impoverishment if our western society were to unlearn the art of convivial coexistence, just because only one kind of labor would be recognized and calculated' (1995, p. 90). This risk might be particularly present in a highly secularized environment, since 'people who consider rationality exclusively as functional rationality,—as being typically modern,—often take religion as irrational', to quote the sociologist Anton Zijderveld (1987, pp. 104–105).

Another critical question can be added: What kind of social bonds or forms of solidarity are reflected in the financial figure? The 'society' that benefits remains unspecified, but citizens in society at large might not regard (all) activities carried out within religious organizations, or (any) admonitions or advice brought up in pastoral care, as beneficial to society. The method always shows a positive contribution: Input of time always generates a social return if a professional equivalent ex-

---

[15] Habermas: 'secular and religious citizens can only fulfill the normative expectations of the liberal role of citizens if they likewise fulfill certain cognitive conditions' (2006, p. 4).

16 Volunteering in Religious Communities

ists, regardless of what is said or done by the actors. The method does not critically address what Cnaan calls externalities: 'by-products of activities that enhance (positive externalities) or damage (negative externalities) the well-being of people or the environment' (2011, p. 387). Cnaan and McLaughlin are aware of these problems, which accompany attempts to quantify social work in monetary terms, but they introduce the argument that neither positive nor negative externalities are reflected in market prices (2011, p. 387). For the time being, Cnaan states that 'the valuation of negative externalities is more problematic than our current knowledge makes possible' (2009, p. 642).

Public and Political Response

That these risks and questions are not only theoretical becomes clear when we look at widely divergent public and political responses to three of the Oikos studies. These responses will help us to discuss the question whether SY and similar methods can be regarded as a suitable way for religious organizations to prove their value to society. The reactions also show that the debate about finding ways to quantitatively assess the accomplishments of religious organizations is indeed not just an academic one, but a political and societal discussion as well. First we will look at how the publication of the report about migrant churches made them visible to the municipality of The Hague (Van der Sar and Visser 2006). Then we will see how an ecumenical organization in the provincial town Lelystad used the outcomes to strengthen their position as a church organization in relation to their municipality, providing themselves with a 'license to operate' (Van der Sar 2009). The responses to the mosque report show a very different attitude (Van der Sar et al. 2009). Here, public debate turned into a discussion about the 'cost and benefit' of (Muslim) migrants when the populist Party for Freedom (PVV) raised the question: 'what does an immigrant cost?'

After the publication about the migrant churches in The Hague in 2006, it became clear to the town council how important migrant churches were as a shelter and crisis centre for various people such as drug addicts, the homeless, victims of human trafficking, people without residence permits and teenagers. As a consequence, secular politicians and policymakers took an interest in these matters; after discussing the results, they took a favourable stance towards the requests by migrant churches for meeting rooms and they actively cooperated in looking for new church buildings. For their part, volunteers in migrant churches realized that they could strengthen their own performance and started to improve their approach to reach people in need of their services.

In Lelystad, a provincial town in the middle of the Netherlands, the interchurch social welfare organization IDO also became more visible to the local municipality. The board of IDO took an active stance by commissioning a study carried out by Oikos in 2009. In their foreword to the report, they expressed their willingness to use the outcome to sustain their work in Lelystad. By showing the value of their work, they wanted to convince the local authorities that it was worth the investment to subsidize their activities (Van der Sar 2009). The board successfully negotiated with the local authorities to continue supporting IDO's diaconal work 'realizing that an investment of one Euro from the municipality would generate the saving of almost 10 € in other parts of their budget'.[16]

Also eye-catching was the report on mosques (Van der Sar et al. 2009), but this evoked a very different set of reactions. The report on mosques, published in 2009, calculated the contribution of all Dutch mosques as saving a minimum of € 150 million per year.[17] This result caused tumultuous reactions, not least in the political arena. The research was commissioned by the Ministry for Home Affairs and Kingdom Relations. In some reactions, the carefully formulated research question was rephrased into a simple counter-question: 'and how much does a mosque cost society?' The populist PVV, led by Geert Wilders, used the opportunity to request the government to calculate 'how much an immigrant costs society', which they assumed to be far more than their contribution.[18] This was the opposite effect of what the cooperating mosques had had in mind. They appreciated the fact that their activities were investigated with exactly the same research method as other religious organizations, instead of the more common research question of 'how well mosques are integrated'. For them, the hope dominated that, in this way, they could make visible what happens within a mosque, and that this could also be regarded as a valuable contribution to society as a whole, as a positive input in the heated public debate about Islam. The often spiteful public remarks clearly showed the reality of the aforementioned risk of reduction of the research method to a simple 'cost-benefit-analysis' in which the religious organization is to 'prove' its functional rationality. The fact that the other reports did not give rise to as many fierce reactions also shows that public and political opinions about the target of social solidarity differ.

The considerations for providing government subsidies to social work carried out under the responsibility of religious organizations are outside the scope of this article. This does not mean that the question is irrelevant. The SY reports bring in information that can be used in discussions about the feasibility of government subsidies, but, as we have seen, the interpretation of this information by various actors differs. Furthermore, the government can choose to provide or deny government grants on the basis of principled or pragmatic considerations (see Davelaar and Smits van Waesberghe 2010; Dierckx et al. 2009).

---

[16] Written by the Board of IDO in the preface to Van der Sar 2009.

[17] Extrapolation to all 475 mosques in the Netherlands of the result of the 16 mosques researched (see Table 1.16).

[18] On 20 July 2009, PVV member of Parliament Sietse Fritsma sent 79 parliamentary questions to the Cabinet, addressed to the Ministers of 12 Departments (numbers 2009Z14076– 86). Normally, the answering of questions from Parliament requires 6 weeks; in this case, it took about 6 months before a reaction to the questions was published.

Concluding Remarks

In highly secularized societies, religious organizations are searching for ways to bring into focus their value to secular citizens who might no longer accept their social relevance automatically, uncritically or unconditionally. This chapter has described the case of a Dutch Christian civil society organization, Oikos, which applied a specific method of measuring the social value of religious organizations. In this context, the advantage of the 'replacement value' method described above has become clear. At a single glance, one can see the vast amounts of money which religious organizations and its volunteers 'save' society, if professional organizations elsewhere in society were to have to do this work. This benefit to society is expressed in a vocabulary which can be understood by a 'secular citizen' (compare Habermas 2006). The method provides religious organizations with an instrument to emphasize their social value, thereby counteracting the process of marginalization from the public sphere. We saw that several Christian organizations (the interchurch organization IDO and migrant churches) have actively used this as a technique to demonstrate their social relevance (trying to obtain government grants or support for their welfare activities). Mosques also wanted to show their social contribution to Dutch society, but did not receive the appreciation they had hoped for.

The SY method is presented by Oikos as an attempt to demonstrate something which otherwise would not become visible. Nevertheless, the use of economic terminology (whether metaphorically or not) does imply a certain risk, both methodologically as well as sociopolitically. Although the method extensively indicates its limitations, it carries the risk of reducing the rationality of a religious organization to its functional meaning. When religious organizations are only appreciated using these norms, there might be a risk of 'commodifying social solidarity', particularly if economic metaphors are taken literally. This not only applies to the method used by Oikos, but also to other existing methods which try to capture the value of voluntary work in monetary terms. Although these studies do not intend to reduce the outcome of 'replacement value' studies to a simple 'cost-benefit-calculation', this is a realistic pitfall, judging by the fierce reactions to the mosque study. Like IDO and the migrant churches, the mosques attempted to prove their legitimacy by means of the SY method; however, this had very different sociopolitical consequences. It is not easy to communicate the subtleties of the notions of reciprocity and gift when an economic denominator is used which derives from another class of economic exchange. Moreover, it is neither evident nor uncontroversial that religious organizations should be considered as primary welfare producers and that their efforts must be quantified at all.

A concrete figure tends to 'stick in the memory' but also easily provokes reactions. These reactions contribute to an ongoing social and political debate about the meaning of solidarity and reciprocity in neo-liberal secular states as well as about the contribution of religious organizations and their volunteers to society as a whole. The outcomes of the SY studies can function as building blocks in these discussions, but they should not replace descriptive qualitative researches about the social benefits of religious organizations.

References

Bernts, T. (Ed.). (2004). *Boodschap aan de kerken? Religie als sociaal en moreel kapitaal* [Message to the churches? Religion as social and moral capital]. Zoetermeer: Meinema.

Brown, E. (1999). Assessing the value of volunteer activity. *Nonprofit and Voluntary Sector Quarterly, 28*(1), 3–17.

Burger, A., Dekker, P., Toepler, S., Anheier, H. K., & Salamon, L. M. (1999). The Netherlands: Key features of the Dutch nonprofit sector. In L. M. Salamon, H. K. Anheier, R. List, S. Toepler, S. Wojciech Sokolowski, et al. (Eds.), *Global civil society: Dimensions of the nonprofit sector* (pp. 145–162). Baltimore: The Johns Hopkins Center for Civil Society Studies.

Cnaan, R. A. (2009). Valuing the contribution of urban religious congregations. *Public Management Review, 11*(5), 641–662.

Cnaan, R. A., & Kang, C. (2011). Toward valuation in social work and social services. *Research on Social Work Practice, 21*(4), 388–396.

Cnaan, R. A., & McLaughlin, T. (2011). Introduction to special section on cost-effectiveness and valuation in social work. *Research on Social Work Practice, 21*(4), 385–387.

Crutzen, O. (2008). *Armoede in Nederland 2008. Onderzoek naar financiële hulpverlening door diaconieën, parochiale caritas instellingen en andere kerkelijke organisaties in Nederland* [Poverty in the Netherlands. Research into financial aid by diaconal, parochial charity institutions and other church organizations in the Netherlands]. Utrecht: Kerk in Actie.

Davelaar, M., & Smits van Waesberghe, E. (2010). *Tussen principes en pragmatisme. Een onderzoek onder Nederlandse gemeenten naar de subsidiëring van levensbeschouwelijke organisaties* [Between principles and pragmatism. A study of the subsidizing of religious and 'ideological' organizations by Dutch municipalities]. Utrecht: Forum and Verwey Jonker Instituut.

Davie, G. (2007). *The sociology of religion*. Los Angeles: Sage Publishers.

Dierckx, D., Vranken, J., & Kerstens, W. (Eds.). (2009). *Faith-based organizations and social exclusion in European cities: National context reports (FACIT)*. Leuven: Acco.

Guera, J. C., Glashouwer, M., & Kregting, J. (2008). *Tel je zegeningen. Het maatschappelijk rendement van christelijke kerken in Rotterdam en hun bijdrage aan sociale cohesie* [Count your blessings. The social yield of Christian churches in Rotterdam and their contribution to social cohesion]. Nijmegen: Nijmegen Institute for Mission Studies.

Habermas, J. (2006). Religions in the public sphere. *European Journal of Philosophy, 14*(1), 1–25.

Handy, F., & Srinivasan, N. (2004). Valuing volunteers: An economic evaluation of the net benefits of hospital volunteers. *Nonprofit and Voluntary Sector Quarterly, 33*(1), 28–54.

Lombo-Visser, R., & van der Sar, J. (2009). *Winst voor jongeren. Het maatschappelijk rendement van Youth for Christ* [Benefit for youngsters. The social yield of Youth for Christ]. Utrecht: Oikos.

Mook, L., Handy, F., Ginieniewicz, J., & Quarter, J. (2007). The value of volunteering for a nonprofit membership association: The case of ARNOVA. *Nonprofit and Voluntary Sector Quarterly, 36*(3), 504–520.

Norris, P., & Inglehart, R. (2004). *Sacred and secular. Religion and politics worldwide*. Cambridge: Cambridge University Press.

Schnabel, P. (Ed.). (2006). *Investeren in vermogen: Sociaal en Cultureel Rapport 2006* [Investing in capital: Social and Cultural Report 2006]. Den Haag: SCP.

Schuyt, C. J. M. (1995). *Tegendraadse werkingen. Sociologische opstellen over de onvoorziene gevolgen van verzorging en verzekering* [Counter-effects. Sociological essays on the unforeseen consequences of care and insurance]. Amsterdam: Amsterdam University Press.

Scott, R. (2011). Making volunteers count. *BMJ Supportive and Palliative Care, 1*(2), 212.

SCP (2011). *The social status of the Netherlands*. Den Haag: SCP. (http://www.scp.nl/english/Topics/P_Z/Social_Support_Act_Wmo). Accessed Oct 2012.

van der Donk, W. B. H. J., Jonkers, A. P., Kronjee, G. J., & Plum, R. J. J. (Eds.). (2006). *Geloven in het publieke domein. Verkenningen van een dubbele transformatie* [Believing in the public domain. Explorations of a double transformation]. Amsterdam: Amsterdam University Press. (Wetenschappelijke Raad voor het Regeringsbeleid).

16 Volunteering in Religious Communities

van der Sar, J. (2004). *Van harte! Onderzoek naar het maatschappelijk rendement van de Protestantse Gemeente in Utrecht* [Sincerely! Study of the social yield of the Protestant Community in Utrecht]. Utrecht: Oikos Foundation.

van der Sar, J. (2009). *IDO—niet voor niets. Een onderzoek naar het maatschappelijk rendement van het Interkerkelijk Diaconaal Overleg in Lelystad* [IDO—not for nothing. A study of the social yield of the Interchurch Social Welfare Committee in Lelystad]. Utrecht: Stichting Oikos.

van der Sar, J., Lombo-Visser, R., & Boender, W. (2009). *Moskeeën gewaardeerd. Een onderzoek naar het maatschappelijk rendement van moskeeën in Nederland* [Mosques valued. A study of social yield of mosques in the Netherlands]. Den Haag: Ministry of Home Affairs and Kingdom Relations.

van der Sar, J., & Schoemaker, T. (2003). *De Hofstad, een cadeautje aan de samenleving* [The Hofstad (The Hague), a gift to society]. Utrecht: Stichting Oikos.

van der Sar, J., & van Rooijen, J. (2012). *Gezien en gewaardeerd—Onderzoek naar het maatschappelijk rendement van zes ouderenorganisaties in Veldhoven* [Seen and appreciated—study into the social yield of six elderly organizations in Veldhoven]. Utrecht: Stichting Oikos.

van der Sar, J., & Visser, R. (2006). *Gratis en waardevol: Rol, positie en maatschappelijk rendement van migrantenkerken in Den Haag* [Free and valuable: Role, position and social yield of migrant churches in The Hague]. Den Haag: Stichting Oikos (commissioned by SKIN and STEK).

van Tienen, M., Scheepers, P., Reitsma, J., & Schilderman, H. (2011). The role of religiosity for formal and informal volunteering in the Netherlands. *VOLUNTAS: International Journal of Voluntary and Nonprofit Organizations, 22,* 365–389.

Zijderveld, A. C. (1987). *De samenleving als schouwspel. Een sociologisch leer- en leesboek* [Society as spectacle. A sociological textbook]. Gravenhage: VUGA.

Index

2011 Egyptian revolution, 283

A

Abrahamic philosophical tradition, 60
Abrahamic religions, 11, 63
Abrahamic religions *See also* Judaism;
    Christianity; Islam, 11
Active citizenship, 193, 194, 212
Advocacy, 86, 139, 141, 176, 244, 247, 250,
    256, 284, 294, 297
Age, 85, 87, 130, 134
    cohorts, 101
    distribution, 153
    groups, 99, 153
    secular, 194, 202, 206, 213, 214
Altruism, 1, 5, 9, 11, 80, 99–101, 134, 139,
    149, 150, 156
    and volunteering, 149, 150
Altruistic act, 54
Ambiguity, 10, 199, 214, 257
    orchestrated, 251–254
American pragmatism, 178
Anheier, Helmut, 107
Arendt, Hannah, 149, 152, 211
ar-Rahim
    the Merciful, 60
ar-Rahman
    the Beneficent, 60
Authenticity, 155–159, 204, 272
    ethics of, 194, 206
Autonomous, 2, 27, 38, 39, 159, 160, 170, 176
    architecture, 177
    decision, 30
    human being, 31
    subject, 23
Autonomy, 32, 105, 123, 140
    human, 32, 33, 38

B

Beirut/Lebanon, 16, 265, 270
Benefits
    of C/P communities, 16
    of employment, 35
    of pragmatic approach, 242
    of Tsedakah, 47
    of volunteering, 5
Biblical tradition, 63
Bonhoeffer, Dietrich, 26
Bottom-up processes, 171
Bourdieu field, 308
Bringing theology back in, 164
By-products, 339
    reward as, 156

C

Cairo, 16, 47, 287, 292, 296, 300
Calling
    Lutheran doctrine of, 158–160
Callon, Michel, 178, 180–182, 187
Campus Crusade for Christ *SeeCru*, 221
Casanova, José, 3, 6, 8, 147, 220, 241
Case study, 14, 15, 91, 171
    Schulen's parish church, 172–174
Case study organizations, 284, 287–290, 292,
    297–299, 302
Catholic, 35, 78, 85, 107, 124, 331
Celebrants (priests), 169, 171, 173
Charismatic authority, 338
Charismatic/Pentecostal (C/P), 16, 263, 264,
    267
    believers, 268, 279
    bonding capital, 269
    groups, 265, 269
    mega churches, 267
    rituals, 264
Charitable activities, 64, 65, 245

L. Hustinx et al. (eds.), *Religion and Volunteering*, Nonprofit and Civil Society Studies,
DOI 10.1007/978-3-319-04585-6, © Springer International Publishing Switzerland 2015

346   Index

Charitable organizations, 23, 42, 53, 141
Charity, 37, 42, 47, 59, 61, 83
Christianity, 24, 28, 31, 78, 148, 191,
    196–198, 218, 228, 232
Christian socio-political group, 172
Christian theology, 2, 7, 23, 31
Church attendance, 6, 14, 114, 137–139, 151
Churches
    Anglican, 124
    Catholic, 124, 159, 163, 171, 267, 331
    in Australia, 124
    Uniting, 124, 131
Church hierarchy, 169, 182
Civic
    action, 16, 242, 246, 248, 251
    commitment, 16, 188, 211, 283, 291, 292,
        300, 302
    culture, 285
Civic dimension
    crime, 201, 205, 209, 211, 212
Civic engagement, 1, 77, 93, 121, 137
Civil
    sphere, 247
Civil society, 3, 4, 7, 9, 15, 17, 66, 86, 92, 151,
        164, 187, 204, 211, 283, 285
    in egypt, 285, 287
Civil society organizations (CSOs), 162, 284,
        285, 300, 332
Civil society regimes, 5
Class, 122, 250, 273, 276, 315, 319, 322, 341
Club-style volunteering, 246
Cnaan, Ram, 1, 7, 24, 139, 329
Collective efficacy, 13, 129, 140, 141
    and congregational bridging, 137, 138
Commandment, 12, 25, 34, 42, 43, 47, 54
Commitment, 8, 14, 24, 26, 28, 30, 36–38, 48,
        211, 214, 232, 241, 245, 263, 331
Commodification, 176
Communication, 15, 187, 208, 218, 223, 248,
        250
Communication style, 264, 280
Community Holistic Circle Healing, 195
Community service, 128, 129, 134, 136, 284,
        288, 293, 297
Community use, 171
Confessional identity, 263
Consequences of volunteering, 1, 5, 15
Consolation, 27, 37, 39
Contingency, 5, 176, 178, 181, 184, 220
Cost-benefit-analysis, 340
Country of Birth, 130, 134
Cross-national analysis, 116
Cross-national variation, 107, 115
Cru, 221, 222, 225–229, 231, 232

Cultural repertoires, 248
Cultural sociology, 164, 248, 250

D
Davie, Grace, 164, 170
Default relationship, 2, 3
Democracy, 86, 89, 164, 193, 247, 285
Democratic, 77, 86, 92, 153, 187, 191, 285
Democratization, 180, 285
De-politicize, 4
Deregulation, 48
Desolation, 27, 37
De Tocqueville, Alexis, 241, 251
Development, 66, 86, 99, 138, 331
    economic, 89, 104
    of christian personhood, 218
    of ZAKA, 50, 51
    scale, 127
Dictatorship
    military, 285
Discernment, 11, 27, 28, 37
Doctrine, 90
    Luther's, 161
    political, 71
    religious, 79
    Salafi, 294
Doctrine of the calling
    Lutheran, 158–160
Donations, 44, 66, 68, 223, 288, 299, 302
Double effect, 263, 278, 279
Duty, 12, 42, 43, 52, 59, 62, 99, 106, 295
Duty-centered perspective, 59

E
Economic Development, 86, 89, 104, 223,
        256, 286
Economic man, 149, 151
Economy, 48, 67, 68, 69, 299, 311, 314
Ecumenical, 17, 219, 221, 223, 263, 331, 339
Education level, 85, 87, 106, 130, 131, 134
Egoism, 101, 104, 149, 150, 161
Egypt, 16, 53, 70, 283–286
Elections, 53, 71, 286, 293–297, 299
Embeddedness, 170, 173
Empathy, 61, 116, 270
Episodic volunteering, 4
Erasmus, Desiderius, 32
Erving Goffman, 250
Esping-Andersen, Gosta, 104, 107
Ethnic hierarchies, 322
Ethnography, 15, 17, 179, 251, 264, 280, 309,
        314, 324
Europe, 6, 7, 9, 44, 147, 152, 221, 272, 285,
        330, 333

Index

European welfare states, 329
Evangelical Christianity, 220, 223
Evangelicalism, 130
Evangelism, 15, 217, 223, 233
Everyday life, 148, 152, 154
Everyday practices, 221, 234
Exclusion, 28, 30, 255, 264, 266, 312
Exhortations, 62, 63

F
Fabric committees, 169, 171, 173, 179, 181
Faith-based organizations (FBOs), 16, 284,
    331–333
    Islamic, 283
Fieldwork, 17, 45, 287, 300, 310, 311, 316,
    318, 322
Formal legal dimension
    crime, 201
Formal volunteering, 12, 82, 83, 85, 87, 93,
    121
For-profit, 329
Four Spiritual Laws (pamphlet), 225, 228
Freedom, 2, 31–35, 60, 155, 159, 160
Free will, 4, 10, 11, 23–25, 27, 28, 30–33, 36,
    38, 155
Functional solidarity, 338
Functions of religion, 297
Fundamentalist, 53, 54, 289

G
Gallup World Poll, 12, 82, 102
Genealogies, 148
God-pleasing deed, 63
God's grace, 28, 38, 159
Grace, 26, 27, 33–35, 158
Groupism, 244
Group solidarity, 82, 91
Group style, 15, 248, 250, 257

H
Haredi community, 12, 43–46, 50, 53, 54
Healing justice, 192, 195, 197, 198
Hebrew Bible, 47
Hegemony, 17, 152, 312, 314, 322
Heritage values, 175, 176
Heteronomy, 39
Heuristic, 27
Hindu, 13, 79, 85, 87, 91, 107
Holy Spirit, 265, 267, 268, 273–278, 280
Homelessness, 243, 250, 251, 253–256
Human being, 24, 27, 28, 30–35, 37, 39, 63, 205
    fundamental respect for, 61

Hussein Ali Montazeri, 72

I
Ibn as-sabil, 62
Ibn Rushd, Averroës, 59
Ignatius of Loyola, 35, 37, 38
IMPACT, 221, 223, 225–227, 230–232
Incarnation, 28–30
Inclusion
    in volunteering, 321–323
Individual-centred perspective, 64
Individualism, 4, 48, 101, 115, 164, 197
Individualized volunteering, 4, 98, 100, 254
Individual virtue, 61
Inglehart, Ronald, 101, 103, 147, 161
In-group bias, 82
Institutionalization, 9, 38, 64–66
Instrumentality, 122, 155
Instrumentalization, 4
Insufficient, 63
Intangible effects, 330
Interconnectedness, 28, 192, 196
Internal and external values, 157
Interpersonal dimension
    crime, 201, 205
Interrelatedness, 28
InterVarsity Christian Fellowship (IVCF), 221,
    222, 225–231
Islam, 2, 6, 60, 65, 69, 70, 72, 226, 228, 229,
    289, 294, 340
Islamic Sharia Law, 294
Islamic theological tradition, 60, 61, 63
Islamic world, 61
Islamist movement, 283, 284
Islamist political groups, 288
Islamists, 283, 293, 299, 302
Israel, 12, 16, 43, 46, 48, 51, 53, 267, 305,
    308, 310, 312, 314, 318
    inHaredi community, 45, 46
    in volunteerism, 43–45

J
Jesus Christ (of Nazareth), 28–30, 37
Jewish, 12, 13, 26, 41–43, 45, 47, 49–52, 54,
    85, 87, 312–314, 321
Jewish tradition, 41, 42, 47, 52
Jews, 43, 52, 89
    Ashkenazi, 16, 311, 312, 314, 315, 317
    Mizrahi, 313, 314, 322
    secular, 47
    ultra-orthodox, 46, 312
Johns Hopkins Comparative Nonprofit Sector
    Project, 106, 108

348   Index

Jon Sobrino, 26
Joshua Project, 225
Judaism, 2, 12, 41, 51, 78, 255
Justice system, 192–197, 199, 208, 210

K
Khorasani, Akhund, 73
Kingdom of God, 28–30, 274
Koran, 2

L
Latour, Bruno, 177, 178
Law, 2, 11, 34, 45
    emergency, 286
    Jewish, 42, 50, 51
    rule of, 194, 207, 210
    violation of, 201
Laypersons, 180, 184
Local actors, 171, 180, 181, 184, 257, 264
Local associations, 173, 179, 181, 184
Local knowledge, 174, 179, 185–187
Love
    neighborly, 2, 11, 149
Lutheran theology, 149, 154, 158, 159, 161

M
Managerial, 17, 319
    ideology, 319
    practices, 316, 323
Mandatory volunteering, 4
Martin Luther
    Lutheran, 31, 35, 38
Massignon, Louis, 63
Mediation, 321
    victim-offender, 191, 199–201, 203, 205, 207, 208
Mediators, 192, 211, 212
Middle East, 11, 221, 232, 265, 274, 283
MirzaShirazi, 69
Missional church, 218
Mitzvah, 42, 50, 52
Modernity, 3, 6, 7, 24, 31, 36, 147, 148, 275
Monetary value, 329, 330
Mony/Monetary terms, 329, 330, 332, 333, 335, 338, 339, 341
Mosques, 287, 288, 294, 296, 298, 299, 301, 332–336, 340, 341
    in Cairo, 16
    Salafi, 297
Motivation to volunteer (MTV), 13, 97–99, 104, 115
    Acts of Compassion, 98
    alturistic, 100, 104, 106, 107, 109, 112, 114

duty to the poor, 99
egoistic motivation, 150, 161
functionalist approach, 233
instrumental, 113
motivational accounts, 97, 112, 117
self-interested, 106, 112
selflessness, 99
social-constructionist approach, 97, 112
Volunteer Functions Inventory, 97, 123
Muhammad, 67
Multilevel linear regression, 108
Multilevel model, 82
Muslim, 61, 62, 67, 72, 85, 225, 230, 296, 339
    African American, 252
    beliefs, 258
    communities, 274, 279
    Muslim Brotherhood, 287, 289, 296, 298, 301
    rural areas, 279
Muslim Brotherhood *See* under Muslim, 16
Muslim moral philosophy, 59
Muslim theology
    compassion in, 59–61

N
National
    aristocracy, 315
    space, 17, 315, 319
    unity, 280, 316, 317, 322
    will, 315, 316, 318, 323
National Church Life Survey (NCLS), 126, 128, 138
Neighbour, 25, 26, 33, 34, 268
Neoliberalism, 313, 319
Neo-Tocquevillian synthesis, 245, 246, 248, 250
    religion and solidarity, 241, 242
Network, 92
    arguments, 114
    hypothesis, 2
    parish church as, 178–180
    religious, 80
    Salafi, 300
    social, 62, 80
    spillover, 103
    worldwide, 38
New Testament, 2, 149
Nina Eliasoph, 3, 245, 248, 308, 318
Non-denominational Christianity, 219, 221, 232
Nongovernmental organizations (NGOs), 222, 247, 307
    Belgian, 200
    political, 286

Index

umbrella and intermediary, 309
Non-profit
   organizations, 45, 48, 51, 54
   sector, 98, 104
Non-profit sector regime
   conservative-corporatist, 108
   CSO workplace, 108, 112, 115
   liberal, 108
   revenue structure, 105, 112, 115
   social democratic, 108
   volunteer labor, 108, 115
Non-religious, 3, 16, 45, 80, 85, 91, 102, 162,
   253, 255, 297
Not-for-profit organizations, 121
   in Australia, 125, 141

O

Oikos Foundation, 331, 333
Oppressed, 63
Orthodox, 11, 78, 85, 263, 269, 317

P

Palestinian citizens of Israel, 312, 314, 321
Parish church, 9, 170, 171
   as a forum, 180–182
   as a network, 178–180
   Schulen's (case study), 172–174
Participant observation, 10, 16, 251, 266, 290,
   310
Participative citizenship, 14, 192
Pastoral care, 333, 335, 337, 338
Peacemaking, 191, 196
Performance
   social, 177
Phenomenological approach, 10, 152
Philanthropy, 61, 108
Philosophical anthropology, 149, 150
Piety, 4, 12, 46, 55, 149, 253
Pillarization, 331
Pillars, 51, 331
Places of public significance, 174
Plug-in volunteering, 233, 245–247, 251
Policy makers, 200, 329, 339
Political activism, 3, 286
Political change, 15, 16, 286, 293, 300
Political ideology, 300
Political participation, 242, 244, 293, 311
Political transformation, 16, 284, 290, 293,
   298
   and FBOs, 284, 285
Politics of religion
   and volunteering, 8–10
Porous boundaries, 247
Post-revolutionary Egypt, 284

Post-secular, 3, 7, 8, 14, 15, 149, 220
Post-secularity, 147, 220
Post-Tocquevillian scenario, 257
   religion and solidarity in, 247, 248
Post war society, 263
Poverty, 16, 28, 36, 53, 287, 300, 302
   reduction, 288, 289, 293, 297, 298–300
Practice, 1, 10, 69, 114, 162, 192, 199, 201,
   220, 241, 267, 294, 308
Pragmatic model, 5, 258
Pragmatist approach, 16, 242, 249
Pre-modern times, 63, 160
Privatization, 48, 231, 243
Problem of goodness, 149, 150, 154, 161
Pro-social, 79, 242
   action, 257
   behavior, 23, 82, 93
Protest, 69, 241, 244, 251, 292
Protestant church, 79, 138, 250, 251, 256, 336
Pseudo-participation, 180
Public action, 258
Public sphere, 6, 7, 9, 73, 148, 182, 187, 204,
   205, 265
Putnam, Robert, 121, 247

Q

Qualitative methodology, 264
Qur'an, 60, 62

R

Radical Islamist groups, 294
Ramadan, 61, 65
Ranking system, 333, 337
Rational Choice, 81
Rationality
   functional, 338, 340
   substantial, 338
Reasoning, 60, 173, 174, 178, 180, 254
Relational ministry, 219, 220, 226, 227
Religion
   definition of, 8, 42
   individual religiosity, 23, 78, 102, 107,
      109, 114
   religious conviction, 2, 9, 114, 253, 255
   religious membership, 82, 107, 114
   religious practice, 1, 9, 15, 78, 100, 148,
      151, 198, 280, 322
   religious socialization, 102
   religious teaching, 116, 250, 255
   religious worship, 87, 114
Religious actor, 15, 25, 234, 242, 243, 247,
   256, 279
Religious affiliation, 55, 77, 85, 87, 91,
   124, 192
   and service attendance, 79, 80

350 Index

Religious associational life, 242
Religious belief, 1, 3, 6, 7, 23, 99, 116, 125,
    134, 137, 194, 202, 212, 213, 243,
    249, 258, 324
Religious calling, 2
Religious capital, 297
Religious change, 2, 6, 8, 13
Religious communities, 5–7, 9, 17, 100, 192,
    263, 277, 280, 332
Religious context, 13, 80, 81, 102, 113, 115,
    148
  devout societies, 102
  national religious culture, 103, 114
  religious networks, 79, 91, 114
  religious network spillover, 103
  secular societies, 92, 98, 103, 161, 219
Religious conviction *See under* Religion, 2
Religious culture, 16, 102, 103, 114, 248, 249,
    251, 264, 274, 280
Religious devoutness, 80, 92
Religious diversity, 77, 81, 85, 89, 91, 107,
    225
Religious foundations
  of neighborly love, 2
Religious identity, 15, 45, 46, 55, 89, 91, 124,
    229, 241, 243, 250, 252, 255, 258,
    279
Religious leaders, 15, 49, 65, 69, 70, 72, 252,
    272, 294
Religious minority, 77, 85, 89, 91
  group affiliation, 82
Religious networks *See* under Religious
  context, 2
Religious norms, 59, 79, 80, 90, 234
Religious organizations, 9, 17, 45, 79, 125,
    140, 284, 287, 330–332, 334, 337,
    339
Religious plurality, 6
Religious social capital, 242, 256
Religious spill-over effect, 3
Replacement value, 330, 332, 333, 336, 341
Responsibility, 11, 12, 26, 28, 33, 47, 52, 63,
    65, 67, 73, 79, 195, 288
Restorative justice, 9, 14, 191–194, 196, 197,
    199, 201, 205
  in secular age, 202–204, 206
  moderate version of, 14, 194
Restorative practices, 192
Restorative spirituality, 194, 209, 210
Return of religion, 6, 8, 147
Rewards, 14, 52, 54, 150, 155, 157
  as unexpected by-products, 156, 157
Righteousness, 12, 33, 34, 159
Ritual, 41, 42, 47, 49, 51, 254, 264, 267, 272, 273

S
Sabbath, 42, 51, 55
Sacred canopy, 242, 243
Sa'di of Shiraz, 64
Salafi movement, 16, 288, 293, 294, 297, 300
Salamon, Lester, 86
Samaritan, 25, 26, 99
Samir Khalaf, 269, 275
Sawatsky, Jarem, 195, 197, 198, 209
Scale model, 185, 187
  Schulen, 182, 188
Scholars, 67, 69, 73
  Islamic, 12
  of religion and volunteering, 2
  Sunni, 66
Science and Technology Studies (STS), 180
Sectarian welfare regime, 274, 280
Secular
  age, 194, 202
    restorative justice in, 202–206
  organizations, 1, 5, 129, 136, 140, 141, 298
  society, 6–9, 14, 17, 148, 162, 164, 229,
    332, 333
Secularism, 149, 210, 220, 231, 313, 323, 324
Secularity, 8, 194, 202, 258
Secularity *See also* Post-secularity, 213
Secularization, 2, 4–9, 14, 98, 147, 162, 164,
    170, 202, 241, 330
Semitic, 63
Service attendance, 13, 77, 114
  and religious affiliation, 79, 80
Service provision, 104, 105, 286, 296
Setting, 15, 16, 100, 179, 226, 244, 248, 249,
    253, 256
  and methodology, 309–311
Seyyed Mohammad Tabatabai, 68
Short-term mission (STM), 217, 218, 221
  history of, in United States, 222, 223
  preparing for, 224–227
  voluntarism, 15
Sin, 32, 37, 47, 49
Sincere self, 155, 157, 160
Situated action, 248
Situated identities, 248
Situational inequality, 61
Social activism, 3, 66
Social benefit, 331–333, 337
Social capital
  as bonding, 122
  as bridging, 9, 122
  definition, 121
  relationship between bonding and bridging,
    138, 139
Social engineering, 180

Social imaginary/ ies, 204, 219, 220, 233
Social life, 62, 77, 170, 173, 202, 244
Social origins theory, 104, 105, 107
Social relations, 61, 79
Social Return On Investment (SROI), 333
Social safety net, 12, 62, 64, 65, 71, 73
Social solidarity, 5, 16, 241, 242, 245–247,
 280, 281, 331, 341
Social yield
 SY-method, 335, 336
Sociology of religion, 81, 82, 243
Socio-political structure, 264
Sola Gratia, 32, 158, 159
Solidarity *See* Social solidarity, 4
Spatial agency, 14, 175–178, 183, 187
Spiritual aspects, 60
Spiritual family, 269, 271
Spirituality, 8, 15, 36, 38, 197, 198, 255
 rediscovery of, 192, 193
Spiritual justice, 193
Spiritual nature/dimension, 60, 192–194,
 199, 210
Sunni, 65, 279
Sura, 60
Sweden, 151, 153, 160, 162, 163
Synagogue, 46, 47, 255

T
Talmud, 42, 47, 52
Taylor, Charles, 194, 202, 204
The Netherlands, 17, 171, 245, 331–333, 336,
 339
Theological framework, 9, 148, 149, 152, 153,
 161
Theology, 4, 10, 33
Theology *See also* Christian theology; Muslim
 theology; Lutheran theology, 14
The road/wayfarer, 62
Third cultural space
 religious motivation for volunteering,
 274–276
Third sector, 44, 83, 84, 308, 314
Thomas Aquinas, 31
Thomas Hobbes, 31
Thuiszorg, 331, 335, 336
Till, Jeremy, 176, 182, 188
Torah studies, 49, 50
Tourism, 15, 46, 217, 222, 233
Traditionalism, 276, 322
Trust, 30, 36, 101, 122, 129, 150, 197, 211,
 273
Tsedakah, 47, 51

U
Ultra-orthodox, 12, 43, 44, 46, 53, 312
Uncertainty, 93, 171, 177, 181, 257, 317
Unitary actor model, 5, 16, 242, 243, 247, 248,
 251, 253
United States, 44
 STM in, overview and history of, 222, 223
Unpaid, 4, 24, 30, 35, 39, 82, 105, 106, 149,
 152, 154, 160, 245
Unselfish aid work, 61

V
Value patterns
 altruistic individualism, 101
 national, 13
 post-materialism, 107
 post-materialist values, 107
 solidary individualism, 101
van Broeckhoven, Egied, 29
van der Sar, Jaap, 333, 340
Vicarious religion, 170, 188
Victim-offender mediation, 191, 199–201,
 203, 205, 207, 208
Voluntarism, 15, 16, 93, 116, 218, 233, 243
Voluntary associations, 241, 242, 245, 247,
 256, 276
Voluntary labor, 338
Voluntary non-profit organizations (VNPOs),
 43, 44
Volunteering
 and religion, 1–3
 antecedents of, 5, 324
 as a free choice, 2
 definition of, 1, 10, 42, 308
 expressive, 105
 likelihood of, 13, 77, 80, 81, 83, 86, 87, 89,
 90–92, 134
 management of, 318
 meaning of, 6, 35, 148, 149, 151–154, 157,
 160, 164
 motivations, 11, 13, 24, 98, 100,
 134–136 336
 motives for, 5, 12, 14, 157
 predictors, 133, 134, 151
 promotion of, 323
 public perception of, 4
 religious perspective on, 11, 160, 161
 service-oriented, 104
 traditional, 100, 117
 value of, 41, 55, 333
Volunteer mobilization, 91
Volunteers
 recruitment, 97, 140
 religious, 264

352   Index

secular, 9, 103, 114
use of, 299
Volunteer work, 4, 24, 61, 64, 67, 71, 72, 78, 337

W
Waqf system, 67
Waqfsystem, 66
Weber, Max, 163, 285, 338
Welfare state, 48, 65, 92
Welfare state regimes, 98, 107, 112, 113
Welfare state *See also* Welfare state regimes, 8
Welfare system, 1, 44, 48
Whiteness, 314, 315
Wilders, Geert, 340
Wilson, John, 3, 5, 6
World Values Survey, 13, 78, 83, 93, 98, 105, 113

Worldview
religious, 207
spiritual, 191, 193, 194, 197, 202, 214
Worship, 79, 85, 91, 228, 232, 274
Wuthnow, Robert, 2, 5, 23, 79, 98, 99, 103, 116, 148, 151, 217, 222, 223, 245, 247, 254

Y
Yad Sarah, 51–54

Z
ZAKA, 48–53
Zakat al-fitr, 65

CPSIA information can be obtained at www.ICGtesting.com
Printed in the USA
LVOW02*1220210714

395261LV00002BA/3/P